# Statistical Methods

*Statistical Methods: An Introduction to Basic Statistical Concepts and Analysis*, Second Edition is a textbook designed for students with no prior training in statistics. It provides a solid background of the core statistical concepts taught in most introductory statistics textbooks. Mathematical proofs are deemphasized in favor of careful explanations of statistical constructs.

The text begins with coverage of descriptive statistics such as measures of central tendency and variability, then moves on to inferential statistics. Transitional chapters on z-scores, probability, and sampling distributions pave the way to understanding the logic of hypothesis testing and the inferential tests that follow. Hypothesis testing is taught through a four-step process. These same four steps are used throughout the text for the other statistical tests presented including *t* tests, one- and two-way ANOVAs, chi-square, and correlation. A chapter on nonparametric tests is also provided as an alternative when the requirements cannot be met for parametric tests.

Because the same logical framework and sequential steps are used throughout the text, a consistency is provided that allows students to gradually master the concepts. Their learning is enhanced further with the inclusion of "thought questions" and practice problems integrated throughout the chapters.

New to the second edition:

- Chapters on factorial analysis of variance and non-parametric techniques for all data
- Additional and updated chapter exercises for students to test and demonstrate their learning
- Full instructor resources: test bank questions, PowerPoint slides, and an Instructor Manual

**Cheryl Ann Willard** serves on the faculty of the Psychology Department at Lee College in the Houston, Texas area. She has been teaching courses in psychology and statistics for over 25 years and continues to take great joy in witnessing her students develop new skills and apply them in new and creative ways.

# Statistical Methods

## *An Introduction to Basic Statistical Concepts and Analysis*

### Second Edition

Cheryl Ann Willard

Routledge
Taylor & Francis Group

NEW YORK AND LONDON

Second edition published 2020
by Routledge
52 Vanderbilt Avenue, New York, NY 10017

and by Routledge
2 Park Square, Milton Park, Abingdon, Oxon, OX14 4RN

*Routledge is an imprint of the Taylor & Francis Group, an informa business*

© 2020 Taylor & Francis

The right of Cheryl Ann Willard to be identified as author of this work
has been asserted by her in accordance with sections 77 and 78 of the
Copyright, Designs and Patents Act 1988.

All rights reserved. No part of this book may be reprinted or reproduced
or utilised in any form or by any electronic, mechanical, or other means,
now known or hereafter invented, including photocopying and recording,
or in any information storage or retrieval system, without permission in
writing from the publishers.

*Trademark notice*: Product or corporate names may be trademarks or
registered trademarks, and are used only for identification and explanation
without intent to infringe.

First edition published by Pyrczak Publishing 2010

*Library of Congress Cataloging-in-Publication Data*
A catalog record for this book has been requested

ISBN: 978-0-367-20351-1 (hbk)
ISBN: 978-0-367-20352-8 (pbk)
ISBN: 978-0-429-26103-9 (ebk)

Typeset in Minion
by Apex CoVantage, LLC

Visit the eResources: www.routledge.com/9780367203528

To Jim,
a constant source of loving support.

# Contents

# Tables

# Preface

When I first started teaching statistics over 25 years ago, I noticed immediately that students were trying to write down everything I said. It was soon clear that they were having difficulty understanding their textbook. I tried switching books on several occasions, but that didn't seem to help. Finally, I started preparing handouts for the students so that, instead of focusing on recording my every word, they could concentrate on understanding the meaning of the words. The handouts became more and more elaborate, and students commented that they were more helpful than their textbook. That is how *Statistical Methods* came into being, with my students as the primary source of inspiration.

# Acknowledgments

As always, I am grateful to my students who have continued to play an important role in the development of this text with their thoughtful questions and comments. I would like to thank my friend, colleague, and poet extraordinaire, Jerry Hamby, Professor of English at Lee College, for his discerning eye, and for allowing me to intrude upon his day on many occasions with no complaint. I would also like to thank Hannah Shakespeare and Matt Bickerton and the rest of the team at Routledge for being so responsive to all of my queries, and for providing the materials that I needed to move forward. Most importantly, I would like to thank my incredibly talented husband and partner of over 40 years, James Willard. Not only did he create all of the cartoon illustrations in the text, but he also learned and performed all of the techniques presented in the text. I wanted the viewpoint of a non-statistician to check the book for clarity and he performed that role with diligence and enthusiasm, providing many helpful suggestions along the way. The book would not be the same without his considerable insight.

# Introduction

*Statistical Methods* is designed for students with no prior training in statistics. Core statistical concepts are taught using hypothetical examples that students can relate to from experiences in their own lives. The same logical framework and sequential steps are used for teaching hypothesis testing throughout the text, providing a consistency that allows students to gradually master the concepts. Their learning is enhanced further with the inclusion of "thought questions" and practice problems integrated throughout the chapters. All told, students come away with a solid foundation in the basic statistical concepts taught in an introductory course and a greater appreciation for scientific inquiry in general.

## FEATURES

Each chapter follows a similar structure and includes the following elements:

- *Explanation of Concepts.* Each chapter begins with a careful explanation of the statistical concepts relevant to that chapter. The writing style is designed to enable students to grasp basic ideas without getting lost in technical jargon.
- *Examples.* Following the explanation of concepts are examples that illustrate the applications of the ideas discussed.
- *"Your Turn" Exercises.* Within the chapters, problems or questions are presented that give students the opportunity for their own hands-on learning experience.
- *Glossary.* Each chapter contains terms that normally appear in statistics texts. These terms are in boldface type and italicized. They are defined in the text and appear in the glossary in Appendix A.
- *Tips.* Boxes containing helpful pointers to students are included in the chapters. These are often mnemonics for remembering concepts, precautions warning against commonly made mistakes, or other ways of looking at a concept that provide additional clarification.
- *Graphics.* The book contains the typical charts, normal distribution curves, and scatterplots found in most statistics texts. In addition, the "Tip" boxes and "Your Turn" exercises have their own graphic that students will come to recognize.
- *Cartoons.* Several chapters contain cartoons and illustrations that bring a bit of light-heartedness to what is frequently perceived by students as a heavy subject.

- *Instructions for Excel* (New). Many of the chapters that involved statistical tests now include instructions for how to perform the operations in Microsoft Excel.
- *Additional Practice Problems* (New). All chapters now include extra problems for students to work. These problems are very similar to the kinds of questions that will likely be on exams.

## NEW TO THIS EDITION

The second edition of *Statistical Methods* represents significant changes in terms of additions to both the text and supplemental materials for instructors. These changes include the following:

- A new chapter on Factorial Analysis of Variance.
- A new chapter on Nonparametric Statistics for Ordinal Data.
- Expanded coverage on the topics of *power* and *effect size* in the chapter on Hypothesis Testing.
- Answers to the "Your Turn" learning checks are now placed at the end of the chapters.
- Instructions for using Excel for data analysis are included at the end of many of the chapters.
- Additional practice problems are included at the end of all chapters. A new appendix includes answers to the odd-numbered items.

For instructors:

- A test bank is provided for all chapters which includes multiple choice questions, short-answer essays, and problems.
- Thoroughly developed PowerPoint presentations are included for all chapters.
- Answers to even-numbered end-of-chapter problems are provided. This is helpful for instructors who want to assign graded homework.
- Learning objectives are provided for all chapters.

# 1
# Introduction to Statistics

## HOW STATISTICS ADDS UP

Congratulations! You are about to embark on an exciting adventure into the world of statistics. Perhaps, for you, this is unexplored territory. Even so, you probably have some ideas (and possibly some misconceptions) about what a course in statistics might be like. Sometimes students enter the course a bit apprehensive due to a perception of themselves as having poor math skills. If you have similar concerns, you can take comfort in knowing that most of the mathematical computations involved in statistics are not difficult. Although some of the formulas that you will use look rather ominous, their computation is simply a matter of breaking them down. Essentially, you need to know how to add, subtract, multiply, divide, work with signed numbers, find square roots (with a calculator), and know the order of mathematical operations. If you can carry out these functions, then you can rest assured that you have the prerequisite math ability to complete this book successfully. If you have not had a math course in a while and are feeling a bit rusty, there is a review at the end of this chapter that outlines some of the rules of computation. This will help to familiarize you with the types of calculations you will be performing as you study statistics.

## WHY STATISTICS MATTERS: A CASE FOR STUDYING STATISTICS

Over and above statistical formulas, you will learn the basic vocabulary of statistics, how statistics is used in research, the conceptual basis for the statistical procedures used, and how to interpret research results in existing literature. Learning to understand and appreciate statistics will help you to better understand your world. We are exposed to statistics on a daily basis. We cannot watch the evening news, read a newspaper, or even listen to a sporting event without reference to some sort of statistical outcome. In addition to being able to make sense of these everyday facts and figures, there are other reasons for studying statistics.

- *Statistical procedures are used to advance our knowledge of ourselves and the world around us.* It is by systematically studying groups of people, gathering scores, and analyzing the results statistically that we learn about how humans perform under differing situations, what their reactions and preferences are, and how they respond to different treatments and procedures. We can then use this knowledge to address a wide variety of social and environmental issues that affect the quality of people's lives.
- *Statistics helps to strengthen your critical thinking skills and reasoning abilities.* Some of what we hear in the news or read in magazines or on the Internet may contain false or misleading information. Consider these tabloid claims that were published online in the *Weekly World News:*

  Women's Hot Flashes Cause Global Warming (8/19/2003)
  The Sun Will Explode in Less Than 6 Years (9/19/2002)
  Your Social Security Number Predicts Your Future (5/25/2001)

  Understanding statistical protocol and rules of conduct enable us to evaluate the validity of such assertions to see if they stand up to scientific scrutiny. Without research evidence to support various claims, theories, and beliefs, we would have no way to separate fact from mere opinion or to protect ourselves from scam artists and quacks.
- *Statistics enables you to understand research results in the professional journals of your area of specialization.* Most fields of study publish professional journals, many of which contain articles describing firsthand accounts of research. Such publications enable professionals to remain abreast of new knowledge in their respective areas of expertise. However, for students who have not taken a course in statistics, the results sections of such articles probably look like ancient hieroglyphics. For example, you may see results reported as follows:

Males were significantly more competitive against other males versus females. Reject $H_0$, $t(53) = 3.28$, $p < .01$.
There was no significant relationship between gender and level of creativity. Fail to reject $H_0$, $\chi^2 (3, n = 73) = 5.23$, $p > .05$.

The way in which the terms *significantly* or *significant* are used, and the numbers and symbols at the end of the above phrases, may make little sense to you now. However, if you return to this section after you have worked through this book, you should be able to explain them with ease. Thus, learning statistics can help you to discuss research results with your friends and colleagues confidently. It is a step toward becoming a knowledgeable and competent professional in your area of study.

## *STATISTICS* AND OTHER STATISTICAL TERMS

We will now lay some groundwork by becoming acquainted with some terminology that will come up repeatedly as you study statistics. ***Research***, a systematic inquiry in search of knowledge, involves the use of statistics. In general, ***statistics*** refers to procedures used as researchers go about organizing and analyzing the information that is collected. Usually, a set of scores, referred to as ***data***, will be collected. Before the scores have undergone any type of statistical transformation or analysis, they are called ***raw scores***.

More often than not, researchers want to draw conclusions about the characteristics of an entire group of persons, plants, animals, objects, or events that have something in common. This group is referred to as the ***population***. Populations can be broadly defined, such as gorillas in the wild, or more narrowly defined, such as high school seniors in the state of Kentucky. In either case, populations are generally larger in scope than researchers can realistically access in their entirety. Consequently, only a ***sample***, or subset, of the population will be used in the study, the results of which will then be generalized to the population as a whole. Because conclusions are to be drawn about a population based on sample data, it is important that the sample be representative of the population, meaning that it should reflect the characteristics of the population as much as possible in all aspects relevant to the study. Suppose you wanted to know the overall rate of satisfaction of the students at your college with regard to educational experience. If you asked only students who attended night classes, this would not be a representative sample of the population of students at large. Perhaps many students who take night classes work during the day and are tired when they come to class. This might influence their degree of satisfaction. You would want to include *some* night students in your sample, but it should not consist of *only* night students, or *only* students taking particular courses, or *only* first-year college students, and so on. You would want a proper mix of students.

How do you obtain a suitable cross-section of students for your sample? There are several sampling procedures that can be used in research, but the most basic is called ***random sampling***, which means that all members of a population have the same chance of being selected for inclusion in the sample. One way of achieving this would be to use a computer software program that generates random numbers. You could first assign each of the members of your population a unique number and then get a computer to generate as many random numbers as you need for your sample. Those members of the population whose numbers match those generated by the computer would make up your sample.

Tip!

Technically, random sampling should be done *with replacement*. If all members of the population have the same chance of being included in the sample, this would mean that once a name has been selected, it should then be placed back into the population pool before the next name is chosen. If this were not done, the probabilities of being selected for each subsequent candidate would be changed and all members would not have the same chance of being selected. In actuality, sampling is usually done *without replacement* of names, thus eliminating the possibility of repeatedly selecting the same participant. However, any error produced by this deviation from true random sampling is minor because in an actual population, which is usually very large, the probability of drawing the same person's name more than once is quite small.

While there are other sampling procedures that researchers sometimes use, random sampling (or variations thereof) is basic to many of the statistical procedures that will be covered in this book and will therefore be assumed in our research process.

Because populations are often very large (e.g., "individuals who suffer from depression"), researchers usually do not have lists of names identifying all members of the population of interest. Consequently, samples are normally drawn from only the portion of the population that is accessible, referred to as the ***sampling frame***. Still, as long as some sort of randomizing process is used, such as random assignment to different groups (discussed under "Experimentation"), the validity of the study remains intact. However, researchers should note any limitations of their sample that should be taken into consideration in generalizing results to the population at large.

Statistical procedures can be broken down into two different types. ***Descriptive statistics*** sum up and condense a set of raw scores so that overall trends in the data become apparent. Percentages and averages are examples of descriptive statistics. ***Inferential statistics*** involve predicting characteristics of a population based on data obtained from a sample. A definition of statistics in general was previously given as the procedures used for organizing and analyzing information. More narrowly, a ***statistic*** is a numerical value that originates from a sample, whereas a ***parameter*** is a numerical value that represents an entire population. Parameters are usually inferred from samples rather than being calculated directly. However, it cannot be assumed that the values predicted by a sample will reflect the population values exactly. If we drew another sample from the same population, we would likely get a somewhat different value. Even though we may be using a representative sample, we still do not have all the information that we would have if we were measuring the population itself. Thus, a certain amount of error is to be expected. The amount of error between a sample statistic and a population parameter is referred to as ***sampling error***. Inferential statistics are used to assess the amount of error expected by chance due to the randomness of the samples.

Tip!

A mnemonic for remembering statistics and parameters is that the two Ss belong together and the two Ps belong together. We speak of <u>s</u>ample <u>s</u>tatistics and <u>p</u>opulation <u>p</u>arameters.

👉 Your Turn! 👈

### I. Statistical Terms

Read the scenario below and then fill in the blanks with the appropriate statistical terminology.

After reading a book about the relationship between sleep deprivation and accidents,[1] the CEO of a large multinational corporation becomes curious about the amount of sleep his own 120,000 employees obtain. He hired a research consultant

**Your Turn!**
(continued)

who surveyed a subset of the company's employees. The researcher used a selection procedure that helped to ensure that those chosen to participate in the study were representative of the company's employees in general.

A. The entire 120,000 employees are referred to as the _population_.
B. The _sample_ is made up of the employees who were actually surveyed.
C. The procedure used to make sure that the selected participants were representative of the company is called _sampling frame_.
D. The values that the researcher obtained from the sample are called _Descriptive Stats_.
E. The researcher will use the values obtained from the sample to make predictions about the overall sleep patterns of the company employees. Predicting population characteristics in such a manner involves the use of _inferential_.
F. In all likelihood, the values obtained from the selected employees will not predict with complete accuracy the overall sleep patterns of the company's employees due to _Sampling error_.

## MEASUREMENT

Statistics involves the measurement of variables. A **variable** is anything that varies or that can be present in more than one form or amount. Variables describe differences. These can be differences in individuals, such as height, race, or political beliefs. Variables are also used to describe differences in environmental or experimental conditions, such as room temperature, amount of sleep, or different drug dosages.

Variables themselves are variable in that there are several different types. **Qualitative variables** differ in kind rather than amount – such as eye color, gender, or the make of automobiles. **Quantitative variables** differ in amount – such as scores on a test, annual incomes, or the number of pairs of shoes that people own.

Variables can be further described as being either discrete or continuous. **Discrete variables** cannot be divided or split into intermediate values, but rather can be measured only in whole numbers. Examples include the number of touchdowns during a football game or the number of students attending class. That number may vary from day to day – 21 students one day, 24 the next – but you will never see $22^1/_2$ students in class.

**Continuous variables**, on the other hand, *can* be broken down into fractions or smaller units. A newborn baby can weigh 7 pounds, 7.4 pounds, 7.487 pounds, or 7.4876943 pounds. Continuous variables could continue indefinitely, but they are reported only to a certain number of decimal places or units of measurement. Whatever number is reported is assumed to include an interval of intermediate values bounded by what is referred to as **real limits**. The upper and lower boundaries of a value's real limits will extend beyond the reported value by one-half of the unit of measurement in either direction. For instance, if the unit of measurement is in whole numbers in feet, 6 feet is assumed to include all intermediate values from 5.5 feet (lower limit) to 6.5 feet (upper limit).

### Determining Real Limits

We will want to establish both lower and upper real limits. To determine a lower real limit, subtract half of the unit of measurement from the reported value. Then, add half of the unit of measurement to the reported value to determine the upper limit. Here is how:

1. Identify the unit of measurement. If the value reported is a whole number, the unit of measurement is 1. If the value reported has a decimal, examine the digits after the decimal to identify the unit of measurement.
2. Using a calculator, divide the unit of measurement in half.
3. For lower limits (LL), subtract the value obtained in Step 2 from the reported value.
4. For upper limits (UL), add the value obtained in Step 2 to the reported value.

|  | Whole numbers | Tenths | Hundredths | Thousandths |
|---|---|---|---|---|
| Reported value | 94 | 94.5 | 94.53 | 94.538 |
| Unit of measurement | 1 | .1 | .01 | .001 |
| Lower Limit (LL) | 93.5 | 94.45 | 94.525 | 94.5375 |
| Upper Limit (UL) | 94.5 | 94.55 | 94.535 | 94.5385 |

### For Example

Fifteen is a whole number, rather than a fraction or decimal. So the unit of measurement is 1. Half of 1 is .5. Therefore,

Lower Limit of 15 is → 15 − .5 = 14.5
Upper Limit of 15 is → 15 + .5 = 15.5

The unit of measurement reported in the value of 6.8 is tenths (or 1/10 = .1). Half of .1 = .05. Therefore,

Lower Limit of 6.8 is → 6.8 − .05 = 6.75
Upper Limit of 6.8 is → 6.8 + .05 = 6.85

The unit of measurement reported in the value of 2.95 is hundredths (or 1/100 = .01). Half of .01 = .005. Therefore,

Lower Limit of 2.95 is → 2.95 − .005 = 2.945
Upper Limit of 2.95 is → 2.95 + .005 = 2.955

Tip!

*Looking forward!* Real limits will be used in later chapters for determining a type of average, called the median, and a type of variability, called the range.

## Your Turn!

### II. Discrete or Continuous Variables

Identify whether each of the situations below reflects a discrete *or* a continuous variable.

A. Number of traffic fatalities in Chicago in a given year: _Contiuns_
B  Length of time it takes to get to school: _____
C. The speed of an automobile: _____
D. Academic major: _quactivic_
E. Answers on a true/false test: _____
F. Volume of liquid in a container: _Contiay_

### III. Real Limits

Find the lower and upper limits for the following continuous variables:

A. 9 gallons of gas
   Lower Limit _8.5_
   Upper Limit _9.5_
B. 6.3 seconds to solve a word problem
   Lower Limit _6.25_
   Upper Limit _6.35_
C. 31.28 tons of sand
   Lower Limit _31.275_
   Upper Limit _31.285_

## Scales of Measurement

When measuring variables, you will end up with a set of scores. These scores will have certain mathematical properties that determine the types of statistical procedures that are appropriate to use for analyzing the data. These properties can be sorted into four different scales of measurement: nominal, ordinal, interval, and ratio – with each scale providing increasingly more information than the last.

- *Nominal Scale.* The least-specific measurement scale is the **nominal scale**, which simply classifies observations into *different categories*. Religion, types of trees, and colors are examples of variables measured on a nominal scale. You can see that these variables have no quantitative value. Sometimes, numbers are assigned arbitrarily to nominal data. For example, the students in your class have student ID numbers. But it would not make any sense to calculate an average for those numbers because they do not have any real quantitative value. The numbers are used only to differentiate one student from another. Therefore, there are few statistical operations that can be performed with nominally scaled data.
- *Ordinal Scale.* We are provided with a bit more information using the **ordinal scale**. In addition to classifying observations into different categories, this scale also permits

*ordering, or ranking, of the observations.* An example of a variable measured on an ordinal scale is a horse race with the horses arriving at the finish line in different amounts of time so that there will be first-, second-, and third-place winners. The first-place horse may have come in .5 seconds before the second-place horse and .75 seconds before the third-place horse. However, this information remains unspecified on an ordinal scale. Ordinal scales do not indicate how much difference exists between observations. The ordinal scale only provides information about which observation is "more than or less than," but not how much "more than or less than."

- *Interval Scales.* With **interval scales**, on the other hand, there is *equal distance between units* on the scale. Temperature in degrees Fahrenheit is measured on an interval scale. The difference between 10°F and 30°F is the same as the difference between 40°F and 60°F (20°F in each case). However, on an interval scale, there is an *arbitrary zero point* as opposed to an absolute, or real, zero point. An absolute-zero point indicates an absence of the quality being measured; an arbitrary zero point does not. Zero degrees F (0°F) does not mean an absence of the quality of temperature. It is simply one degree warmer than −1°F and one degree cooler than 1°F. Because interval scales lack a true zero point, it is not appropriate to make ratio or proportion statements such as "90° is twice as hot as 45°." This is not a valid statement because the true zero point is not known.

  As another example, suppose we are measuring intelligence. In the rare event that a person does not answer any of the questions correctly, this does not mean that the person has zero intelligence. It is possible that if easier questions were asked, the person might have been able to answer some of them. Thus, a zero on the test does not represent a complete absence of intelligence. Consequently, we cannot say that a person who scores 100 has twice the intelligence of a person who scores 50 because, without an absolute-zero point, we do not know where each person's actual ability begins.

- *Ratio Scale.* On **ratio scales**, the real, *absolute-zero point* is known. Speed, for example, is measured on a ratio scale, and so we can make ratio statements like "Jorge is twice as fast as Miguel." A zero on this scale means *none* – we know the beginning point. Other examples of variables measured on a ratio scale include height, weight, and the number of dollars in your wallet.

While there is a technical difference between interval and ratio measurements (i.e., the lack of an absolute zero on the interval scale), most researchers treat them the same for the purpose of statistical analyses.

Knowing the properties of the different scales of measurement is important because the types of statistical procedures that legitimately can be used for a data set will be determined by the scale on which it is measured. Most inferential statistics require an interval or ratio level of measurement. But we will also look at some techniques that are appropriate to use with nominal- or ordinal-level data.

**Tip!**

Here is a mnemonic for remembering the four scales of measurement (**N**ominal, **O**rdinal, **I**nterval, **R**atio):

**N**othing **O**rdinary **I**nterests **R**achel

## Your Turn!

### IV. Scales of Measurement

Identify the scale of measurement for the following variables:

A. Military rank _ordinal_
B. Reaction time _ratio_
C. Intelligence test score _ordinal_
D. Telephone numbers _nominal_
E. Annual income _interval_
F. Eye color _nominal_
G. Letter grades _ordinal_
H. Temperature in degrees Fahrenheit _interval_
I. Distance traveled _ratio_
J. Degrees longitude _interval_
K. Social Security number _nominal_
L. Academic degree (i.e., AA, BS, MA, PhD) _ordinal_

## EXPERIMENTATION

As we have seen, statistics help researchers to analyze the results of their studies. In general, researchers want to discover relationships between variables. This is often accomplished through *experimentation*, a research technique that involves manipulating one or more variables to see if doing so has an effect on another variable. The manipulated variable is called the *independent variable*. The variable that is measured to see if it has been affected by the independent variable is called the *dependent variable*.

For instance, a researcher who is interested in the ways in which music affects behavior conducts a study to see whether background music improves balance. One group of participants listens to smooth jazz while balancing a dowel rod on the forefinger of their dominant hand. Another group balances the dowel rod without listening to music. The balancing durations of both groups are then measured and analyzed statistically to see if there is a significant difference between them.

In the above example, the smooth jazz background music was the independent variable that was manipulated by the researcher. One group was exposed to this treatment; the other group was not. The dependent variable measured by the researcher was the balancing duration of the dowel rod. Notice that the scores for two groups are being compared. In an experiment, there will usually be a *control group* that is not exposed to the experimental treatment and that is used as a baseline for comparison with the *experimental group*, which *does* receive the experimental treatment. In this experiment, the group that was exposed to smooth jazz was the experimental group, and the group that did not have background music was the control group.

Researchers must also consider *extraneous variables*. These are variables that could have an unintended effect on the dependent variable if not controlled. For example, suppose that balancing durations were longer for the smooth jazz group than for the control group. Suppose further that the control group was doing its balancing in a cold room while the smooth jazz group was in a comfortable room. How could we be certain that it was the smooth jazz music, rather than the more comfortable room temperature, that was responsible for the improved performance? Room temperature would be an extraneous variable that should be controlled, or maintained at the same level, for both groups. In fact, except for the influence of the independent variable, all other conditions should have been exactly the same for both groups as much as possible. This allows us to deduce that it was, in fact, the music and not some outside influence that was not controlled, that accounted for better balancing. As you can imagine, there are usually a number of such extraneous variables that have to be controlled in an actual experiment. If an experiment *is* well controlled, it may be inferred that the independent variable was probably the cause of changes in the dependent variable.

The composition of the groups is one type of extraneous variable that has to be controlled. As we have seen, in most instances researchers do not have access to entire populations, so true random sampling is not an option. However, the integrity of the research can still be maintained if **random assignment** is used. This means that all participants

---

👉 Your Turn! 👈

### V. Independent and Dependent Variables

For each of the experiments described below, identify the independent and dependent variables.

A. The reaction time of 60 males is measured after they have consumed 0, 1, 2, or 3 ounces of alcohol.

_____reaction time_____ Independent Variable
_____are_____ Dependent Variable

B. While completing a basic math test, one group listened to classical music, another group listened to hard rock music, and a third completed the test in silence. The number of problems correctly answered by each group was then assessed.

_____silence_____ Independent Variable
_____styles_____ Dependent Variable

C. An environmental psychologist is interested in studying the effect of room temperature on creativity.

_____creativity_____ Independent Variable
_____temptrature_____ Dependent Variable

D. Three groups are given a memory test after being deprived of differing amounts of sleep.

_____with sleep_____ Independent Variable
_____no sleep_____ Dependent Variable

E. Each boy in a group of 5-year-old boys is given a glass of soda with real sugar. Each boy in another group of boys of the same age is given soda with artificial sweetener. The activity level of each group of boys is then measured.

_____boys_____ Independent Variable
_____soda_____ Dependent Variable

involved in the experiment have an equal chance of being assigned to any one of the groups. This helps to eliminate bias due to preexisting differences between participants by randomly spreading out those differences among the various groups so that the groups are equivalent.

## NONEXPERIMENTAL RESEARCH

Much of the research discussed in this book is based on the principles of experimentation, in which an experimenter manipulates an independent variable to determine its effect on a dependent variable. However, we will also examine some nonexperimental research in which variables that already exist in different values are passively observed and analyzed rather than being actively manipulated.

For example, *correlation research* involves using statistical procedures to analyze the degree of relationship between two variables. Many educators have determined that there is a relationship between class absences and course grades, such that the more absences students have, the lower their grades tend to be for those courses. Even though this relationship exists, correlation does not allow us to make the claim that absences *caused* the lower grades. While the absences (and the consequent missing of lectures and class discussions) *may* have contributed to the lower grades, there may be other outside factors that could be influencing both class absences and grades, such as illness, work, or extracurricular activities. Because we are only passively observing rather than manipulating and

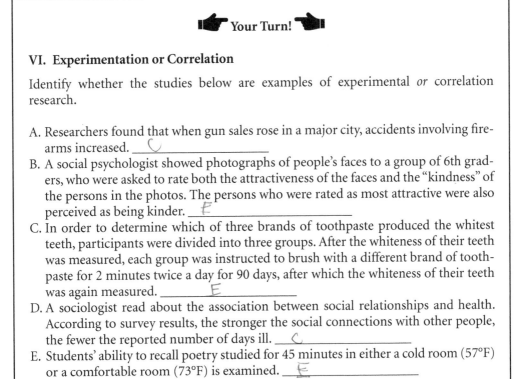

👉 **Your Turn!** 👈

### VI. Experimentation or Correlation

Identify whether the studies below are examples of experimental *or* correlation research.

A. Researchers found that when gun sales rose in a major city, accidents involving fire-arms increased. __C__

B. A social psychologist showed photographs of people's faces to a group of 6th graders, who were asked to rate both the attractiveness of the faces and the "kindness" of the persons in the photos. The persons who were rated as most attractive were also perceived as being kinder. __E__

C. In order to determine which of three brands of toothpaste produced the whitest teeth, participants were divided into three groups. After the whiteness of their teeth was measured, each group was instructed to brush with a different brand of toothpaste for 2 minutes twice a day for 90 days, after which the whiteness of their teeth was again measured. __E__

D. A sociologist read about the association between social relationships and health. According to survey results, the stronger the social connections with other people, the fewer the reported number of days ill. __C__

E. Students' ability to recall poetry studied for 45 minutes in either a cold room (57°F) or a comfortable room (73°F) is examined. __E__

controlling the variables involved, causal inferences may *not* be made. Only experimental research allows the inference of cause-and-effect relationships. Correlation research is discussed further in a later chapter.

## MATH REVIEW

To conclude this chapter, let us review some basic mathematical operations that will be encountered as you work through this book. If you are already comfortable with these procedures, then you will move through this section quickly. If the material seems unfamiliar to you, be sure to study it carefully.

### Rounding

When using a calculator and working with continuous variables, rounding off numbers will usually be necessary – but doing so introduces some error. Waiting to round until the final answer produces less error than rounding in the middle of a calculation. However, in some cases, when learning statistical formulas, it is easier to round before the end of the problem as well as rounding the final answer. Ask your instructor how much error due to rounding is acceptable.

In this text, values are generally rounded to two decimal places (to the nearest hundredth). To accomplish this, if the first digit of the numbers to be dropped is less than 5, simply drop them. If the first digit of the numbers to be dropped is 5 or greater, round up. One exception is if a calculation results in a whole number. In this case, it is optional to add zeros in the decimal places.

9.34782 rounds to 9.35
123.39421 drops to 123.39
74.99603 rounds to 75 or 75.00

### Proportions and Percentages

A proportion is a part of a whole number that can be expressed as a fraction or as a decimal. For instance, in a class of 40 students, six earned As. The proportion of the class that received As can be expressed as a fraction (6/40) or as a decimal (.15).

To change a fraction to a decimal, simply divide the numerator by the denominator:

$6/40 = 6 \div 40 = .15$

To change a decimal (proportion) to a percentage, simply multiply by 100 (or move the decimal point two places to the right) and place a percent sign (%) after the answer:

$.1823 \times 100 = 18.23\%$

To change a percentage to a proportion (decimal), remove the percent sign and divide by 100 (or move the decimal point two places to the left):

$15\% = 15 \div 100 = .15$
$23.68\% = 23.68 \div 100 = .2368$

 Your Turn!

## VII. Rounding

Round to the nearest hundredth:

A 13.614 = _13.600_          F. 0.675 = _0.7_
B. 0.049 = _0.000_           G. 12.0650 = _12_
C. 1.097 = _1.1_             H. 4.0050 = _4_
D 6.9101 = _6.9_             I. 1.995 = _2_
E. 3.6248 = _3.6_            J. 99.555 = _99.6_

## VIII. Proportions and Percentages

A. Convert 3/25 to a decimal proportion: _.12_
B. Convert 2/3 to a percentage: _66.6%_
C. Twenty-six out of 31 students completed the course. What proportion completed the course? _.6_
D. Four out of 48 students in a biology class had green eyes. What percentage of students had green eyes? _8.5%_
E. Of 36 students in a chemistry class, eight were nursing majors. What percentage of the students in the class was majoring in nursing? _22.2%_

## Signed Numbers

Numbers with the presence of either a positive or a negative sign are called signed numbers. If no sign is present, the number is assumed to be positive. The following rules will help you determine how to add, subtract, multiply, and divide signed numbers:

- *Addition.* When adding values that include both *positive and negative* numbers: (a) add all the positive numbers, (b) add all the negative numbers, and (c) determine the difference between the two sums, using the sign of the larger number for the result.

$$(-6) + (-8) + (10) + (-7) + (5) + (-1) = 15 + (-22) = -7$$

When adding *only negative* values, add as if they are positive and then attach a negative sign in the result.

$$(-3) + (-17) + (-42) + (-18) + (-5) + (-21) = -106$$

- *Subtraction.* Change the sign of the value to be subtracted, and add (using above rules of addition).

$$(-14) - (-5) = -14 + 5 = -9$$
$$20 - (-4) = 20 + 4 = 24$$
$$52 - (+73) = 52 + (-73) = -21$$

- *Multiplication.* Multiplication will be indicated either by a times sign ($\times$) or two values beside each other in parentheses. If two values with the same sign are to be multiplied, the result will be positive.

$-12 \times (-3) = 36$
$(-7)(-7) = 49$

If two values with the *opposite sign* are to be multiplied together, the result will be negative.

$(-7)(7) = -49$

- *Division.* If the numerator and the denominator both have the same sign, the result will be positive.

$(-15) \div (-3) = 5$

If the numerator and the denominator have *opposite signs*, the result will be negative.

$6 \div (-3) = -2$

---

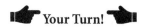 **Your Turn!**

**IX. Signed Numbers**

Perform the calculations as required for the following numbers:

A. $(-48) \div 4 =$ _____ ⁻12
B. $(-4)(-9) =$ _____ 36
C. $(-9) + (-16) + (26) + (13) + (-2) + (-22) =$ _____ ⁻16
D. $59 - (-36) =$ _____ 95
E. $(-96) \div (-12) =$ _____ 8
F. $(-13) + (-6) + (-9) + (-2) + (-14) + (-8) =$ _____ ⁻52
G. $(7)(-11) =$ _____ ⁻77
H. $(-24) - (-17) =$ _____ ⁻7

---

## Order of Operations

You may remember the mnemonic "*Please Excuse My Dear Aunt Sally*" from your childhood days as the order in which mathematical operations should be completed. It is still relevant today and translates as *Parentheses, Exponents, Multiplication, Division, Addition, Subtraction.* Some rules follow:

- Compute all values that are in parentheses first. Brackets and parentheses may be used interchangeably, but parentheses may also be nested inside brackets. If this kind of nesting occurs, compute values in the innermost parentheses first.

$7 \times [4 - (3 \times 6)]$
$= 7 \times (4 - 18)$
$= 7 \times (-14)$
$= -98$

$-3 + [(2 \times 4) - (7 \times 7)] + 8$
$= -3 + (8 - 49) + 8$
$= -3 + (-41) + 8$
$= -36$

- Exponents are next. Exponents are numbers that are raised slightly above and to the right of another number, and they tell you how many times to multiply that number by itself. The only exponent we will be using is 2. In other words, some of our values will need to be squared. To square a number means to multiply that number by itself. "Six squared" means "six times six" and is written as $6^2$.

$$4 + (9 \times 3) + (6 - 4^2)$$
$$= 4 + 27 + (6 - 16)$$
$$= 4 + 27 + (-10)$$
$$= +21$$

- After parentheses and exponents have been taken care of, multiplication and division (from left to right) are next. Addition and subtraction (from left to right) are performed last.

$$(-7 + 4^2) \times 2 - [(3 \times 6) \div 2]$$
$$= (-7 + 16) \times 2 - (18 \div 2)$$
$$= 9 \times 2 - 9$$
$$= +9$$

Order is important because the same numbers with parentheses and brackets in different places would result in a different amount, as shown below.

$$-7 + [(4^2 \times 2) - (3 \times 6)] \div 2$$
$$= -7 + [(16 \times 2) - 18] \div 2$$
$$= -7 + (32 - 18) \div 2$$
$$= -7 + (14) \div 2$$
$$= -7 + 7$$
$$= 0$$

---

 **Your Turn!**

### X. Order of Operations

Compute the values for the following numbers:

A. $(-15 + 17) \times 3 - [(4^2 \times 9) \div 3] =$ ___ -4 ~~46~~ 2
B. $-15 + [(17 \times 3) - (4^2 \times 9)] \div 3 =$ _2_
C. $6 + 4 \times 4 \div 2 =$ _14_
D. $5 + 4 \times (13 + 25) \div 8 - 24 =$ _0_

---

### Summation Operator

The Greek letter *sigma* ($\Sigma$) is used as a symbol for the summation operator. This is a frequently used notation in statistics that tells you to add the value of whatever variable(s) follows to the right of the symbol. Variables are often represented as $X$ or $Y$. Remember to keep the order of operations in mind when using the summation operator.

### For Example

Suppose you have the following $X$ and $Y$ scores:

| $X$ | $Y$ | $X^2$ | $XY$ | $(X-3)$ | $(Y+2)$ | $(Y+2)^2$ |
|---|---|---|---|---|---|---|
| 6 | 4 | 36 | 24 | 3 | 6 | 36 |
| 5 | 7 | 25 | 35 | 2 | 9 | 81 |
| 9 | 2 | 81 | 18 | 6 | 4 | 16 |
| 8 | 1 | 64 | 8 | 5 | 3 | 9 |
| 28 | 14 | 206 | 85 | 16 | 22 | 142 |

Here is how summation operations would be performed:

$\Sigma X = 28$ — Simply add all of the $X$ values.

$(\Sigma X)^2 = 784$ — Remember, parentheses first. Sum the $X$ values. Then, square the sum of the $X$ values.

$\Sigma X^2 = 206$ — Here, exponents come first. Square each $X$ value first, then find the sum of the $X^2$ column.

$\Sigma XY = 85$ — Multiplication comes before addition. Thus, multiply each $X$ value by each $Y$ value $(XY)$, then add the column for the $XY$ values.

$\Sigma(X-3) = 16$ — Subtract 3 from each $X$ value, then add the $(X-3)$ column.

$\Sigma(Y+2)^2 = 142$ — Parentheses first, then exponents, then addition. Thus, add 2 to each $Y$ value, then square the $(Y+2)$ values, and finally sum the $(Y+2)^2$ column.

---

**☞ Your Turn! ☜**

### XI. Summation

| $X$ | $Y$ | $X^2$ | $Y^2$ | $XY$ | $(X-1)$ | $(X-1)^2$ |
|---|---|---|---|---|---|---|
| 4 | 1 | | | | | |
| 6 | 3 | | | | | |
| 2 | 6 | | | | | |
| 8 | 4 | | | | | |
| 5 | 2 | | | | | |

**Your Turn!**
(continued)

Perform the requested summations for the above values:

A. $\Sigma X =$ _____ 25
B. $\Sigma Y =$ _____ 16
C. $\Sigma X^2 =$ _____ 145
D. $\Sigma Y^2 =$ _____ 66
E. $\Sigma XY =$ _____ 70
F. $(\Sigma X)(\Sigma Y) =$ _____ 400
G. $(\Sigma X)^2 =$ _____ 625
H. $\Sigma X^2 + \Sigma Y^2 =$ _____ 211
I. $\Sigma X^2 + (\Sigma Y)^2 =$ _____ 401
J. $\Sigma(X - 1) =$ _____ 20
K. $\Sigma(X - 1)^2 =$ _____ 100

**Answers to "Your Turn!" Problems**

**I. Statistical Terms**

A. Population
B. Sample
C. Random sampling
D. Statistics
E. Inferential statistics
F. Sampling error

**II. Discrete or Continuous Variables**

A. Discrete
B. Continuous
C. Continuous
D. Discrete
E. Discrete
F. Continuous

**III. Real Limits**

A. LL = 8.5          UL = 9.5
B. LL = 6.25         UL = 6.35
C. LL = 31.275       UL = 31.285

(*Continued*)

Answers to "Your Turn!" Problems
(continued)

## IV. Scales of Measurement

A. Ordinal
B. Ratio
C. Interval
D. Nominal
E. Ratio
F. Nominal
G. Ordinal
H. Interval
I. Ratio
J. Interval
K. Nominal
L. Ordinal

## V. Independent and Dependent Variables

A. IV – Amount of alcohol
   DV – Reaction time
B. IV – Music type or lack of music
   DV – Score on math test
C. IV – Room temperature
   DV – Creativity score

D. IV – Amount of sleep deprivation
   DV – Memory score
E. IV – Type of sweetener
   DV – Activity level

## VI. Experimentation or Correlation

A. Correlation
B. Correlation
C. Experimentation
D. Correlation
E. Experimentation

## VII. Rounding

A. 13.61
B. 0.05
C. 1.10
D. 6.91
E. 3.62
F. 0.68
G. 12.07
H. 4.01
I. 2.00
J. 99.56

Answers to "Your Turn!" Problems
(continued)

## VIII. Proportions and Percentages

A. .12
B. 66.67%
C. .84
D. 8.33%
E. 22.22%

## IX. Signed Numbers

A. −12
B. +36
C. −10
D. +95
E. +8
F. −52
G. −77
H. −7

## X. Order of Operations

A. −42
B. −46
C. 14
D. 0

## XI. Summation

A. 25
B. 16
C. 145
D. 66
E. 76
F. 400
G. 625
H. 211
I. 401
J. 20
K. 100

*Additional Practice Problems*

**Answers to odd numbered problems are in Appendix C at the end of the book.**

1. Identify the following as either continuous or discrete variables.
   a. Number of desks in a classroom   *discreate*
   b. Distance from the earth to the moon   *(continued)*
   c. Amount of time that your phone holds a charge   *Continuos*
   d. How many pearls there are on a necklace   *discreate*
2. Determine the lower and upper limits for the values listed below.
   a. Hiking distance: 12.332 miles   *L12.3315   up 12.3325*
   b. Words typed per minute: 48 words   *(47.5)   48.5)*
   c. Time spent studying per week: 28.5 hours   *28.45   28.55*
   d. Amount of water consumed in a day: 1.83 liters   *1.825   1.835*
3. Identify the scale of measurement for the following variables:
   a. The number on football jerseys   *Nominal*
   b. Scores on ability tests (IQ, GRE, SAT)   *Ordinal*
   c. Shirt size (small, medium, large)   *Ordinal*
   d. Reaction time   *ration*
4. Research participants watched the same situational comedy either alone or with other participants. All participants then rated the funniness of the program. What are the independent and dependent variables?   *participants being with someone*
5. One group of students studied for their exam while listening to music. Another group studied in silence. Exam scores for the two groups were then compared. What are the independent and dependent variables?   *Studying   listening to music*
6. After drinking a beverage that contained 100, 200, or 300 mg of caffeine, research participants were asked to hold a pencil halfway inside of a tube while trying not to touch the tube with the pencil. The tube measured 8 mm in diameter, 2 mm larger than the pencil. The number of times that the participants touched the tube with the pencil was recorded. What are the independent and dependent variables?
7. Round the numbers below to the nearest hundredth.
   a. 3.5151   *3.5*
   b. 64.5891   *64.6*
   c. 19.67843   *19.7*
   d. 36.998   *37*
   e. 3.86492   *3.9*
8. Write the following percentages as decimal proportions.
   a. 1%   *0.01*
   b. 28%   *.28*
   c. 112%   *1.12*
   d. 364.7%   *3.647*
9. In an English class of 35 students, 28 are female. In a history class of 60 students, 42 are male. Which class has a higher percent of females?   *English*
10. There were 98 questions on Diego's final psychology exam. He answered 85 of them correctly. Sofia answered 72 out of 80 questions correctly on her final geometry exam. Who scored higher?   *Sofia*
11. Perform the calculations required for the following signed numbers:
    a. $(-12) - (-8) =$   *-4*
    b. $10 + (-11) + 5 + (-5) =$   *-1*
    c. $(6)(-2) =$   *-12*

    d. $(-4)(-5) =$

    e. $(-28) \div (7) =$

    f. $(-80) \div (-20) =$

12. Using the correct order of operations, solve the following equations:

    a. $(24 \div 8)^2 + (13 + 4) + 5^2 =$

    b. $[(23 - 17) - (69 \div 3)^2 + 6^2] =$

    c. $[4^2 + (9 \div 3 + 3^2)] - 6^2 =$

13. Summation Operators:

| $X$ | $Y$ | $X^2$ | $Y^2$ | $XY$ | $(X-1)$ | $(X-1)^2$ |
|---|---|---|---|---|---|---|
| 3 | 2 | | | | | |
| 6 | 4 | | | | | |
| 5 | 4 | | | | | |
| 14 | 10 | | | | | |

    a. $\Sigma X =$

    b. $\Sigma Y =$

    c. $\Sigma X^2 =$

    d. $\Sigma Y^2 =$

    e. $\Sigma XY =$

    f. $(\Sigma X)(\Sigma Y) =$

    g. $(\Sigma X)^2 =$

    h. $\Sigma X^2 + \Sigma Y^2 =$

    i. $\Sigma X^2 + (\Sigma Y)^2 =$

    j. $\Sigma(X - 1) =$

    k. $\Sigma(X - 1)^2 =$

## Note

1 Coren, S. (1996). *Sleep thieves: An eye-opening exploration into the science and mysteries of sleep.* New York: Simon and Schuster.

# Organizing Data Using Tables and Graphs

## ORGANIZING DATA

Once we have embarked on our fact-finding expedition and have gathered a set of scores, we will want to organize them in a way that promotes understanding. Raw, unorganized scores are not very impressive, as follows:

Raw, Unorganized Leadership Scores of 35 Managers:

| 54 | 43 | 48 | 50 | 52 | 44 | 49 |
|----|----|----|----|----|----|----|
| 44 | 46 | 51 | 42 | 50 | 46 | 50 |
| 51 | 55 | 57 | 48 | 53 | 51 | 48 |
| 46 | 52 | 50 | 45 | 55 | 49 | 53 |
| 48 | 50 | 49 | 51 | 48 | 43 | 52 |

As we can see, not much helpful information can be gleaned from this set of scores. It would be advantageous to arrange the scores into a *frequency distribution*, a table that gives organization to a set of raw scores so that patterns in how the scores are *distributed* may be detected. Some frequency distributions elaborate on the frequency information to show further details, while others provide only basic frequency information.

## SIMPLE FREQUENCY DISTRIBUTIONS

A *simple frequency distribution* simply lists the frequencies with which each raw score occurs. A tally mark is shown in one column for each individual score, and then the tally marks are counted and placed into a frequency column. The notation for raw scores is the letter $X$, frequency is designated by an $f$, and the total number of scores is represented by the uppercase letter $N$ if we are working with population scores or a lowercase letter $n$ if we are working with scores from a sample. A simple frequency distribution for the above scores is shown as follows:

Simple Frequency Distribution for the Leadership Scores:

| X | Tally | f |
|---|---|---|
| 57 | \| | 1 |
| 56 | | 0 |
| 55 | \|\| | 2 |
| 54 | \| | 1 |
| 53 | \|\| | 2 |
| 52 | \|\|\| | 3 |
| 51 | \|\|\|\| | 4 |
| 50 | |\|\|\| | 5 |
| 49 | \|\|\| | 3 |
| 48 | |\|\|\| | 5 |
| 47 | | 0 |
| 46 | \|\|\| | 3 |
| 45 | \| | 1 |
| 44 | \|\| | 2 |
| 43 | \|\| | 2 |
| 42 | \| | 1 |
| | | $N = 35$ |

We can see that a frequency distribution provides a structure so that general trends in the arrangement of the scores can be seen at a glance, including the highest and lowest scores, where each score falls in the distribution, and the frequency of each score.

## To Create a Simple Frequency Distribution:

1. Create labels for three columns, as follows: X, Tally, and f.
2. Locate the highest and lowest scores in the unorganized list of scores.
3. Beginning with the highest score at the top, list the score values in descending order in the X column of your frequency distribution. Do not skip any values even if there are no occurrences of some of the values in your list of scores. Stop at the lowest obtained score.
4. Underline the first score in your unorganized list and place a tally mark for that score in the Tally column of your frequency distribution. Underlining the scores helps you

to keep track of your place on the list. Continue this process until all the scores in your list have been underlined.

5. Count the number of tally marks for each score and record this number in the $f$ column.

6. Total the scores in the $f$ column. The sum should be equal to the total number of scores ($N$).

The scores on a hypothetical statistics quiz will be used to illustrate several components of a frequency distribution.

## For Example

Raw Scores on a 10-Point Statistics Quiz:

| | | | | |
|---|---|---|---|---|
| 8 | 3 | 5 | 6 | 10 |
| 6 | 9 | 8 | 9 | 6 |
| 5 | 7 | 10 | 5 | 8 |
| 7 | 8 | 3 | 8 | 10 |
| 6 | 7 | 8 | 7 | 6 |
| 10 | | | | |

Simple Frequency Distribution of Scores for the Statistics Quiz:

| X | Tally | f |
|---|---|---|
| 10 | \|\|\|\| | 4 |
| 9 | \|\| | 2 |
| 8 | ⅣⅠ \| | 6 |
| 7 | \|\|\|\| | 4 |
| 6 | ⅣⅠ | 5 |
| 5 | \|\|\| | 3 |
| 4 | | 0 |
| 3 | \|\| | 2 |
| | | N = 26 |

The highest score was 10 and the lowest score was 3. Notice that even though there were no occurrences of 4, it is included in the list of scores.

 **Your Turn!**

## I. Simple Frequency Distribution

Construct a simple frequency distribution for the following raw scores of 20 students who took a medical terminology quiz.

| | | | |
|---|---|---|---|
| 23 | 21 | 22 | 25 |
| 21 | 23 | 20 | 18 |
| 17 | 19 | 26 | 21 |
| 21 | 18 | 23 | 23 |
| 22 | 25 | 21 | 18 |

| X | Tally | f |
|---|---|---|
| 26 | \| | 1 |
| 25 | \|\| | 2 |
| 24 | \|...\| | 0 |
| 23 | \|\|\|\| | 4 |
| 22 | \|\| | 2 |
| 21 | ⊬⊬ | 5 |
| 20 | \| | 1 |
| 19 | \| | 1 |
| 18 | \|\|\| | 3 |
| | | |
| 17 | \| | |
| | | N = 20 |

## RELATIVE FREQUENCY DISTRIBUTIONS

In a simple frequency distribution, the frequency refers to *how many times* a particular score occurs, whereas in a **relative frequency distribution**, the frequency refers to the *proportion of time* that the score occurs. Relative frequency (Rel. *f*) is found by dividing the score's frequency by *N*:

$$\text{Rel.} f = \frac{f}{N}$$

## To Create a Relative Frequency Distribution:

Simply add a column to the simple frequency distribution table and do the math. (Tally marks are usually eliminated in the final presentation.)

## For Example

Relative Frequency Distribution for Scores on the Previously Mentioned Statistics Quiz

| X | f | Rel. f |
|---|---|---|
| 10 | 4 | .15 |
| 9 | 2 | .08 |
| 8 | 6 | .23 |
| 7 | 4 | .15 |
| 6 | 5 | .19 |
| 5 | 3 | .12 |
| 4 | 0 | .00 |
| 3 | 2 | .08 |
| | $N = 26$ | 1.00 |

We can see that in the above distribution, the relative frequency of a score of 6 was .19. In other words, the score of 6 occurred 19% of the time.

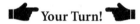 Your Turn!

## II. Relative Frequency Distribution

Construct a relative frequency distribution for the medical terminology quiz.

| X | f | Rel. f |
|---|---|---|
| 26 | 1 | .04 |
| 25 | 2 | .08 |
| 24 | 0 | .00 |
| 23 | 4 | .15 |
| 22 | 2 | .08 |
| 21 | 5 | .19 |
| 20 | 1 | .04 |
| 19 | 1 | .04 |
| 18 | 3 | .12 |
| 17 | 1 | .04 |
| | $N =$ 26 | |

## CUMULATIVE FREQUENCY DISTRIBUTIONS

Another type of distribution table is the ***cumulative frequency distribution***, which indicates the frequency of scores that fall at or below a particular score value. This type of table is useful if you want to know how many people scored below a certain value on a test. To arrive at the answer, you simply need to add the frequencies of the scores below the score of interest.

### To Create a Cumulative Frequency Distribution:

1. Begin with a simple frequency distribution table.
2. Add a cumulative frequency (*cf*) column to the table.
3. Work from the bottom up in the *f* and *cf* columns. Take the bottom score in the *f* column and enter that number in the corresponding space in the *cf* column. Then take that number (in the *cf* column) and add it to the next number up in the *f* column and record the total in the next space up in the *cf* column. Take the last number entered in the *cf* column and add it to the next number up in the *f* column. Repeat this process until the *cf* column is complete. The number at the top of the *cf* column should be equal to *N*.

### For Example

Cumulative Frequency Distribution for Scores on the Statistics Quiz:

| X | f | cf | |
|---|---|-----|---|
| 10 | 4 | 26 | (the *cf* at the top is equal to *N*) |
| 9 | 2 | 22 | |
| 8 | 6 | 20 | |
| 7 | 4 | 14 | |
| 6 | 5 | 10 | |
| 5 | 3 | 5 | (*cf* of 2 below + *f* of 3 = 5) |
| 4 | 0 → 2 | | (because no students scored 4, the *cf* is still 2) |
| 3 | 2 ↘ 2 | | |
| N = 26 | | | |

Tip!

The cumulative frequency distribution will also be used in the next chapter when we calculate a measure of central tendency called the median.

 **Your Turn!**

### III. Cumulative Frequency Distribution

Construct a cumulative frequency distribution for the medical terminology quiz.

| X | f | cf |
|---|---|---|
| 26 | 1 | 2~ |
| 25 | 2 | 19 |
| 24 | 0 | 17 |
| 23 | 4 | 17 |
| 22 | 2 | 13 |
| 21 | 5 | 11 |
| 20 | 1 | 6 |
| 19 | 1 | 5 |
| 18 | 3 | 4 |
| 17 | 1 | 1 |
| | N = 25 | |

## PERCENTILE RANK

You can also include a column for percentile ranks in your cumulative frequency distribution table. **Percentile rank (P.R.)** gives a bit more information than just frequency by indicating the *percentage* of scores that fall at or below a given score in a distribution. The percentile rank is calculated by dividing the cumulative frequency (*cf*) for each score by *N* and multiplying by 100:

$$P.R. = \frac{cf}{N} \times 100$$

## For Example

Percentile Rank for Scores on the Statistics Quiz:

| X | f | cf | P.R. |
|---|---|---|---|
| 10 | 4 | 26 | 100.00 |
| 9 | 2 | 22 | 84.62 |
| 8 | 6 | 20 | 76.92 |
| 7 | 4 | 14 | 53.85 |
| 6 | 5 | 10 | 38.46 |
| 5 | 3 | 5 | 19.23 |
| 4 | 0 | 2 | 7.69 |
| 3 | 2 | 2 | 7.69 |
| | N = 26 | | |

In the distribution above, the percentile rank of a student who scored 8 is 76.92. In other words, about 77% of the students scored at or below that score and only 23% of the students achieved scores above 8.

---

 **Your Turn!**

### IV. Percentile Ranks

Determine the percentile ranks for the medical terminology quiz.

| X | f | cf | P.R. |
|---|---|----|------|
| 26 | 1 | 20 | $10$ |
| 25 | 2 | 19 | $95$ |
| 24 | 0 | 17 | $85$ |
| 23 | 4 | 17 | $75$ |
| 22 | 2 | 13 | $65$ |
| 21 | 5 | 11 | $55$ |
| 20 | 1 | 6 | $30$ |
| 19 | 1 | 5 | $25$ |
| 18 | 3 | 4 | $20$ |
| 17 | 1 | 1 | $3$ |
| $N = 20$ | | | |

---

## COMBINING THE TABLES!

It is helpful to create separate frequency distributions when you are first learning about the various ways in which raw scores can be represented in tables. Discussing the types of frequency distributions individually allows you to digest one concept at a time before moving on to the next concept. In reality, it is not necessary or desirable to create separate distributions. Rather, it is more efficient to simply create one table with a number of different columns.

## For Example

The distribution below illustrates all of the different components of the frequency distribution that we have discussed for the statistics quiz.

Frequency Distribution for Scores on the Statistics Quiz Referred to Previously:

| X | f | Rel. f | cf | P.R. |
|---|---|--------|----|------|
| 10 | 4 | .15 | 26 | 100.00 |
| 9 | 2 | .08 | 22 | 84.62 |
| 8 | 6 | .23 | 20 | 76.92 |
| 7 | 4 | .15 | 14 | 53.85 |
| 6 | 5 | .19 | 10 | 38.46 |
| 5 | 3 | .12 | 5 | 19.23 |
| 4 | 0 | .00 | 2 | 7.69 |
| 3 | 2 | .08 | 2 | 7.69 |

 **Your Turn!**

## V. Combining the Tables!

Complete the columns that follow for the raw scores below:

| 29 | 33 | 32 | 34 |
|----|----|----|----|
| 32 | 32 | 31 | 32 |
| 33 | 32 | 32 | 33 |
| 32 | 31 | 34 | 32 |
| 31 | 33 | 33 | 31 |

| X | Tally | f | Rel. f | cf | P.R. |
|---|-------|---|--------|----|------|
| 34 | | | | | |
| 33 | | | | | |
| 32 | | | | | |
| 31 | | | | | |
| 30 | | | | | |
| | | | | | |

## GROUPED FREQUENCY DISTRIBUTIONS

The scores in all the previous frequency distributions were ungrouped, meaning that each raw score in the table was listed separately. However, ungrouped frequency distributions can be cumbersome if there are too many scores that vary widely over a large span. The data become unremarkable and any patterns that may exist in the scores are not readily apparent, as shown below.

Raw Scores from an Ungrouped Simple Frequency Distribution:

| X | f | X | f | X | f |
|---|---|---|---|---|---|
| 81 | 1 | 69 | 3 | 57 | 3 |
| 80 | 2 | 68 | 4 | 56 | 3 |
| 79 | 0 | 67 | 2 | 55 | 1 |
| 78 | 1 | 66 | 3 | 54 | 0 |
| 77 | 2 | 65 | 9 | 53 | 2 |
| 76 | 1 | 64 | 8 | 52 | 1 |
| 75 | 3 | 63 | 4 | 51 | 0 |
| 74 | 5 | 62 | 5 | 50 | 0 |
| 73 | 4 | 61 | 6 | 49 | 3 |
| 72 | 2 | 60 | 4 | 48 | 2 |
| 71 | 0 | 59 | 6 | 47 | 1 |
| 70 | 4 | 58 | 4 | 46 | 1 |
| | | | | $N = 100$ | |

Due to the large number of scores, it is difficult to extract any meaningful information from the preceding distribution in its ungrouped state. *Grouped frequency distributions*, on the other hand, combine scores into groups, referred to as *class intervals*, thus condensing the data and making overall trends more apparent.

**For Example**

Below is a grouped frequency distribution for the scores contained in the preceding ungrouped simple frequency distribution.

| Class interval | f |
|---|---|
| 81–83 | 1 |
| 78–80 | 3 |
| 75–77 | 6 |
| 72–74 | 11 |
| 69–71 | 7 |
| 66–68 | 9 |
| 63–65 | 21 |
| 60–62 | 15 |
| 57–59 | 13 |
| 54–56 | 4 |
| 51–53 | 3 |
| 48–50 | 5 |
| 45–47 | 2 |
| | $N = 100$ |

We can see in the grouped frequency distribution that most of the scores are in the middle range, while just a few are very high or very low.

Before we begin discussing the actual steps for constructing a grouped frequency distribution, let us first examine a few new terms and some ground rules that will be involved.

### New Terms

- *Class intervals* refer to groups of scores, such as 6–7, 21–23, or 55–59.
- *Interval size*, symbolized by $i$, refers to the number of scores in the class interval. For example, $i = 3$ for the class interval of 21–23 because there are three scores in the interval.
- The *range*, symbolized by $R$, refers to the amount of spread in a distribution of scores. It is determined by subtracting the lower limit (LL) of the lowest score from the upper limit (UL) of the highest score. (See "Determining Real Limits" in Chapter 1.)

$$R = X_{UL-High} - X_{LL-Low}$$

For example, if the lowest score in a distribution is 53 and the highest score is 81, then the range for that distribution would be 29 ($R = 81.5 - 52.5$).

### Ground Rules

There is no magical formula as to how many class intervals to use or the number of scores to include in your class intervals. We do, however, want to keep the number of class intervals both meaningful and manageable. Too few intervals obscure the data so that trends cannot be detected, while too many intervals defeat our purpose of manageability. In general, the more scores there are, the greater the number of intervals that will be used. To learn how to construct grouped frequency distributions, let us use the following ground rules:

- We will use between 10 and 20 class intervals.
- We will use interval sizes ($i$) of 2, 3, or 5.
- Begin the class interval column at the bottom of the distribution with a multiple of $i$ while making sure that your first interval will encapsulate the lowest score in the distribution. For instance, if $i = 3$ in a distribution where the lowest raw score is 31, the first class interval should be 30–32 because 30 is a multiple of 3 and 31 is not.
- The largest scores go at the top of the distribution.

Tip!

The ground rules for constructing grouped frequency distributions vary somewhat from one author to another. Likewise, symbols sometimes vary from one text to another, as do formulas (but they lead you to the same conclusions). There tends to be a lack of standardization in textbooks regarding statistical notation and methods. This is something to be aware of if you see different statistical protocols in other textbooks.

## Finally, the Steps

1. Locate the highest and lowest scores in the distribution and find the range of scores.
2. Determine the size of the class interval ($i$) by trial and error, keeping the preceding ground rules in mind. *Divide the range (Step 1) by potential i values (2, 3, or 5).* This will tell you approximately how many class intervals would result. (Remember, we want between 10 and 20 class intervals.)

   - Suppose the highest score in our distribution is 64 and the lowest is 23. The range, then, is $64.5 - 22.5 = 42$.
   - Experiment by dividing the range by potential $i$ values:

     $42 \div 2 = 21$ (too many)
     $42 \div 3 = 14$ (just right)
     $42 \div 5 = 8.4$ (not enough)

   - In this case, we would use 3 as our interval size with a result of approximately 14 class intervals.

3. Create labels for three columns as follows: Class interval, Tally, and $f$.
4. Using lined paper, count down the number of spaces needed to accommodate all of your class intervals. It is a good idea to add a couple of extra spaces because the division in Step 2 only approximates the number of class intervals.
5. Start at the bottom space of the class interval column and begin creating your class intervals. *Remember that your first entry should begin with a multiple of i and should contain the lowest score in the data set.* You may need to begin with a value that is lower than the lowest score to accomplish this.

## For Example

Bowling Scores of a High School Gym Class:

| | | | | |
|---|---|---|---|---|
| 82 | 128 | 110 | 140 | 127 |
| 109 | 92 | 119 | 142 | 111 |
| 126 | 85 | 124 | 138 | 92 |
| 83 | 114 | **146** | 112 | 86 |
| 98 | 132 | 128 | 95 | 120 |
| 122 | 115 | 92 | 116 | 119 |
| **79** | 113 | 81 | 112 | 115 |

*Step 1:* Find the range. The high score is 146 and the low score is 79.
Thus, $R = 146.5 - 78.5 = 68$.

*Step 2:* Determine the size of the class interval ($i$) by trial and error.
$68 \div 2 = 34$ (too many)
$68 \div 3 = 22.67$ (too many)
$68 \div 5 = 13.60$ (just right, $i = 5$)

*Step 3*: Create labels. ⟶

| Class interval | Tally | f |
|---|---|---|
| 145–149 | \| | 1 |
| 140–144 | \|\| | 2 |
| 135–139 | \| | 1 |
| 130–134 | \| | 1 |
| 125–129 | \|\|\|\| | 4 |
| 120–124 | \|\|\| | 3 |
| 115–119 | Ж | 5 |
| 110–114 | Ж \| | 6 |
| 105–109 | \| | 1 |
| 100–104 |  | 0 |
| 95–99 | \|\| | 2 |
| 90–94 | \|\|\| | 3 |
| 85–89 | \|\| | 2 |
| 80–84 | \|\|\| | 3 |
| 75–79 | \| | 1 |
|  |  | N = 35 |

*Steps 4 & 5*: Beginning at the bottom, create your class intervals. ⟶

Tip!

Do not forget to begin your first entry at the bottom with a multiple of *i*. Failure to do so is a common student error.

---

👉 **Your Turn!** 👈

## VI. Grouped Frequency Distribution

Construct a grouped frequency distribution for the following raw scores on a 70-point statistics exam:

| | | | | |
|---|---|---|---|---|
| 52 | 49 | 45 | 25 | 61 |
| 42 | 53 | 54 | 47 | 49 |
| 56 | 69 | 60 | 68 | 66 |
| 65 | 50 | 51 | 57 | 40 |
| 51 | 37 | 52 | 50 | 55 |

$R =$  45

$i =$ 3

**☞ Your Turn! ☜**
(continued)

| Class interval | Tally | f |
|---|---|---|
| 61-74 | l | 1 |
| 61-K6 | H | 2 |
| 63-65 | l | 1 |
| 60-62 | ll | 2 |
| 57-59 | | 1 |
| 54 - 56 | (ll) | 3 |
| 51-53 | HH | 5 |
| 48-50 | (lll) | 4 |
| 48 - 45 | (ll) | 3 |
| 42 - 44 | l | 1 |
| 39-41 | l | 1 |
| 36-38 | l | |
| 33-35 | 6 | 6 |
| 31-32 | 6 | 6 |
| 3-23 | 6 | 6 |
| 27-31 | l | 1 |
| 24-2 | | |
| | | |
| | | |
| | | N = 2 |

## GRAPHIC REPRESENTATION OF DISTRIBUTIONS

The information from a frequency distribution can also be illustrated in the form of a graph, providing us with a pictorial view of the data. Graphs are usually displayed on two axes, one horizontal and one vertical. The horizontal axis is the X-axis, also called the baseline or **abscissa**, and it usually represents the values or categories of the variable being measured, such as scores on a test or military rank. The vertical axis is the Y-axis, also called the **ordinate**, and it usually represents the frequencies of those values or categories. Three of the most commonly used graphs of distributions are bar graphs, histograms, and frequency polygons. Which type of graph to use will depend upon the characteristics of the variable being measured.

**Bar graphs** are used for qualitative variables that differ in kind. These would include data measured on nominal or ordinal scales. In this type of graph, the bars are spatially separated to illustrate their discontinuous, or categorical, nature. The heights of the bars reflect the frequencies of the event.

**For Example**

This bar graph shows the frequencies of seven different types of therapy received by 140 clients at a mental health clinic in one month:

**Types of Therapy**

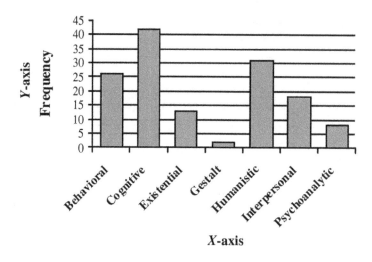

The *X*-axis shows the different types of therapy offered. The *Y*-axis shows the number of clients (*f*) who received each type of therapy.

**Tip!**

For *nominal* data, the order of the bars is a matter of personal preference. Academic major, for example, has no particular order. If the categories are psychology, criminal justice, nursing, and political science, the order in which they are shown on the graph does not matter. If *ordinal* data are being used, on the other hand, the natural order of the variable should be reflected. For example, if academic year were being measured, the natural order would be freshman, sophomore, junior, and senior.

*Histograms* are used for quantitative variables that differ in amount. These would include data measured on interval or ratio scales. Histograms are similar to bar graphs except that the bars touch each other to reflect the continuous nature of the measured variable (i.e., different amounts of the same variable).

**For Example**

The histogram below represents the number of days 100 employees were absent over a 12-month period.

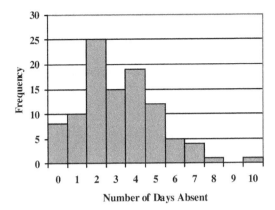

Frequency / Number of Days Absent

*Frequency polygons* are also used for quantitative data; dots, corresponding to the appropriate frequency, are used instead of bars. The dots are then connected by a straight line.

### For Example

The following frequency polygon represents the number of days 100 employees were absent over a 12-month period.

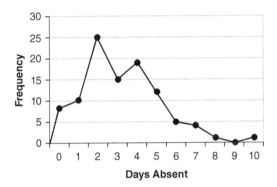

Frequency / Days Absent

An advantage of using frequency polygons over histograms is that they allow you to compare different distributions. For example, if you wanted to compare scores for male athletes and female athletes, both sets of scores could be shown on a frequency polygon, one in the color red and one in the color blue. The lines would be superimposed so that the general trends of both sets of scores would be apparent.

### TYPES AND SHAPES OF FREQUENCY POLYGONS

Thus far, we have been discussing *empirical distributions*, which are based on frequencies of actual scores. *Theoretical distributions*, on the other hand, are based on the mathematical probability of the frequencies of scores in a population. Theoretical polygons are drawn with smooth lines without dots because actual scores are not represented. An indispensable theoretical distribution that we will use extensively throughout this text is the *normal distribution curve*, sometimes referred to as the *bell curve* because it is shaped like a bell, as illustrated:

### The Normal Distribution Curve

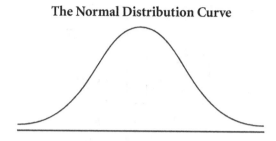

## Some important characteristics of the bell curve are as follows:

- It is symmetrical, with the left and right sides being mirror images of each other.
- It is based on an infinite number of cases. Therefore, the tails are *asymptotic*, meaning that they never touch the baseline (i.e., a theoretical normal distribution can never have a frequency of zero).
- The most frequently occurring scores are in the middle.
- The least frequently occurring scores are farthest from the middle.

The reason that the normal distribution is so important is that when many events in nature are measured (including various characteristics of human beings), the scores will often distribute themselves into this shape. The area under the curve represents the entire population that was measured. Most people will fall in the middle (that is why more space is devoted to this area), and just a few people will fall at the extremes. Take height, for example. A few people are very tall, a few people are very short, but by and large, most people are of average height and fall in the middle. The normal distribution will be revisited in later chapters.

*Skewed distributions*, on the other hand, are not symmetrical. Instead, they have scores that tend to stack up at either the high or low end of the distribution and trail off at the other end.

In a *positively skewed distribution*, there are more low scores than high scores.

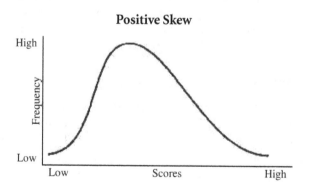

Positive Skew

In a *negatively skewed distribution,* there are more high scores than low scores:

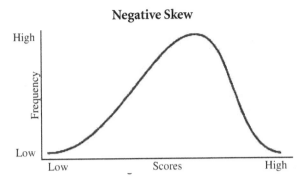

For example, the ages of college students would result in a *positively skewed distribution* because there would be fewer high scores (i.e., most students who attend college are under the age of 30). A distribution for the ages of grandparents, on the other hand, would have a *negative skew* because there would be fewer young ages.

**Tip!**

It is a common error to confuse the two types of skews. In this context, positive and negative have nothing to do with good and bad. Think of the skew in terms of the direction of the tail. In a positively skewed distribution, the tail extends to the right toward the positive end. In a negatively skewed distribution, the tail extends to the left toward the negative end.

**The child of a statistician.**

**Your Turn!**

## VII. Skewed Distributions

Imagine these variables being graphed along the *X*-axis and indicate whether they would result in distributions that are positively *or* negatively skewed.

| Variable | Direction of skew |
|---|---|
| A. Age at death | N |
| B. Baldness among children (excluding newborn infants) | P |
| C. Muscle tone of couch potatoes | P |
| D. Roller skate purchases for elderly people | P |
| E. Muscle tone of professional athletes | N |
| F. Incomes of high school dropouts | P |
| G. Scores on an easy test | N |
| H. Caloric intake of thin people | P |

## Answers to "Your Turn!" Problems

### I. Simple Frequency Distribution

| Score (X) | Tally | Frequency (f) |
|---|---|---|
| 26 | \| | 1 |
| 25 | \|\| | 2 |
| 24 | | 0 |
| 23 | \|\|\|\| | 4 |
| 22 | \|\| | 2 |
| 21 | ̶|̶|̶|̶|̶| | 5 |
| 20 | \| | 1 |
| 19 | \| | 1 |
| 18 | \|\|\| | 3 |
| 17 | \| | 1 |
| | | N = 20 |

### II. Relative Frequency Distribution

| Score (X) | f | Rel. f |
|---|---|---|
| 26 | 1 | .05 |
| 25 | 2 | .10 |
| 24 | 0 | .00 |

Answers to "Your Turn!" Problems
(continued)

| Score (X) | f | Rel. f |
|---|---|---|
| 23 | 4 | .20 |
| 22 | 2 | .10 |
| 21 | 5 | .25 |
| 20 | 1 | .05 |
| 19 | 1 | .05 |
| 18 | 3 | .15 |
| 17 | 1 | .05 |
| | N = 20 | 1.00 |

## III. Cumulative Frequency Distribution

| Score (X) | f | cf |
|---|---|---|
| 26 | 1 | 20 |
| 25 | 2 | 19 |
| 24 | 0 | 17 |
| 23 | 4 | 17 |
| 22 | 2 | 13 |
| 21 | 5 | 11 |
| 20 | 1 | 6 |
| 19 | 1 | 5 |
| 18 | 3 | 4 |
| 17 | 1 | 1 |
| | N = 20 | |

## IV. Percentile Ranks

| Score (X) | f | cf | P.R. |
|---|---|---|---|
| 26 | 1 | 20 | 100 |
| 25 | 2 | 19 | 95 |
| 24 | 0 | 17 | 85 |
| 23 | 4 | 17 | 85 |
| 22 | 2 | 13 | 65 |
| 21 | 5 | 11 | 55 |
| 20 | 1 | 6 | 30 |
| 19 | 1 | 5 | 25 |
| 18 | 3 | 4 | 20 |
| 17 | 1 | 1 | 5 |
| | N = 20 | | |

(Continued)

**Answers to "Your Turn!" Problems**
(continued)

## V. Combining the Tables!

| X | Tally | f | Rel. f | cf | P.R. |
|---|-------|---|--------|-----|------|
| 34 | || | 2 | .10 | 20 | 100 |
| 33 | |||| | 5 | .25 | 18 | 90 |
| 32 | |||| ||| | 8 | .40 | 13 | 65 |
| 31 | |||| | 4 | .20 | 5 | 25 |
| 30 | | 0 | .00 | 1 | 5 |
| 29 | | | 1 | .05 | 1 | 5 |

## VI. Grouped Frequency Distribution

$R = 69.5 - 24.5 = 45$
$45 \div 3 = 15$. Thus, $i = 3$

| Class Interval | Tally | f |
|----------------|-------|---|
| 69–71 | | | 1 |
| 66–68 | || | 2 |
| 63–65 | | | 1 |
| 60–62 | || | 2 |
| 57–59 | | | 1 |
| 54–56 | ||| | 3 |
| 51–53 | |||| | 5 |
| 48–50 | |||| | 4 |
| 45–47 | || | 2 |
| 42–44 | | | 1 |
| 39–41 | | | 1 |
| 36–38 | | | 1 |
| 33–35 | | 0 |
| 30–32 | | 0 |
| 27–29 | | 0 |
| 24–26 | | | 1 |
| | | N = 25 |

## VII. Skewed Distributions

A. Negative
B. Positive
C. Positive
D. Positive
E. Negative
F. Positive
G. Negative
H. Positive

*Additional Practice Problems*

**Answers to odd numbered problems are in Appendix C at the end of the book.**

1. Identify the appropriate type of graph that should be used for the variables listed below:
   a. military rank    *postiu*
   b. intelligence scores  *postive*
   c. annual income    *negatine*
   d. eye color      *bell*
   e. letter grades
   f. a comparison of life expectancy rates for males and females  *bell*
   g. puppy weights  *negatine*
2. Under what circumstances would you use a bar graph, histogram, and frequency polygon?
3. Discuss the differences between empirical and theoretical distributions.
4. Discuss the characteristics of the normal distribution curve.
5. The high score on a final exam in history was 84 and the low score was 22. Assume the professor constructs a grouped frequency distribution for the class.
   a. What is the range?
   b. What size of class interval should be used?
   c. What should the first entry be at the bottom of the distribution?
6. For the following set of scores, first construct a simple frequency distribution. Then include columns for relative frequency, cumulative frequency, and percentile rank.

| | | | |
|---|---|---|---|
| 25 | 30 | 23 | 27 |
| 28 | 22 | 27 | 28 |
| 26 | 29 | 29 | 23 |
| 25 | 26 | 26 | 25 |

7. Given the following cumulative frequency distribution:

| X | f | cf |
|---|---|---|
| 21 | 2 | 11 |
| 20 | 3 | 9 |
| 19 | 2 | 6 |
| 18 | 3 | 4 |
| 17 | 0 | 1 |
| 16 | 1 | 1 |

   a. What is $N$?
   b. What is the cumulative frequency of a score of 18?
   c. What is the percentile rank of a score of 19?
   d. What is the relative frequency of a score of 20?
8. Construct a grouped frequency distribution for the following set of scores:

| | | | |
|---|---|---|---|
| 55 | 93 | 67 | 84 |
| 68 | 77 | 82 | 81 |
| 48 | 56 | 46 | 65 |
| 82 | 51 | 79 | 80 |
| 90 | 73 | 84 | 91 |

# 3

# Measures of Central Tendency

## CENTRAL TENDENCY

We learned in the last chapter that one way of describing frequency distributions is in terms of the shape of their curves. Another way of describing them is in terms of their *central tendency*, which is a single value that describes the most typical or representative score in an entire distribution. Three commonly used measures of central tendency are the *mode*, the *median*, and the *mean*.

## THE MODE

The *mode (MO)* specifies the score value with the highest frequency in a set of scores. To determine the mode, simply arrange the scores in descending order (or create a frequency distribution if there are numerous scores). Once they are arranged so, it is easy to see at a glance which score occurred with the greatest frequency. No calculations are necessary.

## For Example

In the set of scores below,

73, 73, 72, 70, 68, 68, 68, 68, 59, 59, 59, 55

the mode is 68 and is written as follows: $MO = 68$.

    If you are working with a grouped frequency distribution, the mode would be the *midpoint* of the class interval with the greatest frequency. The midpoint is simply the middle score in a class interval. In the following grouped frequency distribution, the mode would be 25.

| Class intervals | Midpoint | f | Class intervals | Midpoint | f |
|---|---|---|---|---|---|
| 36–38 | 37 | 8 | 21–23 | 22 | 20 |
| 33–35 | 34 | 11 | 18–20 | 19 | 16 |
| 30–32 | 31 | 18 | 15–17 | 16 | 12 |
| 27–29 | 28 | 26 | 12–14 | 13 | 7 |
| 24–26 | 25 | 32 | 9–11 | 10 | 3 |

The class interval with the most frequently occurring scores is 24–26, with a frequency count of 32. The midpoint of that class interval is 25. Thus, $MO = 25$.

**Tip!**

---

Notice that the mode is not a frequency, but rather the value that occurs most often.

---

The mode is easy to find quickly. However, there are some drawbacks to using the mode. One is that the mode ignores all scores other than those occurring most frequently, thus casting much information aside. In addition, the mode is not always reliable. A change in one value can have a dramatic effect on the mode. Consider the following distribution of scores on a 20-point quiz: 20, 20, 20, 20, 18, 17, 15, 15, 13, 12, 11, 11, 8, 8, 8. The mode is 20. However, if one more student scored 8, rather than 20, the mode would then become 8. We would like to have a more stable measure of the typical score in a data set.

---

 **Your Turn!**

### I. Simple Frequency Distribution and Mode

A. Create a simple frequency distribution table for the following ages, reported by 24 high school seniors, at which they received their first romantic kiss. What is the mode of this distribution?

13, 15, 16, 15, 17, 14, 15, 13, 15, 16, 12, 14,
16, 15, 13, 15, 16, 15, 14, 16, 15, 12, 14, 15

| X | Tally | f |
|---|-------|---|
| 17 | ⲓ⅃⅃⅃ ⅃⅃⅃ ⅃⅃⅃ ⅃⅃ | 1 |
| 16 | ⅃⅃⅃ ⅃⅃⅃⅃⅃ ⅃ | 5 |
| 15 | ⅃⅃⅃⅃ ⅃⅃⅃ ⅃⅃⅃ | 9 |
| 14 | ⅃⅃⅃⅃ ⅃⅃⅃⅃⅃⅃ | 4 |
| 13 | ⅃⅃⅃ ⅃⅃⅃⅃ ⅃⅃ | 3 |
| 12 | ⅃⅃⅃⅃ ⅃⅃⅃⅃⅃ | 2 |

$MO = $ ~~15~~

(*Continued*)

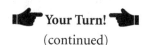 **Your Turn!**
(continued)

B. What is the mode for the following grouped frequency distribution?

| Class interval | Midpoint | f |
|---|---|---|
| 95–99 | 97 | 3 |
| 90–94 | 92 | 2 |
| 85–89 | 87 | 5 |
| 80–84 | 82 | 3 |
| 75–79 | 77 | 10 |
| 70–74 | 72 | 12 |
| 65–69 | 67 | 7 |
| 60–64 | 62 | 4 |
| 55–59 | 57 | 3 |
| 50–54 | 52 | 0 |
| 45–49 | 47 | 2 |

$MO =$ _____ *Fh*

## Graphic Representations of Mode

The mode can be graphed on a frequency polygon and will be at the highest peak, indicating the greatest frequency.

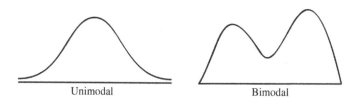

Unimodal                    Bimodal

If the distribution has only one peak, it is referred to as a **unimodal distribution**. A **bimodal distribution** is also possible, in which case it will have two modes – and two peaks. If a distribution has two scores with high frequencies (even if the frequencies are not exactly the same) with no other high frequencies in between, it is considered to be bimodal.

## THE MEDIAN

The second measure of central tendency that we will consider is the **median** *(Mdn)*, which is the middle point in a distribution. Half the scores are above this middle point and half are below it. We will look at two different methods for determining the median.

### Counting Method

If you are working from a short list of scores, then the procedure for locating the median involves simple counting. But that procedure will differ slightly depending on whether you are working with an odd or even number of scores.

To find the median for an *odd* number of scores:

- Arrange the scores in descending order from highest to lowest.
- The location of the median will be the score that has an equal number of scores above and below as determined by:

$$\frac{N+1}{2}$$

### For Example

For the following distribution of an *odd* number of scores:

26, 25, 24, 20, <u>18,</u> 17, 17, 15, 12

$$\frac{9+1}{2} = 5$$

We are looking for the 5th score. Thus, the median is 18 (i.e., *Mdn* = 18). Note that 5 is not the median, but rather the location of the median.

To find the median for an *even* number of scores:

- Arrange the scores in order from highest to lowest.
- Divide the distribution in half and draw a line between the two scores that separate the distribution into halves.
- Add the two middle scores that surround the halfway point and divide by 2. The resulting value will be the median.

### For Example

For the following distribution of an *even* number of scores:

$$92, 91, 90, 90, 87, 82, \Big| 77, 75, 75, 70, 68, 60$$

Middle Scores

$$Mdn = \frac{82+77}{2} = 79.5$$

The median may or may not be an actual score in the distribution. It is the center point that has half the scores above it and half below it.

**Tip!**

---

 **Your Turn!**

## II. Median: Counting Method

A. Last year, 11 employees of a lawnmower manufacturing company retired. Their retirement ages are listed below. What was the median retirement age?

65, 67, 73, 64, 78, 60, 56, 70, 62, 66, 65

*Mdn* = _____

B. Determine the median number of haircuts given on one Saturday by each of 12 stylists at Pro Cut Salon:

10, 8, 21, 7, 15, 8, 5, 14, 10, 7, 3, 17

*Mdn* = _____

---

## Formula Method

The formula method for determining the median is used when you are working from a grouped frequency distribution and the cumulative frequency of the scores has been included. The formula is as follows:

$$Mdn = LL + \left( \frac{50\% \text{ of } N - cf_{below}}{f_{wi}} \right) i$$

where: LL = lower limit of the class interval that contains the median

$N$ = number of scores

$cf_{below}$ = cumulative frequency below the class interval that contains the median

$f_{wi}$ = frequency of scores in the interval that contains the median

$i$ = size of class interval

**For Example**

| Class interval | f | cf |
|---|---|---|
| 42–44 | 4 | 124 → N |
| 39–41 | 8 | 120 |
| 36–38 | 10 | 112 |
| 33–35 | 11 | 102 |
| 30–32 | 8 | 91 |
| 27–29 | 18 | 83 |
| 24–26 ————— | 17 ————— | 65 |
| 21–23 | 16 | 48 |
| 18–20 | 10 | 32 |
| 15–17 | 11 | 22 |
| 12–14 | 5 | 11 |
| 9–11 | 6 | 6 |

According to our definition of the median, we are looking for the point that divides the distribution in half. Because $N = 124$, we are looking for the 62nd case. This will be found in the class interval of 24–26, where the cumulative frequency is 65, because 65 is the first *cf* number that can possibly contain the 62nd case. Thus, the 62nd case (i.e., the median) will fall somewhere within that class interval.

The elements of the formula are as follows:

- The lower limit of the interval that contains the median is 23.5.
- $N$ is 124. We have already established that 50% of $N = 62$, which is the point that divides the distribution in half.
- The *cf* below the interval that contains the median is 48.
- The frequency of scores in the interval that contains the median ($f_{wi}$) is 17.
- The size of the class interval is 3.

**Tip!**

Once you learn what the abbreviations stand for, it is easy to identify these values in the language of the formula. In other words,

LL = 23.5
50% of $N$ = 62
$cf_{below}$ = 48
$f_{wi}$ = 17
$i$ = 3

Applying these values to the formula results in the following median outcome:

$$Mdn = 23.5 + \left( \frac{62 - 48}{17} \right)(3)$$

$$= 23.5 + 2.47$$

$$= 25.97$$

The median is usually more informative as a measure of central tendency than is the mode, and it does not have the instability of the mode. However, the median still does not consider all scores and has limited use in further calculations.

---

 **Your Turn!**

### III. Median: Formula Method

Determine the median points earned by 60 college football teams during the first game of the season as reported below:

| Class intervals | $f$ | $cf$ |
|-----------------|-----|------|
| 60–64 | 2 | 60 |
| 55–59 | 1 | 58 |
| 50–54 | 0 | 57 |
| 45–49 | 5 | 57 |
| 40–44 | 0 | 52 |
| 35–39 | 7 | 52 |
| 30–34 | 13 | 45 |
| 25–29 | 12 | 32 |
| 20–24 | 8 | 20 |
| 15–19 | 5 | 12 |
| 10–14 | 0 | 7 |
| 5–9 | 5 | 7 |
| 0–4 | 2 | 2 |

$$Mdn = LL + \left( \frac{50\% \text{ of } N - cf_{below}}{f_{wi}} \right) i$$

$Mdn = \underline{\quad 27.67 \quad}$

## THE MEAN

Finally, we get to the **mean**, which is the sum total of all of the scores in a distribution divided by the total number of scores. The symbols for the mean and for the number of scores are dependent on whether you are working with population or sample data. The symbol for a population mean is the Greek symbol $\mu$ (pronounced "mew"). Two common symbols for the sample mean are the letter $M$ and $\overline{X}$ (pronounced "X-bar"). We will use the symbol $M$ because it is this symbol that is often reported in professional journals. An uppercase $N$ is used if the scores are from a population, and a lowercase $n$ is used if the scores are from a sample. The formula for the mean is as follows:

For a population,                    For a sample,

$$\mu = \frac{\Sigma X}{N} \qquad\qquad M = \frac{\Sigma X}{n}$$

Notice that the calculations for both the population and the sample mean are the same. Only the symbols are different.

### For Example

Let us calculate the mean for the following set of scores from a population:

78, 63, 42, 98, 87, 52, 72, 64, 75, 89

$$\mu = \frac{\Sigma X}{N} = \frac{720}{10} = 72$$

The mean for the following set of scores from a sample involves the same set of calculations:

3, 8, 6, 9, 10, 17, 5, 8, 1

$$M = \frac{\Sigma X}{n} = \frac{67}{9} = 7.44$$

### Mean for a Simple Frequency Distribution

To calculate the mean for scores that have been arranged into a simple frequency distribution, the formula is modified as follows:

For a population,                    For a sample,

$$\mu = \frac{\Sigma\, fX}{N} \qquad\qquad M = \frac{\Sigma\, fX}{n}$$

where: $fX$ = frequency of the score multiplied by the score itself.

## For Example

Let us calculate the mean for the following scores from a sample arranged into a simple frequency distribution table:

| X | f | fX | X | f | fX |
|---|---|---|---|---|---|
| 48 | 1 | 48 | 41 | 4 | 164 |
| 47 | 4 | 188 | 40 | 6 | 240 |
| 46 | 2 | 92 | 39 | 3 | 117 |
| 45 | 4 | 180 | 38 | 0 | 0 |
| 44 | 9 | 396 | 37 | 1 | 37 |
| 43 | 8 | 344 | 36 | 2 | 72 |
| 42 | 5 | 210 | 35 | 1 | 35 |
| | | | | $n = 50$ | $\Sigma fx = 2123$ |

$$M = \frac{\Sigma fX}{n} = \frac{2123}{50} = 42.46$$

Remember the order of mathematical operations. Multiplication comes before addition. Thus, the frequency of each score is multiplied by the score itself first (fX). Then, sum (Σ) the fX values.

**Tip!**

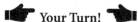 **Your Turn!**

### IV. Mean for a Simple Frequency Distribution

Following are the number of nonsense syllables (out of 20) correctly recalled after rehearsal by 73 sample participants. Calculate the mean.

| X | f | fX |
|---|---|---|
| 17 | 1 | 17 |
| 16 | 0 | 0 |
| 15 | 3 | 45 |
| 14 | 2 | 28 |
| 13 | 4 | 52 |
| 12 | 8 | 96 |
| 11 | 12 | 132 |
| 10 | 13 | 130 |
| 9 | 6 | 54 |
| 8 | 8 | 64 |
| 7 | 5 | 35 |

**Your Turn!**

(continued)

| X | f | fX |
|---|---|---|
| 6 | 3 | 18 |
| 5 | 4 | 20 |
| 4 | 2 | 8 |
| 3 | 1 | 3 |
| 2 | 0 | 0 |
| 1 | 1 | 1 |

$$M = \frac{\Sigma \, fX}{n}$$

$M =$ _____ 7.3

## Mean for a Grouped Frequency Distribution

The procedure for calculating the mean for scores that have been arranged into a grouped frequency distribution is the same as for a simple frequency distribution except that you use the midpoint of each class interval for X.

## For Example

Let us calculate the mean for the following scores from a sample arranged into a grouped frequency distribution:

| Class interval | Midpoint (X) | f | fX |
|---|---|---|---|
| 36–38 | 37 | 4 | 148 |
| 33–35 | 34 | 3 | 102 |
| 30–32 | 31 | 1 | 31 |
| 27–29 | 28 | 4 | 112 |
| 24–26 | 25 | 7 | 175 |
| 21–23 | 22 | 6 | 132 |
| 18–20 | 19 | 6 | 114 |
| 15–17 | 16 | 2 | 32 |
| 12–14 | 13 | 0 | 0 |
| 9–11 | 10 | 3 | 30 |
| | | $n = 36$ | $\Sigma fX = 876$ |

$$M = \frac{\Sigma fX}{n} = \frac{876}{36} = 24.33$$

### Advantages of the Mean

- The mean is the measure of central tendency that is used most often in statistics because it is the only one of the three that takes every score value into consideration. It is therefore the only one that can be used for additional statistical operations.
- The sample mean ($M$) is also an unbiased estimate of the population mean ($\mu$) and is therefore important in inferential statistics.

### Mean ($M$) as an Unbiased Estimate of $\mu$

Here is an explanation of an unbiased estimate of the population mean. Remember that with inferential statistics, we use sample statistics to estimate population parameters.

Suppose we were to select a random sample of people from a population, measure them on some dependent variable, and then calculate a mean. If we used that sample mean to estimate the population mean, our estimate would probably not be exactly equal to the population mean. It might either underestimate or overestimate the population mean. This would be the sampling error referred to in Chapter 1.

If we drew another sample from the same population and again calculated a mean, it would again probably be somewhat different from the actual population mean. And if we repeated this process over and over, our sample means would likely continue to be somewhat off. However, there would be no systematic pattern in our deviations from the population mean. Errors in both directions (overestimates and underestimates) would balance out. Thus, there would be no systematic bias in our sample estimates of the population mean, even though any particular estimate might be somewhat off due to sampling error.

In later chapters, we will learn ways to measure the amount of sampling error to be expected when estimating population parameters.

## WHEN TO USE WHICH MEASURE OF CENTRAL TENDENCY

In determining which measure of central tendency to use for a set of scores, the scale of measurement and the shape of the distribution need to be considered.

### Scale of Measurement

- While the *mode* can be used for all scales (nominal, ordinal, interval, ratio), it is the *only* measure of central tendency that can be used for nominal variables, and that is its typical use.
- The *median* can be used for all scales except nominal. (It makes no sense to determine the median for categorical variables such as the median color of automobiles.)
- The *mean* can be used only for variables measured on interval or ratio scales.

### Shape

- For approximately normally shaped distributions, the mean is preferred.
- For skewed distributions, use the median. This is because the mean is affected by extreme scores and the median is not. Such extreme scores are referred to as **outliers**.

## For Example

Given the following data set, the mean is 74.11:

36, 54, 56, 70, 72, 91, 91, 95, 102

However, if the last score of 102 were replaced with 802, the mean would be affected by that extreme score and would be pulled in that direction to result in a value of 151.89. On the other hand, the median would not be affected by the outlier and in both cases would result in a value of 72, which more accurately reflects the central tendency of the entire distribution.

## THE POSITION OF CENTRAL TENDENCIES IN FREQUENCY POLYGONS

In a *normal distribution*, all three measures of central tendency would be in the middle of the distribution and all would have the same value. The mode will always be at the peak, reflecting the highest frequency. The median divides the distribution in half, and the mean balances out the high and low scores.

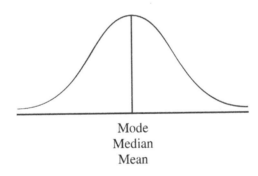

Mode
Median
Mean

In *skewed distributions*, the mode would again be at the peak; the mean would be located toward the tails in the direction of the skew (having been affected by either high or low extreme scores); and the median would be between the mode and the mean (so that half the scores lie above it and half below it).

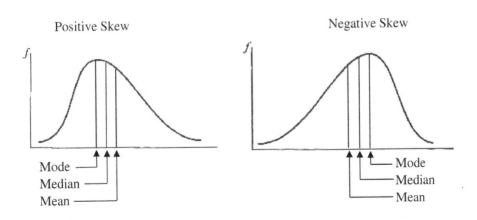

**Your Turn!**

## V. Median/Mean Comparison

Following is a sample distribution of 15 annual incomes:

18,000
21,000
23,500
27,275          A. What is the median?
28,925              *31,650* (handwritten)
29,400          B. What is the mean?
29,900              *50,067.4* (handwritten)
31,650          C. Which is the more appropriate measure of central
34,500              tendency to use for this distribution? _____ Why?
38,900
38,955              *its positively skewed* (handwritten)
39,780              *so mean wont* (handwritten)
40,621              *be effected* (handwritten)
164,980
183,625

---

**Answers to "Your Turn!" Problems**

### I. Simple Frequency Distribution and Mode

A.  | $X$ | $f$ |
|----|----|
| 17 | 1 |
| 16 | 5 |
| 15 | 9 |
| 14 | 4 |
| 13 | 3 |
| 12 | 2 |

$MO = 15$

B. $MO = 72$

### II. Median: Counting Method

A. 78, 73, 70, 67, 66, **65**, 65, 64, 62, 60, 56

$$\frac{11+1}{2} = 6 \qquad \text{Sixth score is 65, thus } Mdn = 65.$$

**Answers to "Your Turn!" Problems**
(continued)

B. 21, 17, 15, 14, 10, <u>10, 8</u>, 8, 7, 7, 5, 3

$$Mdn = \frac{10+8}{2} = 9$$

### III. Median: Formula Method

$$Mdn = LL + \left( \frac{50\% \text{ of } N - cf_{below}}{f_{wi}} \right) i$$

$$= 24.5 + \left( \frac{30-20}{12} \right)(5)$$

$$= 28.67$$

### IV. Mean for a Simple Frequency Distribution

| X | f | fX | |
|---|---|---|---|
| 17 | 1 | 17 | |
| 16 | 0 | 0 | |
| 15 | 3 | 45 | |
| 14 | 2 | 28 | |
| 13 | 4 | 52 | |
| 12 | 8 | 96 | |
| 11 | 12 | 132 | |
| 10 | 13 | 130 | $M = \dfrac{\Sigma fX}{n} = \dfrac{703}{73} = 9.63$ |
| 9 | 6 | 54 | |
| 8 | 8 | 64 | |
| 7 | 5 | 35 | |
| 6 | 3 | 18 | |
| 5 | 4 | 20 | |
| 4 | 2 | 8 | |
| 3 | 1 | 3 | |
| 2 | 0 | 0 | |
| 1 | <u>1</u> | <u>1</u> | |
| | 73 | 703 | |

### V. Median/Mean Comparison

A. 31,650

B. 50,067.40

C. The median is more appropriate because the distribution is positively skewed. The mean would be affected by the two extremely high salaries. The median would not be affected by those values.

### Additional Practice Problems

**Answers to odd numbered problems are in Appendix C at the end of the book.**

1. Define the three most common measures of central tendency and discuss their advantages and disadvantages.
2. What is meant by the statement, "The sample mean is an unbiased estimate of the population mean?"
3. Discuss the locations of the mode, median, and mean in the normal distribution and in skewed distributions.
4. In a negatively skewed distribution, Tyron's score was the same as the median, Jorge's score was the same as the mode, and Geraldine's score was the same as the mean.
   a. Who scored the highest?
   b. Who scored the lowest?
5. In a distribution of scores, the mode was 68, the median was 59, and the mean was 47. What shape is the distribution?
6. In a distribution of scores, the median was 60, the mean was 98, and the mode was 42. What is the shape of the distribution?
7. Which measure of central tendency should be used when reporting the annual income of US households and why?
8. Dr. Hardnose is known for his difficult tests. The biology mid-term exam was no exception and many of the students obtained low scores. What measure of central tendency should be used to reflect the performance of the class and why?
9. One of the presenters at an auto show wanted to know what color of motor vehicle is preferred. She asked the participants to choose from: black, white, blue, red, green, and tan. Which measure of central tendency should be reported?
10. Why is it inappropriate to use the mean as a measure of central tendency in distributions that are skewed?
11. What two factors need to be considered when deciding which measure of central tendency to report?
12. Decide which measure of central tendency should be used in the following situations:
    a. It is the only measure of central tendency that can be used for data measured on a nominal scale.
    b. It can only be used for data measured on interval and ratio scales.
    c. It can be used for all scales of measurement except nominal.
    d. It should be used for distributions that are positively skewed.
    e. It should be used for distributions that are negatively skewed.
    f. It should be used for normally shaped distributions.
13. Given the following set of scores: 6, 8, 3, 7, 9, 3, 7, 4, 7
    a. what is the mode?
    b. what is the median?
    c. what is the mean?
14. Given the following set of scores: 8, 10, 10, 7, 12, 10, 8, 10, 7, 9
    a. what is the mode?
    b. what is the median?
    c. what is the mean?

15. The annual incomes for the employees of a new hat company are listed below (in thousandths).

| | | | |
|---|---|---|---|
| 65 | 33 | 52 | 47 |
| 72 | 73 | 68 | 65 |
| 58 | 49 | 18 | 59 |
| 31 | 62 | 61 | 74 |
| 42 | 27 | 54 | 52 |
| 80 | 78 | 66 | 22 |

Construct a grouped frequency distribution table. Using the table, determine the median, mean and mode, adding additional columns as needed.

**4**

# Measures of Variability

## VARIABILITY

In the previous chapter, we used single values to describe the most representative scores in an entire distribution of scores. A further way that we can describe distributions is in terms of their *variability*, or the amount of spread among the scores. Measures of variability provide information about how similar or different the scores are in relationship to other scores in the distribution.

Both of the distributions below have the same mean; however, they are quite different in the variability of their scores.

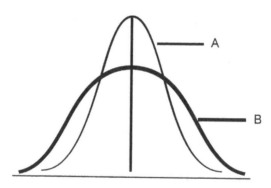

- Distribution A shows greater similarity among the scores. The scores are closer together, indicating less spread.
- Distribution B shows a greater amount of spread, or variability, among the scores.

Just as there are different ways of expressing central tendency, there are also different ways of expressing variability. Three common measures of variability are the *range*, the *interquartile range*, and the *standard deviation*.

## THE RANGE

The *range* (R) was discussed in Chapter 2 as one of the steps involved in constructing a grouped frequency distribution. To refresh your memory, the range is determined by subtracting the lower limit of the lowest score from the upper limit of the highest score.

$$R = X_{UL-High} - X_{LL-Low}$$

## For Example

For the following set of scores,

3, 3, 5, 7, 7, 7, 8, 9

$R = 9.5 - 2.5 = 7$

---

 **Your Turn!**

### I. Range

A. Determine the range for the following set of scores:

3, 3, 3, 3, 4, 5, 5, 6, 6, 6, 6, 7, 10, 11, 11, 11

$R = \underline{\phantom{9}}$

B. Replace the last score of 11 in the above distribution with a score of 54, and calculate the range.

$R = \underline{52}$

---

As you can tell from your calculations, the range can be problematic if there are extreme scores in the distribution. This is because the range only considers the scores at the ends of the distribution, and a single extreme score can give a false impression of the true amount of variability of the scores.

## INTERQUARTILE RANGE

A second measure of variability is the **interquartile range** (*IQR*), which describes the range of scores from the middle 50% of a distribution. To determine the interquartile range, we first divide the distribution into four equal parts, which produces three **quartiles**, as shown below.

**Quartiles**

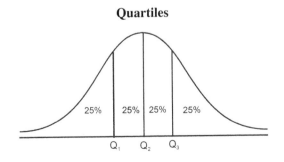

25%   25% 25%   25%

$Q_1$   $Q_2$   $Q_3$

$Q_1$ = the point at or below which 25% of the scores lie
$Q_2$ = the point at or below which 50% of the scores lie
$Q_3$ = the point at or below which 75% of the scores lie

**Tip!**

> The second quartile should seem familiar to you. It is the median (i.e., the point in a distribution that splits the scores into two equal parts).

## Steps for Determining the Interquartile Range

1. Arrange scores in order from low to high.
2. Divide the distribution of scores into four equal parts.[1]
3. Find the points below which 25% of the scores and 75% of the scores lie.
4. Identify the two scores that surround these points.
5. Determine the means of each of these two pairs of scores to determine $Q_1$ and $Q_3$.
6. Subtract $Q_1$ from $Q_3$. The resulting value is the interquartile range, which, as you can see, is simply the distance between the third and first quartiles. Here is a formula for accomplishing these steps:

$$IQR = Q_3 - Q_1$$

## For Example

Compute the interquartile range for the following scores:

85, 115, 90, 90, 105, 100, 110, 110, 95, 110, 95, 100

| 25% of the scores lie below this point. | 75% of the scores lie below this point. |
|---|---|

85  90  90 ‖ 95  95  100  |  100  105  110 ‖ 110  110  115

$$Q_1 = \frac{90 + 95}{2} = 92.50 \qquad\qquad Q_3 = \frac{110 + 110}{2} = 110$$

$$IQR = Q_3 - Q_1 = 110 - 92.50 = 17.50$$

Thus, the range of the middle 50% of the distribution is 17.50.

 Your Turn!

**II. Interquartile Range**

Determine the *IQR* for the following set of scores:

36, 42, 30, 7, 51, 29, 45, 35, 44, 53, 32, 50, 28, 43, 33, 29

*IQR* = ___15___

The interquartile range compensates for the sensitivity of the range to extreme scores by not including them in the computation. You may recall from the last chapter that the median is the preferred measure of central tendency for skewed distributions because it is not sensitive to extreme scores. It is for this reason that the interquartile range is also preferred if the distribution is skewed. However, for normally shaped distributions, the mean is the preferred measure of central tendency, and the standard deviation, discussed next, is the preferred measure of variability.

## STANDARD DEVIATION

The **standard deviation** first requires calculating a value called the variance. Mathematically, the standard deviation is the square root of the variance.

We will look at two different formulas for the standard deviation: a definitional formula and a computational formula. **Definitional formulas** are written the way that statistics are defined. These formulas usually involve more computations but are helpful when initially learning statistics because they guide the learner through the process of what is measured. **Computational formulas**, on the other hand, are easier to use with a handheld calculator and will result in the same mathematical conclusions.

### Definitional Formula

The definitional formula for the population standard deviation is as follows:

$$\sigma = \sqrt{\frac{\Sigma (X - \mu)^2}{N}}$$

If you actually have access to population data, or if you are just working with a group of scores such as the exams from a statistics class, and you have no need to estimate the standard deviation of a population, then the above formula applies and the standard deviation would be symbolized by $\sigma$. Conversely, if you only have access to sample data but are really interested in knowing the standard deviation of a population, then a slight adjustment has to be made in the formula and a different symbol, *s*, is used. We will return to this issue after discussing how to calculate a standard deviation.

The standard deviation is based on deviation scores. To *deviate* means to depart from a standard, the standard in this case being the mean. Thus, we are interested in a measure that considers the amount by which scores deviate from the mean of a distribution. **Deviation scores** are obtained by subtracting the mean from the raw scores in a distribution. In the above formula, notice that the operation inside the parentheses is asking for a deviation score $(X - \mu)$.

The operations under the square root symbol are asking you to sum the squared deviation scores and to divide by *N*. You should recognize that this is the process for obtaining a mean. In fact, the resulting value *is* a mean; it is the mean, or average, of the squared deviations, also known as the **variance** (symbolized by $\sigma^2$). Usually, to obtain a mean, we simply sum the scores and divide by *N*. The reason that we first have to square the deviation scores is that if we simply added them without squaring them first, the sum of the deviation scores would be zero. This is because the positive and negative values would cancel each other out. (You will note this when you work through an example.) The variance is an important measure of variability for the more advanced statistics that we will cover in Chapter 13. But for our present purposes, we need to return our data to their original unsquared unit of measurement, which is why we need to obtain the square root of the variance to finally arrive at the standard deviation.

One other term will come up in later chapters. The numerator in the formula for the standard deviation is called **sum of squares** (SS), which gives you the sum of the squared deviations, a measure of total variability. Used alone, SS is not very informative, but you could encounter it in rewritten formulas for the variance and standard deviation as shown below:

| sum of squares | variance | standard deviation |
|:---:|:---:|:---:|
| $SS = \Sigma (X - \mu)^2$ | $\sigma^2 = \dfrac{SS}{N}$ | $\sigma = \sqrt{\dfrac{SS}{N}}$ |

**Tip!**

These symbols and formulas may seem a bit confusing at the moment. However, after you have worked on a few problems, they will become familiar, and you should be able to recognize them with ease.

## Guide for Definitional Formula for Population Standard Deviation

1. Using the appropriate notation, create four columns as follows:

   - $X$
   - $\mu$
   - $(X - \mu)$
   - $(X - \mu)^2$

2. List the raw scores under $X$.
3. Calculate the mean ($\mu$) for the second column.
4. Subtract the mean from each raw score to find the deviation score.

5. Square each deviation score and then sum the squared deviations. This value is the numerator in the standard deviation formula. It is also the sum of squares (*SS*).
6. Divide *SS* by *N*. This value is the variance ($\sigma^2$).
7. Obtain the square root of the variance to arrive at the standard deviation ($\sigma$).

## For Example

| $X$ | $\mu$ | $(X - \mu)$ | $(X - \mu)^2$ |
|---|---|---|---|
| 17 | 21.4 | −4.4 | 19.36 |
| 24 | 21.4 | 2.6 | 6.76 |
| 22 | 21.4 | 0.6 | .36 |
| 26 | 21.4 | 4.6 | 21.16 |
| 18 | 21.4 | −3.4 | 11.56 |
| $\Sigma X = 107$ | $\mu = \dfrac{\Sigma X}{N} = \dfrac{107}{5} = 21.4$ | $\Sigma(X - \mu) = 0$ | $\Sigma(X - \mu)^2 = 59.20$ |

Notice that the sum of the deviation scores equals zero [$\Sigma(X - \mu) = 0$], which is why we need to square the deviation scores in the last column.

Finally, we can insert our values into the formula for the standard deviation.

$$\sigma = \sqrt{\frac{\Sigma(X - \mu)^2}{N}} = \sqrt{\frac{59.20}{5}} = \sqrt{11.84} = 3.44$$

**Tip!**

The sum of squares (*SS*) value for this example is 59.2, the variance ($\sigma^2$) is 11.84, and the standard deviation ($\sigma$) is 3.44.

What does the standard deviation tell us? It tells us that the raw scores in the distribution varied, on average, about 3.44 points from the mean. Larger values indicate greater variability. Smaller values indicate less variability. A standard deviation of 0 would indicate no variability (i.e., that everyone scored at the mean).

 **Your Turn!**

### III. Population Standard Deviation (Definitional Formula)

Using the definitional formula, determine the sum of squares, the variance, and the standard deviation for the following numbers of cups of coffee consumed by each of the workers at a print shop on a given day:

3, 3, 0, 1, 1, 2, 2, 2, 6, 0

*(Continued)*

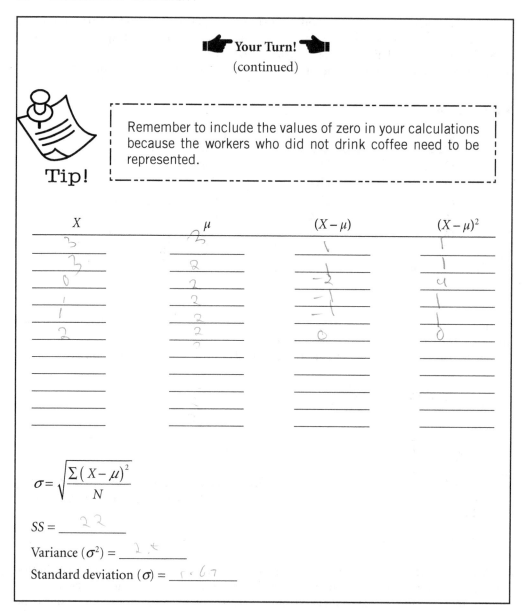

**Your Turn!**
(continued)

**Tip!**

Remember to include the values of zero in your calculations because the workers who did not drink coffee need to be represented.

| X | $\mu$ | $(X - \mu)$ | $(X - \mu)^2$ |
|---|---|---|---|
| 3 | 2 | 1 | 1 |
| 3 | 2 | | 1 |
| 0 | 2 | -2 | 4 |
| 1 | 2 | -1 | 1 |
| 2 | 2 | 0 | 0 |
| | 2 | | |

$$\sigma = \sqrt{\frac{\Sigma (X - \mu)^2}{N}}$$

SS = _____ 22

Variance ($\sigma^2$) = _____ 2.t

Standard deviation ($\sigma$) = _____ r.67

## Computational Formula

While definitional formulas facilitate understanding of what the standard deviation actually measures, you will find that computational formulas are easier to use. The computational formula does not require that means and deviation scores be calculated, but simply makes use of the raw scores. For this reason, it is also referred to as the *raw score* formula. The formula and the formula guide are shown below, followed by the same example provided earlier.

$$\sigma = \sqrt{\frac{\Sigma X^2 - \frac{(\Sigma X)^2}{N}}{N}}$$

where: $\Sigma X^2$ = sum of the squared raw scores

$(\Sigma X)^2$ = square of the sum of the raw scores

### Guide for Computational Formula for Population Standard Deviation

1. Create two columns, $X$ and $X^2$, and list the raw scores under $X$.
2. Square the individual raw scores and place these values in the $X^2$ column.
3. Sum the $X$ column to obtain $\Sigma X$.
4. Sum the $X^2$ column to obtain $\Sigma X^2$.
5. Place these values into the formula along with the appropriate $N$.
6. Square the sum of the raw scores and divide the result by $N$ to determine $\dfrac{(\Sigma X)^2}{N}$.
7. Subtract this result from $\Sigma X^2$. This value is SS.
8. Divide SS by $N$. This value is the variance ($\sigma^2$).
9. Find the square root of the variance to obtain the standard deviation ($\sigma$).

### For Example

Here is the computational workup for the standard deviation of the scores presented in the original example:

| $X$ | $X^2$ |
|---|---|
| 17 | 289 |
| 24 | 576 |
| 22 | 484 |
| 26 | 676 |
| 18 | 324 |
| $\Sigma X = 107$ | $\Sigma X^2 = 2349$ |

$$\sigma = \sqrt{\dfrac{\Sigma X^2 - \dfrac{(\Sigma X)^2}{N}}{N}}$$

$$\sigma = \sqrt{\dfrac{2349 - \dfrac{(107)^2}{5}}{5}} = \sqrt{\dfrac{2349 - 2289.8}{5}} = \sqrt{\dfrac{59.20}{5}} = \sqrt{11.84} = 3.44$$

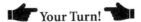

(labels: Sum of Squares → 59.20, Variance → 11.84, Standard Deviation → 3.44)

Notice that the resulting sum of squares, variance, and standard deviation are the same as those calculated by the definitional formula.

---

### 👉 Your Turn! 👈

### IV. Population Standard Deviation (Computational Formula)

Using the computational formula, calculate the standard deviation for the same problem that you worked earlier that referred to the number of cups of coffee consumed. The scores are repeated below:

3, 3, 0, 1, 1, 2, 2, 2, 6, 0

*(Continued)*

**Your Turn!**
(continued)

| X | X² |
|---|---|
| 3 | 9 |
| 3 | 9 |
| 0 | 0 |
| 1 | 1 |
| 1 | 1 |
| 2 | 4 |
| 2 | 4 |
| 2 | 4 |
| ( | 36 |
| 6 | 0 |

$$\sigma = \sqrt{\dfrac{\Sigma X^2 - \dfrac{(\Sigma X)^2}{N}}{N}}$$

## USING SAMPLES TO ESTIMATE POPULATION STANDARD DEVIATIONS

More often than not, researchers have access only to samples, not to entire populations. We saw in the previous chapter that the sample mean ($M$) is an unbiased estimate of the population mean ($\mu$). However, the same is not true of the sample standard deviation, which is said to be a biased estimate of the population standard deviation. In particular, the sample standard deviation tends to underestimate the value of $\sigma$.

Look at this more closely. Samples are, by definition, smaller than populations, and you are more likely to find more deviant scores in a larger group than in a smaller one. For instance, you are more likely to find a person with an IQ of 120 or higher in a group of 500 than in a group of 20. Thus, samples do not reflect the true variability of their parent populations. For this reason, if you are using sample data to estimate the population standard deviation, an adjustment in the standard deviation formula is necessary. Specifically, you will need to use $n - 1$, rather than $N$, in the denominator. The lowercase $n$ reflects the fact that you are using sample data. In addition, subtracting one (1) has the effect of increasing the size of the resulting standard deviation value, thus correcting for the underestimation.

As discussed earlier, the standard deviation symbol when using sample data to estimate the population standard deviation is a small $s$. We will compare $\sigma$ and $s$ for the following set of scores:

| X | X² |
|---|---|
| 36 | 1296 |
| 30 | 900 |
| 42 | 1764 |
| 29 | 841 |
| 40 | 1600 |
| $\Sigma X = 177$ | $\Sigma X^2 = 6401$ |

Using $N$ in the denominator:

$$\sigma = \sqrt{\dfrac{\Sigma X^2 - \dfrac{(\Sigma X)^2}{N}}{N}}$$

$$= \sqrt{\dfrac{6401 - \dfrac{(177)^2}{5}}{5}}$$

$$= 5.20$$

Using $n - 1$ in the denominator:

$$s = \sqrt{\dfrac{\Sigma X^2 - \dfrac{(\Sigma X)^2}{n}}{n-1}}$$

$$= \sqrt{\dfrac{6401 - \dfrac{(177)^2}{5}}{5-1}}$$

$$= 5.81$$

**Tip!**

The $n - 1$ adjustment goes in the denominator only. The $n$ value in the numerator is not adjusted.

The same adjustment ($n - 1$) in the denominator applies to the definitional formula for the sample standard deviation.

Notice the increased size of the standard deviation with the adjustment in the denominator. This adjustment is referred to as **degrees of freedom** (*df*), and it is a correction factor used to estimate population values more accurately. Degrees of freedom will also be used for more advanced statistics and usually will be calculated based on sample size and/or the number of data sets included in the computation of a statistic.

 **Your Turn!**

## V. Sample Standard Deviation

Using the computational formula, calculate the standard deviation for the following scores from a sample that will be used to estimate the standard deviation of a population: 4, 3, 2, 1.

| $X$ | $X^2$ |
|-----|-------|
| 4   | 16    |
| 3   | 9     |
| 2   | 4     |
| 1   | 1     |

$$s = \sqrt{\dfrac{\sum X^2 - \dfrac{(\sum X)^2}{n}}{n-1}}$$

$s = \underline{\ 1.29\ }$

## SUMMARY OF MEASURES OF VARIABILITY

The following is a recap of the formulas that we have used for measuring variability:

### 1. The Range

$$R = X_{\text{UL-High}} - X_{\text{LL-Low}}$$

### 2. Interquartile Range

$$IQR = Q_3 - Q_1$$

### 3. Sum of Squares

    A. Definitional Formula

        (for population)                               (for sample)

$$SS = \Sigma(X - \mu)^2 \qquad \text{or} \qquad SS = \Sigma(X - M)^2$$

    B. Computational Formula

        (for population)                               (for sample)

$$SS = \Sigma X^2 - \frac{(\Sigma X)^2}{N} \qquad \text{or} \qquad SS = \Sigma X^2 - \frac{(\Sigma X)^2}{n}$$

### 4. Standard Deviation

    A. Definitional Formulas

        (for population)                               (for sample)

$$\sigma = \sqrt{\frac{\Sigma(X - \mu)^2}{N}} \qquad \text{or} \qquad s = \sqrt{\frac{\Sigma(X - M)^2}{n-1}}$$

B. Computational Formulas

(for population)                                 (for sample)

$$\sigma = \sqrt{\dfrac{\sum X^2 - \dfrac{(\sum X)^2}{N}}{N}}$$   or   $$s = \sqrt{\dfrac{\sum X^2 - \dfrac{(\sum X)^2}{n}}{n-1}}$$

C. The standard deviation can also be abbreviated:

(for population)                                 (for sample)

$$\sigma = \sqrt{\dfrac{SS}{N}}$$   or   $$s = \sqrt{\dfrac{SS}{n-1}}$$

---

 **Answers to "Your Turn!" Problems**

**I. Range**

A. $R = 11.5 - 2.5$       B. $R = 54.5 - 2.5$
  $= 9$                        $= 52$

**II. Interquartile Range**

7  28  29  29  ‖  30  32  33  35  |  36  42  43  44  ‖  45  50  51  53

$$Q_1 = \frac{29 + 30}{2} = 29.5 \qquad Q_3 = \frac{44 + 45}{2} = 44.5$$

$$IQR = Q_3 - Q_1$$
$$= 44.5 - 29.5$$
$$= 15$$

**III. Population Standard Deviation (Definitional Formula)**

| $X$ | $\mu$ | $(X - \mu)$ | $(X - \mu)^2$ |
|---|---|---|---|
| 3 | 2 | 1 | 1 |
| 3 | 2 | 1 | 1 |
| 0 | 2 | −2 | 4 |
| 1 | 2 | −1 | 1 |
| 1 | 2 | −1 | 1 |
| 2 | 2 | 0 | 0 |

(*Continued*)

☞ **Answers to "Your Turn!" Problems** ☜
(continued)

| $X$ | $\mu$ | $(X - \mu)$ | $(X - \mu)^2$ |
|:---:|:---:|:---:|:---:|
| 2 | 2 | 0 | 0 |
| 2 | 2 | 0 | 0 |
| 6 | 2 | 4 | 16 |
| 0 | 2 | −2 | 4 |

$$\sum (X - \mu)^2 = 28$$

$$\sigma = \sqrt{\frac{\sum (X - \mu)^2}{N}} = \sqrt{\frac{28}{10}} = \sqrt{2.8} = 1.67$$

$SS = 28$

$\sigma^2 = 2.8$

$\sigma = 1.67$

### IV. Population Standard Deviation (Computational Formula)

| $X$ | $X^2$ |
|:---:|:---:|
| 3 | 9 |
| 3 | 9 |
| 0 | 0 |
| 1 | 1 |
| 1 | 1 |
| 2 | 4 |
| 2 | 4 |
| 2 | 4 |
| 6 | 36 |
| 0 | 0 |

$\Sigma X = 20 \quad \Sigma X^2 = 68$

$$\sigma = \sqrt{\frac{\sum X^2 - \frac{(\sum X)^2}{N}}{N}}$$

$$= \sqrt{\frac{68 - \frac{(20)^2}{10}}{10}}$$

$$= \sqrt{2.8}$$

$$= 1.67$$

### V. Sample Standard Deviation

| $X$ | $X^2$ |
|:---:|:---:|
| 4 | 16 |
| 3 | 9 |
| 2 | 4 |
| 1 | 1 |

$\Sigma X = 10 \quad \Sigma X^2 = 30$

$$s = \sqrt{\frac{\sum X^2 - \frac{(\sum X)^2}{n}}{n-1}} = \sqrt{\frac{30 - \frac{(10)^2}{4}}{4-1}} = \sqrt{1.67} = 1.29$$

## Using Microsoft Excel for Data Analysis[2]

### Activating the Data Analysis ToolPak

If you are using Excel for the first time for the purpose of statistical analyses, you may need to load the add-in tool that allows these functions. If this applies to you, follow the steps below for either a PC or a Mac.

Steps for a PC:

1. Launch Excel and open a spreadsheet.
2. Go to the **File** tab in the left-hand corner; then choose **Options**.
3. From the Excel Options window, select **Add-ins** and highlight the **Analysis ToolPak**.
4. Click on the **Go** button. This has to be done first; then click **OK**.

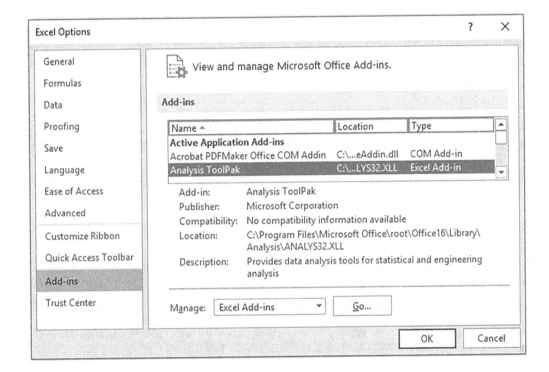

5. Go to the **Data** tab. The ribbon should now include a choice for **Data Analysis** on the right side.

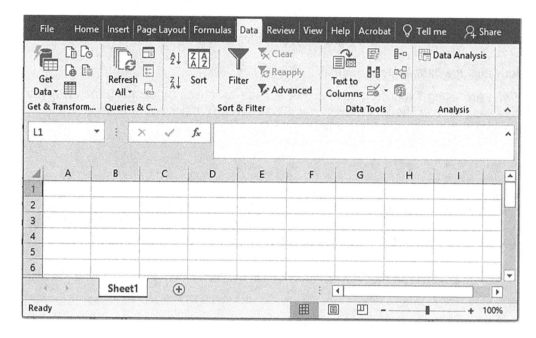

Steps for a Mac:

1. Launch Excel and open a spreadsheet.
2. Go to the **Tools** menu that runs across the very top of the screen. Choose **Excel Add-ins** and then check the **Analysis ToolPak** box. Click **OK**.
3. Go to the **Data** tab. The ribbon should now include a choice for **Data Analysis** on the right side as shown above. (You may need to quit and then re-launch Excel).

### General Instructions for Excel

There may be some variations in appearance depending on whether you use a Mac computer or a PC and depending on which version of Excel you are using. For example, if you are using a Mac, some of the dialog boxes may appear in the right column rather than in the middle of the screen, and you may need to click on **Done** instead of **OK**. There were substantial changes in Excel in 2007 and as long as you are using that or a later version, the differences should be minor and you should be able to navigate through the Excel exercises without much difficulty.

- *Excel Spreadsheets.* Open Excel to a blank workbook which will contain spreadsheets. Initially, there will be one spreadsheet, identified as **Sheet 1** in the lower left corner. You will also see a plus sign that allows you to create additional sheets related to the same project (see above image). If you use your mouse to right click on **Sheet 1**, you will be presented with different options, including one which allows you to rename the spreadsheet.
- *Entering Data.* Spreadsheets contain gridlines that are made up of cells. Cells are labeled according to column letters that run across the top of the spreadsheet, and row numbers that run along the left side of the spreadsheet. You will be entering data into the cells; a group of cells is referred to as a range. The range of cells that contain the scores below is A1 to A5.

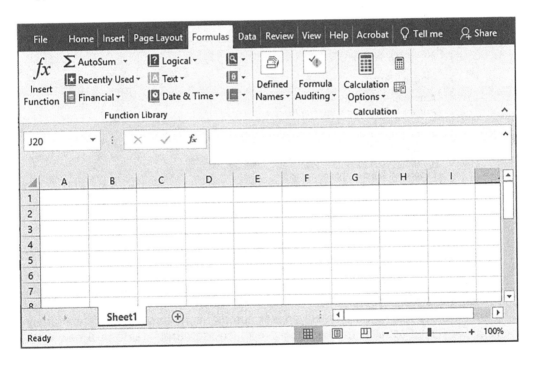

- *Primary Tools.* We will use two primary methods for analyzing data. One of these makes use of the **Data Analysis** command referred to above which is accessed from the **Data** tab. The other method involves use of the functions tool. To access this tool, go to the **Formulas** tab, then choose the **Insert Function (fx)** command from the ribbon. These tools will not be demonstrated here but will be used repeatedly throughout the chapters as we use Excel for performing the analyses for various types of statistical problems.

- *Column Width.* For many of the Excel exercises, you will probably need to expand the column width in order to accommodate all of the input and output data. If so, select the column or columns that need to be increased in width. From the **Home** tab, click on the down arrow of the **Format** command and choose **Autofit Column Width**. The columns will expand so that you can now see all of the content.

### Using Excel for Descriptive Statistics

In the first chapter, you learned that descriptive statistics seeks to summarize and describe data. Measures of central tendency and measures of variability are some of the descriptive statistics that can be obtained using Excel. Although these and other descriptive statistics will be included in the output that will result from these instructions, we will focus on the standard deviation. We will start with a sample standard deviation that uses $n - 1$ in the formula to get an unbiased estimate of the population standard deviation. Let's look at the example used in this chapter when you learned this formula under the section *Using Samples to Estimate Population Standard Deviations*. Follow the steps below:

- Enter the data into a spreadsheet by typing the scores (36, 30, 42, 29, 40) into the first column, beginning with cell A1 and ending in cell A5.
- Click on the **Data** tab and then on the **Data Analysis** command. A Data Analysis dialog box will appear.
- Select **Descriptive Statistics** and click **OK**.

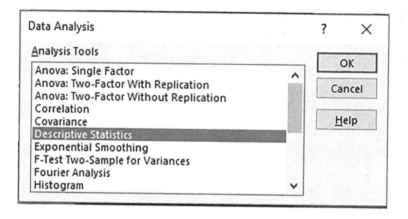

- With the cursor in the **Input Range** of the Descriptive Statistics dialog box, drag your mouse over the scores in column A of the spreadsheet. Only the cells that contain the scores should appear in the Input Range window (the dollar signs are references used by Excel and will appear automatically in some statistical analyses). For **Output options**, the default is to place the output table in a new worksheet. If you prefer, you can include the output table on the same spreadsheet by checking **Output Range** and typing in any empty cell location. Let's enter C1 to keep our output on the same worksheet. Finally, check the **Summary statistics** box and then click **OK**.

The resulting output table provides you with various kinds of information, including the mean, mode, median, sample standard deviation, and sample variance (you will probably need to expand the column width to see all of the output). Notice that the sample standard deviation is 5.81, the same value that you obtained by hand calculations.

| ◢ | A | B | C | D | E |
|---|---|---|---|---|---|
| 1 | 36 | | *Column1* | | |
| 2 | 30 | | | | |
| 3 | 42 | | Mean | 35.4 | |
| 4 | 29 | | Standard Error | 2.6 | |
| 5 | 40 | | Median | 36 | |
| 6 | | | Mode | #N/A | |
| 7 | | | Standard Deviation | 5.813776741 | |
| 8 | | | Sample Variance | 33.8 | |
| 9 | | | Kurtosis | -2.667798747 | |
| 10 | | | Skewness | -0.073280334 | |
| 11 | | | Range | 13 | |
| 12 | | | Minimum | 29 | |
| 13 | | | Maximum | 42 | |
| 14 | | | Sum | 177 | |
| 15 | | | Count | 5 | |

If you want to obtain a population standard deviation without the $n - 1$ adjustment factor, a few more steps are required.

- In the output table, place your cursor in the cell that contains the value for the sample standard deviation (cell D7).
- Go to the **Formulas** tab, then choose the **Insert Function (fx)** command from the ribbon.
- From the **Insert Function** dialog box, click the dropdown arrow that allows you to select a category; select **Statistical**. From the **Select a function** window, scroll down and highlight **STDEV.P**. Click **OK**. A **Function Arguments** box will appear. (This will be called **Formula Builder** on a Mac).

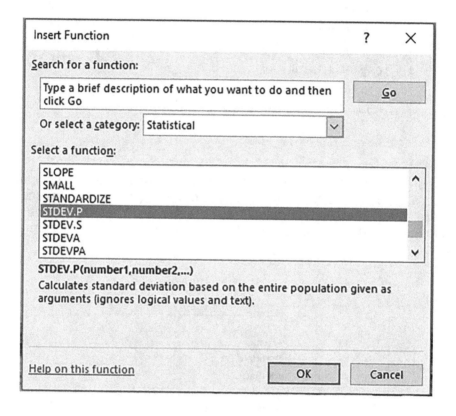

- With the cursor in the **Number 1** box, drag your mouse over the scores in column A of the spreadsheet. The cell range A1:A5 should appear in the **Number 1** window. Click **OK**.

| Function Arguments | | | ? X |
|---|---|---|---|

STDEV.P

| **Number1** | A1:A5| | ▦ | = {17;24;22;26;18} |
|---|---|---|---|
| Number2 | | ▦ | = number |

= 3.440930107

Calculates standard deviation based on the entire population given as arguments (ignores logical values and text).

**Number1:** number1,number2,... are 1 to 255 numbers corresponding to a population and can be numbers or references that contain numbers.

Formula result = 3.440930107

Help on this function

| OK | Cancel |
|---|---|

- The population standard deviation will now be displayed in the table. For this example, that value is 5.20, the same value shown in your text using the $\sigma$ formula.

---

## Additional Practice Problems

### Answers to odd numbered problems are in Appendix C at the end of the book.

1. What is the preferred measure of variability for distributions that are skewed? Why?
2. Why is the range sometimes problematic as a measure of variability?
3. What is a disadvantage and advantage of using definitional formulas?
4. What is meant by the statement that "the sample standard deviation is a biased estimate of the population standard deviation"? What can be done about it?
5. Explain the difference between $s$ and $\sigma$ including the reason for the adjustment in $s$.
6. Mathematically, how are the variance and standard deviation related?
7. The standard deviation of a distribution of scores was 0. What can you conclude?
8. A set of scores follows: 36, 42, 28, 39, 27, 51, 32, 45, 59, 34, 71, 68.
   a. Determine the range.
   b. Determine the $IQR$.
9. Calculate the range for the following scores: .48, .72, .81, .68, and .39. (Hint: you may need to revisit the topic of real limits from chapter 1.)
10. Calculate the range for the following scores: 2.5, 6.8, 3.4, 4.4, and 5.6. (Hint: you may need to revisit the topic of real limits from chapter 1.)
11. Use the definitional formula to calculate $SS$, $\sigma^2$, and $\sigma$ for the following set of scores from a population: 7, 10, 13, 9, and 6.

12. Use the computational formula to calculate $SS$, $s^2$, and $s$ for the following set of scores from a sample: 23, 42, 38, 29, 51, 37, and 44.
13. A set of scores follows: 6, 7, 8, 9, 10.
    a. Using the computational formula, calculate $\sigma$.
    b. Calculate $s$.
    c. Which is larger? Explain.

### Notes

1  If a distribution does not divide evenly into four equal parts, there are procedures that may be used for determining $Q_1$ and $Q_3$ similar to those used for arriving at the median. For the sake of simplicity, we will use only those distributions whose numbers of scores are wholly divisible by four.
2  Used with permission from Microsoft.

# z-Scores and Other Standard Scores

## Z-SCORES

The standard deviation discussed previously describes an average amount that an entire distribution of scores deviates from the mean. A *z-score*, on the other hand, describes how far a particular raw score deviates from the mean in standard deviation units. Positive z-scores reflect deviations above the mean, and negative z-scores reflect deviations below the mean.

The relationship between raw scores and z-scores is illustrated below. Raw scores are shown directly below the baseline, with a mean of 50 and a standard deviation of 5 points. The corresponding z-scores are underneath the raw scores. A z-score distribution has a mean of zero and a standard deviation of one.

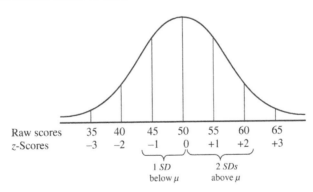

| Raw scores | 35 | 40 | 45 | 50 | 55 | 60 | 65 |
|---|---|---|---|---|---|---|---|
| z-Scores | −3 | −2 | −1 | 0 | +1 | +2 | +3 |

If the mean of a distribution is 50 and the standard deviation is 5, a z-score of +2.00 would tell us that the person scored 2 standard deviations (or 10 raw score points) above the mean, with a raw score of 60. A z-score of −1.00 would tell us that the person scored 1 standard deviation (or 5 raw score points) below the mean, with a raw score of 45. Someone who earned a score of 50 had no deviation from the mean.

## CONVERTING RAW SCORES TO Z-SCORES

Raw scores are simply points that need comparative information in order to be intelligible. A raw score of 60 points on a history test has no meaningful interpretation in and of itself. If there were 65 points available on the test, then a raw score of 60 sounds quite good. But if there were 100 points on the test, then there is less cause for celebration. It would also be instructive to know how others performed on the test. If it was an easy test and the mean was 63, then a score of 60 is not so impressive – especially if the standard deviation was 1.5 because that would mean that a person who earned 60 scored two standard deviations below the mean.

In other words, raw scores become most meaningful by comparison with the mean and standard deviation of the entire distribution of scores. If we convert a raw score into a z-score, then we can determine that person's standing relative to the rest of the group because z-scores tell us how many standard deviations a raw score is above or below the mean. Raw scores can be converted into z-scores using the formula below:

$$z = \frac{X - \mu}{\sigma}$$

This formula tells us how to find out to what extent the raw score deviates from the mean in standard deviation units.

## For Example

Jose scored 60 on his history test. The class mean was 49, and the standard deviation was 7. What is Jose's equivalent z-score?

$$z = \frac{60 - 49}{7} = +1.57$$

Thus, a raw score of 60 converts to a z-score of +1.57, meaning that Jose scored 1.57 standard deviations above the mean. This situation is illustrated in the following graph:

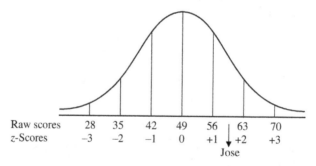

| Raw scores | 28 | 35 | 42 | 49 | 56 | 63 | 70 |
| z-Scores | −3 | −2 | −1 | 0 | +1 | +2 | +3 |

Jose

The z-score can also be used to compare scores from different distributions.

## For Example

Jason wants two master's degrees, one in psychology and one in business administration. Therefore, he had to take two departmental entrance exams. His score for the psychology exam was 109. The mean for all psychology applicants this year was 93 with a standard

Tip!

In this case, we would need to transform both scores into z-scores in order to see Jason's relative standing in both courses.

deviation of 12. Jason's score in business administration was 56. The mean for this group was 52 with a standard deviation of 6. On which test was Jason's performance superior?

Psychology

$$z = \frac{109 - 93}{12} = +1.33$$

Business Administration

$$z = \frac{56 - 52}{6} = +.67$$

Although Jason's performance was above the mean for both entrance exams, his standing was higher in psychology than in business administration in comparison to the other applicants.

## DETERMINING RAW SCORES FROM Z-SCORES

We can also do the reverse and determine the raw score, given a z-score, using the following formula.

$$X = \mu + z(\sigma)$$

---

 **Your Turn!**

### I. Converting Raw Scores to z-Scores

Latisha is taking four courses this semester. She earned the following scores on her midterm exams:

| Course | Latisha's score | Class mean | Class standard deviation |
|---|---|---|---|
| Sociology | $X = 82$ | $\mu = 78$ | $\sigma = 4$ |
| English | $X = 58$ | $\mu = 52$ | $\sigma = 2$ |
| Math | $X = 89$ | $\mu = 104$ | $\sigma = 8$ |
| Art history | $X = 73$ | $\mu = 70$ | $\sigma = 6$ |

A. What are Latisha's equivalent z-scores?

| Course | Latisha's z-score |
|---|---|
| Sociology | 1·U G |
| English | 3.0 6 |
| Math | −1.15 |
| Art history | 3ᴄ |

B. In which course was her best performance compared to the rest of the class?

English

C. In which course was her worst performance?

Math

## For Example

Given: $z = -.75$, $\sigma = 4$, $\mu = 26$, what is the equivalent raw score?

$X = 26 + (-.75)(4)$
$\quad = 23$

Again, this relationship between raw scores and z-scores can be shown graphically:

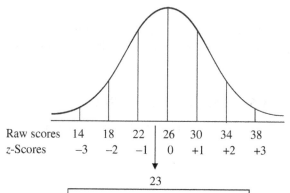

| Raw scores | 14 | 18 | 22 | 26 | 30 | 34 | 38 |
|---|---|---|---|---|---|---|---|
| z-Scores | −3 | −2 | −1 | 0 | +1 | +2 | +3 |

23

A z-score of −.75 translates into a
raw score of 23 for this distribution.

---

👉 **Your Turn!** 👈

### II. Determining z-Scores and Raw Scores

The midterm exam in Anatomy and Physiology had a mean of 73 and a standard deviation of 12.

A. The raw scores are listed below for three students. What are their equivalent z-scores?

| Marisol | $X = 84$ | $z =$ 1.2 |
|---|---|---|
| Twila | $X = 70$ | $z =$ −2.5 |
| Juan | $X = 90$ | $z =$ 1.42 |

B. The z-scores are listed below for three students. What are their equivalent raw scores?

| Brenda | $z = +1.25$ | $X =$ 78 |
|---|---|---|
| Patrick | $z = -.75$ | $X =$ 64 |
| Jeff | $z = +.50$ | $X =$ 29 |

## OTHER STANDARD SCORES

A z-score is a type of standard score. **Standard scores** are scores that are expressed relative to a specified mean and standard deviation. The specified mean for a z-score scale is 0 and the standard deviation is 1. However, z-scores can be awkward to work with because half of the scores will have negative values. In addition, most values will be between −3.00 and +3.00 and therefore require decimals to add greater precision.

We can transform z-scores into other types of standard scores with different means and standard deviations that are more convenient to use. Such transformations do not alter the shape of the original distribution or the relative position of any of the scores in the distribution. Common standard scores and their means and standard deviations include the following:

| | | |
|---|---|---|
| z-score | $\mu = 0$ | $\sigma = 1$ |
| Wechsler IQ | $\mu = 100$ | $\sigma = 15$ |
| SAT subscales | $\mu = 500$ | $\sigma = 100$ |
| T-score | $\mu = 50$ | $\sigma = 10$ |

T-scores are often used when it is desirable to eliminate negative numbers that can be confusing when communicating test results.

### Transformed Standard Scores (*TSS*)

Any set of z-scores may be altered from its original scale and changed into a set of **transformed standard scores** (TSS) using the formula below in which a new mean and standard deviation are specified.

$$TSS = \text{specified } \mu + z \,(\text{specified } \sigma)$$

Tip!

Raw scores have to be converted to z-scores before using this formula.

### For Example

Wechsler IQ ($\mu = 100$, $\sigma = 15$)

Suppose a class of students taking a course in psychological measurement took the Wechsler IQ test. The class mean was 102 and the standard deviation was 12. Conrad's raw score was 98. What is his equivalent standardized Wechsler IQ score?

$$z = \frac{98 - 102}{12} = -.33$$

Specified $\mu$ | Specified $\sigma$

Wechsler IQ $= 100 + (-.33)(15) = 95.05$

You can see in the diagram below that Conrad's position in the distribution has not changed as a result of the transformation. His equivalent raw score, z-score, and IQ score are all located in the same relative position.

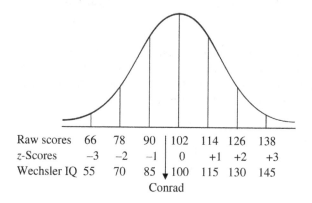

| Raw scores | 66 | 78 | 90 | 102 | 114 | 126 | 138 |
| z-Scores | −3 | −2 | −1 | 0 | +1 | +2 | +3 |
| Wechsler IQ | 55 | 70 | 85 | 100 | 115 | 130 | 145 |

Conrad

### SAT ($\mu = 500$, $\sigma = 100$)

For a given distribution of scores with a mean of 148 and a standard deviation of 18, Najma scored 166. What is her equivalent standardized SAT score?

$$z = \frac{166 - 148}{18} = +1.00$$

Specified $\mu$    Specified $\sigma$

SAT = 500 + 1.00(100)

= 600

### T-score ($\mu = 50$, $\sigma = 10$)

For a given distribution of scores with a mean of 60 and a standard deviation of 5, Marie scored 78. What is her equivalent t-score?

$$z = \frac{78 - 60}{5} = +3.60$$

Specified $\mu$   Specified $\sigma$

T = 50 + 3.60(10)

= 86

The relationship between the transformed distributions discussed previously can be shown graphically in a polygon.

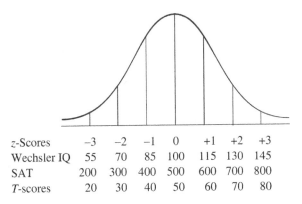

| z-Scores | −3 | −2 | −1 | 0 | +1 | +2 | +3 |
|---|---|---|---|---|---|---|---|
| Wechsler IQ | 55 | 70 | 85 | 100 | 115 | 130 | 145 |
| SAT | | 200 | 300 | 400 | 500 | 600 | 700 | 800 |
| T-scores | | 20 | 30 | 40 | 50 | 60 | 70 | 80 |

You can see that the mean in each case is in the center of the distribution. The standard deviation is shown in the increments specified by each scale.

---

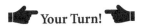 **Your Turn!**

### III. Transformed Standard Scores

A. In a raw score distribution with a mean of 80 and a standard deviation of 10, Lyle scored 92. What is his equivalent *T*-score?

_____

B. Emanuel's raw Wechsler IQ score was 84 in a distribution with a mean of 78 and a standard deviation of 6. What was Emanuel's equivalent standardized Wechsler IQ score?

_____

C. If the mean of a set of raw SAT scores was 101.6 with a standard deviation of 12.2, and Victoria scored 93.1, what was her equivalent standardized SAT score?

_____

D. You are creating a new test of creativity called ZONE, which you have decided to standardize. You have specified the new mean as 200 and the standard deviation as 25. The mean of the raw score distribution is 42 with a standard deviation of 4. Georgia's raw score is 50. What is her standardized ZONE creativity score?

_____

---

**Answers to "Your Turn!" Problems**

### I. Converting Raw Scores to z-Scores

A. Sociology = +1.00
   English = +3.00
   Math = −1.88
   Art history = +.50
B. English
C. Math

*(Continued)*

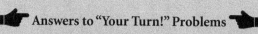

**Answers to "Your Turn!" Problems**

(continued)

### II. Determining z-Scores and Raw Scores

A. Marisol = +.92
  Twila = −.25
  Juan = +1.42

B. Brenda = 88
  Patrick = 64
  Jeff = 79

### III. Transformed Standard Scores

A. Lyle

$$z = \frac{92 - 80}{10} = +1.20$$

$$T = 50 + 1.20(10)$$
$$= 62$$

B. Emanuel

$$z = \frac{84 - 78}{6} = +1.00$$

$$IQ = 100 + 1.00(15)$$
$$= 115$$

C. Victoria

$$z = \frac{93.1 - 101.6}{12.2} = -.70$$

$$SAT = 500 + (-.70)(100)$$
$$= 430$$

D. Georgia

$$z = \frac{50 - 42}{4} = +2.00$$

$$ZONE = 200 + 2.00(25)$$
$$= 250$$

---

## Using Microsoft Excel for Data Analysis

If you are using Excel for the first time for statistical analysis, you may need to load the add-in tool that allows these functions. The information for loading the Data Analysis ToolPak as well as general instructions for using Excel for data analysis are at the beginning of the Excel section in Chapter 4.

### Converting Raw Scores to z-Scores in Excel

Excel can easily convert raw scores into z-scores by simply entering the information needed for the z-score formula $(X - \mu/\sigma)$ and making use of the functions tool. You will not need to enter any data into the spreadsheet itself but, before you start, make sure that your cursor is in the cell where you want to show the resulting z-score. Follow the steps below:

1. Go to the **Formulas** tab, then choose the **Insert Function (fx)** command from the ribbon.

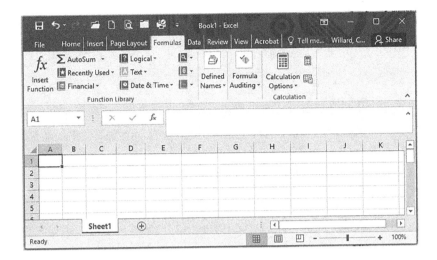

2. From the **Insert Function** dialog box, click the dropdown arrow that allows you to select a category; select **Statistical**. From the **Select a function** window, scroll down and highlight **STANDARDIZE**. Click **OK**. A **Function Arguments** box will appear. (This will be called **Formula Builder** on a Mac).

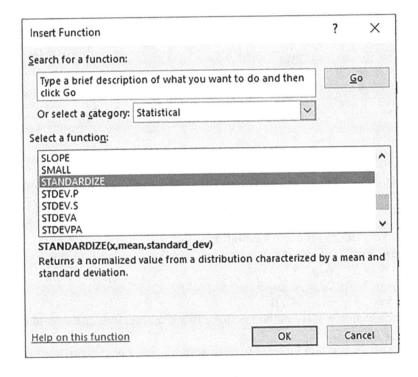

3. For the **Function Arguments** (or **Formula Builder**) dialog box, you will enter a raw score, a mean and a standard deviation. We will use the example from Jose's history test from this chapter where you first learned how to use the *z*-score formula. After entering these values for this example, click **OK**.

| Function Arguments | | ? ☒ |
|---|---|---|
| STANDARDIZE | | |

| | X | 60 | 🔢 | = 60 |
|---|---|---|---|---|
| | Mean | 49 | 🔢 | = 49 |
| | Standard_dev | 7 | 🔢 | = 7 |

= 1.571428571

Returns a normalized value from a distribution characterized by a mean and standard deviation.

Standard_dev is the standard deviation of the distribution, a positive number.

Formula result = 1.571428571

Help on this function            OK            Cancel

4. The z-score value will now appear in the cell where your cursor was placed before you engaged the functions tool.

| | A | B | C |
|---|---|---|---|
| 1 | 1.571429 | | |
| 2 | | | |
| 3 | | | |
| 4 | | | |

### Additional Practice Problems

**Answers to odd numbered problems are in Appendix C at the end of the book.**

1. Juanita took up running when she was 60 years old and has participated in a 5K race every year since. She is now 64. Her race times (in minutes) as well as the means and standard deviations for her age group are listed below.
   First year: $X = 34$, $\mu = 30$, $\sigma = 2$
   Second year: $X = 36$, $\mu = 43$, $\sigma = 4$
   Third year: $X = 39$, $\mu = 38$, $\sigma = 5$
   Fourth year: $X = 37$, $\mu = 42$, $\sigma = 3$
   a. In which year was Juanita's performance the best in comparison to others in her age group?
   b. In which year was Juanita's performance the worst in comparison to others in her age group?
2. You scored at the mean on your first statistics test. What is your z-score?
3. What are the mean and standard deviation for a z-distribution?
4. Harry's score was 66 on an exam that had a mean of 57 and a standard deviation of 6. Find and interpret Harry's z-score.
5. Brenda's score was 90 on both her geology and math exams. The class mean for the geology exam was 87 with a standard deviation of 6. The class mean for the math exam was 82 with a standard deviation of 8. Calculate and interpret Brenda's z-scores.

6. The average weight of a popular brand of cookies is 14.3 ounces with a standard deviation of .4 ounces. Jasmin purchases a box of the cookies. Having recently learned about means, standard deviations, and z-scores in her statistics class, she takes them home and puts them on the scale. Jasmin's cookies weigh 14.8 ounces. How did Jasmin's cookies compare with the average weight for that brand of cookies?

7. There were four exams in Liam's sociology class. He scored 68 on the first exam, 72 on the second, 80 on the third, and 65 on the fourth. The means and standard deviations for the exams are listed below.

| Exam # | Mean | Standard Deviation |
|--------|------|--------------------|
| 1 | 72 | 5 |
| 2 | 66 | 4 |
| 3 | 75 | 6 |
| 4 | 68 | 3 |

a. On which exam was Liam's performance the best in comparison to the rest of the class?
b. On which exam was Liam's performance the worst in comparison to the rest of the class?

8. A distribution of scores has a $\mu = 75$ and a $\sigma = 8$. What is the z-score for the following $X$ values?
a. 95
b. 63
c. 75
d. 82

9. Students taking a college prep course take a practice SAT test. The mean for the class was 108 with a standard deviation of 11. Using the same $\mu$ and $\sigma$ of the standardized SAT test, the course tutor transforms the students' raw scores into SAT-like scores. The raw scores for three of the students are listed below. What is their equivalent SAT-like score?
a. Student A: $X = 112$
b. Student B: $X = 96$
c. Student C: $X = 120$

10. A personality psychologist is developing a new personality inventory, which she calls FLEX, designed to measure resilience. The new assessment will be standardized with a mean of 70 and a standard deviation of 12. She administers the inventory to a pilot group of volunteers. The mean for the group is 89 and the standard deviation is 8.
a. Preston scored 82. What is his FLEX score?
b. Kaleb scored 92. What is his FLEX score?

11. A set of scores has a mean of 65.83 and a standard deviation of 5.41. Erica scored 1.12 standard deviations below the mean and Gianna scored 1.08 standard deviations above the mean.
a. What was Erica's raw score?
b. What was Gianna's raw score?

12. A set of raw scores follows: 12, 11, 10, 9, 8, 7
a. What is the z-score for a raw score of 9?
b. What is the z-score for a raw score of 12?

13. A set of scores follows: 8, 7, 6, 5
a. What is the z-score for a raw score of 5?
b. What is the z-score for a raw score of 7?

14. Which score is higher: a Wechsler IQ score of 112 or an SAT score of 600? Explain.

# 6
# Probability and the Normal Distribution

## PROBABILITY

Probability, or chance, is a familiar concept that we have been using since elementary school. We all know, for instance, that if we toss a coin into the air, the probability of the coin coming up heads is .50. We also know that, given four choices, the probability of getting a question correct on a multiple choice exam by just guessing is .25. Probability is also important in inferential statistics because it allows us to make decisions about the results of our research. It helps us to determine if the results of a study are more likely due to the effects of chance (i.e., probability) or to the effects of specific treatment procedures.

*Probability* is the mathematical likelihood of an event occurring, and it is expressed as a proportion. In statistics, the terms *probability* and *proportion* are used interchangeably. For example, the proportion of times that an event will occur is the same as the probability of the event occurring. Probability is determined by dividing the number of items of interest by the total number of possible outcomes.

$$p(\text{item of interest}) = \frac{\text{number of items of interest}}{\text{number of possible outcomes}}$$

We will use $p$ to symbolize both probability and **proportion**, and parentheses around the item of interest.

### For Example

What is the probability of drawing a queen (Q) from a deck of 52 cards?

$$p(Q) = \frac{4}{52} = .08$$

The item of interest in this example is a queen. There are four items of interest in a deck of cards and 52 possible outcomes. Thus, the probability of drawing a queen is .08 (rounded up).

## More Examples

There were 76 healthy babies delivered in the month of December at Camden Hospital; 41 girls and 35 boys. The names had been decided before birth for 36 of the girls and 34 of the boys.

- What proportion of the babies are male?

$$p(\text{male}) = \frac{35}{76} = .46$$

- What proportion of the babies are named female?

$$p(\text{named female}) = \frac{36}{76} = .47$$

- If you randomly selected a baby from this nursery, what would be the probability that the baby was: female, named, unnamed, or a named male?

$$p(\text{female}) = \frac{41}{76} = .54$$

$$p(\text{named}) = \frac{70}{76} = .92$$

$$p(\text{unnamed}) = \frac{6}{76} = .08$$

$$p(\text{named male}) = \frac{34}{76} = .45$$

---

 **Your Turn!**

### I. Practicing with Probability and Proportion

Forty-four of the 61 members of the Yahoo Optimist Club are 50 years of age or older. Seventeen are under 50 years old. Of those aged 50 and over, 32 are married. Of those under age 50, 15 are married. Suppose you selected a member at random.

A. What is the *probability* that the member would be
   1. < 50 years old: _____
   2. married: _____.77_____
   3. married and ≥ 50 years old: _____

B. What *proportion* of the club is
   1. unmarried: _____
   2. married and < 50 years old: _____

## THE NORMAL DISTRIBUTION

The normal distribution was briefly encountered in an earlier chapter. Here, we will examine it in greater detail. It is a bell-shaped curve of probabilities and proportions whose units of measurement are in $z$-scores. Other important characteristics of the normal distribution are:

- The tails are asymptotic (i.e., they never touch the baseline); this is because the normal distribution is based on an infinite number of cases.
- The area under the curve is equal to 1.
- The proportion of the area that lies between the mean and a $z$-score of +1.00 is .3413.
- .1359 of the area lies between $z$-scores of +1.00 and +2.00.
- .0215 of the area lies between $z$-scores of +2.00 and +3.00.
- .0013 of the area lies beyond a $z$-score of +3.00.
- Because the distribution is symmetrical, the same proportions that apply to the right side of the distribution (positive $z$-values) also apply to the left (negative $z$-values).

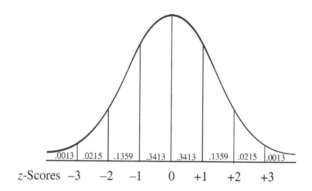

The theoretical normal distribution is important in the social sciences because the distributions of many human characteristics, when measured, approximate normally shaped empirical distributions. A few people will score very high and a few people will score very low. But most people are average and will score in the middle. Thus, we can apply our knowledge of the mathematical properties and known probabilities of the theoretical distribution to answer questions about probability for our empirically derived distributions.

## RELATIONSHIP BETWEEN THE NORMAL DISTRIBUTION AND PROBABILITY/ PROPORTIONS/PERCENTAGES

Because of the precise relationship between the normal distribution and $z$-score values, we can use it to determine probabilities, proportions, and percentages of specified $z$-scores. Keep the following points in mind:

- *Proportions* and *probability* are interchangeable terms.
- Proportions can be translated into percentages by multiplying by 100 and adding a percent sign (%):

  For example: $.1359 \times 100 = 13.59\%$

- Likewise, percentages can be translated into proportions by dropping the percent sign and dividing by 100:

For example : $13.59 \div 100 = .1359$

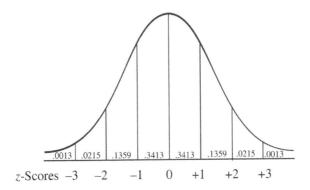

| | | | | | | | | |
|---|---|---|---|---|---|---|---|---|
| | .0013 | .0215 | .1359 | .3413 | .3413 | .1359 | .0215 | .0013 |

$z$-Scores  $-3$  $-2$  $-1$  $0$  $+1$  $+2$  $+3$

## Other Examples

- The *probability* of obtaining a $z$-score between $-1.00$ and $+1.00$ is .6826.
- The *proportion* of the population that will have a $z$-score below $-3.00$ is .0013.
- The *percentage* of the population that will have a $z$-score between $+2.00$ and $+3.00$ is 2.15%.

## THE Z-TABLE

A $z$-score usually will not be a whole number, but tables have been constructed that identify precise proportions under the curve associated with specific $z$-score values. Table 1 near the end of this book, the Table of the Normal Distribution Curve, is one such listing. We can also refer to this table as the $z$-table. Notice that we will refer to four columns in the table, as follows:

- Column A – indicates a particular $z$-score value.
- Column B – indicates the proportion in the body of the curve (i.e., the larger portion).
- Column C – indicates the proportion in the tail (i.e., the smaller portion).
- Column D – indicates the proportion between the mean and the $z$-score value in Column A. (Remember that the mean of a $z$-scale is 0 and it is located in the center of the distribution.)

Let us examine the proportions in the chart for a particular $z$-score, say $+1.25$, which will be found in Column A. Column B tells us that .8944 proportion of the curve lies below that $z$-score value. Column C tells us that .1056 proportion of the curve lies above that $z$-score value. And Column D tells us that .3944 proportion of the curve lies between the mean and that $z$-score value.

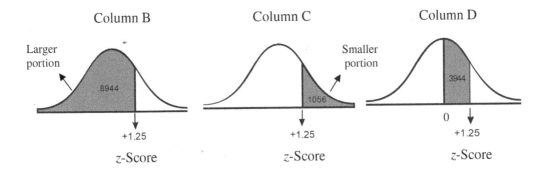

Notice that the proportions for columns B and C, when added together, equal 1 because these two columns together encompass the entire distribution.

**Tip!**

To find *p* values in the *z*-table that are:

- above a positive number, look in Column C (tail).
- below a positive number, look in Column B (body).
- number, look in Column B (body).
- below a negative number, look in Column C (tail).

The *z*-table can be used to answer a number of questions about probabilities, proportions, and percentages.

### Probabilities/Proportions/Percentages for Specified *z*-Scores

We may be interested in knowing the proportion of the normal distribution that is associated with particular *z*-scores.

### For Example

What proportion of the normal distribution is associated with *z*-scores greater than +2.50? The proper notation for this question is:

$p(z > +2.50) = ?$

**Tip!**

It is helpful to sketch a picture of the normal distribution curve when answering questions about *z*-scores, proportions, and probabilities.

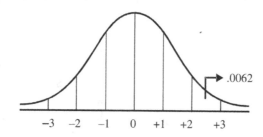

To find this proportion, look in Column C (in the tail) of the *z*-table. You will see that .0062 of the distribution is associated with *z*-scores greater than +2.50. Remember that this value is not only a proportion but also a probability. Hence, the probability of obtaining a *z*-score value greater than +2.50 is also .0062. Keep in mind that this value can be changed into a percentage by simply multiplying by 100 and adding a percent sign. Accordingly, we can say that .62% of the scores in a normal distribution are above a z-score value of +2.50, which, as you can tell, is a very low probability of occurrence.

$p(z > +2.50) = .0062$

## Other Examples Are as Follows

$p(z < +2.00) = .9772$ (look in the body, Column B)
$p(z < -1.50) = .0668$ (look in the tail, Column C)
$p(z > -1.23) = .8907$ (look in the body, Column B)

### z-Scores for Specific Probabilities/Proportions/Percentages

In the previous section, you were given a z-score and asked to find the associated proportion, probability, or percentage. However, you may also be given a proportion or percentage and asked to find the associated z-score. In this case, follow the steps below:

- If you are given a percentage, translate it into a proportion by dividing by 100 because the language of the z-table is in proportions.
- Next, look in Column B or Column C for the *closest* proportion.
- Then look in Column A for the corresponding z-score.

### For Example

What z-score value is associated with the lowest 10% of the distribution?

- First, translate 10% into a proportion ($10 \div 100 = .1000$).
- Next, look in Column C, the tail, for the proportion closest to .1000, which is .1003.
- Finally, look in Column A for the z-score that corresponds to the lowest .1003 of the distribution. This z-score is 1.28. We know that the z-score will be negative because we were interested in the *lowest* 10% of the distribution.

−1.28 is the z-score associated with the lowest 10% of the scores.

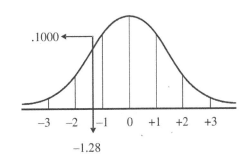

### Another Example

What z-score separates the lowest 75% from the highest 25% of the distribution?

- In this case, we can locate the z-score associated with either the lower .7500 ($75 \div 100$) or the upper .2500 ($25 \div 100$).
- The closest proportion to .7500 is .7486 (Column B). The closest proportion to .2500 is .2514 (Column C).

Thus, +.67 is the z-score that separates the lowest 75% of the distribution from the upper 25%.

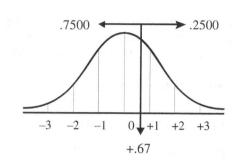

---

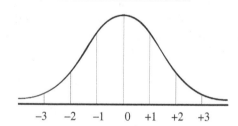Your Turn!

**II. Practicing with the z-Table**

A. Determine the proportions associated with the following z-scores.

1. $p(z > -.55) =$ _____ 7088

2. $p(z > +.87) =$ _____ .1922

3. $p(z < +3.11) =$ _____ .9991

4. $p(z > +.55) =$ _____ .2912

B. Determine the z-scores associated with the following percentages.

1. What z-score value is associated with the highest 2.5% of the scores?

_____ +1.2 6

2. What z-score separates the lowest 40% from the highest 60% of the distribution?

_____ .25 .25

### Probabilities/Proportions/Percentages for Specified Raw Scores

When you are conducting research, the initial data collected will be in the form of raw scores. However, if the raw scores of a normally shaped empirical distribution are converted into z-scores, we can use the normal distribution z-table to find probabilities and proportions associated with our empirical distribution.

### For Example

For the following set of problems, a normally distributed set of scores has a $\mu = 68$ and a $\sigma = 6$.

1. What is the *probability* of obtaining a score greater than 58? Because we are looking for the probability associated with a raw score ($X$) greater than 58, the correct notation for this problem would be:

$p(X > 58) =$

The raw score will first have to be converted to a z-score so that you can refer to the z-table.

**Tip!**

$$z = \frac{X - \mu}{\sigma} = \frac{58 - 68}{6} = -1.67 \qquad\qquad p(X > 58) = .9525$$

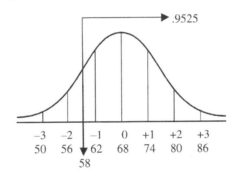

2. What *proportion* of the population is expected to score less than 60?

$$z = \frac{60 - 68}{6} = -1.33 \qquad\qquad p(X < 60) = .0918$$

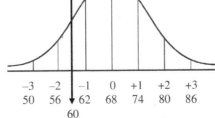

3. What *percentage* of scores can be expected to score higher than 74?

$$z = \frac{74 - 68}{6} = +1.00$$

$$p(X > 74) = .1587$$

$$.1587 \times 100 = 15.87\%$$

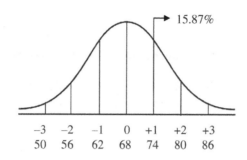

15.87%

| −3 | −2 | −1 | 0 | +1 | +2 | +3 |
|----|----|----|----|----|----|----|
| 50 | 56 | 62 | 68 | 74 | 80 | 86 |

---

### 👉 Your Turn! 👈

### III. Probabilities/Proportions/Percentages for Specified Raw Scores

A normally distributed set of scores has a $\mu = 80$ and a $\sigma = 12$.

A. What *proportion* of the population can be expected to score above 86?

_____ : 80 86

B. What is the *probability* of obtaining a score less than 95? __.89 44__

C. What *percentage* of scores can be expected to be above 77? __59·17__

---

### Probabilities/Proportions/Percentages *Between* Two Raw Scores

We can also start with two raw scores from a normally shaped empirical distribution and find the probabilities and proportions between those two score values.

### For Example

A normally distributed set of scores has a $\mu = 75$ and a $\sigma = 12$. What *proportion* of the population scored between 63 and 87?

$$p(63 < X < 87) =$$

Notice that in the notation above, we are looking for the proportion of scores greater than 63 and less than 87 (i.e., 63 is less than the value we are interested in and the value we are interested in is less than 87. We are interested only in the proportion associated with the scores between these two values).

**Tip!**

Both raw scores will first have to be converted to z-scores.

$$z = \frac{63 - 75}{12} = -1.00 \qquad\qquad z = \frac{87 - 75}{12} = +1.00$$

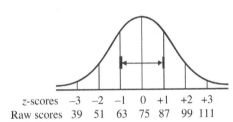

z-scores  −3  −2  −1   0  +1  +2  +3
Raw scores  39  51  63  75  87  99  111

- Look up the proportion between the mean and each of the z-scores (Column D).
- Add these two proportions.

| | |
|---|---|
| Proportion between mean and +1.00 | .3413 |
| Proportion between mean and −1.00 | +.3413 |
| | .6826 |

Thus, $p(63 < X < 87) = .6826$

## Another Example

Same $\mu = 75$
$\sigma = 12$

What is the *probability* that a randomly selected score would fall between 81 and 93?

z-scores  −3  −2  −1   0  +1  +2  +3
Raw scores  39  51  63  75  87  99  111

$$z = \frac{81 - 75}{12} = +.50 \qquad\qquad z = \frac{93 - 75}{12} = +1.5$$

- First, look in Column D for the proportion between the mean and z-score of +1.50 (.4332).
- Then, subtract from it the proportion between the mean and a z-score of +.50 (.1915).

.4332 − .1915 = .2417
Thus, $p(81 < X < 93) = .2417$.

The percentage of scores that would fall between the range of 81 and 93 is 24.17%.

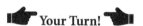

> If the proportions you are interested in lie on both sides of the mean, *add* the two areas together. If the proportions you are interested in lie on only one side of the mean, *subtract* the smaller portion from the larger one.

**Tip!**

---

### Your Turn!

#### IV. Probabilities/Proportions/Percentages *Between Two* Raw Scores

A. A normally distributed set of scores has a $\mu = 45$ and a $\sigma = 12$. What is the *probability* that a randomly selected score will fall between 24 and 54? ___·7333___

B. A normally distributed set of scores has a $\mu = 100$ and a $\sigma = 16$. Determine both the *proportion* and the *percentage* of scores that can be expected to fall between 110 and 125. ___20.49___

---

## Locating Raw Scores From Given Proportions or Percentages

In the last chapter, we used a formula that allowed us to determine what the raw score would be for a given z-score.

Here is the formula: $X = \mu + z(\sigma)$

We can also use this formula to determine the raw score(s) associated with specified proportions or percentages.

### For Example

A normally shaped distribution resulted in $\mu = 100$ and $\sigma = 20$. What raw score separates the lower 20% from the upper 80% of the distribution?

- First, look in the z-table for the proportion *closest* to .2000 in Column C (or we could look for the proportion closest to .8000 in Column B). Then, find the corresponding z-score. In this case, the corresponding z-score is −.84. (The negative sign does not appear in the table. However, we know that all of the z-scores in the lowest 50% of the distribution have negative signs).

- Once we have located the z-score associated with the specified proportion, we then use the formula to convert that z-score into a raw score.

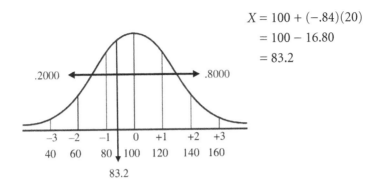

$$X = 100 + (-.84)(20)$$
$$= 100 - 16.80$$
$$= 83.2$$

Thus, 83.2 is the raw score that separates the lower 20% from the upper 80% of the distribution.

---

👉 **Your Turn!** 👈

### V. Locating Raw Scores from Given Proportions or Percentages

A. A normally shaped distribution has a $\mu = 90$ and a $\sigma = 12$. What score separates the lower 10% of the distribution from the upper 90%? _76.14_

B. Given a normally shaped distribution with $\mu = 74$ and a $\sigma = 8$, what score separates the lower 75% of the distribution from the upper 25%? _79.35_

---

## Locating Extreme Raw Scores in a Distribution

Yet another use of the z-table is to find the extreme scores in a normally shaped distribution.

## For Example

A normally shaped distribution resulted in $\mu = 79$ and $\sigma = 20$. What raw scores are so extreme that they will be achieved by only 1% of the population?

**Tip!**

Because the question does not specify high or low extreme scores, we assume both are of interest, .5% at each end.

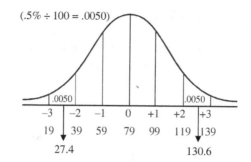

- First, change the .5% into a proportion by dividing by 100 (.5% ÷ 100 = .0050).
- Because extremes appear in the tails, look in Column C of the z-table. Notice that .0050 is not shown and that two proportions are equally near (.0049 and .0051). Because we are looking for the scores that fall within the .5% (.0050) extremes, we would choose .0049 because .0051 falls outside these extremes. The corresponding z-score for .0049 is 2.58.
- We are interested in both extremes. Therefore, we will use both positive and negative z-scores.

$$X = \mu + z(\sigma)$$

$X = 79 + (-2.58)(20) \quad X = 79 + (+2.58)(20)$

$\quad\quad = 79 - 51.6 \quad\quad\quad\quad\quad = 79 + 51.6$

$\quad\quad = 27.40 \quad\quad\quad\quad\quad\quad = 130.60$

The raw scores 27.4 and 130.6 are so extreme that they will be achieved by only 1% of the population.

---

 **Your Turn!**

## VI. Locating Extreme Raw Scores in a Distribution

A normally shaped distribution has a $\mu$ = 100 and a $\sigma$ = 15. What raw scores are so extreme that they are achieved by only 5% of the population?
_____ and _____

---

 **Answers to "Your Turn!" Problems**

### I. Practicing With Probability and Proportion

A. 1. $p(<50) = \dfrac{17}{61} = .28$

2. $p(\text{married}) = \dfrac{47}{61} = .77$

3. $p(\text{married} \geq 50) = \dfrac{32}{61} = .52$

**Answers to "Your Turn!" Problems**

(continued)

B. 1. $p(\text{unmarried}) = \dfrac{14}{61} = .23$

   2. $p(\text{married} < 50) = \dfrac{15}{61} = .25$

## II. Practicing with the z-Table

A. Proportions
   1. $p(z > -.55) = .7088$       2. $p(z > +.87) = .1922$
   3. $p(z < +3.11) = .9991$      4. $p(z > +.55) = .2912$

B. z-scores
   1. Highest 2.5% (equivalent proportion is $2.5 \div 100 = .0250$);
      look in Column C of z-table → $+1.96$
   2. $(40 \div 100 = .4000)$ → look in Column C (.4013 is closest to .4000) → $-.25$, or
      $(60 \div 100 = .6000)$ → look in Column B (.5987 is closest to .6000) → $-.25$

## III. Probabilities/Proportions/Percentages for Specified Raw Scores

A. $z = \dfrac{86 - 80}{12} = +.50$    B. $z = \dfrac{95 - 80}{12} = +1.25$    C. $z = \dfrac{77 - 80}{12} = -.25$

$p(X > 86) = .3085$      $p(X < 95) = .8944$      $p(X > 77) = .5987$

                                                         $.5987 \times 100 = 59.87\%$

## IV. Probabilities/Proportions/Percentages *Between* Two Raw Scores

A. Proportion between mean and $-1.75$    $.4599$
   Proportion between mean and $+ .75$    $+ \underline{.2734}$
                                              $.7333$

B. Proportion between mean and $+1.56$    $.4406$
   Proportion between mean and $+.63$    $- \underline{.2357}$
                                          $.2049 → 20.49\%$

## V. Locating Raw Scores From Given Proportions or Percentages

A. Closest proportion to .1000 is .1003; look in Column C → z-score $= -1.28$
   $X = 90 + (-1.28)(12)$
      $= 90 - 15.36$
      $= 74.64$

B. Closest proportion to .7500 is .7486; look in Column B → z-score $= +.67$
   $X = 74 + (+.67)(8)$
      $= 74 + 5.36$
      $= 79.36$

## VI. Locating Extreme Raw Scores in a Distribution

$X = 100 + (-1.96)(15)$        $X = 100 + (+1.96)(15)$
   $= 100 - 29.40$             $= 100 + 29.40$
   $= 70.60$                   $= 129.40$

## Additional Practice Problems

**Answers to odd numbered problems are in Appendix C at the end of the book.**

1. The Table of the Normal Distribution Curve is made up of four columns. Briefly describe what each column contains.
2. Locate the probabilities associated with the following:
   a. $p(z > +1.25)$
   b. $p(z > -2.10)$
   c. $p(z < -1.87)$
   d. $p(z < +2.68)$
3. Locate the z-scores associated with the following:
   a. lowest 40% of the normal distribution
   b. highest 56% of the normal distribution
   c. highest 12.5% of the normal distribution
4. What z-score separates the highest 35% of the normal distribution from the lowest 65%?
5. What z-score separates the lowest 25% of the normal distribution from the highest 75%?
6. Given a normal distribution with a $\mu = 82$ and $\sigma = 8$, determine the following proportions:
   a. $p(X > 93)$
   b. $p(X > 72)$
   c. $p(X < 63)$
   d. $p(X < 104)$
7. Given a normal distribution with a $\mu = 37$ and $\sigma = 4$, what proportion of the population can be expected to score
   a. greater than 40?
   b. greater than 25?
   c. less than 32?
   d. less than 39?
8. Given a normal distribution with a $\mu = 112$ and $\sigma = 10$, what percentage of the population can be expected to score
   a. lower than 100?
   b. higher than 90?
9. A normal distribution has a $\mu = 50$ and $\sigma = 5$.
   a. What proportion of the population can be expected to obtain scores between 42 and 53?
   b. What is the proper notation for the above question and answer?
10. A normal distribution has a $\mu = 84$ and $\sigma = 6$.
    a. What proportion of the population can be expected to obtain scores between 72 and 89?
    b. What is the proper notation for the above question and answer?
11. A normal distribution has a $\mu = 57$ and $\sigma = 8$. What is the probability that a randomly selected score would fall between 59 and 71?
12. A normal distribution has a $\mu = 36$ and $\sigma = 3$. What is the probability that a randomly selected score would fall between 28 and 32?
13. Given a normal distribution with a $\mu = 40$ and $\sigma = 4$, what raw score separates the upper 68% of the distribution from the lower 32%?
14. Given a normal distribution with a $\mu = 96$ and $\sigma = 12$, what raw score separates the lower 56% of the distribution from the upper 44%?
15. A normally shaped distribution has a $\mu = 71$ and $\sigma = 6$. What raw scores are so extreme that they will be achieved by only 9% of the population?
16. A normally shaped distribution has a $\mu = 34$ and $\sigma = 4$. What raw scores are so extreme that they will be achieved by only 3% of the population?

# 7

# Sampling Distribution of Means

## WHAT *IS* A SAMPLING DISTRIBUTION?

As we have discussed previously, inferential statistics are used to predict characteristics of a population based on sample data. We use sample statistics to estimate population parameters. However, statistics vary from one sample to the next. If we drew ten random samples from the same population, measured them on some dependent variable, and computed their means, we could easily end up with ten different means. How do we know if our sample statistics are accurate estimates of population parameters? We determine this by using a ***sampling distribution***, a theoretical probability distribution that represents a statistic (such as a mean) for all possible samples of a given size from a population of interest. Let us examine the ***sampling distribution of means*** to illustrate.

Imagine a population of interest and, from that population, we draw a random sample of a certain size. We will use $n = 60$. We measure our sample on some characteristic, calculate a mean, and record it. We then repeat the process of drawing additional samples of the same size from the same population and recording their means. We do this until *all possible samples* of size $n = 60$ have been drawn from the population and their means recorded. We then plot all of these means in a frequency distribution, called the sampling distribution of the means.

Of course, this is not done in actuality. The sampling distribution of means is a *theoretical* distribution, and we only imagine theoretical distributions. We do not actually construct them. Neither does it make sense to undertake such an endeavor. If we could study every possible sample in a population, we could more easily just calculate the mean for the population to begin with. However, as you know, we usually do not have access to populations. Fortunately, statisticians have been able to identify the important characteristics of sampling distributions so that we do not have to actually construct them. These characteristics are described in the central limit theorem.

## THE CENTRAL LIMIT THEOREM

The ***central limit theorem*** states that (1) as the size of the sample ($n$) increases, the shape of the sampling distribution of means approximates the shape of the normal distribution; (2) the mean of the sampling distribution of means will equal the population mean ($\mu$); and (3) the standard deviation will equal $\sigma / \sqrt{n}$. These ideas are discussed more fully below.

- *Shape.* Even if the shape of the population distribution from which a sample is drawn is *not* normal, if the sample size is large (i.e., $n = 60$ or more), the sampling distribution itself will be normal in shape.
- *Mean.* If we literally added up all of the means from our sampling distribution of means and divided by whatever number constituted *all possible samples*, we would obtain the mean of the sampling distribution of means, called the **expected value**, which would be equal to $\mu$. Remember that sample means are unbiased estimates of the population mean. They do not systematically either overestimate or under-estimate the population mean. Errors in one direction are balanced by errors in the other direction. Thus, when all sample means are averaged, the resulting value should be equal to the population mean ($\mu$). Furthermore, any particular sample mean, in actual application, is *expected* to be close in value to the population mean, hence the expected value.
- *Standard Deviation.* The standard deviation of the sampling distribution of means is called the **standard error of the mean** ($\sigma_M$), or simply *standard error*. It is called *error* because, while any particular sample mean is expected to be close in value to the popu-lation mean, it is not expected to be exact. Most of the sample means will vary some-what in value from $\mu$ just because of chance, or random sampling error. The standard error ($\sigma_M$) represents the amount that a sample mean ($M$) is expected to vary from the population mean ($\mu$).

The formula for the standard error of the mean is a function of the population standard deviation and sample size, as shown below:

$$\sigma_M = \frac{\sigma}{\sqrt{n}}$$

Note the fact that as the size of the sample increases, the amount of standard error decreases. For instance, the standard deviations shown below are identical, but the sample sizes are different. Look what happens to the size of the standard error when $n$ goes from 25 to 100.

Give:  $\sigma = 16$            $\sigma = 16$
       $n = 25$            $n = 100$

$$\sigma_M = \frac{16}{\sqrt{25}} = 3.2 \qquad\qquad \sigma_M = \frac{16}{\sqrt{100}} = 1.6$$

Thus, larger samples generally produce less sampling error.

## PROBABILITIES, PROPORTIONS, AND PERCENTAGES OF SAMPLE MEANS

The sampling distribution of means can be used to determine the probabilities, proportions, and percentages associated with particular sample means. This is similar to our previous use of the normal distribution curve to determine these figures for particular raw scores. But because we are now dealing with sample means rather than raw scores, the formulas involved are modified as follows:

$$z = \frac{M - \mu}{\sigma_M} \qquad \text{and} \qquad M = \mu + (z)(\sigma_M)$$

In the sampling distribution of means, sample means, rather than raw scores, run along the baseline and $z$-scores are in standard error units rather than standard deviation units. In the sampling distribution below, $\mu = 80$, $\sigma = 14$, and $n = 49$. Using the appropriate formula, we find the standard error $(\sigma_M)$ to be 2. Thus,

$$\sigma_M = \frac{16}{\sqrt{49}} = 2$$

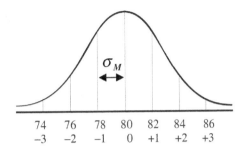

| 74 | 76 | 78 | 80 | 82 | 84 | 86 |
|----|----|----|----|----|----|----|
| −3 | −2 | −1 | 0 | +1 | +2 | +3 |

We can now use the sampling distribution of means to answer questions about probabilities, proportions, and percentages.

**For Example**

1. Given the previous normally shaped distribution with $\mu = 80$ and $\sigma_M = 2$,

   A. What is the probability that an obtained sample mean will be below 81?

   - Convert the given sample mean to a $z$-score:

   $$z = \frac{M - \mu}{\sigma_M} = \frac{81 - 80}{2} = +.50$$

   - Then, locate in the $z$-table the probability associated with sample means below a $z$-score of +.50 (column B):

   $$p(M < 81) = .6915$$

   Notice that the correct notation now specifies a sample mean ($M$) rather than a raw score ($X$).

   B. What proportion of the sample means can be expected to have a value greater than 83?

   $$z = \frac{M - \mu}{\sigma_M} = \frac{83 - 80}{2} = +1.50 \qquad\qquad p(M < 83) = .0668$$

A. .6915

B. .0668

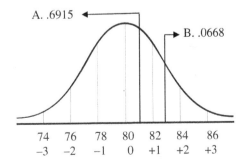

| 74 | 76 | 78 | 80 | 82 | 84 | 86 |
|----|----|----|----|----|----|----|
| −3 | −2 | −1 | 0 | +1 | +2 | +3 |

2. Given a normally shaped population distribution with $\mu = 95$ and $\sigma = 5$, a sample size of $n = 25$ is drawn at random.

A. The probability is .05 that the mean of the sample will be above what value?

- First, find the standard error: $\sigma_M = \dfrac{5}{\sqrt{25}} = 1$

- Next, find the $z$-score associated with the closest proportion above .0500, which is 1.65.
- Finally, use the formula to convert the $z$-score to a sample mean:

$$M = \mu + (z)(\sigma_M)$$
$$= 95 + (+1.65)(1)$$
$$= 96.65$$

B. What range of sample means would be expected to occur in the middle of the distribution 70% of the time?

**Tip!**

We need to identify the $z$-scores associated with the extreme 30% in the tails (i.e., .1500 at each end).

$$M = \mu + (z)(\sigma_M)$$
$$M = 95 + (-1.04)(1) \quad M = 95 + (+1.04)(1)$$
$$= 93.96 \qquad\qquad = 96.04$$

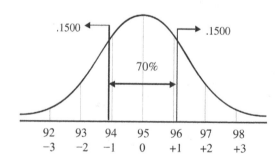

Thus, 70% of the time, we can expect to draw sample means that fall within the range of 93.96 and 96.04.

Tip!

> When working out problems that deal with the sampling distribution of means, be sure to pay attention to what kind of values you are being asked to find: proportions, probabilities, or sample means. This will determine which formula to use.

- In the first set of "Your Turn!" questions that follow, you are given a sample mean and are *asked for a proportion or probability*. This requires that the sample mean be changed into a z-score so that you can use the z-table to find the proportion or probability of interest:

$$z = \frac{M - \mu}{\sigma_M}$$

- In the second set of questions, you are given a probability or percentage and are *asked for the value of a sample mean (or means)*. This requires first looking in the z-table to locate the z-score associated with the given probability or percentage and then using the formula for finding the value of the mean:

$$M = \mu + (z)(\sigma_M)$$

---

### 👉 Your Turn! 👈

### I. Finding Probability or Proportion of Given Sample Means

Given a normal distribution with $\mu$ = 100 and $\sigma$ = 12, a sample of $n$ = 36 is drawn at random.

A. What is the probability that the sample mean will fall above 99?  .50 | .6915

B. What proportion of the sample means will have a value less than 95? (.006)

### II. Finding Sample Means from Given Probabilities or Percentages

The Wechsler IQ test is normally distributed and has a known $\mu$ = 100 and a $\sigma$ = 15. A sample of $n$ = 25 is drawn at random.

A. The probability is .04 that the mean of the sample will be below what value? 94.75

B. What middle range of sample IQs will be expected to occur 95% of the time? 99.12    105

## FORMULA SUMMARY

The formulas that you were introduced to in this chapter are summarized below:

$z = \dfrac{X - u}{\sigma}$ tells how much a particular raw score deviates from the mean of a population in standard deviation units.

$z = \dfrac{M - u}{\sigma_M}$ tells how much a particular sample mean deviates from the population in standard error units.

$X = \mu + (z)(\sigma)$ – use when being asked for a raw score value.
$M = \mu + (z)(\sigma_M)$ – use when being asked for the value of a sample mean.

μ!

  **Answers to "Your Turn!" Problems**

### I. Finding Probability or Proportion of Given Sample Means

A. $\sigma_M = \dfrac{\sigma}{\sqrt{n}} = \dfrac{12}{\sqrt{36}} = 2$ $z = \dfrac{M - \mu}{\sigma_M} = \dfrac{99 - 100}{2} = -.50$ $p(M > 99) = .6915$

B. $z = \dfrac{M - \mu}{\sigma_M} = \dfrac{95 - 100}{2} = -2.50$ $p(M < 95) = .0062$

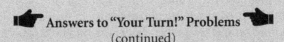

## Answers to "Your Turn!" Problems
### (continued)

### II. Finding Sample Means from Given Probabilities or Percentages

A. $\sigma_M = \dfrac{\sigma}{\sqrt{n}} = \dfrac{15}{\sqrt{25}} = 3$ $\quad M = \mu + (z)(\sigma_M)$

$= 100 + (-1.75)(3)$

$= 94.75$

B. Need to identify the extreme 5%, 2½% at each end. The z-score associated with .0250 is ±1.96. Thus,

$M = \mu + (z)(\sigma_M)$ $\qquad\qquad M = \mu + (z)(\sigma_M)$

$\quad = 100 + (-1.96)(3)$ $\qquad\qquad = 100 + (+1.96)(3)$

$\quad = 94.12$ $\qquad\qquad\qquad\quad = 105.88$

---

### Additional Practice Problems

**Answers to odd numbered problems are in Appendix C at the end of the book.**

1. What is a sampling distribution and what is its purpose?
2. Briefly discuss the characteristics outlined by the central limit theorem.
3. Why is it important to exercise caution when using a sample mean to make a prediction about the population mean?
4. The Wechsler IQ has a $\mu = 100$ and a $\sigma = 15$.
   a. Compute $\sigma_M$ for a sample size of $n = 120$.
   b. Compute $\sigma_M$ for a sample size of $n = 50$.
   c. How is $\sigma_M$ affected by sample size?
5. Explain what is meant by the standard error of the mean. How is it related to sample size? What are the practical implications of this relationship?
6. Given a normally shaped population distribution with $\mu = 88$ and $\sigma = 12$, what is the probability that an obtained sample of size $n = 36$ will have a mean that is
   a. above 92?
   b. above 87?
   c. below 87?
7. An assessment instrument on assertiveness has been standardized with a mean of 90 and a standard deviation of 20. A large manufacturing company administers the test to its sales force. If $n = 64$, determine
   a. $p(M < 92)$
   b. $p(M < 86)$
   c. $p(M < 96)$
8. Given a normal population distribution with $\mu = 62$ and $\sigma = 15$,
   a. what is the probability of obtaining a sample mean less than 61 if $n = 53$?
   b. what proportion of sample means can be expected to score above 59 if $n = 36$?

9. Given a normal population distribution with $\mu = 71$ and $\sigma = 14$,
   a. what is the probability of obtaining a sample mean greater than 76 if $n = 44$?
   b. what proportion of sample means can be expected to be below 76 if $n = 24$?

10. A population is normally distributed with $\mu = 36$ and $\sigma = 8$. A sample of $n = 25$ is drawn at random.
    a. The probability is .05 that the sample mean will be above what value?
    b. The probability is .01 that the sample mean will be below what value?

11. A random sample of size $n = 63$ is drawn from a normally distributed population with $\mu = 106$ and $\sigma = 18$.
    a. The probability is .10 that the mean of the sample will be below what value?
    b. The probability is .04 that the mean of the sample will be above what value?

12. A population distribution is normally shaped with $\mu = 83$ and $\sigma = 13$. If samples of size $n = 36$ are drawn at random, what range of sample means would be expected to occur in the middle of the distribution 90% of the time?

13. A normally shaped population distribution has a $\mu = 73$ and a $\sigma = 11$. If samples of size $n = 22$ are drawn at random, what range of sample means would be expected to occur in the middle of the distribution 95% of the time?

# 8

# Hypothesis Testing

## HYPOTHESIS TESTING

Now that we have examined the properties of the normal distribution and you have an understanding of how probability works, let us look at how it is used in hypothesis testing. **Hypothesis testing** is the procedure used in inferential statistics to estimate population parameters based on sample data. The procedure involves the use of statistical tests to determine the likelihood of certain population outcomes. In this chapter, we will use the z-test, which requires that the population standard deviation ($\sigma$) be known.

Tip!

> The material in this chapter provides the foundation for all other statistical tests that will be covered in this book. Thus, it would be a good idea to read through this chapter, work the problems, and then go over it again. This will give you a better grasp of the chapters to come.

Hypothesis testing usually begins with a research question such as the following:

## Sample Research Question

Suppose it is known that scores on a standardized test of reading comprehension for fourth graders is normally distributed with $\mu = 70$ and $\sigma = 10$. A researcher wants to know if a new reading technique has an effect on comprehension. A random sample of $n = 25$ fourth graders are taught the technique and then tested for reading comprehension. A sample mean of $M = 75$ is obtained. Does the sample mean ($M$) differ enough from the population mean ($\mu$) to conclude that the reading technique made a difference in level of comprehension?

Our sample mean is, obviously, larger than the population mean. However, we know that some variation of sample statistics is to be expected just because of sampling error. What we want to know further is if our obtained sample mean is different enough from the population mean to conclude that this difference was due to the new reading technique and not just to random sampling error.

## HYPOTHESIS TESTING STEPS

The process of hypothesis testing can be broken down into four basic steps, which we will be using throughout the remainder of this text:

1. Formulate hypotheses.
2. Indicate the alpha level and determine critical values.
3. Calculate relevant statistics.
4. Make a decision and report the results.

Let us examine each of these steps separately and apply them to our research question.

### Step 1: Formulate Hypotheses

There will be two mutually exclusive hypotheses: either the new reading technique does not have an effect on comprehension, or it does. Both cannot be true. These competing hypotheses are referred to as the null hypothesis and the alternative hypothesis, respectively.

The **null hypothesis** (symbolized by $H_0$) attributes any differences between our obtained sample mean and the population mean to chance. $H_0$ can be expressed in different ways depending on the research question. It can be described as a statement of

- *chance* (i.e., any differences found are simply due to chance, or random sampling error)
- *equality* (i.e., there is no true difference between our obtained statistic and the population parameter being predicted; they are essentially equal)
- *ineffective treatment* (i.e., the independent variable had no effect)

The **alternative hypothesis** (symbolized by $H_1$), also called the research hypothesis, is the opposite of the null. $H_1$ describes

- *true differences* (rather than just chance differences)
- *the effectiveness of treatment* (of the independent variable)

For our example, the null hypothesis states that the new reading technique does not have an effect on comprehension, that there is no true difference between the mean of the population ($\mu$) and the mean of the sample ($M$), and that any differences found are due simply to chance, or random sampling error. In symbolic form, the null hypothesis for this example would be written as follows:

$$H_0 : \mu = 70$$

In essence, $H_0$ states that the new reading technique would not change the mean level of reading comprehension. The population mean ($\mu$) would still be 70.

The alternative hypothesis, on the other hand, states that the new reading technique does have an effect on comprehension and that differences between $M$ and $\mu$ are more than chance differences. For our example, the alternative hypothesis would be written as follows:

$$H_1 : \mu \neq 70$$

$H_1$ predicts that the mean for reading comprehension *would* be different for the population of fourth graders who were taught to read using the new technique (i.e., $\mu$ would not be equal to 70).

## Directionality of the Alternative Hypothesis

$H_1$ may be stated in either a nondirectional or directional format.

- A ***nondirectional alternative hypothesis*** merely states that the value of $\mu$ is something other than the value predicted in $H_0$; the direction of expected differences is not specified. The value of $\mu$ could be higher or it could be lower.
- A ***directional alternative hypothesis*** specifies the direction of expected difference and is used when researchers have reason to believe that a treatment will either *increase* or *decrease* a mean score.

Thus, $H_1$ could alternatively be written as

- $H_1: \mu \neq 70$ (nondirectional) (for $H_0: \mu = 70$)
- $H_1: \mu > 70$ (directional) (for $H_0: \mu \leq 70$)
- $H_1: \mu < 70$ (directional) (for $H_0: \mu \geq 70$)

Symbolically, the alternative hypothesis is written as the opposite of the null hypothesis. In the first case ($H_1: \mu \neq 70$), the alternative hypothesis predicts that the mean of the population would not equal 70 after use of the new reading technique. In the second case ($H_1: \mu > 70$), the alternative hypothesis predicts that the mean of the population would increase after use of the new reading technique. The third case ($H_1: \mu < 70$) predicts that $\mu$ would decrease, a prediction that a researcher is unlikely to make because a new reading technique would be designed to *improve* scores, not decrease them. A different research question, however, such as one dealing with a medication to treat pain, may predict a decrease in the mean pain score ($\mu$) after treatment. Notice the fact that the equal to sign under the greater than and less than signs ($\geq$ and $\leq$) will always be associated with the null hypothesis when using directional alternative hypotheses.

In our research problem, we are simply asking whether the new reading technique made a difference in reading comprehension. We are not predicting whether reading scores increased or decreased. Thus, we are using a nondirectional alternative hypothesis ($H_1: \mu \neq 70$).

## The Backwards Logic of Hypothesis Testing

Although it may seem backwards, it is the null hypothesis ($H_0$) that is tested and assumed to be true – but the hope is that it can be rejected, thereby giving indirect support to the alternative hypothesis ($H_1$). This is because the statistical tools used for hypothesis testing can only demonstrate a hypothesis to be false, rather than prove one to be true.

To illustrate, suppose the candy store at your local mall has a large bin full of jelly beans. You love jelly beans but are allergic to the blue ones. The clerk claims that there are no blue jelly beans in the bin. You stick the scoop in and pull out a mound full of jelly beans. Upon examination, you find that there are indeed no blue jelly beans in your sample. Have you thus proved the clerk's claim that there are no blue jelly beans in the bin? Of course not. You could replace the jelly beans, draw out another scoop, then another, and another, and another, and still find no blue jelly beans. Even then, the clerk's claim that there are no blue jelly beans in the bin has not been proven. There is always a possibility that a blue jelly bean is hiding somewhere in the bunch. On the other hand, if you pull out a single blue jelly bean in your sample, then you have demonstrated the clerk's claim to be false.

So it is with hypothesis testing. We can more readily show a hypothesis to be false than to prove one to be true. We attempt to show the falsity of the null hypothesis so that we can reject it and thereby, in roundabout fashion, confirm what we believed to be true all along in our alternative hypothesis.

Accordingly, how do we know whether to reject our $H_0$ that $\mu = 70$, thereby giving support to our $H_1$ that $\mu \neq 70$? We must first determine what the sampling distribution of means would look like if the null hypothesis were true, if $\mu = 70$.

If $\mu = 70$, we know that the mean of the sampling distribution of means would also be 70. (This is the expected value that was discussed in the last chapter.) We can then determine the likelihood of obtaining sample means close to or far away from that value by looking in the z-table for such probabilities. If our obtained sample mean has a low probability of occurrence if $H_0$ is true (if $\mu = 70$), then we would reject $H_0$. If our obtained sample mean has a high probability of occurrence, then we would fail to reject $H_0$.

First, we have to specify what we mean by a low or high probability of occurrence. We do this in Step 2.

## Step 2: Indicate the Alpha Level and Determine Critical Values

The **alpha level** (symbolized by $\alpha$) is a probability level set by the researcher that defines the point at which $H_0$ should be rejected. Most often, the alpha level is set at .05 or .01, and occasionally at .001. The alpha level also defines the point at which the critical region begins.

The **critical region** is the area of a sampling distribution in which score outcomes are highly unlikely (i.e., have a low probability of occurrence). Remember that alpha levels are probability levels. Thus, when $\alpha = .05$ and if $H_0$ were true, the probability of obtaining a sample value that falls in the critical region would be .05 or less. Scores in this area are unlikely to have occurred by chance and therefore lead to rejection of $H_0$. This area of rejection is separated from the area of nonrejection by **critical values**, values that designate the point of rejection of $H_0$.

For example, the following illustrates a sampling distribution in which the chosen alpha level is $\alpha = .05$ and the alternative hypothesis is **nondirectional**.

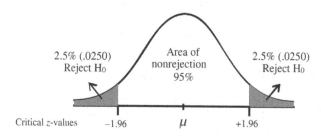

The shaded area represents the critical region that leads to rejection of $H_0$. Sample means that fall in these areas have a 5% or less likelihood of occurring by chance alone if $H_0$ is true. This low probability makes $H_0$ unreasonable enough to be rejected. In this case, the alternative hypothesis that scores this extreme (this far away from $\mu$) are probably due to something other than chance makes more sense. In experimental research, "something other than chance" refers to the effect of an independent variable.

Remember that statements of probability are also statements of proportion. The .05 alpha level not only represents a low probability of sample means falling in these regions of rejection but also the proportion of scores that can be expected to fall in these areas by chance alone. Because our alternative hypothesis is nondirectional, this proportion is divided in two, with .0250 at each end. The critical values of ±1.96 separate these regions of rejection from the rest of the distribution.

Where do you find these critical values? If you look in the z-table, you will see that these values are the z-scores associated with the extreme 2.5% (.0250) of the normal distribution curve.

The following illustrates the sampling distribution for which the researcher specifies an $\alpha = .01$ and the alternative hypothesis is nondirectional.

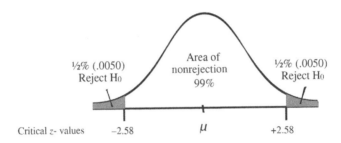

In this case, sample means that fall in the areas of rejection have a 1% or less likelihood of occurring by chance alone if $H_0$ is true. The critical values that separate the areas of rejection are ±2.58. These are the z-scores associated with the extreme ½% (.0050) of the normal distribution curve.

When the alternative hypothesis is nondirectional, we use what is referred to as a **two-tailed test**. This simply means that we are interested in sample means that fall in either tail of the rejection region.

If a **_directional alternative hypothesis_** is specified, the entire rejection area is contained in one end of the distribution. If $H_1$ specifies that $\mu$ would be greater than (>) a particular value, then the rejection region would be in the right tail only. If $H_1$ specifies that $\mu$ would be less than (<) a particular value, then the rejection region would be in the left tail only. Because interest is only in one tail of the distribution, the proportion associated with the alpha level is not divided in half. The following diagrams illustrate both situations, one with $\alpha = .05$, and the other with $\alpha = .01$.

$H_1: \mu >$ value specified in $H_0$

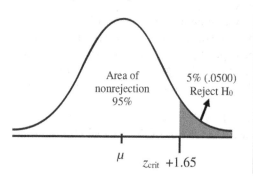

$H_1: \mu <$ value specified in $H_0$

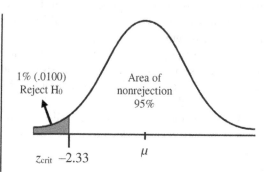

Directional alternative hypotheses call for a ***one-tailed test***, in which case sample means must fall in the tail specified by $H_1$ before $H_0$ can be rejected. In the above illustration on the left with $\alpha = .05$, the critical value for rejecting $H_0$ is +1.65 (abbreviated "$z_{crit}$"). In the illustration on the right with $\alpha = .01$, the critical value is −2.33.

**Tip!**

> If you are using a one-tailed test, the critical value for reject-
> ing $H_0$ will be only positive (+) or negative (−), depending on
> the direction specified in $H_1$. For a two-tailed test, the critical
> values to be considered will be both positive and negative (±).

It is more difficult to reject $H_0$ using a two-tailed test because the rejection region is divided in two and distributed in both tails. And, of course, the farther into the tails we have to go, the more extreme our obtained mean has to be to fall in the rejection region.

Likewise, an alpha level of .01 is more rigorous than an alpha level of .05. Again, the obtained sample would have to show a greater difference from $\mu$, reflecting less probability of just a chance difference.

For our example, we will use an $\alpha = .05$. In Step 1, we used the nondirectional alternative hypothesis $H_1: \mu \neq 70$. Thus, we will be conducting a two-tailed test and our critical $z$-values are ±1.96.

## Step 3: Calculate Relevant Statistics

Once we have established the ground rules for the $z$-test in the first two steps, it is now time to examine our data. It was reported earlier in our research question that our obtained mean for a sample of $n = 25$ fourth graders was $M = 75$ after they were taught the new reading technique. A $\sigma = 10$ was also reported. Now, we need to calculate the relevant statistics, which in this case is a $z$-score. We will use the following formula to transform our obtained sample mean into a $z$-score.

$$z_{obt} = \frac{M - \mu}{\sigma_M}$$

Because we are using a $z$-statistic, the kind of test we are performing is referred to as a $z$-test. We will use the subscript *obt* to distinguish our obtained $z$-score value from the critical $z$-value used as the criterion for rejecting $H_0$. To use the formula, we first need to compute the standard error ($\sigma_M$). We can then determine $z_{obt}$.

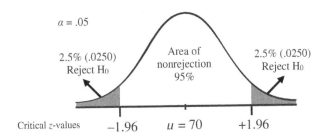

$$\sigma_M = \frac{\sigma}{\sqrt{n}} = \frac{10}{\sqrt{25}} = 2 \qquad\qquad z_{obt} = \frac{75-70}{2} = +2.50$$

## Step 4: Make a Decision and Report the Results

Finally, we must decide whether to reject the null hypothesis that $H_0$: $\mu = 70$. We are using an $\alpha = .05$ and a nondirectional alternative hypothesis. The sampling distribution for this example is shown below.

$\alpha = .05$

2.5% (.0250)
Reject H₀

Area of
nonrejection
95%

2.5% (.0250)
Reject H₀

Critical $z$-values    $-1.96$     $u = 70$     $+1.96$

For our example, the $z_{crit}$ values are $\pm1.96$, meaning that in order to reject $H_0$, we would need a sample mean that converted to an obtained $z$-value beyond 1.96 (in either direction). Our obtained $z$-score was $+2.50$, which falls in the rejection region. Thus, we will reject $H_0$: $\mu = 70$. We will reject the null hypothesis because if it were true that $\mu = 70$, there would be only a 5% or less chance that we would have obtained a sample mean as far from that value as the one we obtained (i.e., $M = 75$). The alternative hypothesis that $H_1$: $\mu \neq 70$ for the population of fourth graders using the new reading technique makes more sense. We conclude, therefore, that the new reading technique did have an effect on reading comprehension.

**Tip!**

In order to reject $H_0$, your obtained $z$-value has to be more extreme than the critical $z$-value.

## Results Format

When reporting the outcome of research, we will use the following customary format:

The new reading program had a significant effect on reading comprehension. Reject $H_0$, $z = +2.50$, $p < .05$.

Notice that

- the word *significant* has been used in the conclusion. In statistical language, **significant** simply means a greater-than-chance result (i.e., the new reading program had a greater-than-chance effect on reading comprehension). If a null hypothesis has been rejected, then the results are said to be significant.
- the z-score that is reported is the *obtained* value of z, rather than the $z_{crit}$ value.
- the p stands for probability. Here, if $H_0$ were true, the probability would be less than .05 of obtaining a sample mean that falls in the critical region. Use the alpha level ($\alpha$) that has been preset by the researcher as the p value. If $z_{obt}$ is less extreme than $z_{crit}$, p will be greater than (>) the alpha level and we will "fail to reject $H_0$." If $z_{obt}$ is more extreme than $z_{crit}$, p will be less than (<) the alpha level and we will "reject $H_0$."

**Tip!**

Note that the words *proved* or *disproved* have not been used when the null hypothesis has been rejected or retained. Mathematical formulas may be proven, but experimental hypotheses may not be. This is because there is always some probability that our results occurred because of chance. Thus, we either *reject* the null hypothesis as being extremely unlikely, or we *fail to reject* it. But we cannot *prove* or *disprove* it.

## SUMMARY OF PROBLEM

The following summarizes the steps that we have carried out for this problem.

### Sample Research Question

Given $\mu = 70$, $\sigma = 10$, and $n = 25$, did the new reading technique have an effect on comprehension?

### Step 1: Formulate Hypotheses

$H_0: \mu = 70$
$H_1: \mu \neq 70$

### Step 2: Indicate the Alpha Level and Determine Critical Values

$\alpha = .05$
$z_{crit} = \pm 1.96$

### Step 3: Calculate Relevant Statistics

Given:  $n = 25$     $\mu = 70$     $\sigma = 10$     $M = 75$

$$\sigma_M = \frac{\sigma}{\sqrt{n}} = \frac{10}{\sqrt{25}} = 2$$

$$z_{obt} = \frac{M - \mu}{\sigma_M} = \frac{75 - 70}{2} = +2.50$$

**Step 4: Make a Decision and Report the Results**

The new reading program had a significant effect on reading comprehension. Reject $H_0$, $z = +2.50, p < .05$.

## EFFECT SIZE FOR A Z-TEST

We will examine a bit further what it means when we reject a null hypothesis at a given alpha level ($\alpha$). We conclude that our result is statistically significant and probably not due to chance. In other words, we decide that our treatment was effective. However, this does not inform us as to how effective our treatment was. Did it make a huge difference or very little difference? Really, statistical significance only indicates that the results *may* be important but further scrutiny should be employed. We saw in a previous chapter that increasing the sample size will produce less standard error. Lower standard error values result in greater differences in our obtained test statistic making it more likely that $H_0$ will be rejected. If the sample size is increased enough, even small differences may be statistically significant. That is not to say that these differences have any practical significance that is useful in the real world. Many researchers have argued that an index that provides the size of an effect would allow for a more meaningful interpretation of results. Moreover, the American Psychological Association (APA) recommends including a measure of effect size when reporting the results of research.[1] Hence, when we reject a null hypothesis, we will also include a measure of effect size in our results. *Effect size* indicates the magnitude of a treatment effect.

One popular measure of effect size is Cohen's $d$, devised by Jacob Cohen.[2] The formula for this measure involves comparing mean differences and dividing by the standard deviation. As applied to the $z$-test, the formula is as follows:

| General formula, | For our research problem, |
|---|---|
| $$d = \frac{|M - \mu|}{\sigma}$$ | $$d = \frac{|75 - 70|}{10} = .5$$ |

The two vertical bars around $M - \mu$ are used to indicate that we are only interested in the absolute value of the difference without regard to sign. Thus, $d$ values will always be expressed as positive numbers. The following guidelines are often used for judging the size of $d$:

- $d = .20$ to $.49$ – Small effect
- $d = .50$ to $.79$ – Moderate effect
- $d = .80$ and above – Large effect

For our problem, what this value tells us is that our effect size is one-half of a standard deviation, a moderate effect.

## ASSUMPTIONS

Statistical procedures that test hypotheses about populations are referred to as **parametric tests**. Such tests should live up to certain assumptions in order for the results to be well founded. The general assumptions for the $z$-test are as follows:

- *Independent and random selection of participants.* Subjects cannot be sampled twice nor can their scores influence any other scores. Random sampling from the population of interest generally takes care of this requirement.

- *Normality.* The characteristic being measured is approximately normally distributed in the population. This is necessary because we are using the normal distribution table (i.e., the z-table) to determine the probability associated with our obtained z-scores. However, if our sample is reasonably large, normality can be assumed.
- *Interval or ratio scores.* Since we use a mean to calculate the z-score, a dependent variable that can be measured on an interval or ratio scale is necessary. A mean cannot be calculated for nominal- or ordinal-level data.
- *σ is known.* We need to know the value of the population standard deviation ($\sigma$) in order to calculate the standard error for use in the formula for the z-test.

---

 **Your Turn!**

## I. Hypothesis Testing with the z-Test

A. *Research Question.* A standardized productivity scale has a $\mu = 25$ and a $\sigma = 5$. The CEO of Company A wants to know if employee participation in company decisions has an effect on productivity. A sample of $n = 75$ employees who participated in the decision-making process was administered the productivity scale with a result of $M = 27$. Does participation in company decisions have an effect on productivity? Use $\alpha = .01$ and a two-tailed test.

Step 1: Formulate Hypotheses

$$H_0 : \mu = 25$$
$$H_1 : \mu \ne 25$$

Step 2: Indicate the Alpha Level and Determine Critical Values

$$a = .01$$
$$z_{crit} = \pm 2.58$$

Step 3: Calculate Relevant Statistics

$$\sigma_M = .58$$
$$z_{obt} = +3 \text{ (ces)}$$

Step 4: Make a Decision and Report the Results

Participation in charce making process

$$H_0, z_{obt} = +3.45, p < .01$$

B. Now calculate Cohen's *d* and, using the guidelines suggested previously, indicate the size of the effect.

$$d = .40 \quad \text{Small effect}$$

## ERRORS

Hypothesis testing involves making a decision to either reject the null hypothesis or not to reject it. However, we can also be either right or wrong in our decision to reject or not to reject. That is, the null hypothesis could really be true and we could reject it, which would be an error. Alternatively, the null hypothesis could really be false and we could fail to reject it – also an error. Thus, two types of error are possible whenever we make a decision either to reject or not reject $H_0$.

- A *Type I error* is rejecting a null hypothesis that is in reality true (i.e., saying that treatment had an effect when it actually did not).
- A *Type II error* is the failure to reject a null hypothesis that is in reality false (i.e., saying that treatment did not have an effect when it actually did).

Remember, when we reject $H_0$ using an $\alpha = .05$, we are saying that our obtained statistic is unlikely to have occurred by chance alone (i.e., it would have occurred less than 5% of the time) if $H_0$ were true. Such an unlikely event leads us to reject $H_0$ and to conclude instead that our independent variable had an effect. However, we could be wrong (Type I error). In fact, we know that using a .05 alpha level will result in scores in the rejection region 5% of the time just by chance alone (without the influence of an independent variable). Thus, the probability of obtaining a Type I error is defined by the alpha level.

If we are using $\alpha = .05$, we could lower the probability of making a Type I error by lowering the alpha level, say to .01. As can be seen in the graphs below, using $\alpha = .01$ reduces the rejection region and we would therefore be rejecting $H_0$ less often. However, using $\alpha = .01$ rather than $\alpha = .05$ simultaneously increases the probability of a Type II error – failing to reject a false null hypothesis.

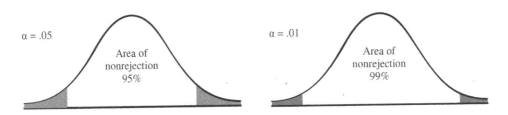

Because we cannot test actual populations, we have to rely on samples that introduce the possibility of error. We never know whether an error (either Type I or Type II) has been committed, but researchers want to keep the *risk* of error at a minimum. If we reject a null hypothesis, we want to be relatively certain that our results were real and not due to sampling error. The possibility of error associated with an alpha level of .05 is usually the greatest amount of risk that a researcher is willing to accept. If the consequences of making a Type I error are serious, then a lower alpha level may be chosen. However, this will also have to be weighed against the seriousness of making a Type II error.

## For Example

Suppose a neurologist, for some curious reason, believed that a tablespoon of sugar taken within 10 minutes of a stroke would decrease the possibility of paralysis. Because a tablespoon of sugar is unlikely to cause serious complications (even if the doctor is wrong), and because the potential benefit would be great if it did work, the doctor would probably want to minimize the possibility of not discovering the effectiveness of this intervention. Thus, she would want to minimize the possibility of a Type II error. In this case, an alpha level of .05 might be chosen, making it easier to reject $H_0$.

## Another Example

Assume another researcher believes that moderate drinking helps to prevent relapse in people who struggle with alcoholism. In this case, the researcher would want to take care to minimize the possibility of a Type I error – rejecting a true $H_0$. It would be a sobering mistake to say that moderate drinking is effective if in fact it leads to more serious alcohol problems. Thus, a more stringent alpha level (.01, or even .001) would likely be chosen, making it harder to reject $H_0$.

Researchers attempt to weigh the consequences and reach a balance between the two types of errors. Alpha levels of .05, .01, and .001 are commonly accepted as achieving this aim.

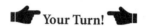 **Your Turn!**

## II. Thought Questions About Error

A. Does the probability of a Type II error increase or decrease as we move from an alpha level of .01 to .05? Explain. the probility of a type II error descrese ar the alpha level inceess fom .11 to .o5 this is becass a.05 alpha level makss the Ho

B. Given the same alpha level, does the probability of a Type I error increase *or* decrease as we move from a one-tailed test to a two-tailed test? Explain. Given the same alpha level the probaility of a type I error decrase as we nelc from a one toired teda to a two toirst tedt this is becase the rejerlion reyion in a two foiled ef rt

C. Suppose a researcher wants to test a new drug that she believes will promote concentration. However, the drug has some potentially dangerous side effects. Would you choose an $\alpha = .05$ or an $\alpha = .001$? Why? a = .0c1 bi Should Minimire the probility of a type i error becase of the potentlerny fangerool sse effecss of the drug

# POWER

The **power** of a statistical test refers to its ability to reject a null hypothesis that is in fact false. In other words, power makes it more likely that a treatment that actually exists will be detected. The size of the differences between obtained sample means and hypothesized population mean values will, of course, influence whether the null hypothesis will be rejected. Larger differences make the detection of statistical significance more likely, thus increasing power. Additionally, the chosen alpha level, directionality of the alternative hypothesis, sample size, and variability of the scores will all affect the power of a test. Each of these is discussed separately below.

*Alpha Level.* Choosing a less rigorous alpha level, such as .05 instead of .01, will increase power, making it more likely that the null hypothesis will be rejected. However, keep in mind that this will also increase the likelihood of a Type I error (and decrease the likelihood of a Type II error). This is why the circumstances of the research situation have to be considered when deciding on what alpha level to use.

*Directionality of the alternative hypothesis.* A similar case can be made when discussing a one- or two-tailed test. Other things being equal, a one-tailed test is more likely to detect statistical significance because the rejection region is larger. If $\alpha = .05$, the rejection region encompasses the entire 5%. If a two-tailed test was being used, that 5% rejection region would be split in half, with each half moving further into the tails of the distribution making it more difficult to reject $H_0$. Again, one has to look at the research situation. Unless there is reason to know the likely direction of a statistical result based on previous studies, researchers will generally choose the tougher standard and use a two-tailed test.

*Sample size.* We saw in the last chapter that larger samples generally produce less sampling error. Reduced sampling error will result in larger obtained test statistics. To illustrate, let's look at the example with the same standard deviations but with different sample sizes:

$$\sigma_M = \frac{s}{\sqrt{n}} = \frac{16}{\sqrt{25}} = 3.2$$

$$\sigma_M = \frac{s}{\sqrt{n}} = \frac{16}{\sqrt{100}} = 1.6$$

Now, let's look at the effect of $\sigma_M$ on $z_{obt}$:

$$z_{obt} = \frac{M - \mu}{\sigma_M} = \frac{17 - 12}{3.2} = 1.56$$

$$z_{obt} = \frac{M - \mu}{\sigma_M} = \frac{17 - 12}{1.6} = 3.13$$

You can see that the standard deviations, sample means, and population means all remained the same. The only difference was the sample size which, when increased, resulted in a larger obtained test value. Larger obtained test values extend further into the tail of the distribution making rejection of the null hypothesis more likely.

*Variability of the data.* We have learned that the standard deviation is a measure of the variability of scores. Greater variability increases the amount of standard error making rejection of the null hypothesis less likely. Let's look at another example to illustrate. This time, we will change only the standard deviation.

$$\sigma_M = \frac{s}{\sqrt{n}} = \frac{2}{\sqrt{9}} = .67$$

$$\sigma_M = \frac{s}{\sqrt{n}} = \frac{5}{\sqrt{9}} = 1.67$$

The standard deviation of 2 in the first instance reflects less variability among the scores than the greater variability shown in the second case with a standard deviation of 5. The smaller standard deviation produced a smaller amount of standard error. Now, let's look at how a smaller amount of standard error affects the obtained sample statistic.

$$z_{obt} = \frac{M - \mu}{\sigma_M} = \frac{10 - 8}{.67} = 2.99$$

$$z_{obt} = \frac{M - \mu}{\sigma_M} = \frac{10 - 8}{1.67} = 1.20$$

You can see that the means are the same; only the standard error is different. The result is a larger obtained $z$-value and a greater likelihood of rejecting the null hypothesis, again increasing power.

## A LOOK FORWARD

The ideas presented in this chapter lay the groundwork for upcoming chapters. The $z$-test is a valid test in its own right but is not commonly used because, in reality, we usually do not have access to population standard deviations. Thus, in future chapters we will build on the concepts of hypothesis testing presented in this chapter using other types of statistical tests.

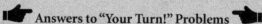 **Answers to "Your Turn!" Problems**

### I. Hypothesis Testing With the $z$-Test

A. Step 1:        Step 2:              Step 3:

$H_0: \mu = 25$      $\alpha = .01$          $\sigma_M = .58$
$H_1: \mu \neq 25$      $z_{crit} = \pm 2.58$      $z_{obt} = +3.45$

Step 4:

Participation in the decision-making process significantly affected productivity. Reject $H_0$, $z_{obt} = +3.45$, $p < .01$.

B. $d = .40$, small effect

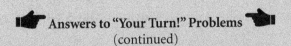

**Answers to "Your Turn!" Problems**
(continued)

### II. Thought Questions About Error

A. The probability of a Type II error decreases as the alpha level *increases* from .01 to .05. This is because a .05 alpha level makes the $H_0$ easier to reject and we would be failing to reject it less often.

B. Given the same alpha level, the probability of a Type I error *decreases* as we move from a one-tailed test to a two-tailed test. This is because the rejection region in a two-tailed test is split in two and falls farther into the extremes, making it more difficult to reject $H_0$. Thus, we would be rejecting a $H_0$ that is actually true less often.

C. $\alpha = .001$. We should minimize the probability of a Type I error because of the potentially dangerous side effects of the drug. (We want to make it more likely that any differences found are due to treatment and not chance, hence the lower $\alpha$.)

---

## Using Microsoft Excel for Data Analysis

If you are using Excel for the first time for statistical analysis, you may need to load the add-in tool that allows these functions. The information for loading the Data Analysis ToolPak as well as general instructions for using Excel for data analysis are at the beginning of the Excel section in Chapter 4.

### One-Sample z-Test in Excel

To use Excel for a one-sample z-test, we will be providing formula instructions for Excel to use for the necessary calculations. To demonstrate the procedures, we'll work with the sample research question from this chapter. First, type in the information shown below in column A of the spreadsheet that will be needed for the calculations. Also type in the summary information in column B that was provided for this problem.

|   | A | B | C |
|---|---|---|---|
| 1 | Sample mean | 75 | |
| 2 | Population mean | 70 | |
| 3 | Population SD | 10 | |
| 4 | n | 25 | |
| 5 | z crit (two-tailed at .05) | | |
| 6 | Standard error | | |
| 7 | z obt | | |
| 8 | | | |

Rather than using the table at the back on your text, Excel will determine your $z_{crit}$ values. We are using a nondirectional test and an alpha level of .05. Since it is a two-tailed test, remember that you have to divide that .05 in half to obtain the $z_{crit}$

values associated with the extreme 2.5% of the normal distribution. With your cursor in cell B5, type the following exactly as written: =ABS(NORMSINV(.025))

| | A | B | C | D |
|---|---|---|---|---|
| 1 | Sample mean | 75 | | |
| 2 | Population mean | 70 | | |
| 3 | Population SD | 10 | | |
| 4 | n | 25 | | |
| 5 | z crit (two-tailed at .05) | =ABS(NORMSINV(.025)) | | |
| 6 | Standard error | | | |
| 7 | z obt | | | |
| 8 | | | | |

After you hit the enter key, $z_{crit}$ (1.959964) will appear in the cell. If you were using a one-tailed test, you would use .05 instead of .025. For an alpha level of .01, you would use .005 for a two-tailed test and .01 for a one-tailed test.

Next, we want to calculate the standard error of the mean using the formula $\sigma_M = \sigma / \sqrt{n}$. In essence, we will be instructing Excel to divide the population standard deviation by the square root of $n$ by grabbing those values from the cells where they are located. For this example, with your cursor in cell B6, type the following exactly as written: =B3/SQRT(B4)

| | A | B | C |
|---|---|---|---|
| 1 | Sample mean | 75 | |
| 2 | Population mean | 70 | |
| 3 | Population SD | 10 | |
| 4 | n | 25 | |
| 5 | z crit (two-tailed at .05) | 1.959964 | |
| 6 | Standard error | =B3/SQRT(B4) | |
| 7 | z obt | | |
| 8 | | | |

After you hit the enter key, the standard error (2) will appear in the cell.

Lastly, we need to calculate our obtained z-value using the formula $z_{obt} = (M - \mu) / \sigma_M$. With your cursor in cell B7, type the following exactly as written: = (B1–B2)/B6

| | A | B | C |
|---|---|---|---|
| 1 | Sample mean | 75 | |
| 2 | Population mean | 70 | |
| 3 | Population SD | 10 | |
| 4 | n | 25 | |
| 5 | z crit (two-tailed at .05) | 1.959964 | |
| 6 | Standard error | 2 | |
| 7 | z obt | =(B1-B2)/B6 | |
| 8 | | | |

After hitting the enter key, you will see the value for $z_{obt}$ (2.5).

|  | A | B | C |
|---|---|---|---|
| 1 | Sample mean | 75 | |
| 2 | Population mean | 70 | |
| 3 | Population SD | 10 | |
| 4 | n | 25 | |
| 5 | z crit (two-tailed at .05) | 1.959964 | |
| 6 | Standard error | 2 | |
| 7 | z obt | 2.5 | |
| 8 | | | |

## Additional Practice Problems

**Answers to odd numbered problems are in Appendix C at the end of the book.**

1. Discuss the difference between the null hypothesis and the alternative hypothesis.
2. Discuss the difference between directional and nondirectional alternative hypotheses.
3. Explain what is meant by the alpha level and the critical region of a sampling distribution and how they are related.
4. A new activity program is being developed to determine its effectiveness in influencing the amount of time that children spend watching television, which is currently $\mu = 30$ hours per week. In symbolic form, write the notation for both the null hypothesis and the alternative hypothesis for:

   a. a nondirectional hypothesis test.
   b. a directional test that specifies that the program would reduce the number of hours spent in front of the television.
5. If our obtained sample mean is close in value to the population mean, is $H_0$ or $H_1$ more likely to be supported? Explain.
6. What are two conditions that researchers control that influence the likelihood of rejecting the null hypothesis?
7. For the values listed below, indicate whether to reject or fail to reject the null hypothesis, and whether the obtained probability is greater than or less than alpha.

|  | $z_{crit}$ | $z_{obt}$ | $\alpha$ |
|---|---|---|---|
| a. | −2.33 | −2.07 | .01 |
| b. | ±1.96 | −2.38 | .05 |
| c. | +1.65 | +1.83 | .05 |
| d. | ±2.58 | +2.54 | .01 |

8. For the values listed below, indicate whether the obtained $z$-value is significant (S) or nonsignificant (NS).

|  | $z_{crit}$ | $ss_{obt}$ |
|---|---|---|
| a. | ±2.58 | −2.47 |
| b. | −1.65 | −2.13 |
| c. | +2.33 | +2.40 |
| d. | +3.10 | +3.00 |

9. What is a Type I error and how is it related to the alpha level?
10. What is a Type II error? What can researchers do to make a Type II error less likely to occur?
11. A psychology professor has developed a workshop designed to reduce the apprehension of students taking university courses for the first time. All incoming freshmen take a standardized apprehension assessment which has resulted in a normal distribution with $\mu = 80$ and $\sigma = 12$. A random sample of $n = 44$ new freshmen who attended the professor's workshop obtained a $M = 76$.

  a. Using the four-step hypothesis testing procedure, test at $\alpha = .05$ using a one-tailed test.
  b. What was the size of the effect?
  c. If an alpha level of $\alpha = .01$ was used, would the statistical decision remain the same? Explain.
  d. Based on your answers to "c" above, how is the power of a statistical test related to the alpha level that is set by the researcher?

12. A cognitive psychologist has developed a new technique which he believes will influence the ability to concentrate while performing difficult cognitive tasks. A standardized test of logical reasoning is normally distributed and has a $\mu = 36$ and a $\sigma = 8$. A random sample of $n = 18$ adults is taught the concentration technique and then administered the logic test. A sample mean of $M = 38$ was obtained. Use the hypothesis testing procedure with $\alpha = .05$ to determine the effectiveness of the concentration technique.

13. A standardized mood assessment has a $\mu = 65$ and a $\sigma = 15$. Higher scores reflect a more positive mood state. A pop music producer, interested in how music affects peoples' mood, hires a research company to assess this relationship. As a part of the study, the research company obtains a random sample of $n = 40$ adults and administers the mood assessment while they are listening to soft piano music. The mean for the sample was $M = 69$.

  a. Using a two-tailed test and $\alpha = .05$, use the four-step hypothesis testing procedure to test the music producer's hypothesis that music affects mood.
  b. Given the same $\alpha = .05$, but using a one-tailed test hypothesizing that the music would improve the mood of the listeners, would the outcome have been the same? Explain.
  c. Based on your answer to "b" above, how is the power of a statistical test related to the directionality of the research hypothesis?

## Notes

1  American Psychological Association. (2001). *Publication manual of the American Psychological Association* (5th ed.). Washington, DC: American Psychological Association.
2  Cohen, J. (1988). *Statistical power analysis for the behavioral sciences* (2nd ed.). Hillsdale, NJ: Lawrence Erlbaum Associates.

# One-Sample $t$ Test

## THE $t$-STATISTIC

Now that we have established the foundational concepts for hypothesis testing, we are ready to build further on these ideas. Previously, we used the $z$-statistic in testing hypotheses about the population mean ($\mu$). However, the $z$-test requires knowing the value of the population standard deviation ($\sigma$) – information that is, in fact, not usually known. A standard deviation is needed to calculate the standard error, which is needed in turn for the $z$-score formula. Even though we cannot calculate the population standard deviation directly, remember that we can estimate it by using $n - 1$ in the standard deviation formula presented in Chapter 4:

$$s = \sqrt{\frac{SS}{n-1}}$$

We can then use this estimate in the formula for the standard error. Instead of using $\sigma_M = \frac{\sigma}{\sqrt{n}}$, we use $s_M = \frac{s}{\sqrt{n}}$.

The statistic used to test hypotheses about population means when $\sigma$ is not known is called the $t$-statistic, which is given by the formula:

$$t_{obt} = \frac{M - \mu}{s_M}$$

Notice that the only difference between this formula and the $z$-score formula is the use of the estimated standard error in the denominator in place of the actual standard error.

## THE $t$-DISTRIBUTION

Whenever we engage in hypothesis testing, we will use a sampling distribution of some kind. The **$t$-distribution**, like the $z$-distribution, is theoretical, symmetrical, and bell-shaped, but the appearance of the curve changes according to the size of the sample. The $z$-distribution is based on an infinite number of cases resulting in what we refer to as the normal distribution curve. However, with small samples the curve will be shaped differently. The *t*-distribution is actually a family of curves, one for each sample size. The particular *t*-distribution that we use will be based on the degrees of freedom associated with the sample.

We encountered the term *degrees of freedom* (*df*) when we used $n - 1$ in the denominator of the formula for estimating the population standard deviation from sample data. This corrected for the underestimation of the sample standard deviation. We also use *df* when estimating other population parameters to increase the accuracy of our estimates. The particular *df* to use will vary from one statistical procedure to another depending on the sample size and the number of data sets used to estimate a population parameter. When using the *t*-distribution for a single sample, *df* will also be $n - 1$, the size of the sample minus 1. For instance, if your sample size is 16, *df* will be 15.

## Shape of the *t*-Distribution

The *t*-distribution is used in the same way that we used the normal distribution, except that the curves of the *t*-distribution depart from normality as *df* decrease. The illustration below shows what the curves look like for three different $df \rightarrow 5, 15$, and infinity.

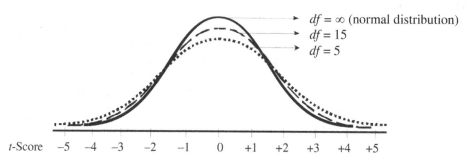

The *t*-scores are shown along the baseline, just like *z*-scores. Notice that the curves become flatter with smaller *df* and that the *t*-values extend farther into the tails. As *df* increase, the *t*-distribution looks more and more like the normal distribution. When *df* are infinite, there is no difference in shape between the *t*-curve and the normal distribution curve.

**Tip!** Because smaller samples result in a distribution that is flatter and more spread out, more extreme *t*-values would be required to reject H₀ (i.e., we would have to go farther into the tails to reach significance with smaller samples).

## Critical Values for the *t* -Distribution

To determine the critical values for the *t*-distribution, we will use Table 2 near the end of this book. This table shows the critical values of *t* that would be necessary for rejecting the null hypothesis. Some important features of the table are as follows:

- In the left column, various degrees of freedom (*df*) are listed.
- The first row across the top lists various levels of significance for a one-tailed test.

- The second row across the top lists various levels of significance for a two-tailed test. When using the table for the normal distribution curve, you were required to divide the proportion associated with the alpha level in half for two-tailed tests. This is not necessary for the table used to determine critical values for the *t*-distribution.
- The remaining columns in the body of the table list the critical values necessary for rejecting $H_0$ at the significance levels identified at the top of each column.

In order to reject $H_0$, your obtained *t*-value will have to exceed the value listed in the chart. However, the chart is abbreviated, and the critical values are not shown for all *df*. If the *df* for your particular research problem are not shown, then use the critical values associated with the *next-lowest df*. For instance, if your sample size is 54, actual *df* would be 53 ($n - 1$), which is not shown. In this case, you would use 40 to ensure that your obtained *t*-value falls inside the critical region.

The "Your Turn!" exercise below will give you some practice working with this table and will reinforce some ideas that were covered in the last chapter.

 Your Turn!

## I. Practicing With the *t*-Table

For each of the obtained *t*-values given below, determine the *t*-critical value and decide if $H_0$ should be rejected. For the one-tailed tests, assume that the researcher is looking for score increases.

| | df | α level | One or two-tailed test | $t_{obt}$ | $t_{crit}$ | Reject $H_0$ Y/N |
|---|---|---|---|---|---|---|
| A. | 11 | .01 | two-tailed | 4.32 | _____ | _____ |
| B. | 80 | .05 | two-tailed | 1.04 | _____ | _____ |
| C. | 24 | .05 | one-tailed | 2.18 | _____ | _____ |
| D. | 24 | .01 | one-tailed | 2.18 | _____ | _____ |
| E. | 42 | .05 | one-tailed | 1.87 | _____ | _____ |
| F. | 42 | .05 | two-tailed | 1.87 | _____ | _____ |
| G. | 19 | .01 | two-tailed | 3.06 | _____ | _____ |
| H. | 19 | .001 | two-tailed | 3.06 | _____ | _____ |

Tip!

Notice that, given the same degrees of freedom and alpha level, it is more difficult to reject the null hypothesis using a two-tailed test than a one-tailed test. In addition, observe that the null hypothesis is more difficult to reject as we move from a .05 to a .01 alpha level, and it is even more difficult to reject at $\alpha = .001$.

**ONE-SAMPLE $t$ TEST**

The ***one-sample t test*** is a test of a hypothesis about a population mean ($\mu$) when the population standard deviation ($\sigma$) is not known. This test is used when researchers want to know (1) if a sample is representative of a population and/or (2) if a particular treatment or condition has a significant effect. We will use the same four-step procedure that we used for the $z$-test, beginning with a research question.

## Sample Research Question (Two-Tailed Test)

The population mean on a standardized test of critical thinking is $\mu$ = 53. A group of faculty members at a small community college underwent a 10-week training program to learn techniques designed to help students develop their critical thinking skills. After the training, the new techniques were implemented in the classrooms. The mean critical thinking score for a sample of $n$ = 87 students exposed to the new techniques was $M$ = 55 with $SS$ = 6013. Do the results suggest that the training program had a significant effect? Use a two-tailed test and $\alpha$ = .05.

## Step 1: Formulate Hypotheses

$H_0: \mu = 53$
$H_1: \mu \neq 53$

The null hypothesis asserts that the critical thinking scores in the population, after implementation of the new techniques, would still be 53. We are using the non-directional alternative hypothesis that the population mean would be some value other than the one specified in $H_0$.

## Step 2: Indicate the Alpha Level and Determine Critical Values

$\alpha = .05$
$df = 86$
$t_{crit} = \pm 2.000$

The actual $df$ is 86 (i.e., $n-1$). However, this value is not shown in the $t$-distribution table. Thus, we will use the next-lowest $df$, which is 60, for which the chart indicates a value of 2.00.

## Step 3: Calculate Relevant Statistics

Because $\sigma$ is not known, we will need to estimate it from our sample data. For this problem, rather than calculating the standard deviation from the raw scores, you are given the value for $SS$ (sum of squares). We will use this value for calculating the estimated population standard deviation($s$):

$$s = \sqrt{\frac{SS}{n-1}} = \sqrt{\frac{6013}{87-1}} = 8.36$$

Before we can determine our obtained $t$-value, we first need to calculate the standard error using the estimated standard deviation above:

$$S_M = \frac{s}{\sqrt{n}} = \frac{8.36}{\sqrt{87}} = .90$$

Finally, we can calculate the $t$-statistic:

$$t_{obt} = \frac{M - \mu}{S_M} = \frac{55 - 53}{.90} = +2.22$$

### Step 4: Make a Decision and Report the Results

The *t*-distribution for this example is below:

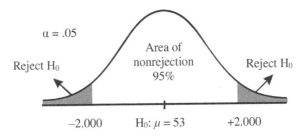

The $t_{crit}$ values are ±2.000. To reject H$_0$, we need a sample mean with an obtained *t*-value beyond 2.000 in either direction. Our obtained *t*-value was +2.22, which falls in the rejection region. Thus, we reject the null hypothesis.

### Proper Format

The format for reporting the results of a one-sample *t* test is as follows:

> Students taught by the faculty who participated in the training program scored significantly higher on the critical-thinking assessment than did the general population. Reject H$_0$, $t(86) = +2.22$, $p < .05$.

Note that

- our obtained probability is less than .05. In other words, if the null hypothesis were true (i.e., if $\mu = 53$), our obtained sample mean would have occurred by chance less than 5% of the time. This unlikely event leads us to reject the null hypothesis and to conclude instead that the critical-thinking training program significantly influenced students' scores.
- the *t*-value reported is the *obtained t*, not the critical *t*.
- the number in parentheses after *t* is the *actual* degrees of freedom, not the lower *df* listed in the chart.

### EFFECT SIZE FOR A ONE-SAMPLE *t* TEST

Because our results were significant, we need to ask how significant they were. Here again, we will use Cohen's *d* to measure the size of the effect, as we did in the last chapter for the *z*-test. However, the formula as applied to a one-sample *t* test will change slightly, as shown below, because for the *t* test we used an estimated population standard deviation (*s*) in lieu of an actual population standard deviation ($\sigma$).

General formula:

$$d = \frac{|M - \mu|}{s}$$

For our current problem:

$$d = \frac{|55 - 53|}{8.36} = .24$$

The critical-thinking scores of the students showed an improvement of about one-fourth of a standard deviation (.24) above the mean of the general population.

As a reminder, the guidelines recommended by Cohen in the last chapter are repeated below:

- $d = .20$ to $.49$ – Small effect
- $d = .50$ to $.79$ – Moderate effect
- $d = .80$ and above – Large effect

Thus, the results of our *t* test can be interpreted as exhibiting a small effect size.

### Another Sample Research Question (One-Tailed Test)

Remember, if a problem indicates that a researcher is looking for score increases or decreases, then assume a one-tailed test. If the researcher is simply looking for an effect with no indication of direction, then assume a two-tailed test.

A well-known sandwich chain puts 9 grams of protein on its sandwiches. A customer complained to the home office that a particular outlet was putting "hardly any meat" on its sandwiches. A random sample of $n = 16$ sandwiches from the sandwich shop in question were weighed. The results showed a $M = 7.9$ with $s = 2.1$. Did the shop put significantly less protein on its sandwiches? Test at $\alpha = .05$.

### Step 1: Formulate Hypotheses

$H_0: \mu \geq 53$
$H_1: \mu < 53$

### Step 2: Indicate the Alpha Level and Determine Critical Values

$\alpha = .05$
$df = 15$
$t_{crit} = -2.131$

### Step 3: Calculate Relevant Statistics

$$S_M = \frac{s}{\sqrt{n}} = \frac{2.1}{\sqrt{16}} = .53$$

$$t_{obt} = \frac{M - \mu}{S_M} = \frac{7.9 - 9}{.53} = -2.08$$

### Step 4: Make a Decision and Report the Results

The sandwich shop did not put a significantly less amount of protein on its sandwiches. Fail to reject $H_0$, $t(15) = -2.08$, $p > .05$.

### ASSUMPTIONS

The same assumptions that apply to the *z*-test also apply to the *t* test, with one exception. The applicable assumptions include the following:

- Independent and random selection of participants.
- The dependent variable is normally distributed in the population of interest.
- The dependent variable can be measured on an interval or ratio scale.

The only assumption that pertains to the *z*-test that does not pertain to the *t* test is that the population standard deviation ($\sigma$) is known. Because we are estimating the population standard deviation for the *t* test, this requirement does not apply.

 Your Turn!

## II. One-Sample $t$ Test

A. *Research Question.* The mean score for golfers at the Country Oaks Golf Course is $\mu = 83$. The manager wonders if posting a red flag at hazard sites (e.g., sand traps, ponds, gullies) will improve scores. After posting the flags at all such sites, she obtains a random sample of 25 golfers whose mean was $M = 81$ with $SS = 788$. Do the data indicate that the flags improved golf scores? (*Note:* Lower scores reflect better performance in golf.) Use a one-tailed test with $\alpha = .05$.

Step 1: Formulate Hypotheses (Be careful!)

Step 2: Indicate the Alpha Level and Determine Critical Values

Step 3: Calculate Relevant Statistics

Step 4: Make a Decision and Report the Results

B. Calculate Cohen's $d$ and indicate the size of the effect.

C. Work problem A above, except use an $\alpha = .01$ rather than .05. (*Hint:* Only Steps 2 and 4 will change.)

 Tip!

Keep the context of the problem in mind when thinking about how to interpret results. While scores below the mean usually indicate worse performance, this is not always the case, as in golf. Here, a negative *t*-value would indicate *improved* performance of a certain size because the goal in golf is to score below par.

The table below will help you to determine how to write your hypotheses (Step 1 in the hypothesis testing procedure) when using a one-or two-tailed test, as well as the direction of your $t_{crit}$ values (Step 2).

| Test | Hypotheses | $t_{crit}$ |
|---|---|---|
| Two-tailed | $H_0: \mu =$ value specified in problem <br> $H_1: \mu \neq$ value specified in problem | $t_{crit} = \pm$ value in chart |
| One-tailed, left | $H_0: \mu \geq$ value specified in problem <br> $H_1: \mu <$ value specified in problem | $t_{crit} = -$ value in chart |
| One-tailed, right | $H_0: \mu \leq$ value specified in problem <br> $H_1: \mu >$ value specified in problem | $t_{crit} = +$ value in chart |

Remember, in order to reject $H_0$, your obtained *t*-value has to be more extreme than the $t_{crit}$ value and in the same direction as the alternative hypothesis.

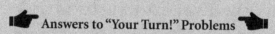 **Answers to "Your Turn!" Problems**

### I. Practicing With the *t*-Table

| | $t_{crit}$ | Reject $H_0$ | | $t_{crit}$ | Reject $H_0$ |
|---|---|---|---|---|---|
| A. | 3.106 | Y | E. | 1.684 | Y |
| B. | 2.000 | N | F. | 2.021 | N |
| C. | 1.711 | Y | G. | 2.861 | Y |
| D. | 2.492 | N | H. | 3.883 | N |

### II. One-Sample *t* Test

A. Step 1:

$H_0: \mu \geq 83$
$H_1: \mu < 83$

Step 2:

$\alpha = .05 \; df = 24$
$t_{crit} = -1.711$

Step 3:

$s = 5.73$
$s_M = 1.15$
$t_{obt} = -1.74$

Step 4:

There was a significant improvement in golf scores after posting red flags in hazard zones. Reject $H_0$, $t(24) = -1.74$, $p < .05$.

B. $d = .35$, small effect size

C. Step 1: Same as A above.

Step 2:

$\alpha = .01 \; df = 24$
$t_{crit} = -2.492$

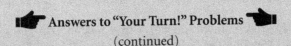

**Answers to "Your Turn!" Problems**
(continued)

Step 3: Same as A above.

Step 4:

There was no significant improvement in golf scores after posting red flags in hazard sites. Fail to reject $H_0$, $t(24) = -1.74, p > .01$.

---

## Using Microsoft Excel for Data Analysis

If you are using Excel for the first time for statistical analysis, you may need to load the add-in tool that allows these functions. The information for loading the Data Analysis ToolPak as well as general instructions for using Excel for data analysis are at the beginning of the Excel section in Chapter 4.

### Sample Research Question

Let's use a new example to learn the procedures involved in using Excel for a one-sample $t$ test. A sales consultant has developed a new set of protocols and practices that she believes will increase sales. The consultant is hired for another year by a company that she has worked with for several years. Last year, the sales force for this company averaged $500 per day in sales. The consultant trains a random sample of eight sales associates to use the new approach. Their average daily sales for a one-month period of time were: 520, 466, 582, 549, 488, 572, 515, and 551. Did the sales consultant's new method improve sales? Test at $\alpha = .05$ using a one-tailed test.

### One-Sample $t$ Test in Excel

Type in the scores in column A of the spreadsheet as well as the information show below that will be used in the analysis. Also type in the population mean (given in the problem), the sample size, and $df$ in column C. Recall that $df = n - 1$ for a one-sample $t$ test.

|   | A | B | C | D |
|---|---|---|---|---|
| 1 | 520 | | Sample mean | |
| 2 | 466 | | Population mean | 500 |
| 3 | 582 | | Sample SD | |
| 4 | 549 | | n | 8 |
| 5 | 488 | | df | 7 |
| 6 | 572 | | t crit (one-tailed at .05) | |
| 7 | 515 | | Standard error | |
| 8 | 551 | | t obt | |

We will now proceed to instruct Excel to perform the remaining operations:

1. **Sample Mean**. Place your cursor in cell D1 to activate it. Go to the **Formulas** tab, then choose the **Insert Function (fx)** command from the ribbon. From the **Insert Function** dialog box, click the dropdown box that allows you to select a category; select **Statistical**. From the **Select a function** window, highlight **AVERAGE** and click **OK**.

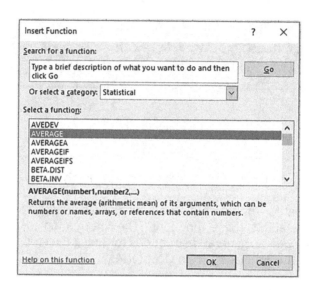

With your cursor in the **Number 1** window of the **Functions Arguments** dialog box, drag your mouse over the scores in column A of the spreadsheet. The cell range A1:A8 should appear in the window. Before clicking **OK**, notice in the lower left corner a "formula result" that shows the result of your actions, in this case the sample mean (530.375). After clicking **OK**, this result will also be shown in the spreadsheet.

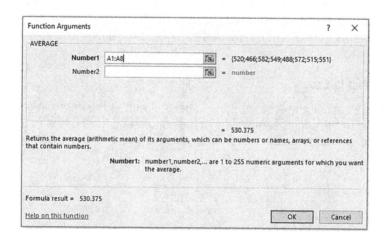

2. **Sample Standard Deviation**. Place your cursor in cell D3 to activate it. Then follow all of the actions in Step 1 above, except from the **Insert Function** dialog box, select **STDEV.S** instead of **AVERAGE**. After clicking **OK** from the **Function Arguments** dialog box, the sample standard deviation (40.45081) will be shown in the spreadsheet.

3. **Critical *t*-value**. Rather than using the table at the back of your text, Excel will determine your $t_{crit}$ values. With your cursor in cell D6, click on the **Insert Function (fx)** command from the ribbon. From the **Select a function** window of the **Insert Function** dialog box, scroll down and highlight **T.INV**. This is the function that will provide the values for $t_{crit}$ for a given area of the distribution.

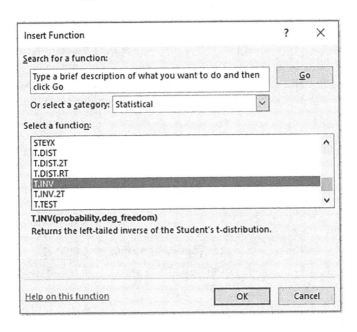

Notice that below the **Select a function** window, you are told what information will be provided: "Returns the left-tailed inverse of the Student's t-distribution." What that means is that the probability value that you will specify in the next dialog box has to include all of the area to the left of the critical value that Excel will provide. Since we are looking for improved sales using a one-tailed test at an alpha level of .05, the area to the left of the critical value would be .95. In the **Function Arguments** dialog box, type in .95 in the **Probability** window and 7 in the **Deg_freedom** window. Click **OK** and the $t_{crit}$ value (1.894579) will be shown on the spreadsheet.

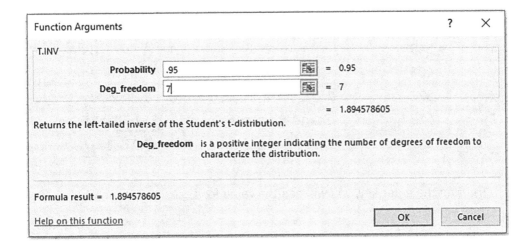

In a different example, if we were using a one-tailed test and looking for a *decrease* in scores at the same alpha level, we would use the probability level of .05 instead of .95. This would result in a negative $t_{crit}$ value because all of the critical values to the left of .05 will be negative. If we were conducting a two-tailed test instead of a one-tailed test, we would select **T.INV.2T** instead of **T.INV** in the **Insert Function** dialog box and then, in the **Function Arguments** dialog box, we would enter whatever alpha level is being used.

4. **Standard Error.** Next, we want to calculate the estimated population standard error of the mean using the formula $s_M = s / \sqrt{n}$. In essence, we will be instructing Excel to divide the sample standard deviation by the square root of *n* by grabbing those values from the cells where they are located. For this example, with your cursor in cell D7, type the following exactly as written: =D3/SQRT(D4)

| | A | B | C | D | E |
|---|---|---|---|---|---|
| 1 | 520 | | Sample mean | 530.375 | |
| 2 | 466 | | Population mean | 500 | |
| 3 | 582 | | Sample SD | 40.45081 | |
| 4 | 549 | | n | 8 | |
| 5 | 488 | | df | 7 | |
| 6 | 572 | | t crit (one-tailed at .05) | 1.894579 | |
| 7 | 515 | | Standard error | =D3/SQRT(D4) | |
| 8 | 551 | | t obt | | |

After you hit the enter key, the standard error (14.30152) will appear in the cell.

5. **Obtained *t*-value.** Finally, we will calculate our obtained *t*-value using the formula $t_{obt} = (M - \mu) / s_M$. With your cursor in cell D8, type the following exactly as written: =(D1–D2)/D7

| | A | B | C | D | E |
|---|---|---|---|---|---|
| 1 | 520 | | Sample mean | 530.375 | |
| 2 | 466 | | Population mean | 500 | |
| 3 | 582 | | Sample SD | 40.45081 | |
| 4 | 549 | | n | 8 | |
| 5 | 488 | | df | 7 | |
| 6 | 572 | | t crit (one-tailed at .05) | 1.894579 | |
| 7 | 515 | | Standard error | 14.30152 | |
| 8 | 551 | | t obt | =(D1-D2)/D7 | |

After hitting the enter key, you will see the value for $t_{obt}$.

| | A | B | C | D |
|---|---|---|---|---|
| 1 | 520 | | Sample mean | 530.375 |
| 2 | 466 | | Population mean | 500 |
| 3 | 582 | | Sample SD | 40.45081 |
| 4 | 549 | | n | 8 |
| 5 | 488 | | df | 7 |
| 6 | 572 | | t crit (one-tailed at .05) | 1.894579 |
| 7 | 515 | | Standard error | 14.30152 |
| 8 | 551 | | t obt | 2.1239 |

For our example, the null hypothesis is that the new training would not change or would decrease sales performance ($H_0$: $\mu \leq \$500$). The alternative hypothesis is that the new training would improve sales and that after training, sales numbers would increase over last year's average ($H_1$: $\mu > \$500$). Remember that it is always the null hypothesis that is being tested but we are really hoping to reject it and thereby gain support for the alternative hypothesis. Since our obtained *t*-value is greater than $t_{crit}$, we can reject the null hypothesis. The study indicated that sales were significantly higher than last year after the training in new sales techniques.

---

### Additional Practice Problems

**Answers to odd numbered problems are in Appendix C at the end of the book.**

1. Compare the shape of the *t*-distribution with the normal distribution as related to sample size. How does this affect the ability to reject the null hypothesis?
2. Given the specifications that follow, determine $t_{crit}$ and whether $H_0$ should be rejected for a one-sample *t* test, $\alpha = .05$, one-tailed. Assume the researcher is looking for score improvements as indicated by higher scores.

| | n | $t_{obt}$ |
|---|---|---|
| a. | 61 | 1.83 |
| b. | 23 | 1.52 |
| c. | 5 | 2.08 |
| d. | 31 | 1.97 |

3. Given the specifications that follow, determine $t_{crit}$ and whether $H_0$ should be rejected for a one-sample *t* test, $\alpha = .01$, two-tailed.

|     | $n$ | $t_{obt}$ |
| --- | --- | --- |
| a.  | 7   | 2.98 |
| b.  | 29  | 3.00 |
| c.  | 17  | 1.87 |
| d.  | 41  | 2.94 |

4. Suppose the body mass index (BMI) for adult males aged 20–39 in the United States is 28.4. A fitness coach at the Forever Fitness Health Club believes that the BMI of his clientele in this age range would be lower.
   a. Write the null and alternative hypotheses in words.
   b. Write the null and alternative hypotheses in symbolic notation.

5. The average number of hours that adults sleep in the United States is 6.8. A psychology professor believes that college students get significantly less sleep than the national average.
   a. Write the null and alternative hypotheses in words.
   b. Write the null and alternative hypotheses in symbolic notation.

6. The manager of a large manufacturing company has decided to implement a reward system to determine if it has any effect on worker productivity. The company currently produces an average of 250 gizmos per day.
   a. Write the null and alternative hypotheses in words.
   b. Write the null and alternative hypotheses in symbolic notation.

7. If a *t*-value is obtained that is not in the critical region, is this result better accounted for by $H_0$ or $H_1$? Explain.

8. If a *t*-value is obtained that is in the critical region, is this result better accounted for by $H_0$ or $H_1$? Explain.

9. Given $s = 12$ and $n = 100$, calculate the standard error of the mean.

10. For a one-sample *t* test, $H_0$: $\mu = 73$. Given $M = 68$, $s = 8$, and $n = 16$, what is $t_{obt}$?

11. For a one-sample *t* test, $H_0$: $\mu \leq 40$. Given $M = 35$, $s = 6$, and $n = 10$, what is $t_{obt}$?

12. Given a $\mu = 30$ and a $s_M = 2$, would $H_0$ be rejected if $M = 33$, $n = 23$, and $\alpha = .05$ for a one-sample, two-tailed *t* test?

13. Given a $\mu = 54$ and $s_M = 4$, would $H_0$ be rejected if $M = 48$, $n = 16$, and $\alpha = .05$ for a one-sample *t* test if the researcher believes a treatment will decrease scores?

14. A normally distributed population has a $\mu = 28$. A researcher believes that scores will improve after a treatment procedure. A sample size of $n = 16$ obtains a $M = 34$ with a $s = 8$. Did the treatment procedure significantly increase the scores? Test at $\alpha = .01$.

15. People in the United States report having an average of nine close friends, not counting relatives. A psychologist believes that extroverts have more friends than the national average. The mean for a sample of $n = 25$ extroverts was $M = 11$ with a $s = 6$. Do extroverts have significantly more friends than the general population? Test at $\alpha = .05$.

16. Newborns in the United States sleep an average of 16 hours in a 24-hour period. Staff at the neonatal unit of a large metropolitan hospital recorded the following sleep times for a sample of their newborn infants: 17, 20, 21, 15, 19, 17, 15, 21. Does the average amount of time slept by the sample differ significantly from the population average? Test at $\alpha = .01$.

# Two-Sample *t* Test
## Independent Samples Design

## TWO-SAMPLE *t* TEST: INDEPENDENT SAMPLES DESIGN

In a one-sample *t* test, a sample mean is used to test a hypothesis about a population mean. Often, however, researchers will want to compare the means for two groups. In such cases, **two-sample t tests** can be used instead. We will look at two types of two-sample *t* tests – independent samples design, which we will cover in this chapter, and related samples design, which we will cover in the next chapter.

The **independent samples design** involves two separate and unrelated samples for which each participant provides one score. This design involves testing hypotheses about the difference between two means to determine if those means differ significantly. The independent samples design is also called a *between-subjects design,* highlighting the fact that it is the means *between* samples that are compared. An example of the kind of research question that this type of design addresses is given below:

> A new drug for anxiety is being tested. Two samples are drawn from a population of individuals who suffer from generalized anxiety. Sample 1 receives the anxiety drug and Sample 2 receives a placebo. Is there enough difference between the means of the two samples to conclude significance?

## SAMPLING DISTRIBUTION OF THE DIFFERENCE BETWEEN MEANS

Once again, we will be comparing our obtained difference between means to a theoretical sampling distribution in order to determine if the difference between our means is significant. In this case, the theoretical sampling distribution is referred to as the **sampling distribution of the difference between means**. Imagine some large population from which you draw two samples of size $n_1$ and size $n_2$. You measure each sample on some aspect of behavior and calculate a mean for each sample. You then determine the difference between those means $(M_1 - M_2)$ and record it. You then repeat this process over and over, drawing all possible random samples of size $n_1$ and $n_2$ and recording only the difference between their means.[1] These *difference between means* values are then arranged into a frequency distribution, called the sampling distribution of the difference between means. (Of course, this is not done in actuality, only in theory.)

## CALCULATIONS

The calculations for the two-sample *t* test will be similar to those that we have utilized before and will include a standard error of difference, a *t* test, and degrees of freedom.

### Standard Error of Difference

The standard deviation of the sampling distribution of the difference between means is called the ***standard error of difference between means***, and it is calculated with the formula below:

$$s_{M_1-M_2} = \sqrt{\left(\frac{SS_1 + SS_2}{n_1 + n_2 - 2}\right)\left(\frac{1}{n_1} + \frac{1}{n_2}\right)}$$

Without knowing the population standard deviation ($\sigma$), we cannot calculate $\sigma_{M_1 - M_2}$ directly, but we can estimate it using $s_{M_1-M_2}$. You may recall from Chapter 4 that a standard deviation is the square root of the variance. In this case, the two variances for the two samples are averaged together. This pooled variance is the first term on the left in parentheses under the square root. The value that this formula as a whole produces is the estimated amount of sampling error that can be expected due to chance alone.

### Formula for the *t* Test, Independent Samples Design

Once we have determined the standard error of difference between means, we can use it in the formula for the independent samples *t* test:

$$t_{obt} = \frac{(M_1 - M_2) - (\mu_1 - \mu_2)}{s_{M_1-M_2}}$$

$(M_1 - M_2)$ represents our obtained difference between means, whereas $(\mu_1 - \mu_2)$ represents the hypothesized difference. Because the null hypothesis usually states no difference between means (see "Hypothesis Testing" on the following page), for our purposes $\mu_1 - \mu_2$ will be 0. Thus, we can simplify the formula as follows:

$$t_{obt} = \frac{M_1 - M_2}{s_{M_1-M_2}}$$

If a two-tailed test is used, $t_{obt}$ may be either positive or negative. If a one-tailed test is used, the alternative hypothesis ($H_1$) will specify one of the means to be higher or lower than the other. In this case, the null hypothesis ($H_0$) can be rejected only if the obtained difference between means is in the direction specified by $H_1$.

### Degrees of Freedom

Because two samples are being used, degrees of freedom (*df*) for the independent samples *t* test will be based on two data sets, as follows:

$$df = n_1 + n_2 - 2$$

## HYPOTHESIS TESTING

When means differ, there are, as usual, two opposing explanations for the difference observed:

- The *null hypothesis* ($H_0$) attributes the difference to chance, or random sampling error, and can be variously written as:

    $H_0 : \mu_1 - \mu_2 = 0$   (no [significant] difference between means)

    $H_0 : \mu_1 = \mu_2$   (the two means are [essentially] equal)

- The *alternative hypothesis* ($H_1$) asserts that differences between means are more than chance differences and that treatment *was* effective.

Again, $H_1$ may be *nondirectional* and simply propose that, after treatment, the population means would not be equal:

$H_1 : \mu_1 \neq \mu_2$   $\left( \text{for } H_0 : \mu_1 = \mu_2 \right)$

Alternatively, $H_1$ may be *directional* and specify the direction of expected difference. $H_1$ may specify that the mean for Group 1 would be greater than the mean for Group 2, or that it would be less than the mean for Group 2. These situations are shown, respectively, below:

$H_1 : \mu_1 > \mu_2$   $\left( \text{for } H_0 : \mu_1 \leq \mu_2 \right)$

$H_1 : \mu_1 < \mu_2$   $\left( \text{for } H_0 : \mu_1 \geq \mu_2 \right)$

### Rejecting $H_0$

For a *nondirectional* alternative hypothesis, when a mean difference falls in the critical region in either tail of the sampling distribution, $H_0$ can be rejected. Differences as large as that are unlikely to be due to chance. For a *directional* alternative hypothesis, rejecting $H_0$ requires that the difference value falls in the critical region in the direction specified in $H_1$.

### Sample Research Question

A political science teacher wonders whether there is a difference in knowledge of current events between students who read newspapers and those who watch the news on television. He randomly assigns students to one of two groups. Group 1 is instructed to read only the daily newspapers (either online or hard copies) for the next 30 days, whereas Group 2 is instructed to only watch the nightly news. Both groups are thereafter given a test to assess their knowledge of current events. The following scores are obtained. Conduct a nondirectional *t* test with $\alpha = .05$.

**Tip!**

Remember from Chapter 4 that *SS* refers to sum of squares:

$$SS = \Sigma X^2 - \frac{(\Sigma X)^2}{n}$$

It is the numerator in the formula for the variance. In some problems, *SS* will be provided. If it is not given, however, it will have to be calculated for each sample.

| Newspaper | Television news |
|-----------|-----------------|
| 59 | 36 |
| 48 | 42 |
| 45 | 50 |
| 39 | 37 |
| 52 | 51 |
| 56 | 32 |
| 50 | 47 |
| 41 | 38 |
| 46 | 40 |
| 45 | 31 |
| 48 | |

## Step 1: Formulate Hypotheses

$H_0 : \mu_1 = \mu_2$

$H_1 : \mu_1 \neq \mu_2$

## Step 2: Indicate the Alpha Level and Determine Critical Values

$\alpha = .05$

$df = n_1 + n_2 - 2$

$\quad = 11 + 10 - 2$

$\quad = 19$

$t_{crit} = \pm 2.093$

## Step 3: Calculate Relevant Statistics

| $X_1$ | $X_1^2$ | $X_2$ | $X_2^2$ |
|-------|---------|-------|---------|
| 59 | 3481 | 36 | 1296 |
| 48 | 2308 | 42 | 1764 |
| 45 | 2025 | 50 | 2500 |
| 39 | 1521 | 37 | 1369 |
| 52 | 2704 | 51 | 2601 |
| 56 | 3136 | 32 | 1024 |
| 50 | 2500 | 47 | 2209 |
| 41 | 1681 | 38 | 1444 |
| 46 | 2116 | 40 | 1600 |
| 45 | 2025 | 31 | 961 |
| 48 | 2304 | | |
| $\Sigma X_1 = 529$ | $\Sigma X_1^2 = 25{,}797$ | $\Sigma X_2 = 404$ | $\Sigma X_2^2 = 16{,}768$ |

$n_1 = 11$ $\qquad\qquad$ $n_2 = 10$

$M_1 = 48.09$ $\qquad\quad$ $M_2 = 40.40$

Calculate the sum of squares for each sample.

$$SS = \Sigma X^2 - \frac{(\Sigma X)^2}{n}$$

$$SS_1 = 25,797 - \frac{(529)^2}{11}$$

$$= 356.91$$

$$SS_2 = 16,768 - \frac{(404)^2}{10}$$

$$= 446.40$$

Calculate the standard error of difference.

Calculate the *t*-statistic.

$$s_{M_1-M_2} = \sqrt{\left(\frac{SS_1 + SS_2}{n_1 + n_2 - 2}\right)\left(\frac{1}{n_1} + \frac{1}{n_2}\right)}$$

$$t_{obt} = \frac{(M_1 - M_2)}{s_{M_1-M_2}}$$

$$s_{M_1-M_2} = \sqrt{\left(\frac{356.91 + 446.4}{11 + 10 - 2}\right)\left(\frac{1}{11} + \frac{1}{10}\right)}$$

$$= \frac{(48.09 - 40.40)}{2.83}$$

$$= \sqrt{(42.28)(.19)}$$

$$= +2.72$$

$$= +2.83$$

## Step 4: Make a Decision and Report the Results

Students who read the newspaper scored significantly higher on knowledge of current events than students who watched the evening news. Reject $H_0$, $t(19) = +2.72$, $p < .05$.

**Tip!**

Look at the means for each sample to determine which group scored higher.

## EFFECT SIZE

Once again, if we end up rejecting the null hypothesis, we will want to probe further and ask how significant our results were. As applied to the independent samples *t* test, the formula for Cohen's *d* effect size is as follows:

$$d = \frac{|M_1 - M_2|}{\sqrt{\dfrac{SS_1 + SS_2}{n_1 + n_2 - 2}}}$$

For our problem

$$d = \frac{|48.09 - 40.4|}{\sqrt{\dfrac{356.91 + 446.4}{11 + 10 - 2}}}$$

$$= 1.18$$

To obtain the estimated standard deviation in the denominator, we simply find the square root of the pooled variance that we have already calculated in $s_{M_1-M_2}$. Using Cohen's guidelines, a *d* value of 1.18 suggests a large effect size.

## ASSUMPTIONS

Assumptions of the independent samples *t* test include the following:

- Independent and random selection of participants.
- The dependent variable can be measured on an interval or ratio scale.
- The dependent variable is normally distributed in the populations of interest.
- Homogeneity of variance of the dependent variable in the populations of interest.

The last assumption, ***homogeneity of variance***, is new. This simply means that population variances of the dependent variable are approximately equal $\left(i.e., \sigma_1^2 \approx \sigma_2^2\right)$. This assumption is necessary because the two sample variances in the standard error portion of the *t*-statistic were averaged. If the variances of the population were drastically different, it would not make sense to average our sample variances. There are several statistical procedures that can be used to verify homogeneity of variance. For our purposes, we will take for granted that this assumption has been satisfied.

A penny for your thoughts, sweetie!

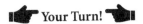

## Your Turn!

### I. Independent Samples *t* Test (nondirectional)

*Research Question.* An industrial/organizational psychologist studying work habits and environment is interested in the effects of music on productivity. He decides to test this relationship by measuring the output of widgets at a large widget manufacturing company. Two samples are obtained and randomly assigned to one of two groups. Group A listens to smooth jazz during the workday. Group B is not exposed to music during the workday. The number of widgets produced over a 40-hour week is recorded and listed on the next page. Does listening to smooth jazz music affect widget productivity? Conduct a nondirectional test with $\alpha = .05$.

| Sample A | Sample B |
|----------|----------|
| 8        | 7        |
| 10       | 6        |
| 9        | 8        |
| 7        | 10       |
| 8        | 7        |
| 11       | 9        |
| 12       |          |

Step 1: Formulate Hypotheses

Step 2: Indicate the Alpha Level and Determine Critical Values

Step 3: Calculate Relevant Statistics

Step 4: Make a Decision and Report the Results

*(Continued)*

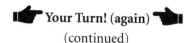

## Your Turn! (again)

(continued)

### II. Independent Samples *t* test (directional)

A. *Research Question.* A sports psychologist read that lack of sleep impairs reaction time and wants to replicate the study. She collected data on two samples. Group 1, made up of 14 participants, was kept awake for 24 hours. Group 2, made up of 11 participants, was allowed to sleep comfortably for 8 hours during the night. The following morning, both groups were given a test of reaction time, with the following results:

$$M_1 = 51 \qquad M_2 = 46$$
$$SS_1 = 328 \qquad SS_2 = 414$$
$$n_1 = 14 \qquad n_2 = 11$$

Reaction time refers to the amount of time it takes to react to a situation. Thus, higher scores indicate worse performance. Conduct a one-tailed test with $\alpha = .05$ to determine if sleep deprivation had a detrimental effect on reaction time.

Step 1: Formulate Hypotheses

Step 2: Indicate the Alpha Level and Determine Critical Values

Tip!

> With a one-tailed *t* test, the $t_{crit}$ value will be in the same direction as the alternative hypothesis.

Step 3: Calculate Relevant Statistics

Step 4: Make a Decision and Report the Results

B. Calculate Cohen's *d* and, using the guidelines suggested previously, indicate the size of the effect.

**Answers to "Your Turn!" Problems**

## I. Independent Samples *t* test (nondirectional)

Step 1:
$H_0: \mu_1 = \mu_2$
$H_1: \mu_1 \neq \mu_2$

Step 2:
$\alpha = .05$
$df = 11$
$t_{crit} = \pm 2.201$

Step 3:
$SS_1 = 19.43$
$SS_2 = 10.83$
$S_{M_1 - M_2} = .92$
$t_{obt} = +1.59$

Step 4:

Listening to smooth jazz music did not significantly affect widget productivity. Fail to reject $H_0$, $t(11) = +1.59$, $p > .05$.

## II. Independent Samples *t* Test (directional)

A.  Step 1:
$H_0: \mu_1 \leq \mu_2$
$H_1: \mu_1 > \mu_2$

Step 2:
$\alpha = .05$
$df = 23$
$t_{crit} = +1.714$

Step 3:
$S_{M_1 - M_2} = 2.29$
$t_{obt} = +2.18$

Step 4:

Sleep-deprived subjects showed a significant increase (and therefore greater impairment) in reaction time. Reject $H_0$, $t(23) = +2.18$, $p < .05$.

B.   $d = .88$, large effect size

---

## Using Microsoft Excel for Data Analysis

If you are using Excel for the first time for statistical analysis, you may need to load the add-in tool that allows these functions. The information for loading the Data Analysis ToolPak as well as general instructions for using Excel for data analysis are at the beginning of the Excel section in Chapter 4.

### Independent Samples *t* Test in Excel

To demonstrate how to use Excel for an independent samples *t* test, we will use the sample research question at the beginning of this chapter about whether current events is best learned via reading the news or watching it on television.

- Enter the scores into columns A and B of the spreadsheet, including the labels in row 1.

| ◢ | A | B |
|---|---|---|
| 1 | Newspaper | Television |
| 2 | 59 | 36 |
| 3 | 48 | 42 |
| 4 | 45 | 50 |
| 5 | 39 | 37 |
| 6 | 52 | 51 |
| 7 | 56 | 32 |
| 8 | 50 | 47 |
| 9 | 41 | 38 |
| 10 | 46 | 40 |
| 11 | 45 | 31 |
| 12 | 48 | |

- Go to the **Data** tab and click on the **Data Analysis** command.
- From the **Data Analysis** dialog box, scroll down and highlight **t-Test: Two Sample Assuming Equal Variances**. Click **OK** and a dialog box for this function will appear.

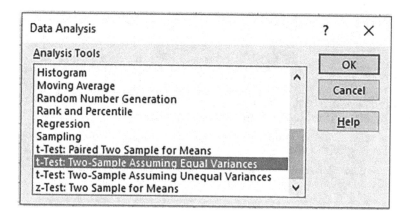

- With your cursor in the window for the **Variable 1 Range**, drag your mouse over the **Newspaper** scores, including the label (A1 through A12). Move your cursor to the window for the **Variable 2 Range** and drag your mouse over the **Television** scores, including the label (B1 through B11). The dollar signs that show up in the window between cell locations are references used by Excel and will automatically appear in some types of statistical analyses.
- Enter 0 in the window for the **Hypothesized Mean Difference**.
- Check the **Labels** box so that the labels for the variables will appear in the output.
- Leave alpha set at .05 which is the default.
- For **Output options**, the default is to place the output table in a new worksheet. If you prefer, you can include the output table on the same spreadsheet by checking **Output Range** and typing in any empty cell number such as D1. For this example, we will leave the **New Worksheet Ply** checked. It is not necessary to enter anything in the window. Excel will simply create a second worksheet where an output table will appear. Click **OK**.

If you look at the bottom left corner, you will see Sheet 1 which contains your input information and Sheet 2 which now contains your output information. You will probably want to expand the width of the columns so that all of the information is visible.

| | A | B | C |
|---|---|---|---|
| 1 | t-Test: Two-Sample Assuming Equal Variances | | |
| 2 | | | |
| 3 | | Newspaper | Television |
| 4 | Mean | 48.09090909 | 40.4 |
| 5 | Variance | 35.69090909 | 49.6 |
| 6 | Observations | 11 | 10 |
| 7 | Pooled Variance | 42.27942584 | |
| 8 | Hypothesized Mean Difference | 0 | |
| 9 | df | 19 | |
| 10 | t Stat | 2.707072161 | |
| 11 | P(T<=t) one-tail | 0.006987186 | |
| 12 | t Critical one-tail | 1.729132812 | |
| 13 | P(T<=t) two-tail | 0.013974371 | |
| 14 | t Critical two-tail | 2.093024054 | |

You can compare Excel's output table with your own calculations for the same problem, including the means for both groups and your obtained t-value (although there will sometimes be some small rounding differences). Critical values are given for both one- and two-tailed tests at whatever alpha level was designated in the **Data Analysis** window. If your obtained t-value exceeds the critical value, then the null hypothesis can be rejected. For this example, our $t_{obt}$ of 2.707 exceeds the $t_{crit}$ of

2.093; thus, we can reject $H_0$. The output table also provides you with the probability (P) of obtaining the resulting $t$-statistic by chance alone if the null hypothesis is true. The P-value of .013974371 (which falls in the rejection region) is less than our alpha level of .05 which is another way of determining that we can reject $H_0$.

---

*Additional Practice Problems*

**Answers to odd numbered problems are in Appendix C at the end of the book.**

1. An independent samples $t$ test involves evaluating the means for two separate and unrelated groups.
   a. Describe in words what the null hypothesis states for a two-tailed independent samples $t$ test.
   b. Describe in words what the alternative hypothesis states for a two-tailed independent samples $t$ test.
2. Why is $\mu_1 - \mu_2$ eliminated from the working formula for the independent samples $t$ test?
3. What is $s_{M_1-M_2}$ and what information is provided by this statistic?
4. What is homogeneity of variance and why is it important that this assumption be met?
5. Based on the summary data that follows, calculate the pooled variance.
$$SS_1 = 163 \qquad n_1 = 12$$
$$SS_2 = 131 \qquad n_2 = 11$$
6. Given the summary data $SS_1=72$, $n_1 = 12$, $SS_2=98$, and $n_2 = 14$, calculate $s_{M_1-M_2}$
7. Based on the summary data below, calculate $t_{obt}$.
$$SS_1 = 324 \quad M_1=32 \quad n_1 = 19$$
$$SS_2 = 251 \quad M_2=28 \quad n_2 = 16$$
8. A researcher is conducting a study involving an intervention which she believes will result in significantly higher scores in group one than in group two. Given the summary data below and $\alpha = .05$, is there evidence to support the researcher's hypothesis?
$$M_1 = 46 \qquad n_1 = 6$$
$$M_2 = 40 \qquad n_2 = 5$$
$$S_{M_1-M_2} = 3.11$$
9. A medical researcher is studying a new medication that he believes will reduce memory errors as reflected in lower scores on a memory test. Group one receives the medication and group two receives a placebo. Summary data for the study are as follows:
$$M_1 = 29 \qquad n_1 = 9$$
$$M_2 = 25 \qquad n_2 = 7$$
$$S_{M_1-M_2} = 2.1$$
   a. Using symbolic notation, write the null and alternative hypotheses for the study.
   b. Using an $\alpha = .05$, what is $t_{crit}$?
   c. Did the new medication in fact reduce memory errors? Based on this example, explain why it is important to designate the direction of expected difference in $H_1$ and $t_{crit}$.
10. Given the summary values that follow, conduct an independent samples $t$ test with $\alpha = .01$, one-tailed. Assume the researcher believes treatment will result in higher scores for group one.
$$M_1 = 13 \qquad n_1 = 6$$
$$M_2 = 10 \qquad n_2 = 5$$
$$S_{M_1-M_2} = 1.25$$

11. The mean for group one, made up of 6 individuals, is 63. The mean for group two, made up of 8 individuals, is 53. $s_{M_1 - M_2} = 4.32$. Is there a significant difference between the means? Use $\alpha = .05$.

12. Based on the summary values that follow, conduct a nondirectional independent samples *t* test with $\alpha = .01$.

$M_1 = 73 \quad n_1 = 19 \quad SS_1 = 284$
$M_2 = 69 \quad n_2 = 16 \quad SS_2 = 302$

13. A cognitive psychologist believes that she can stimulate curiosity by conducting Question and Reflection (Q&R) workshops. Group one participates in the workshop and then takes a standardized curiosity inventory. Group two takes the curiosity test without attending the workshop. The scores for the two groups are listed below. Did the Q&R participants score higher on the curiosity assessment than those who did not attend the workshop? Test with an alpha level of .01.

| Q&R Workshop | No Workshop |
|---|---|
| 17 | 18 |
| 20 | 12 |
| 18 | 16 |
| 18 | 13 |
| 17 | 15 |
| 19 | 17 |
| 22 | |

## Note

1  The size of the two samples can be equal or not, but their sizes must remain the same for each subsequent sample.

# 11
# Two-Sample *t* Test
## Related Samples Design

## TWO-SAMPLE *t* TEST: RELATED SAMPLES DESIGN

Like the independent samples *t* test, the *t* test for a ***related samples design*** also involves making comparisons between two sets of scores. However, with this design, either the scores are from the same subjects (repeated measures) or two samples are related in some other logical way, such as the scores for husbands and wives (matched pairs). Because the computation of the *t*-statistic is the same for both types, we will limit our discussion to the type used most commonly: repeated measures.

A ***repeated measures study*** involves pre- and post-testing of the same subjects after some treatment intervention. This design is also called a *within-subjects design,* highlighting the fact that scores within the same subject group are compared. For example:

> Subjects' anxiety scores before psychotherapy are compared with their anxiety scores after psychotherapy. Is there enough of a mean difference in the pre- and post-conditions to conclude significance?

## SAMPLING DISTRIBUTION OF MEAN DIFFERENCES

As with the other *t* tests, we will want to compare our obtained mean difference to a theoretical sampling distribution to determine if our mean difference is significant. The theoretical sampling distribution for the *independent samples design* discussed previously consisted of the difference between sample means for all possible samples of size $n_1$ and $n_2$. For a *related samples, repeated measures design,* we theoretically draw a sample of subjects of a given size from a population of interest, measure each subject twice on some aspect of behavior, determine the difference between those two raw scores, then calculate the mean of the difference scores and record it. We would then repeat this process for all possible samples of the given size. These mean difference scores are then arranged in a sampling distribution, called the ***sampling distribution of mean differences***. (Again, this is not done in reality, only in theory.)

**Tip!**

Look at the tables below to conceptualize the difference between the *difference between means*, symbolized by $M_1 - M_2$, and the *mean difference*, symbolized by $M_D$.

| Difference between means $(M_1 - M_2)$ | | Mean difference $(M_D)$ | | |
|---|---|---|---|---|
| | | Pre | Post | *Post – pre |
| $X_1$ | $X_2$ | $X_1$ | $X_2$ | difference |
| 3 | 10 | 17 | 24 | 7 |
| 8 | 6 | 21 | 30 | 9 |
| 5 | 11 | 13 | 21 | 8 |
| 4 | 9 | 24 | 22 | −2 |
| $M_1 = 5$ $\quad$ $M_2 = 9$ $\quad\quad$ $M_1 - M_2 = -4$ | | $M_D = \dfrac{\Sigma D}{n} = \dfrac{22}{4} = 5.5$ | | $\Sigma D = 22$ |

*Note: When calculating mean difference values, the pre-test scores are usually subtracted from the post-test scores (see explanation below, under "Calculations").

To determine the difference between means, the mean for each group is calculated separately, and then the difference between the sample means is computed.

To determine the mean difference, the difference between each pre- and post-score is calculated, and then the mean of those difference scores is computed.

## CALCULATIONS

As usual, we will need to calculate a standard deviation value, a $t$ test, and degrees of freedom.

### Standard Error of the Mean Difference

The standard deviation for the sampling distribution of mean differences is called the **standard error of the mean difference** $\left(S_{M_D}\right)$. The actual calculations for both the $t$-statistic and the standard error of the mean difference are the same as for the one-sample $t$ test. Only the symbols are different. This is because in both cases, we are working with only a single mean. The emphasis in the repeated measures design, however, is on the mean of the difference scores provided by each subject rather than on a single sample mean. Here is the formula:

$$S_{M_D} = \frac{S_D}{\sqrt{n}}$$

where $S_D$ is the standard deviation of the difference scores.

The table below illustrates the setup for the calculations necessary for a repeated measures $t$ test:

| Subject | Before ($X_1$) | After ($X_2$) | $D$ | $D^2$ |
|---------|----------------|---------------|-----|-------|
| 1 | 6 | 8 | 2 | 4 |
| 2 | 5 | 4 | $-1$ | 1 |
| 3 | 7 | 9 | 2 | 4 |
| 4 | 10 | 14 | 4 | 16 |
| | | | $\Sigma D = 7$ | $\Sigma D^2 = 25$ |

$$M_D = \frac{\Sigma D}{n} = 1.75$$

Notice the following:

- The same subject provides two scores, one before treatment and one after treatment.
- By convention, the first scores ($X_1$) are usually subtracted from the second scores ($X_2$) to arrive at the difference ($D$) values. This is so that when the mean difference score is calculated, the direction of change in the scores, after the treatment condition, can be determined. A positive mean difference would indicate a tendency toward higher post-test scores, whereas a negative mean difference would indicate a tendency toward lower post-test scores.
- The difference scores will be squared for use in later calculations.
- The mean difference is determined by summing the difference values and dividing by $n$.

## Formulas for One-Sample $t$ Test and Repeated Measures

The following compares the formulas used for the one-sample $t$ test and the repeated measures design. Both are calculated the same way. Only the symbols are different.

| | *One-sample t test* | *Repeated measures t test* |
|---|---|---|
| Sum of squares | $SS = \Sigma X^2 - \dfrac{(\Sigma X)^2}{n}$ | $SS_D = \Sigma D^2 - \dfrac{(\Sigma D)^2}{n}$ |
| Variance | $s^2 = \dfrac{\Sigma X^2 - \dfrac{(\Sigma X)^2}{n}}{n-1}$ <br> or <br> $s^2 = \dfrac{SS}{n-1}$ | $s_D^2 = \dfrac{\Sigma D^2 - \dfrac{(\Sigma D)^2}{n}}{n-1}$ <br> or <br> $s_D^2 = \dfrac{SS_D}{n-1}$ |
| Standard deviation | $s = \sqrt{\dfrac{\Sigma X^2 - \dfrac{(\Sigma X)^2}{n}}{n-1}}$ <br> or <br> $s = \sqrt{\dfrac{SS}{n-1}}$ | $s_D = \sqrt{\dfrac{\Sigma D^2 - \dfrac{(\Sigma D)^2}{n}}{n-1}}$ <br> or <br> $s_D = \sqrt{\dfrac{SS_D}{n-1}}$ |

|  | One-sample t test | Repeated measures t test |
| --- | --- | --- |
| Standard error | $s_M = \dfrac{s}{\sqrt{n}}$ | $s_{M_D} = \dfrac{s_D}{\sqrt{n}}$ |

## Formula and *df* for *t* Test for *Related Samples Design*

The formula for the *related samples t* test is as follows:

$$t_{obt} = \frac{M_D - \mu_D}{s_{M_D}}$$

However, because $H_0$ will assert the population mean difference to be 0 (see below), $\mu_D$ can be eliminated from the formula. Thus, our working formula is

$$t_{obt} = \frac{M_D}{s_{M_D}}$$

Degrees of freedom (*df*) for a *related samples t* test will be the same as for a one-sample *t* test:

$$df = n - 1$$

## HYPOTHESIS TESTING

By now, you are accustomed to the two opposing explanations used in hypothesis testing:

- The *null hypothesis* ($H_0$) attributes a mean difference to chance, or random sampling error, asserting no significant mean difference between pre- and post-assessment.

  $$H_0 : \mu_D = 0$$

- The *alternative hypothesis* ($H_1$) asserts that a mean difference between pre- and post-assessments is due to more than chance, namely the effect of the independent variable. As usual, $H_1$ may be either *nondirectional*:

  $$H_1 : \mu_D \neq 0$$

Alternatively, $H_1$ may be *directional* and specify a direction of expected difference:

$$H_1 : \mu_D > 0 \qquad \text{for } H_0 : \mu_D \leq 0$$
$$H_1 : \mu_D < 0 \qquad \text{for } H_0 : \mu_D \geq 0$$

## Rejecting $H_0$

For a *nondirectional* alternative hypothesis, when a mean difference falls in the critical region in either tail of the sampling distribution, $H_0$ can be rejected. Differences that large are unlikely to be due to chance. Rejecting $H_0$ using a *directional* alternative hypothesis requires that the mean difference falls in the critical region in the direction specified in $H_1$.

## Sample Research Question

A dietician is intrigued when a friend tells her he lost several pounds by eliminating late-night snacks from his diet. The dietician decides to study the "no nighttime snack" diet systematically to determine if such a diet has a significant effect on weight. She obtains a random sample of $n = 8$ late-night snackers, weighs them, instructs them to eliminate food from their diet after 8:00 P.M. for 30 days, weighs them again, and analyzes the results using a two-tailed, related samples *t* test, with $\alpha = .05$.

## Step 1: Formulate Hypotheses

$$H_0 : \mu_D = 0$$
$$H_1 : \mu_D \neq 0$$

## Step 2: Indicate the Alpha Level and Determine Critical Values

$$\alpha = .05$$
$$df = n - 1 = 7$$
$$t_{crit} = \pm 2.365$$

## Step 3: Calculate Relevant Statistics

| Subject | Weight before | Weight after | D* | D² |
|---|---|---|---|---|
| 1 | 156 | 142 | −14 | 196 |
| 2 | 192 | 173 | −19 | 361 |
| 3 | 138 | 140 | 2 | 4 |
| 4 | 167 | 151 | −16 | 256 |
| 5 | 110 | 109 | −1 | 1 |
| 6 | 159 | 151 | −8 | 64 |
| 7 | 171 | 154 | −17 | 289 |
| 8 | 129 | 133 | 4 | 16 |
| | | | $\Sigma D = -69$ | $\Sigma D^2 = 1187$ |

*Remember to use $X_2 - X_1$ to arrive at the difference (*D*) values. In this case, we will end up with a negative difference sum because the dieters weighed less after the treatment condition.

$$M_D = \frac{\Sigma D}{n} = \frac{-69}{8} = -8.63$$

$$s_D = \sqrt{\frac{\Sigma D^2 - \frac{(\Sigma D)^2}{n}}{n-1}} = \sqrt{\frac{1187 - \frac{(-69)^2}{8}}{8-1}} = 9.20$$

$$s_{M_D} = \frac{s_D}{\sqrt{n}} = \frac{9.20}{\sqrt{8}} = 3.25$$

$$t_{obt} = \frac{M_D}{s_{M_D}} = \frac{-8.63}{3.25} = -2.66$$

### Step 4: Make a Decision and Report the Results

Subjects on the "no nighttime snack" diet showed a significant weight loss. Reject $H_0$, $t(7) = -2.66, p < .05$.

## EFFECT SIZE

The formula to determine the effect size for a related samples $t$ test is:

$$d = \frac{|M_D|}{s_D}$$

For our problem,

$$d = \frac{|-8.63|}{9.20} = .94$$

According to the standards suggested by Cohen, an effect size of .94 is considered large.

## ASSUMPTIONS

The assumptions of the repeated measures $t$ test are the same as for the one-sample $t$ test:

- Independent and random sampling from the population of interest.
- The dependent variable is normally distributed in the population of interest.
- The dependent variable can be measured on an interval or ratio scale.

---

 **Your Turn!**

### I. Repeated Samples $t$ Test

**A.** *Research Question.* A psychology professor wants to investigate whether education significantly reduces stereotypes about mental illness. On the first day of her abnormal psychology class of $n = 18$ students, the professor administers a questionnaire designed to assess beliefs about individuals with mental illness. At the end of the semester, the questionnaire is administered again and the difference between the two scores is compared. Lower scores reflect fewer stereotypes. Given $M_D = -3$ and $SS_D = 286$, conduct a one-tailed, repeated measures $t$ test using $\alpha = .05$.

Step 1: Formulate Hypotheses

Step 2: Indicate the Alpha Level and Determine Critical Values

Step 3: Calculate Relevant Statistics

Step 4: Make a Decision and Report the Results

**B.** Calculate Cohen's $d$ and, using the guidelines suggested previously, indicate the size of the effect.

## INDEPENDENT OR REPEATED MEASURES DESIGN: WHICH TO USE

Depending on the nature of the research question, in many cases either an independent or repeated measures design may be used. Given a choice, there are some benefits to using a repeated measures design that are not offered if two separate samples are used.

### Advantages of the Repeated Measures Design

- *Fewer subjects* are required because the same subjects are used in both the "before" and "after" conditions, thus providing for greater economy.
- Fewer subjects means *less variability due to individual differences*, and therefore less sampling error.
- *Developmental changes* that occur over time can be measured using a related samples design because the same subjects are tested more than once.

### Disadvantages of the Repeated Measures Design

There are some drawbacks to the repeated measures design that need to be considered as well, which, if not controlled, have the possibility of confounding the research. Most of these drawbacks fall under the category of ***order effects***, which take place when the order in which the independent variable is presented has an effect on the dependent variable. For example, suppose subjects were shown films of actors role-playing various definitions of sexual harassment. In Condition A, the portrayal of harassment in the film is salient and clear, but in Condition B, the film's portrayal of harassment is more subtle. The order in which the subjects view the films may influence their subsequent evaluation of the degree of sexual impropriety taking place.

Other issues related to the result of ordering might include the lingering effects of a medication persisting from one condition to the next, improved performance due to practice, or boredom setting in while involved in a particular task.

Some of these problems may be dealt with by allowing sufficient time between conditions. Other of these effects can be minimized through a procedure called ***counterbalancing***, wherein participants are exposed to the treatment conditions in different orders. For example, half the subjects would be presented first with Condition A, then B, while the other half would be presented first with Condition B, then A. The purpose of this procedure is to spread out these influences over all the treatment conditions so that they are affected equally.

 **Your Turn!**

### II. Which *t* Test to Use

For each of the following studies, identify whether it would be better to use (a) a one-sample *t* test; (b) a two-sample *t* test, independent samples design; *or* (c) a two-sample *t* test, repeated measures design.

A. A study to evaluate the difference in math skills between 8-year-old boys and 8-year-old girls.

**Your Turn!**
(continued)

B.  A study to evaluate the effectiveness of a new antidepressant by assessing the degree of depression before treatment and then again after taking the medication for 4 weeks.

C.  A researcher is tracking the developmental components of walking by studying the same children at different ages as they advance from sitting unsupported, to crawling, to balancing, to walking.

D.  A college professor reads that the average amount of sleep needed by college freshmen is 8.5 hours. She obtains a sample of 73 freshman students and compares their actual amount of sleep with the reported need for that population.

E.  A cognitive psychologist is studying the effects of visual encoding versus auditory encoding on memory. Different situations are described in writing and presented one at a time on a computer screen. One group of subjects is asked to visualize each situation. Another group is asked to read each situation aloud. Memory of the details of the situations is then tested for both groups and compared.

F.  Mean level of anxiety for a sample of stay-at-home moms is compared to a known population value of 50.

**Answers to "Your Turn!" Problems**

**I. Repeated Samples *t* Test**

A.  Step 1:

$H_0: \mu_D \geq 0$
$H_1: \mu_D < 0$

Step 2:

$\alpha = .05$
$df = 17$
$t_{crit} = -1.740$

Step 3:

$s_D = 4.10$
$S_{M_D} = .97$
$t_{obt} = -3.09$

(*Continued*)

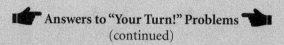

### Answers to "Your Turn!" Problems
### (continued)

Step 4:

Education significantly reduced stereotypical beliefs about mental illness. Reject $H_0$, $t(17) = -3.09, p < .05$.

B.  $d = .73$, moderate effect

### II.  Which *t* Test to Use

A.  Two-sample *t* test, independent samples design
B.  Two-sample *t* test, repeated measures design
C.  Two-sample *t* test, repeated measures design
D.  One-sample *t* test
E.  Two-sample *t* test, independent samples design
F.  One-sample *t* test

---

## Using Microsoft Excel for Data Analysis

If you are using Excel for the first time for statistical analysis, you may need to load the add-in tool that allows these functions. The information for loading the Data Analysis ToolPak as well as general instructions for using Excel for data analysis are at the beginning of the Excel section in Chapter 4.

### Related Samples *t* Test in Excel

To demonstrate how to use Excel for a related samples *t* test, we will use the sample research question in your text pertaining to the "no nighttime snack diet."

- Enter the scores into columns A and B of the spreadsheet. We will include the labels in row one except, since we have used the convention in the text of subtracting the "before" test scores from the "after" test scores, we will reverse the order in Excel which will produce the same sign as our obtained *t*-value.

|  | A | B |
|---|---|---|
| 1 | After | Before |
| 2 | 142 | 156 |
| 3 | 173 | 192 |
| 4 | 140 | 138 |
| 5 | 151 | 167 |
| 6 | 109 | 110 |
| 7 | 151 | 159 |
| 8 | 154 | 171 |
| 9 | 133 | 129 |

- Go to the **Data** tab and click on the **Data Analysis** command.
- From the **Data Analysis** dialog box, scroll down and highlight *t*-**Test: Paired Two Sample for Means**. Click **OK** and a dialog box for this function will appear.

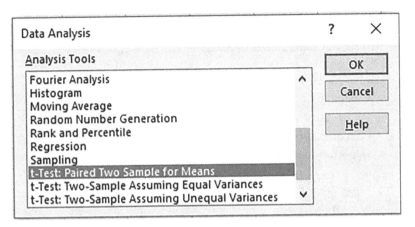

- With your cursor in the window for the **Variable 1 Range**, drag your mouse over the **After** scores, including the label (A1 through A9). Move your cursor to the window for the **Variable 2 Range** and drag your mouse over the **Before** scores, including the label (B1 through B9). The dollar signs that show up in the window between cell locations are references used by Excel and will automatically appear in some types of statistical analyses.
- Enter 0 in the window for the **Hypothesized Mean Difference**.
- Check the **Labels** box so that the labels for the variables will appear in the output.
- Leave alpha set at .05 which is the default.
- For **Output options**, the default is to place the output table in a new worksheet. If you prefer, you can include the output table on the same spreadsheet by checking **Output Range** and typing in any empty cell number such as D1. For this example, we will leave the **New Worksheet Ply** checked. It is not necessary to enter anything in the window. Excel will simply create a second worksheet where an output table will appear. Click **OK**.

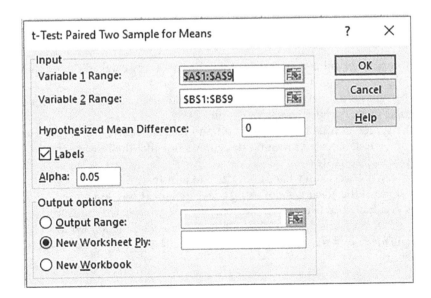

If you look at the bottom left corner, you will see Sheet 1 which contains your input information and Sheet 2 which now contains your output information.

| | A | B | C |
|---|---|---|---|
| 1 | t-Test: Paired Two Sample for Means | | |
| 2 | | | |
| 3 | | After | Before |
| 4 | Mean | 144.125 | 152.75 |
| 5 | Variance | 343.5535714 | 676.5 |
| 6 | Observations | 8 | 8 |
| 7 | Pearson Correlation | 0.970247789 | |
| 8 | Hypothesized Mean Difference | 0 | |
| 9 | df | 7 | |
| 10 | t Stat | -2.653005309 | |
| 11 | P(T<=t) one-tail | 0.016399158 | |
| 12 | t Critical one-tail | 1.894578605 | |
| 13 | P(T<=t) two-tail | 0.032798317 | |
| 14 | t Critical two-tail | 2.364624252 | |

With the exception of a small rounding difference, you can see that Excel calculated the same obtained $t$-value ($-2.653$) as we did. Critical values are given for both one- and two-tailed tests at whatever alpha level was designated in the **Data Analysis** window. If your obtained t-value exceeds the critical value, then the null hypothesis can be rejected. For this example, our $t_{obt}$ of $-2.653$ exceeds the $t_{crit}$ of 2.365; thus, we can reject $H_0$. The output table also provides you with the probability (P) of obtaining the resulting $t$-statistic by chance alone if the null hypothesis is true. The P-value of .032798317 (which falls in the rejection region) is less than our alpha level of .05 which is another way of determining that we can reject $H_0$.

---

## Additional Practice Problems

**Answers to odd numbered problems are in Appendix C at the end of the book.**

1. State in words the null and alternative hypotheses for a two-tailed $t$ test, repeated measures design.
2. Write the symbolic notations for the null and alternative hypotheses for a two-tailed two-sample $t$ test, repeated measures design.
3. Write the symbolic notations for the null and alternative hypotheses for a one-tailed, two-sample $t$ test, repeated measures design. Assume that the researcher is looking for a score decrease in post-testing.
4. What are order effects and what can be done to minimize them?
5. Discuss some of the advantages of using a repeated measures design.
6. Phineas conducted a two-tailed, two-sample $t$ test, repeated measures design with $\alpha = .05$ and $n = 16$. His $t_{obt}$ was +2.04. Phineas concluded the following: "There was no significant mean difference. Reject $H_0$, $t(15) = +2.04$, $p > .05$." What is wrong with his conclusion?

7. Doreen conducted a one-tailed, two-sample $t$ test, repeated measures design with the expectation that post-test scores would be higher than pre-test scores. An alpha level of .01 was used, the sample size was 23, and $t_{obt} = +2.632$. Doreen concluded the following: "The mean difference of the pre- and post-test scores was not significant. Fail to reject $H_0$, $t(22) = +2.632$, $p > .01$." What is wrong with Doreen's conclusion?

8. Marilu conducted a two-sample $t$ test, repeated measures design with $\alpha = .01$. Summary data for her study were as follows: $n = 12$, $M_D = 8$, and $SS_D = 984$. Marilu calculated her $t_{obt}$ value as follows: $t = \dfrac{8}{9.46} = +.85$. What is wrong with this calculation and what is the correct $t_{obt}$?

9. Explain the circumstances under which you would use a one-sample $t$ test, an independent samples $t$ test, and a repeated measures $t$ test.

10. For the studies that follow, indicate which type of $t$ test would be most appropriate, a one-sample $t$ test, an independent samples $t$ test, or a repeated measures $t$ test.

   a. A psychologist is interested in studying how thrill seeking behavior changes over time. He administers a sensation seeking assessment instrument to one group, aged 17 to 21 years old, and to another group, aged 22 to 26 years old.

   b. The average length at birth for girls is $19\frac{3}{4}$ inches. An OB-GYN doctor measures a sample of newborns from the neonatal unit of her hospital to see how they compare.

   c. A study is conducted to evaluate if there is a difference in the level of test anxiety experienced by university freshmen and university seniors.

   d. A researcher studying the effects of alcohol measures the length of time that a group of subjects can balance a dowel rod on the forefinger of their dominant hand. After consuming three alcoholic beverages, the subjects are again given the dowel rod balancing test.

   e. The self-esteem scores of a sample of females attending a private women's college is compared to the known population mean of 25 for females on a standardized self-esteem scale.

   f. A psychologist is interested in studying how thrill seeking behavior changes over time. She administers a sensation seeking assessment instrument to a group of 18-year-olds who take it again at age 25.

11. A particular college entrance test is loaded with difficult vocabulary words. A high school counselor creates a workbook replete with vocabulary lessons that break the words down into prefixes and suffixes. Ten graduating seniors take a practice version of the entrance exam. They then complete the workbook and take another version of the exam. Students' scores are listed below. Was the workbook effective in increasing students' scores on the exam? Conduct a one-tailed, related samples $t$ test with $\alpha = .01$. Determine Cohen's $d$ and interpret the effect size.

| Before Workbook | After Workbook |
|---|---|
| 40 | 58 |
| 45 | 49 |
| 58 | 62 |
| 32 | 52 |
| 48 | 51 |
| 47 | 52 |
| 50 | 57 |
| 52 | 60 |
| 46 | 48 |
| 49 | 53 |

# 12
# Confidence Interval Versus Point Estimation

## CONFIDENCE INTERVAL VERSUS POINT ESTIMATION

We have discussed inferential statistics as procedures used to estimate the parameters of a population. *Estimate* is a definitive word here. Sample statistics are not expected to predict with absolute certainty the parameters of a population because of sampling error. Statistics vary from one sample to another. If we used a single sample mean to estimate the mean of the population, we would be using what is called a point estimate.

A *point estimate* is a single value, based on sample data, that is used to estimate the parameter of a population.

However, the accuracy of our point estimate would remain unknown. Our estimate should be somewhere *close* to the population value, but it would probably not be exact. If we drew another random sample, we would likely get some other (but close) value due to random sampling error. We could be more certain of our estimation by using confidence interval estimation, which takes sampling error into consideration.

A *confidence interval* is a range of values that, with a specified degree of confidence, is expected to include a population parameter.

Let us examine these ideas more closely.

## POINT ESTIMATES

For point estimates of population parameters, the obtained sample values – with no adjustments for standard error – are reported (i.e., the numerator in our working formula for the t-statistic).

- For one-sample $t$ tests, the point estimate for $\mu$ is $M$.
- For two-sample $t$ tests, independent measures design, the point estimate for $\mu_1 - \mu_2$ is $M_1 - M_2$.
- For two-sample $t$ tests, repeated measures design, the point estimate for $\mu_D$ is $M_D$.

While point estimates are straightforward and readily understood, their values can only be expected to be somewhere in the neighborhood of the population values. Confidence intervals specify the boundaries of that neighborhood.

## CONFIDENCE INTERVALS

Because confidence intervals include a range of values, they are not as specific as point estimates. However, they allow us a greater degree of confidence in our estimation. Degree of confidence is expressed as a percentage. The higher the percentage, the greater confidence we can have that the true value of the population parameter will be included in the established interval. Researchers usually want a high degree of assurance, so 95% or 99% confidence levels are frequently used, but other levels can be applied as well.

The specific values to use in the formulas for confidence intervals will be a little different depending on the statistic for which we want to establish confidence, but the general elements are the same. In essence, we will be calculating lower and upper limits for our obtained statistic, using the following basic formulas:

LL = obtained sample statistic − (*t*)(estimated standard error)
UL = obtained sample statistic + (*t*)(estimated standard error)

We know that samples do not predict population parameters with perfect accuracy. Sampling error is to be expected. The last two components of the formula provide a measure of how much sampling error to expect for specified degrees of confidence.

**Tip!**

The lower and upper limits discussed here are different from the lower and upper real limits of continuous variables that were discussed earlier, which were used in the calculation of the range and the median. Here, we are establishing lower and upper limits as boundaries within which population values are expected to lie.

To get a conceptual understanding of confidence intervals, suppose that $\mu$ is the population parameter of interest. Suppose further that we want to include the true value of $\mu$ in our interval about 90% of the time. In a sampling distribution with $df = \infty$, about 90% of the scores lie within plus or minus 1.645 standard errors, as shown in the graph below. The horizontal lines below the graph illustrate 90% confidence intervals for 10 random samples. The means are shown as dots located in the center of the intervals. The boundaries of the intervals extend 1.645 standard errors in either direction of the mean.

**Sampling distribution of means with $df = \infty$**

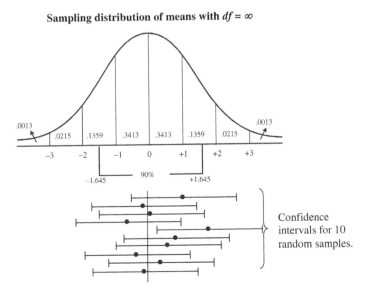

Confidence intervals for 10 random samples.

Notice that only one out of the ten confidence intervals does not include $\mu$, which is what would be expected. In other words, given a 90% confidence level, the true value of the population mean ($\mu$) would be captured in our interval 90% of the time, and 10% of the time it would fail to be captured.

The specific confidence interval formulas for the $t$ tests we have covered are as follows:

- For one-sample $t$ tests:

$$LL = M - t(s_M) \qquad \text{and} \qquad UL = M + t(s_M)$$

- For two-sample $t$ tests, independent samples design:

$$LL = (M_1 - M_2) - t(s_{M_1 - M_2}) \qquad \text{and} \qquad UL = (M_1 - M_2) + t(s_{M_1 - M_2})$$

- For two-sample $t$ tests, repeated measures design:

$$LL = M_D - t(s_{M_D}) \qquad \text{and} \qquad UL = M_D + t(s_{M_D})$$

With these formulas, we will be adding to and subtracting from our obtained sample statistic however many standard errors it would take to encompass a given percentage of the distribution. If we were using a 95% confidence level, then we would use the $t$ values that separate the middle 95% of the distribution from the extreme 5% (i.e., $\alpha = .05$, two-tailed). If we were using a 99% confidence level, we would use the $t$ values that separate the middle 99% of the distribution from the extreme 1% (i.e., $\alpha = .01$, two-tailed). The same degrees of freedom should be used that are appropriate for that particular test.

## ONE-SAMPLE $t$ TEST

### Sample Research Question

The average typing speed for the secretaries of a large company is 52 words per minute. A long-time secretary has developed finger dexterity exercises that she reports have improved her speed dramatically. The owner of the company thus hires a researcher to test the effectiveness of the exercise program. After four weeks of training in the finger exercises, the typing speed of 17 secretaries is measured. The mean number of words per minute was $M = 57$ with $SS = 3600$.

A. What would the point estimate of $\mu$ be after using the finger exercise program?
B. Establish a 90% confidence interval for the mean and write a sentence of interpretation.

◆ ················································································· ◆

A. The point estimate of $\mu$ is $M = 57$.
B. $LL = M - t(s_M)$ $\qquad$ and $\qquad$ $UL = M + t(s_M)$

To use the formulas for establishing confidence intervals, we need values for $M$, $t$, and $s_M$. The value for $M = 57$. For a 90% confidence interval with $df = 16$, the value for $t = \pm 1.746$. We now have to calculate the estimated standard error ($s_M$).

$$s = \sqrt{\frac{SS}{n-1}} = \sqrt{\frac{3600}{17-1}} = 15 \qquad\qquad s_M = \frac{s}{\sqrt{n}} = \frac{15}{\sqrt{17}} = 3.64$$

$$LL = 57 - 1.746(3.64) \qquad\qquad\qquad UL = 57 + 1.746(3.64)$$
$$= 57 - 6.36 \qquad\qquad\qquad\qquad\qquad = 57 + 6.36$$
$$\text{and} \qquad = 50.64 \qquad\qquad\qquad\qquad\qquad\qquad = 63.36$$

## Interpretation

We can be 90% confident that the population mean (after the finger dexterity program) would be between 50.64 and 63.36.

This is what the *t*-distribution would look like for this interval:

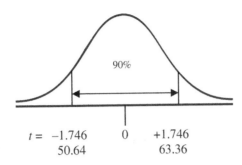

The *t*-values of ±1.746 form the boundaries of the middle 90% of the distribution when *df* = 16.

---

 **Your Turn!**

### I. Confidence Interval for a One-Sample *t* Test

*Research Question.* A history professor was curious about the knowledge of history of graduating seniors in her state. She thus gave a 100-item history test to a random sample of 75 graduating seniors with a resulting $M = 72$ and $SS = 7400$.

A. Make a point estimate of the population mean for that state.

B. Establish a 99% confidence interval for the mean.

C. Write a sentence of interpretation.

---

## TWO-SAMPLE *t* TEST: INDEPENDENT SAMPLES DESIGN

### Sample Research Question

A high school counselor has developed a pamphlet of memory-improving techniques designed to help students in preparing for exams. One group of students is given the pamphlets and instructed to practice the techniques for three weeks, after which their memories are tested. The memories of another group of students, who did not receive the pamphlets, are also tested at this time.

| Memory-pamphlet group | No-pamphlet group |
|---|---|
| $n_1 = 36$ | $n_2 = 40$ |
| $M_1 = 79$ | $M_2 = 68$ |
| $SS_1 = 478$ | $SS_2 = 346$ |

A. Make a point estimate of how much improvement in memory results from following the techniques.

B. Establish a 90% confidence interval around the value for the difference between means and write a sentence of interpretation.

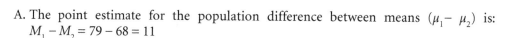

A. The point estimate for the population difference between means $(\mu_1 - \mu_2)$ is:
$$M_1 - M_2 = 79 - 68 = 11$$

B. $\text{LL} = (M_1 - M_2) - t\left(s_{M_1 - M_2}\right)$ and $\text{UL} = (M_1 - M_2) + t\left(s_{M_1 - M_2}\right)$

$$s_{M_1 - M_2} = \sqrt{\left(\frac{SS_1 + SS_2}{n_1 + n_2 - 2}\right)\left(\frac{1}{n_1} + \frac{1}{n_2}\right)}$$

$$= \sqrt{\left(\frac{478 + 346}{36 + 40 - 2}\right)\left(\frac{1}{36} + \frac{1}{40}\right)}$$

$$= \sqrt{(11.14)(.05)}$$

$$= .75$$

$\text{LL} = 11 - 1.671(.75)$ and $\text{UL} = 11 + 1.671(.75)$

$\quad = 11 - 1.25 \qquad\qquad\qquad\qquad = 11 + 1.25$

$\quad = 9.75 \qquad\qquad\qquad\qquad\qquad = 12.25$

## Interpretation

We can be 90% confident that the difference between population means would be between 9.75 and 12.25.

 **Your Turn!**

### II. Two-Sample $t$ Test: Independent Samples Design

*Research Question.* A psychologist is investigating the effects of suggestion on conceptual problem solving. He administers the Concepts Application Test (CAT) to two groups of subjects. Prior to administering the test to one group, the researcher comments that subjects usually report that they enjoy taking the test and that it gives them

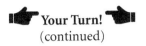

**Your Turn!**
(continued)

a sense of accomplishment. Another group is simply administered the test with no such remarks. The CAT scores for the two groups are presented below:

| CAT with remarks | CAT alone |
|------------------|-----------|
| 49 | 26 |
| 38 | 35 |
| 36 | 40 |
| 42 | 32 |
| 44 | 34 |
| 37 | 30 |
| 47 | |

a. Conduct a two-tailed $t$ test using $\alpha = .05$ and determine the size of the effect.
b. Make a point estimate of the difference between means.
c. If the results are significant, establish a 95% confidence around the difference value and write a sentence of interpretation.

A.  Step 1: Formulate Hypotheses

  Step 2: Indicate the Alpha Level and Determine Critical Values

  Step 3: Calculate Relevant Statistics

  Step 4: Make a Decision and Report the Results

    Effect size

(*Continued*)

👉 **Your Turn!** 👈
(continued)

B. Point Estimate

C. Confidence Interval

Interpretation

## TWO-SAMPLE $t$ TEST: REPEATED MEASURES DESIGN

### Sample Research Question

A promising math tutoring program was developed by a senior math major who also tutored students. His math professors were impressed and decided to test its effectiveness. A comprehensive math test was given at the end of the semester to $n = 45$ students who were struggling in math in the spring semester. Over the summer, they were tutored in the new program and then retested on an alternate form of the test. The mean for the sample of difference scores was $M_D = 12$ with $SS_D = 1648$.

A. Make a point estimate of $\mu_D$.
B. Establish a 90% confidence interval around the difference value and write a sentence of interpretation.

◆ ••••••••••••••••••••••••••••••••••••••••••••••••• ◆

A. The point estimate for $\mu_D$ is: $M_D = 12$

B. $LL = M_D - t\left(s_{M_D}\right)$ and $UL = M_D + t\left(s_{M_D}\right)$

$$s_D = \sqrt{\frac{SS_D}{n-1}} = \sqrt{\frac{1648}{45-1}} = 6.12$$

$$S_{M_D} = \frac{S_D}{\sqrt{n}} = \frac{6.12}{\sqrt{45}} = .91$$

$$LL = 12 - 1.684(.91)$$

and

$$UL = 12 + 1.687(.91)$$

$$= 12 - 1.53$$

$$= 12 + 1.53$$

$$= 10.47$$

$$= 13.53$$

### Interpretation

We can be 90% confident that the increase in scores will be between 10.47 and 13.53.

---

 **Your Turn!**

### III. Two-Sample *t* Test: Repeated Measures Design

*Research Question.* A study is being conducted at a sleep disorders clinic to determine if a regimen of swimming exercises affects the sleep patterns of individuals with insomnia. The number of hours of nightly sleep of 26 insomniac patients is recorded for a two-week period. The patients are then exposed to two weeks of daily swimming exercises, and their sleep is monitored for two more weeks. For this sample of patients, the amount of nightly sleep increased by $M_D = 1.2$ hours with $SS_D = 112$.

a. On the basis of this data, did the swimming regimen affect the amount of sleep? Use a two-tailed test with $\alpha = .05$ and determine the effect size.
b. Make a point estimate of how much sleep increases on average as a result of the swimming regimen.
c. Establish a 95% confidence around the mean difference and write a sentence of interpretation.
d. Establish a 99% confidence around the mean difference and write a sentence of interpretation.

A. Step 1: Formulate Hypotheses

Step 2: Indicate the Alpha Level and Determine Critical Values

*(Continued)*

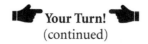
**Your Turn!**
(continued)

Step 3: Calculate Relevant Statistics

Step 4: Make a Decision and Report the Results

Effect size

B.   Point Estimate

C.   95% Confidence Interval

Interpretation

D.   99% Confidence Interval

Interpretation

## DEGREE OF CONFIDENCE VERSUS DEGREE OF SPECIFICITY

As was apparent in the last "Your Turn!" practice exercise, when we increase the level of confidence, we lose specificity. The range of values becomes broader and is thus more likely to include the true population parameters. Conversely, when we reduce the level of confidence, we gain specificity but lose confidence in our estimation. This is illustrated in the normal distribution below.

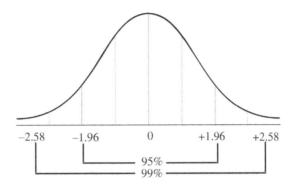

The 95% confidence level establishes a narrower (and more specific) interval of values, while the 99% level provides a wider (and less specific) interval of values.

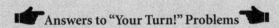

### Answers to "Your Turn!" Problems

**I. Confidence Interval for a One-Sample $t$ Test**

A. $M = 72$
B. LL = 68.94 and UL = 75.06

We can be 99% confident that the population mean would be between 68.94 and 75.06.

**II. Two-Sample $t$ Test: Independent Samples Design**

A. Step 1:      Step 2:      Step 3:
$H_0: \mu_1 = \mu_2$      $\alpha = .05$      $SS_1 = 154.86$
$H_1: \mu_1 \neq \mu_2$      $df = 11$      $SS_2 = 112.83$
      $t_{crit} = \pm 2.201$      $s_{M_1-M_2} = 2.75$
            $t_{obt} = +3.28$

*(Continued)*

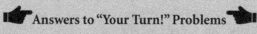

## Answers to "Your Turn!" Problems
(continued)

Step 4:

Subjects who heard positive remarks about taking the CAT scored significantly higher than the group who heard no such remarks. Reject $H_0$, $t(11) = +3.28$, $p < .05$.
   Effect size: $d = 1.83$, large effect

B. $M_1 - M_2 = 9.03$
C. LL = 2.98 and UL = 15.08

We can be 95% confident that the difference between population means would be between 2.98 and 15.08.

## III. Two-Sample $t$ Test: Repeated Measures Design

A. Step 1:          Step 2:          Step 3:
   $H_0: \mu_D = 0$      $\alpha = .05$      $s_D = 2.12$
   $H_1: \mu_D \neq 0$      $df = 25$      $S_{M_D} = .42$
                  $t_{crit} = \pm 2.060$      $t_{obt} = +2.86$

Step 4:

The swimming regimen had a significant effect on sleep. Reject $H_0$, $t(25) = +2.86$, $p < .05$.
   Effect size: $d = .57$, moderate effect

B. $M_D = 1.2$
C. LL $= 1.2 - (2.060)(.42)$          and          UL $= 1.2 + (2.060)(.42)$
      $= .33$                                       $= 2.07$

We can be 95% confident that the increased amount of sleep will be between .33 and 2.07 hours.

D. LL $= 1.2 - (2.787)(.42)$          and          UL $= 1.2 + (2.787)(.42)$
      $= .03$                                       $= 2.37$

We can be 99% confident that the increased amount of sleep will be between .03 and 2.37 hours.

## Using Microsoft Excel for Data Analysis

If you are using Excel for the first time for statistical analysis, you may need to load the add-in tool that allows these functions. The information for loading the Data Analysis ToolPak as well as general instructions for using Excel for data analysis are at the beginning of the Excel section in Chapter 4.

### Confidence Interval for a One-Sample $t$ Test

This chapter looked at confidence intervals for three different kinds of $t$ tests. To calculate these confidence intervals, we will be providing the formulas and instructing Excel to grab the values needed in the formulas from the cells where they are located the spreadsheet. We'll start by using Excel to calculate a confidence interval for the one-sample $t$ test using the example from your text about finger dexterity exercises for typing speed. The formula for the lower limit of the confidence interval for a one-sample $t$ test is: $LL = M - t(S_M)$. The formula for the upper limit is: $UL = M + t(S_M)$.

First, type in the information shown below in column A of the spreadsheet that will be needed for the calculations. Also, type in the summary information in column C that was provided for this problem. We will now instruct Excel to perform the remaining operations:

| | A | B | C |
|---|---|---|---|
| 1 | Mean | | 57 |
| 2 | SS | | 3600 |
| 3 | n | | 17 |
| 4 | t crit | | |
| 5 | Sample SD | | |
| 6 | Standard error | | |
| 7 | Lower Limit | | |
| 8 | Upper Limit | | |
| 9 | | | |

1. **Critical $t$-values.** Rather than using the table at the back of your text, Excel will determine your $t_{crit}$ values. With your cursor in cell C4, go to the **Formulas** tab and click on the **Insert Function (fx)** command from the ribbon. From the **Insert Function** dialog box, scroll down and highlight **T.INV.2T**. This is the function that will provide the $t_{crit}$ values for a two-tailed test. Click **OK**.

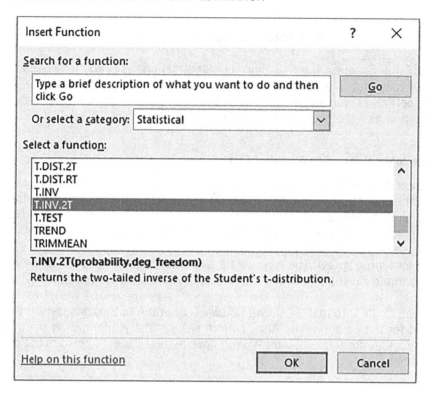

Since we are establishing a 90% confidence interval, we will enter .10 in the probability window of the **Function Arguments** box as well as the appropriate *df* (16 in this case). After clicking **OK**, the $t_{crit}$ values needed for the confidence interval formulas (1.745884) will appear in the cell.

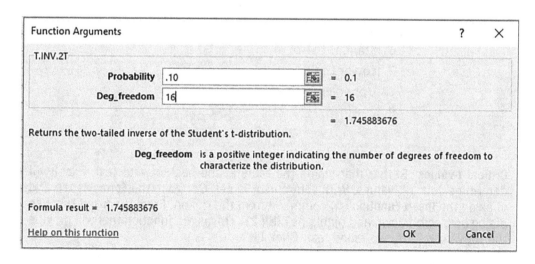

2. **Sample Standard Deviation**. To determine the standard error of the mean needed for the confidence interval formulas, you will first have to obtain the sample standard deviation. With your cursor in cell C5, type the following exactly as written: = SQRT(C2/(C3–1)) and hit the enter key. The sample standard deviation (15) will appear in the cell.

| ⬛ | A | B | C | D |
|---|---|---|---|---|
| 1 | Mean | | 57 | |
| 2 | SS | | 3600 | |
| 3 | n | | 17 | |
| 4 | t crit | | 1.745884 | |
| 5 | Sample SD | | =SQRT(C2/(C3-1)) | |
| 6 | Standard error | | | |
| 7 | Lower Limit | | | |
| 8 | Upper Limit | | | |

3. **Standard Error.** With your cursor in cell C6, type the following exactly as written: = C5/SQRT(C3) and hit the enter key. The standard error (3.638034) will appear in the cell.

4. **Confidence Intervals.** Finally, we can calculate the confidence intervals by instructing Excel to grab the values from the cells needed for the formulas. For the lower limit, place your cursor in cell C7. Type the following exactly as written: = C1-(C4*C6) and hit the enter key. For the upper limit, place your cursor in cell C8. Type the following exactly as written: = C1+(C4*C6) and hit the enter key. Both limits will now appear in the designated cells.

| ⬛ | A | B | C |
|---|---|---|---|
| 1 | Mean | | 57 |
| 2 | SS | | 3600 |
| 3 | n | | 17 |
| 4 | t crit | | 1.745884 |
| 5 | Sample SD | | 15 |
| 6 | Standard error | | 3.638034 |
| 7 | Lower Limit | | 50.64842 |
| 8 | Upper Limit | | 63.35158 |

### Confidence Interval for a Two-Sample $t$ Test: Independent Samples Design

Here again, we will provide Excel with the information it needs to calculate the confidence intervals. The formula for the lower limit of the confidence interval for an independent samples $t$ test is: $LL = (M_1 - M_2) - t(s_{M_1 - M_2})$. The formula for the upper limit is: $LL = (M_1 - M_2) + t(s_{M_1 - M_2})$.

Here, we will use the sample research question pertaining to the pamphlet for memory-improving techniques. Type in the information shown below in column A of the spreadsheet that will be needed for the calculations. Also, type in the summary information in column C that was provided for this problem. Notice that a cell for "df used" is included. Remember that the table for the t-distribution at the back of your book is abbreviated and not all *df* values are included. Be sure to enter the *df* that was used from the table rather than the actual *df* so that your comparison with Excel's output will match (aside from rounding differences).

| | A | B | C |
|---|---|---|---|
| 1 | $M_1$ | | 79 |
| 2 | $M_2$ | | 68 |
| 3 | $SS_1$ | | 478 |
| 4 | $SS_2$ | | 346 |
| 5 | $n_1$ | | 36 |
| 6 | $n_2$ | | 40 |
| 7 | df used | | 60 |
| 8 | t crit | | |
| 9 | Standard error | | |
| 10 | LL | | |
| 11 | UL | | |
| 12 | | | |

1. **Critical *t*-values.** Follow the instructions in step one above for the one-sample *t* test except place your cursor in the cell where you want the *t* values to appear (e.g., C8). We are again establishing a 90% confidence interval and so the probability in the **Function Arguments** dialog box will be .10 and *df* will be 60.

2. **Standard Error.** With your cursor in cell C9, type the following exactly as written: =SQRT((C3+C4)/(C5+C6–2)*(1/C5+1/C6)) and hit the enter key. The standard error (.766608) will appear in the designated cell.

3. **Confidence Intervals.** For the lower limit, place your cursor in cell C10. Type the following exactly as written: =(C1-C2)-C8*C9 and hit the enter key. For the upper limit, place your cursor in cell C11. Type the following exactly as written: =(C1-C2)+C8*C9 and hit the enter key. Both limits will appear in the designated cells. There will be some rounding differences but the values are close to what you calculated by hand.

| | A | B | C |
|---|---|---|---|
| 1 | $M_1$ | | 79 |
| 2 | $M_2$ | | 68 |
| 3 | $SS_1$ | | 478 |
| 4 | $SS_2$ | | 346 |
| 5 | $n_1$ | | 36 |
| 6 | $n_2$ | | 40 |
| 7 | df used | | 60 |
| 8 | t crit | | 1.670649 |
| 9 | Standard error | | 0.766608 |
| 10 | LL | | 9.719267 |
| 11 | UL | | 12.28073 |
| 12 | | | |

### Confidence Interval for a Two-Sample *t* Test: Repeated Measures Design

The formula for the lower limit of the confidence interval for a repeated measures *t* test is: $LL = M_D - t(s_{M_D})$. The formula for the upper limit is: $LL = M_D + t(s_{M_D})$. We will use the sample research question pertaining to the math tutoring program. Type in the information shown below in column A of the spreadsheet that will be needed for the calculations. Also, type in the summary information in column C that was provided for this problem as well as the *df* that was used from the table in the back of your book (rather than the actual *df*).

| | A | B | C |
|---|---|---|---|
| 1 | $M_D$ | | 12 |
| 2 | $SS_D$ | | 1648 |
| 3 | n | | 45 |
| 4 | df used | | 40 |
| 5 | t crit | | |
| 6 | Standard deviation $(s_D)$ | | |
| 7 | Standard error $(s_{M_D})$ | | |
| 8 | LL | | |
| 9 | UL | | |
| 10 | | | |

1. **Critical *t*-values.** Follow the instructions in step one for the one-sample *t* test except place your cursor in the cell where you want the *t* values to appear (e.g., C5). For a 90% confidence interval, the probability in the **Function Arguments** dialog box will be .10 and *df* will be 40.
2. **Standard Deviation.** Here, you will provide Excel with the formula for the standard deviation as well as the locations where the values needed for the calculation are located. With your cursor in cell C6, type the following exactly as written: =SQRT(C2/(C3–1)) and hit the enter key.
3. **Standard Error.** With your cursor in cell C7, type the following exactly as written: =C6/SQRT(C3) and hit the enter key.
4. **Confidence Intervals.** For the lower limit, place your cursor in cell C8. Type the following exactly as written: =C1-C5*C7 and hit the enter key. For the upper limit, place your cursor in cell C9. Type the following exactly as written: =C1+C5*C7 and hit the enter key. Both limits will appear in the designated cells. There will be some rounding differences but the values are close to what you calculated by hand.

| | A | B | C |
|---|---|---|---|
| 1 | $M_D$ | | 12 |
| 2 | $SS_D$ | | 1648 |
| 3 | n | | 45 |
| 4 | df used | | 40 |
| 5 | t crit | | 1.683851 |
| 6 | Standard deviation $(s_D)$ | | 6.120012 |
| 7 | Standard error $(s_{M_D})$ | | 0.912318 |
| 8 | LL | | 10.46379 |
| 9 | UL | | 13.53621 |
| 10 | | | |

### Additional Practice Problems

**Answers to odd numbered problems are in Appendix C at the end of the book.**

1. Define what is meant by a point estimate and a confidence interval and explain the difference between them.
2. What statistics would be used to estimate point estimates for
   a. a one-sample $t$ test?
   b. an independent measures $t$ test?
   c. a repeated measures $t$ test?
3. What statistics would be used to estimate point estimates for
   a. $\mu$?
   b. $\mu_1 - \mu_2$?
   c. $\mu_D$?
4. Given $M = 28$, $n = 10$, and $s_M = 2.2$, construct a
   a. 99% confidence interval for $\mu$.
   b. 95% confidence interval for $\mu$.
   c. 90% confidence interval for $\mu$.
   d. What can be said about the relationship between the width of the confidence interval and level of confidence?
5. A sample was measured with the following scores on the dependent variable: 6, 8,10, 7, 12, and 8. What is the point estimate for $\mu$?
6. One type of treatment resulted in the following scores: 48, 52, 49, 50, 53, 47, and 45. The scores for a second type of treatment were: 34, 40, 38, 45, 41, 37, and 42. What is the point estimate for $\mu_1 - \mu_2$?
7. Pre-test scores were 68, 75, 79, 69, 80, and 70. Post-test scores were 96, 90, 89, 85, 76, and 87. What is the point estimate for $\mu_D$?
8. Based on the summary data below, establish a 90% confidence interval for $\mu$.
   $M = 30$
   $n = 17$
   $SS = 101$
9. Based on the summary data below, establish a 95% confidence for $\mu_1 - \mu_2$
   $M_1 = 72$      $M_2 = 64$
   $n_1 = 9$       $n_2 = 11$
   $SS_1 = 424$    $SS_2 = 347$
10. Based on the summary data below, establish a 99% confidence interval for $\mu_D$.
    $M_D = 27$
    $n = 15$
    $SS_D = 682$
11. A professor in a substance abuse counselor training program surveyed a sample of $n = 25$ students about the age at which they consumed their first alcoholic beverage. The mean age was 13.8 years with a $s_M = 1.11$. Establish a 95% confidence interval for $\mu$ and write a sentence of interpretation.
12. The head of a nursing program is considering the addition of mindfulness training in the curriculum as a way of cultivating cognitive empathy in nursing students. To test the effectiveness of the program, one group of students completes the training program and subsequently takes an empathy assessment. A second group of nursing students takes the assessment without completing the mindfulness training. Summary data for the study are listed below. Higher scores reflect greater cognitive empathy.

| Training | No Training |
|---|---|
| $M_1 = 55$ | $M_2 = 47$ |
| $n_1 = 9$ | $n_2 = 7$ |
| $s_{M_1 - M_2} = 3.28$ | |

a. What is the point estimate for $\mu_1 - \mu_2$?

b. Conduct a two-tailed $t$ test using $\alpha = .05$.

c. Establish a 95% confidence interval for $\mu_1 - \mu_2$ and write a sentence of interpretation.

13. A study was conducted to determine the effectiveness of a new type of exercise designed to help people lose belly fat. The researcher took the waist measurements of a sample of $n = 27$ subjects both before and after the exercise program was implemented. Waist measurement decreased by an average of $M_D = -2.3$ inches with a $s_{M_D} = .81$. Establish a 99% confidence for $\mu_D$ and write a sentence of interpretation.

# 13

# One-Way Analysis of Variance

## INTRODUCTION TO ANALYSIS OF VARIANCE

The purpose of the two-sample $t$-statistic is to examine the difference between two means in order to determine if their differences are likely due to chance (sampling error) or something other than chance (an independent variable). However, the $t$-statistic is limited to comparisons involving only two groups, and sometimes researchers may want to compare more than two groups. For instance, you may want to test the problem-solving abilities of three different age groups: five-year-olds, seven-year-olds, and nine-year-olds. The thought may occur to you to simply compare two groups at a time in such cases. At first glance, this seems like a reasonable solution. Why not use a $t$ test to first compare the means for Groups 1 and 2, and then for Groups 1 and 3, and finally for Groups 2 and 3? As sensible as it sounds, this practice is not acceptable because doing so would create an increased risk of a Type I error.

Remember that a Type I error is rejecting a null hypothesis that is in fact true. Recall also that the probability of a Type I error is defined by the alpha level ($\alpha$). For example, if we reject $H_0$ at $\alpha = .05$, we reject it because our obtained results would be highly unlikely if $H_0$ were true. Such results would occur less than 5% of the time. But this also means that 5% of the time we would be wrong. Thus, the probability of being wrong is .05. Conducting multiple $t$ tests separately increases that probability considerably. **Experiment-wise alpha level** is the term used to refer to this accumulated probability of a Type I error. To minimize this error, we use **analysis of variance**, which allows for the comparison of two, three, four, or more groups simultaneously using only one alpha level and, thus, avoids the buildup of alpha error.

Similar to the $t$-statistic, analysis of variance also has a within-subjects design (akin to the repeated measures $t$ test in which the same subjects are measured on more than one occasion) and a between-subjects design (akin to the independent samples $t$ test involving separate and unrelated samples). Our discussion of analysis of variance will be limited to the between-subjects design.

In addition, while we will be comparing means for more than two groups, the experiments that we analyze will involve only *one* independent variable being manipulated at different levels. For instance, the independent variable of room temperature may be manipulated at the levels of 30°F, 50°F, and 70°F. In another example, time of day may be manipulated at the levels of morning, afternoon, evening, and night. Because we are manipulating only *one* independent variable, the procedure we will be using is referred to as **one-way analysis of variance.**

Finally, the acronym **ANOVA** is used to abbreviate analysis of variance, which gets its name from the fact that the variances of the samples are broken down and analyzed. You are already familiar with the concept of variance, a value that expresses the amount of variability in a distribution of scores. Variability comes about whenever all scores in a distribution are not exactly alike.

## VARIANCE

In ANOVA, total variance is separated into two kinds: *within-treatment variance* and *between-treatments variance*.

- *Within-treatment variance* refers to the variability within a particular sample. There are two sources that contribute to the variability within a sample: individual differences and experimental error. Suppose a study is conducted to evaluate the effectiveness of a new medication in alleviating nausea in cancer patients undergoing chemotherapy. The medication is given to three samples in three different doses: 5 mg, 7 mg, and 9 mg. Within each of these treatment groups, different degrees of nausea will be reported after taking the medication simply because of such factors as differences in body chemistry, tolerance for discomfort, motivation, prior experiences, and a multitude of other characteristics that set individuals apart. Such variations are ascribed to individual differences.

  Experimental error, on the other hand, comes about because of random variations in the experimental situation that could affect measurement of the dependent variable. Such variations might include background noises, transient lapses of attention on the part of the researcher, or inexact measuring instruments. Both of these sources of variance, individual differences and experimental error, are considered to be random error variance, or simply chance because they are unintentional and not the result of planning or design.

- *Between-treatments variance* refers to the variability between the treatment groups. For example, the three groups of cancer patients who received three different dosages of medication probably all have different means. And the same two factors that contributed to within-treatment variance (individual differences and experimental error) also contribute to between-treatments variance. However, there is an additional source that contributes to between-treatments variance: treatment effects. If the three groups of cancer patients who received 5 mg, 7 mg, and 9 mg of the medication subsequently report high, moderate, and mild levels of nausea, respectively, they may indeed be experiencing the effects of the treatment.

### To Summarize

*Between-treatments* variance = Individual differences + Experimental error + Treatment
*Within-treatment* variance = Individual differences + Experimental error

Notice that if there are no treatment effects, between-treatments variance and within- treatment variance would be approximately equal, both being made up of the same factors minus the treatment. Conversely, if treatment *is* effective, then the between-treatments variance would be larger than the within-treatment variance because of the influence of treatment effects.

## THE *F*-STATISTIC

The statistic generated by ANOVA is called the *F*-statistic, which is, essentially, the ratio of between-treatments variance to within-treatment variance.

$$F = \frac{\text{Between} - \text{treatments variance}\left(\text{individual differences, experimental error, treatment effects}\right)}{\text{Within} - \text{treatment variance}\left(\text{individual differences, experimental error}\right)}$$

If the independent variable had no influence on the dependent variable (i.e., if treatment effects were 0), the value of the *F*-statistic would be approximately 1. Conversely, if there *were* treatment effects that created large differences between group means, then the between-treatments variance would be bigger than the within-treatment variance and the value of *F* would be larger than 1. Because both individual differences and experimental error are considered to be the result of chance, or random error, within-treatment variance is also referred to as *error variance* and between-treatments variance is simply referred to as *treatment variance*. Thus, another way of stating the *F*-statistic is:

$$F = \frac{\text{Treatment variance}}{\text{Error variance}}$$

I am certain we have accounted for all extraneous variables.

## HYPOTHESIS TESTING WITH THE *F*-STATISTIC

In conducting an ANOVA, the null and alternative hypotheses will be written as follows:

- The *null hypothesis* predicts that the value of *F* will be 1.00 because, as usual, it asserts no difference between means; that the independent variable had no treatment effect; and that any differences found between means were simply due to chance, or random error. Thus, the null hypothesis can be written as

  $H_0: \mu_1 = \mu_2 = \mu_3 = \mu_k$ (the *k* subscript indicates that there will be as many *μ*s as there are groups)

- The *alternative hypothesis* asserts that there will be significant differences between some of the means. But there are several ways in which the means could differ (i.e., $\mu_1 \neq \mu_2$ and $\mu_1 \neq \mu_3$, but $\mu_2 = \mu_3$ is but one possible scenario for a study with three groups). Thus, we will use the following generic alternative hypothesis:

  $H_1$: Some *μ*s are not equal

## THE *F*-DISTRIBUTION TABLE

If the null hypothesis is true, if means do not differ significantly, the value of *F* will be approximately 1.00. How much larger than 1.00 the *F*-statistic has to be in order to reject $H_0$ will be

---

 **Your Turn!**

### I. Rationale for the *F*-Statistic

A. Why is it inappropriate to use multiple *t* tests in an experiment with more than two groups?

B. What *F*-value is predicted by the null hypothesis? Why? (Include in your response a discussion of the two types of variance involved in the *F*-statistic.)

---

determined by comparing an obtained *F*-value to a theoretical distribution of *F*-values similar to what we have done in the past with *z*-values and *t*-values. The *F*-distribution, like the *t*-distribution, is a family of curves with varying degrees of freedom. You will find the critical values for the *F*-distribution in Tables 3 and 4 near the end of this book. Table 3 applies to an alpha level of .05, and Table 4 applies to an alpha level of .01.

There are several features of each table of which you should take note:

- There will be two *df*: one associated with between-groups variance ($df_{bet}$), which is the numerator in the *F*-statistic, and one associated with within-group variance ($df_{wi}$), the denominator. $Df_{bet}$ runs across the top of the table and $df_{wi}$ runs along the left column.
- Once again, the chart is abbreviated and not all *df* values are shown for the denominator. If the *df* for your particular research problem are not shown, use the next-lowest *df* value.
- If your obtained *F*-value is greater than the critical value listed in the chart, you can reject the null hypothesis because differences between means that large are unlikely to be due to chance. It is more likely that the differences occurred because of the effects of treatment.
- If your obtained *F*-value is less than the listed critical value of *F*, you will fail to reject $H_0$ because differences that small could have occurred by chance alone.

In addition:

- *F*-statistics will not have negative values because they are calculated from ratios of variances, which are squared scores. Thus, *F*-values will only be positive.
- Because only positive *F*-values are possible, there will be no two-tailed tests for the *F*-statistic.

## NOTATIONS FOR ANOVA

Analysis of variance involves working through a series of steps and learning some new notations. After reviewing these notations, we will work through the calculations of ANOVA within the context of an example.

- **Sum of squares (SS)** refers to the sum of the squared deviations of scores from the mean. We will be calculating three SS values: $SS_{total}$, $SS_{wi}$, and $SS_{bet}$.
- **$\Sigma X_{tot}$** refers to the total of all the scores in the study, which is determined by adding the sum of the $X$ scores for each group.
- **$\Sigma X^2_{tot}$** refers to the total of all the squared scores in the study as determined by adding the sum of the squared scores for each group.
- $N$ refers to the total number of scores in all groups.
- $n$ refers to the number of scores in a sample group; particular groups are designated by subscripts.
- $t$ as a subscript refers to individual treatment groups.
- $k$ refers to the number of groups in the study.

### Sample Research Question

A researcher is interested in determining if interactive activities influence the subjective experience of life satisfaction in older individuals. She obtains a random sample of 15 residents from an assisted living residential center, all of whom report only moderate degrees of life satisfaction. The subjects are randomly assigned to one of three interactive conditions: (1) an online chat group, (2) caring for pets, and (3) talking with volunteer students about their life experiences. After three months, the residents are given the Life Satisfaction Questionnaire. Higher scores designate greater life satisfaction. Do the scores indicate significant differences between the three groups? Use $\alpha = .05$.

| Online chat | | Pets | | Students | |
|---|---|---|---|---|---|
| $X_1$ | $X_1^2$ | $X_2$ | $X_2^2$ | $X_3$ | $X_3^2$ |
| 3 | 9 | 8 | 64 | 3 | 9 |
| 3 | 9 | 12 | 144 | 7 | 49 |
| 4 | 16 | 9 | 81 | 10 | 100 |
| 6 | 36 | 7 | 49 | 6 | 36 |
| 4 | 16 | 9 | 81 | 9 | 81 |
| $\Sigma X_1 = 20$ | | $\Sigma X_2 = 45$ | | $\Sigma X_3 = 35$ | |
| $\Sigma X_1^2 = 86$ | | $\Sigma X_2^2 = 419$ | | $\Sigma X_3^2 = 275$ | |
| $n_1 = 5$ | | $n_2 = 5$ | | $n_3 = 5$ | |
| $M_1 = 4$ | | $M_2 = 9$ | | $M_3 = 7$ | |
| | | $\Sigma X_{tot} = 100$ | | | |
| | | $\Sigma X^2_{tot} = 780$ | | | |
| | | $N = 15$ | | | |
| | | $k = 3$ | | | |

## THE CALCULATIONS

The calculations needed for conducting an analysis of variance include the following: sum of squares values, degrees of freedom, mean square values, and the $F$-statistic.

### Sum of Squares (SS)

The first calculations in ANOVA will be three sum of squares values: $SS_{total}$, $SS_{wi}$, and $SS_{bet}$.

- $SS_{total}$ refers to the sum of squares for all of the $N$ scores. We will change the notation in the $SS$ formula that we are used to:

$$SS = \Sigma X^2 - \frac{(\Sigma X)^2}{N}$$

to make it relevant to our current statistical procedure for ANOVA:

$$SS_{total} = \Sigma X_{tot}^2 - \frac{(\Sigma X_{tot})^2}{N}$$

For our research problem,

$$SS_{total} = 780 - \frac{(100)^2}{15}$$
$$= 113.33$$

- $SS_{wi}$ refers to the variability within each group as measured by

$$SS_{wi} = \Sigma \left[ \Sigma X_t^2 - \frac{(\Sigma X_t)^2}{n_t} \right]$$

This formula instructs you to calculate the sum of squares ($SS$) for each treatment group and then to sum each of the $SS$ values. For our research problem,

$$SS_{wi} = \left( 86 - \frac{(20)^2}{5} \right) + \left( 419 - \frac{(45)^2}{5} \right) + \left( 275 - \frac{(35)^2}{5} \right)$$
$$= 6 + 14 + 30$$
$$= 50$$

- $SS_{bet}$ refers to the variability between each group as measured by:

$$SS_{bet} = \Sigma \left[ \frac{(\Sigma X_t)^2}{n_t} \right] - \frac{(\Sigma X_{tot})^2}{N}$$

This formula instructs you to perform the operations in the brackets for each group before subtracting the expression at the end. For our research problem,

$$SS_{bet} = \frac{20^2}{5} + \frac{45^2}{5} + \frac{35^2}{5} - \frac{100^2}{15}$$

$$= 80 + 405 + 245 - 666.67$$

$$= 63.33$$

**Tip!**

We can check our calculations for our sum of squares values because our SS within and SS between variability should equal our SS total variability.

$$SS_{wi} + SS_{bet} = SS_{total}$$

$$50 + 63.33 = 113.33$$

### Degrees of Freedom (*df*)

We will be determining *df* for each of the three *SS* values above according to the following formulas:

- $df_{wi} = N - k$    For our data: $df_{wi} = 15 - 3 = 12$
- $df_{bet} = k - 1$    For our data: $df_{bet} = 3 - 1 = 2$
- $df_{total} = N - 1$    For our data: $df_{total} = 15 - 1 = 14$

$df_{total}$ is not needed in our calculations for ANOVA. However, it also gives us a check because $df_{wi}$ and $df_{bet}$ should equal $df_{total}$. Thus,

$$df_{wi} + df_{bet} = df_{total}$$

$$12 + 2 = 14$$

### Mean Square (*MS*)

You have previously learned that the variance is obtained by dividing *SS* by *df*. In ANOVA, **mean square** is a measure of variance that is also calculated by dividing *SS* by its corresponding *df*. We will calculate the between and within mean squares as follows:

$$MS_{bet} = \frac{SS_{bet}}{df_{bet}}$$

For our data:

$$MS_{bet} = \frac{63.33}{2}$$

$$= 31.67$$

$$MS_{wi} = \frac{SS_{wi}}{df_{wi}}$$  For our data:  $$MS_{wi} = \frac{50}{12}$$
$$= 4.17$$

## F-Statistic

The final calculation in ANOVA is the F-statistic. You have been presented with a couple of different formulations for the F-statistic, the latest being:

$$F = \frac{\text{Treatment variance}}{\text{Error variance}}$$

Let us reformulate it one more time to make it usable for our ANOVA calculations. $MS_{bet}$ is an expression for treatment variance, and $MS_{wi}$ is an expression for error variance. Thus, the working formula we will use for the F-statistic is

$$F = \frac{MS_{bet}}{MS_{wi}}$$  For our data:  $$F_{obt} = \frac{31.67}{4.17} = 7.59$$

We now have to compare our calculated F-value to a critical value of F in order to determine if $H_0$ should be rejected. We obtained an F-value of 7.59 with $df_{wi} = 12$ and $df_{bet} = 2$. We are using an $\alpha = .05$. Consulting the F-distribution table, we find that the critical value for rejecting $H_0$ is 3.88. Because our obtained value exceeds the critical value for F, we will reject the $H_0$ that interactive activities have no effect on life satisfaction.

## Summary Data

Finally, we will arrange our *obtained* values into a summary table that includes the following components:

| Source | SS | df | MS | F | p |
|--------|------|----|-------|------|------|
| Between-treatments | 63.33 | 2 | 31.67 | 7.59 | < .05 |
| Within-treatment | 50.00 | 12 | 4.17 | | |
| Total | 113.33 | 14 | | | |

## Statement of Conclusion

Reject $H_0$. Interactive activities have a significant effect on life satisfaction.

## Note the following:

- Only the SS and df will have totals. MS is not additive.
- The F column will have only one value, and it refers to your obtained F-value rather than the critical F-value.
- The p-value is the alpha level being used. The p, of course, stands for probability. A less-than sign (<) will be used if $H_0$ is rejected and a greater-than sign (>) will be used if it is not.
- Following the summary table, write a verbal statement of your conclusions.

## SUMMARY OF HYPOTHESIS TESTING PROTOCOL FOR ANOVA

At first, ANOVA might seem a bit confusing with all the steps and formulas involved. However, once you have gone through the process of conducting an ANOVA in a structured manner, it becomes quite manageable. The research problem that we just worked through is summarized below using the same four-step process with which you are now well acquainted.

### Step 1: Formulate Hypotheses

$H_0: \mu_1 = \mu_2 = \mu_3$
$H_1:$ some $\mu$s are not equal

### Step 2: Indicate the Alpha Level and Determine Critical Values

$\alpha = .05$

$$df_{wi} = N - k \quad df_{bet} = k - 1$$
$$\phantom{df_{wi}} = 15 - 3 \quad \phantom{df_{bet}} = 3 - 1$$
$$\phantom{df_{wi}} = 12 \quad \phantom{df_{bet}} = 2$$

$F_{crit} = 3.88$

### Step 3: Calculate Relevant Statistics

1. Sum of Squares (SS)

$$SS_{total} = \Sigma X_{tot}^2 - \frac{\left(\Sigma X_{tot}\right)^2}{N}$$
$$= 780 - \frac{(100)^2}{15}$$
$$= 113.33$$

$$SS_{wi} = \Sigma \left[ \Sigma X_t^2 - \frac{\left(\Sigma X_t\right)^2}{n_t} \right]$$
$$= \left( 86 - \frac{(20)^2}{5} \right) + \left( 419 - \frac{(45)^2}{5} \right) + \left( 275 - \frac{(35)^2}{5} \right)$$
$$= 50$$

$$SS_{bet} = \Sigma \left[ \frac{\left(\Sigma X_t\right)^2}{n_t} \right] - \frac{\left(\Sigma X_{tot}\right)^2}{N}$$
$$= \frac{20^2}{5} + \frac{45^2}{5} + \frac{35^2}{5} - \frac{100^2}{15}$$
$$= 63.33$$

2. Mean Square (MS)

$$MS_{bet} = \frac{SS_{bet}}{df_{bet}} = \frac{63.33}{2} = 31.67$$

$$MS_{wi} = \frac{SS_{wi}}{df_{wi}} = \frac{50}{12} = 4.17$$

3. The F-ratio

$$F_{obt} = \frac{MS_{bet}}{MS_{wi}} = \frac{31.67}{4.17} = 7.59$$

## Step 4: Make a Decision and Report the Results

| Source | SS | df | MS | F | p |
|---|---|---|---|---|---|
| Between-treatments | 63.33 | 2 | 31.67 | 7.59 | < .05 |
| Within-treatment | 50.00 | 12 | 4.17 | | |
| Total | 113.33 | 14 | | | |

Interactive activities have a significant effect on life satisfaction → Reject $H_0$.

## EFFECT SIZE FOR ANOVA

One popular measure of effect size for ANOVA is called *eta squared,* symbolized as $\eta^2$. The formula is:

$$\eta^2 = \frac{SS_{bet}}{SS_{total}}$$

As you know, $SS$ is a measure of variability. $SS_{total}$ is a measure of the total variability in the study, while $SS_{bet}$ is a measure of the variability between groups as a result of manipulating the independent variable at different levels. Thus, what eta squared tells us is the proportion of the total variability ($SS_{total}$) that is accounted for by treatment ($SS_{bet}$).

For our data,

$$\eta^2 = \frac{63.33}{113.33} = .56$$

In other words, 56% of all of the score differences in the dependent variable can be explained by treatment (i.e., changing the types of interactive activities).

## WHAT NOW? POST HOC TESTS

Noticeably, the conclusion of our $F$-test that "interactive activities have a significant effect on life satisfaction" is rather vague. It simply tells you that there is a significant difference somewhere among the means, but it does not specify which means differ significantly. Do Groups 1 and 2 differ significantly? Or Groups 2 and 3? Or Groups 1 and 3? Or all of the above? The $F$-statistic does not specify this information. Thus, researchers will usually want to undertake further analysis to determine the source(s) of significance. This is often accomplished by using **post hoc tests**, tests that are conducted after a null hypothesis has been rejected and there are three or more treatment groups. Post hoc tests are used to distinguish which means differ significantly.

### Tukey's Honestly Significant Difference Test

We will use a post hoc test called *Tukey's Honestly Significant Difference test*, or *HSD*. With this test, we will be making multiple comparisons between means, two at a time. Remember that we chose not to use repeated *t* tests for such a comparison because of the increased risk of Type I errors. Tukey's *HSD* test has built-in safeguards that minimize this risk. However, in order to use this test, the sample size (*n*) must be the same for each group.[1]

Tukey's *HSD* formula is as follows:

$$HSD = q\left(\sqrt{\frac{MS_{wi}}{n}}\right)$$

The value for *q* is found in Tables 5 (for $\alpha = .05$) and 6 (for $\alpha = .01$) (near the end of this book). This value is called a *Studentized Range Statistic*, which is how the tables are identified. Notice that we will need two values to use this chart. We will need a value for *k*, the number of treatment groups, which is shown across the top, and one for degrees of freedom, which is shown along the left column. This will be the value for $df_{wi}$. Use the same alpha level that was specified in the problem for the *F*-test.

Three steps are involved for conducting Tukey's *HSD* test:

1. Locate the critical *q* value.

   For our problem: $k = 3$
   $$df_{wi} = 12$$
   $$\alpha = .05$$
   Thus, $q = 3.77$

2. Calculate the *HSD* value.

   $$HSD = q\left(\sqrt{\frac{MS_{wi}}{n}}\right)$$

   $$= 3.77\left(\sqrt{\frac{4.17}{5}}\right)$$

   $$= 3.44$$

3. Compare mean differences and write a verbal conclusion. Mean differences for all sets of means are computed, including comparisons between Groups 1 and 2, 1 and 3, and 2 and 3. You may arrange the means so that only positive difference values are obtained. Only those differences that are greater than the *HSD* value calculated above indicate a significant result.

   $M_2 - M_1 = 9 - 4 = 5*$ (pets and online chat groups)
   $M_2 - M_3 = 9 - 7 = 2$ (pets and student groups)
   $M_3 - M_1 = 7 - 4 = 3$ (students and online chat groups)

   Place an asterisk beside all mean differences that reach significance and write a verbal conclusion.

## For this problem

There was a significant difference in life satisfaction between the pets ($M_2$) and online chat groups ($M_1$), with those caring for pets showing a significant increase in life satisfaction. There were no significant differences between any of the other groups.

## ASSUMPTIONS

You have had previous experience with all the assumptions for ANOVA, independent measures design:

- Independent and random selection of subjects.
- The dependent variable can be measured on an interval or ratio scale.
- The dependent variable is normally distributed in the populations of interest.
- Homogeneity of variance of the dependent variable in the populations of interest.

 **Your Turn!**

### II. Analysis of Variance

*Research Question.* A counseling psychologist conducts a study to determine the effectiveness of different approaches to treating generalized anxiety disorder. Subjects with this disorder are randomly assigned to three groups. One group undergoes cognitive therapy, a second group is trained in biofeedback, and a third untreated group serves as a control. Anxiety scores for each group are listed in the table below. Lower scores indicate lower levels of anxiety.

| *Cognitive* | | *Biofeedback* | | *Control* | |
|---|---|---|---|---|---|
| $X_1$ | $X_1^2$ | $X_2$ | $X_2^2$ | $X_3$ | $X_3^2$ |
| 2 | | 3 | | 8 | |
| 4 | | 4 | | 7 | |
| 5 | | 2 | | 10 | |
| 3 | | 4 | | 6 | |
| 4 | | 3 | | 8 | |
| 6 | | 2 | | 9 | |
| $\Sigma X_1 =$ | | $\Sigma X_2 =$ | | $\Sigma X_3 =$ | |
| $\Sigma X_1^2 =$ | | $\Sigma X_2^2 =$ | | $\Sigma X_3^2 =$ | |
| $n_1 =$ | | $n_2 =$ | | $n_3 =$ | |
| $M_1 =$ | | $M_2 =$ | | $M_3 =$ | |
| | | $\Sigma X_{tot} =$ | | | |
| | | $\Sigma X_{tot}^2 =$ | | | |
| | | $N =$ | | | |
| | | $k =$ | | | |

A. Do the data indicate significant differences between the groups? Use $\alpha = .05$.

Step 1: Formulate Hypotheses

*(Continued)*

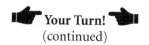 **Your Turn!**
(continued)

Step 2: Indicate the Alpha Level and Determine Critical Values

Step 3: Calculate Relevant Statistics

    1. Sums of Squares (*SS*)

    2. Mean Square (*MS*)

    3. The *F*-ratio

Step 4: Make a Decision and Report the Results

B. Determine the effect size ($\eta^2$).

C. Use Tukey's *HSD* post hoc test to determine which treatments differ significantly.

    1. Locate the critical *q* value.

    2. Calculate *HSD*.

    3. Compare mean differences and write a verbal conclusion.

---

**Answers to "Your Turn!" Problems**

### I. Rationale for the *F*-Statistic

A. Because of the increased risk of a Type I error.

B. An *F*-value of 1 is predicted by the null hypothesis. The *F*-statistic is a ratio of between-treatments variance (made up of individual differences, experimental

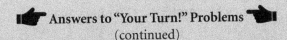

**Answers to "Your Turn!" Problems**
(continued)

error, and treatment effects) to within-treatment variance (made up only of individual differences and experimental error). Because the null hypothesis predicts that there would be no significant treatment effects, then the two types of variance would be approximately equal, resulting in an *F*-value of 1.

## II. Analysis of Variance

A. Step 1:
$H_0: \mu_1 = \mu_2 = \mu_3$
$H_1$: some $\mu$s are not equal

Step 2:
$\alpha = .05$
$df_{wi} = 15$
$df_{bet} = 2$
$F_{crit} = 3.68$

Step 3:
1. $SS_{tot} = 108$
   $SS_{wi} = 24$
   $SS_{bet} = 84$

2. $MS_{bet} = 42$
   $MS_{wi} = 1.6$

3. $F_{obt} = 26.25$

Step 4:
There were significant differences among the treatment groups for generalized anxiety disorder. Reject $H_0$.

| Source | SS | df | MS | F | p |
|---|---|---|---|---|---|
| Between-treatments | 84 | 2 | 42 | 26.25 | <.05 |
| Within-treatment | 24 | 15 | 1.6 | | |
| | 108 | 17 | | | |

B. $\eta^2 = .78$

C. 1. $q = 3.67$
   2. $HSD = 1.90$
   3. $M_1 - M_2 = 4-3 = 1$
      $M_3 - M_1 = 8-4 = 4^*$
      $M_3 - M_2 = 8-3 = 5^*$

While there was no significant difference between the cognitive therapy and biofeedback groups, both of these groups showed significantly lower anxiety than the untreated control group.

## Using Microsoft® Excel for Data Analysis

If you are using Excel for the first time for statistical analysis, you may need to load the add-in tool that allows these functions. The information for loading the Data Analysis ToolPak as well as general instructions for using Excel for data analysis are at the beginning of the Excel section in Chapter 4.

### One-Way ANOVA in Excel

To demonstrate how to use Excel for a one-way ANOVA, we will use the sample research question at the beginning of this chapter that asks if interactive activities influence the experience of life satisfaction in older adults.

- Enter the scores into columns A, B, and C of the spreadsheet, including the labels in row 1.

| ▲ | A | B | C |
|---|---|---|---|
| 1 | Online Chat | Pets | Students |
| 2 | 3 | 8 | 3 |
| 3 | 3 | 12 | 7 |
| 4 | 4 | 9 | 10 |
| 5 | 6 | 7 | 6 |
| 6 | 4 | 9 | 9 |
| 7 | | | |

- Go to the **Data** tab and click on the **Data Analysis** command.
- From the **Data Analysis** dialog box, scroll down and highlight **Anova: Single Factor**. Click **OK** and a dialog box for this function will appear.

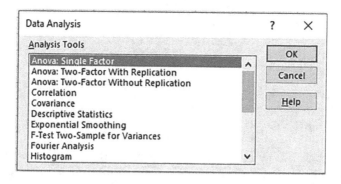

- With your cursor in the window for the **Input Range**, drag your mouse over *all* the scores, including the labels (A1 through C6). The dollar signs that show up in the window between cell locations are references used by Excel and will automatically appear in some types of statistical analyses.
- Check the **Labels** box so that the labels for the variables will appear in the output.
- Leave alpha set at .05 which is the default.

- For **Output options**, the default is to place the output table in a new worksheet. If you prefer, you can include the output table on the same spreadsheet by checking **Output Range** and typing in any empty cell number such as E1. For this example, we will leave the **New Worksheet Ply** checked. It is not necessary to enter anything in the window. Excel will simply create a second worksheet where an output table will appear. Click **OK**.

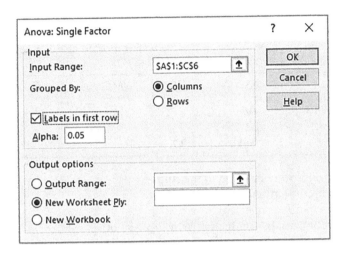

If you look at the bottom left corner, you will see Sheet 1 which contains your input information and Sheet 2 which now contains your output information. You can compare Excel's output table with your own calculations for the same problem. The summary table at the bottom is very much like the one that you created. Included in the table is the $F_{crit}$-value. Since $F_{obt}$ exceeds $F_{crit}$, we can reject the null hypothesis. Also included in the output table is a P-value. This is the actual probability of your obtained $F$-value by chance alone if the null hypothesis is true. The P-value of .0073 (which falls in the rejection region) is less than our alpha level of .05 which is another way of determining that we can reject $H_0$.

| | A | B | C | D | E | F | G |
|---|---|---|---|---|---|---|---|
| 1 | Anova: Single Factor | | | | | | |
| 2 | | | | | | | |
| 3 | SUMMARY | | | | | | |
| 4 | Groups | Count | Sum | Average | Variance | | |
| 5 | Online Chat | 5 | 20 | 4 | 1.5 | | |
| 6 | Pets | 5 | 45 | 9 | 3.5 | | |
| 7 | Students | 5 | 35 | 7 | 7.5 | | |
| 8 | | | | | | | |
| 9 | | | | | | | |
| 10 | ANOVA | | | | | | |
| 11 | Source of Variation | SS | df | MS | F | P-value | F crit |
| 12 | Between Groups | 63.3333333 | 2 | 31.6666667 | 7.6 | 0.00737351 | 3.88529383 |
| 13 | Within Groups | 50 | 12 | 4.16666667 | | | |
| 14 | | | | | | | |
| 15 | Total | 113.333333 | 14 | | | | |
| 16 | | | | | | | |

### Additional Practice Problems

**Answers to odd numbered problems are in Appendix C at the end of the book.**

1. What statistical test should be used if we want to compare the means for several different groups? Why is this test more appropriate than using $t$ tests to compare two groups at a time?

2. In a one-way ANOVA, if $df_{bet}$ = 4 and $df_{wi}$ = 20, how many groups were involved in the study and how many subjects participated?

3. The results of a one-way ANOVA with $\alpha$ = .05 were reported as follows:

| Source | SS | df | MS | F | p |
|---|---|---|---|---|---|
| Between-treatments | 1036 | 2 | 518 | .94 | > .05 |
| Within-treatment | 8272 | 15 | 551.47 | | |
| Total | 9308 | 17 | | | |

   a. How many groups were involved in the study?
   b. How many subjects participated?
   c. Was the null hypothesis rejected?
   d. Should a post hoc test be conducted? Why or why not?

4. What is eta squared and what information does it provide?

5. What does it mean if the null hypothesis of a one-way ANOVA is rejected? What action should be taken next?

6. A one-way ANOVA was conducted at $\alpha$ = .01. The study involved 4 different groups with 10 subjects in each. $F_{obt}$ = 4.14, $df_{wi}$ = 36, and $df_{bet}$ = 3. Can the null hypothesis be rejected?

7. A one-way ANOVA was conducted at $\alpha$ = .05. The study involved three different groups with 12 subjects in each. The means for each group were as follows: $M_1$ = 10.92, $M_2$ = 13.83, and $M_3$ = 14.92. The sum of squares values are shown in the table below.

| Source | SS | df | MS | F | p |
|---|---|---|---|---|---|
| Between-treatments | 102.72 | | | | |
| Within-treatment | 229.50 | | | | |
| Total | 332.22 | | | | |

   a. Assuming $\alpha$ = .05, complete the rest of the table and write a verbal conclusion.
   b. Conduct a Tukey's HSD and indicate which means differ significantly.

8. The summary table below includes partial values for the results of a one-way ANOVA. Complete the rest of the table where indicated with a blank line.

| Source | SS | df | MS | F |
|---|---|---|---|---|
| Between-treatments | _____ | 2 | 324.9 | _____ |
| Within-treatment | 584.2 | ___ | _____ | |
| Total | _____ | 29 | | |

9. The summary table below includes partial values for the results of a one-way ANOVA. Complete the rest of the table where indicated with a blank line.

| Source | SS | df | MS | F |
|---|---|---|---|---|
| Between-treatments | 129.08 | _____ | _____ | _____ |
| Within-treatment | _____ | 21 | _____ | |
| Total | 295.83 | 23 | | |

10. Given the information below for three separate studies, determine $F_{crit}$ and decide if $H_0$ should be rejected.

| | Number of Groups | No. of Subjects in each Group | $F_{obt}$ | $\alpha$ | $F_{crit}$ | Reject $H_0$ Y/N |
|---|---|---|---|---|---|---|
| a. | 3 | 10 | 2.81 | .05 | | |
| b. | 4 | 12 | 16.21 | .01 | | |
| c. | 5 | 7 | 4.76 | .05 | | |

11. For the following scores involving a study with three different groups, calculate $SS_{tot}$, $SS_{wi}$, and $SS_{bet}$.

| Group 1 | Group 2 | Group 3 |
|---|---|---|
| 12 | 8 | 6 |
| 14 | 10 | 3 |
| 10 | 9 | 7 |
| 11 | 8 | 5 |

12. Conduct a one-way ANOVA for the scores below using an $\alpha = .05$. If appropriate, follow up with Tukey's *HSD*.

| Group 1 | Group 2 | Group 3 |
|---|---|---|
| 5 | 6 | 7 |
| 6 | 8 | 9 |
| 8 | 9 | 8 |
| 9 | 10 | 11 |
| 7 | 8 | 6 |

13. A psychologist is studying the effects of noise on concentration. The scores below are the number of errors made on a basic vocabulary test under varying levels of noise. Conduct a one-way ANOVA using an $\alpha = .05$. Follow up with Tukey's *HSD*. (Hint: To make sure that the means for all groups are compared, start with the mean for Group 1 and compare it with all other group means. Then move to Group 2; since it has already been compared with Group 1, it will only need to be compared with the remaining Groups 3

and 4. Now move to Group 3; since it has already been compared with Groups 1 and 2, it will only need to be compared with Group 4.)

| Quiet ($X_1$) | Low Noise ($X_2$) | Moderate Noise ($X_3$) | Loud Noise ($X_4$) |
|---|---|---|---|
| 2 | 3 | 4 | 6 |
| 0 | 1 | 2 | 4 |
| 1 | 2 | 2 | 4 |
| 1 | 1 | 2 | 3 |

## Note

1   There are several post hoc tests that do not require that sample sizes be equal. These can be found in most intermediate and advanced statistics textbooks.

# Factorial Analysis of Variance

## FACTORIAL DESIGN

Previously, we looked at a one-way ANOVA for situations in which we wanted to compare the means for more than two groups. But, although more than two groups were investigated at the same time, only one independent variable was being tested. In actuality, people are often affected by many different variables at the same time that combine to influence their behavior. A ***factorial analysis of variance*** (or factorial ANOVA) allows us to examine such situations.

### Factors and Levels

In research, a ***factor*** refers to any independent variable that can be manipulated at several different levels. The notation for a factorial ANOVA describes how many independent variables (or factors) are being used as well as the number of levels at which each factor is presented. A two-way ANOVA with two independent variables, each being presented at three levels, would be notated as a $3 \times 3$ ANOVA. A three-way ANOVA with three independent variables, the first with three levels, the second with two levels, and the third with three levels would be notated as $3 \times 2 \times 3$. How many numbers there are reflect how many independent variables there are. The value of each number reflects how many levels (or conditions) there are for each of those independent variables. In this chapter, we will focus on two-factor, independent samples designs with equal $n$'s in all conditions. The independent samples design is also referred to as between-subjects designs, akin to the between-subjects design of the independent samples $t$ test and independent samples one-way ANOVA.

### For Example

Do you remember our problem from the last chapter in which we examined if interactive activities (independent variable) influence ratings of life satisfaction (dependent variable) in older people? We looked at three different levels of the independent variable, including (1) an online chat group, (2) caring for pets, and (3) talking with students. Suppose we want to include a second independent variable, personal achievement activities, which we also want to present at three different levels: (1) painting, (2) memorizing and reciting poetry, and (3) writing short stories. You should recognize this as a $3 \times 3$ ANOVA with two independent variables, each being manipulated at three levels each. Such a study would allow us to determine:

- How the different types of *interactive activities* affect degree of life satisfaction.
- How the different types of *personal achievement activities* affect degree of life satisfaction.
- How the different *combinations of interactive activities and personal achievement activities* affect life satisfaction.

The first two situations above would be referred to as "main effects" and the last situation would be referred to as an "interaction." These situations will be discussed after the "Your Turn" exercise below.

 **Your Turn!**

**I. Factors and Levels**

A. How many independent variables are involved in a $4 \times 3 \times 2$ ANOVA?

B. A memory researcher has been studying the chemical properties of a new smart drug (i.e., a nootropic) and has arrived at a chemical composition that has shown promising results in enhancing memory. She is now ready to further her research to include not only three different dosages of the medication (5 mg, 10 mg, and 12 mg), but she also wants to explore how memory might be impacted by listening to music in combination with the medications. In particular, she is interested in the genres of jazz, classical, country, and hip hop.

1. What is the dependent variable?

2. What are the independent variables and how many levels of each are being investigated?

3. What is the correct notation for this study?

## MAIN EFFECTS AND INTERACTIONS

A **main effect** refers to the effect of a single independent variable (factor) on a dependent variable. In a one-way ANOVA, there is only one main effect since there is only one independent variable. In a factorial ANOVA, there are as many main effects as there are factors. Main effects are determined by simply examining the differences among the means for each separate factor. They provide the same information that would be attained by conducting separate one-way ANOVAs for each independent variable.

In addition to main effects, a factorial ANOVA also examines how one independent variable is affected by different levels of other independent variables. These are referred to as *interaction effects*. For example, many prescription medications have side effects. When taken alone, these side effects may not be serious but, when taken in combination with other

**Tip!**

> The term "main effect" is sometimes misinterpreted as meaning "significant effect." The terms are not equivalent. As we have learned in previous chapters, determining significance requires the use of statistical tests to make sure that the differences between means are not just chance differences due to random sampling error.

medications, the effects could be quite harmful. The particular combinations of these medications may interact to produce effects that are different from the side effects of either of the medications acting alone.

Let's look at a hypothetical example. Food scientists from Ancient World Spice Company have been experimenting with a newly discovered spice, yameric, harvested from the root of a yameric tree. Initial taste tests have been favorable and the researchers are now ready to try the spice in various recipes. For the current study, the same vegetable casserole dish is prepared using two different vegetables, cauliflower in one and eggplant in the other. The amount of the spice added was varied under three different conditions, ½ teaspoon, 1 teaspoon, and 1½ teaspoons. Notice that there are two factors involved – the amount of the spice (Factor A) and the vegetable (Factor B). The assignment of factors to A or B variables is arbitrary. The dependent variable for this example is the flavor ratings of the casserole dishes by the sample participants under these varying conditions. Higher scores represent more favorable ratings.

Main effects and interactions can be illustrated via either tables or graphs. For each, we will first consider the situation in which there is no interaction between the amount of the spice and type of vegetable. We will then look at a table and a graph that show an interaction between the two variables.

### Table and Graph With No Interaction

In Table 14.1, means for the dependent variable (flavor ratings) are shown for each condition in the relevant cells. In addition, the mean of the means for each level of the factors is shown in the margins. These margin means are helpful in understanding main effects. The participants who ate the eggplant dish seasoned with yameric gave an overall mean rating of $M_{B_1} = 6$. The overall mean rating for those who ate the cauliflower dish was $M_{B_2} = 8$. The

*Table 14.1* No Interaction

| | | Amount of Spice (A) | | | |
|---|---|---|---|---|---|
| | | ½ t. $(A_1)$ | 1 t. $(A_2)$ | 1½ t. $(A_3)$ | |
| **Vegetable (B)** | Eggplant $(B_1)$ | 3 | 6 | 9 | $M_{B_1} = 6$ |
| | Cauliflower $(B_2)$ | 5 | 8 | 11 | $M_{B_2} = 8$ |
| | | $M_{A_1} = 4$ | $M_{A_2} = 7$ | $M_{A_3} = 10$ | |

difference between these margin means indicates the main effect for Factor B, which would be subjected to a statistical test to determine if the difference is significant. In a similar fashion, the differences between the margin means for the varying amounts of the spices added to the dish, Factor A (e.g., $M_{A_1} = 4$, $M_{A_2} = 7$, $M_{A_3} = 10$), would be compared to determine if the main effect for that factor is significant.

Besides checking for the significance of main effects, we also want to determine if there is any interaction between Factors A and B. That is, does the effect of one independent variable differ depending on the level of the other independent variable? For our example, does the effect of the amount of yameric that was added to the recipe change depending on which vegetable was used? One way to look for an interaction is to examine how the cell means change across different levels of one factor in comparison to the other factor. For Factor B, notice that subjects who ate the recipe prepared with cauliflower consistently gave 2-point higher ratings than those who ate the same dish prepared with eggplant. This was true regardless of the *amount* of the spice that was added (Factor A). Similarly, increasing the amount of the spice (Factor A) consistently increased the ratings by 3 points regardless of *which* vegetable was used (Factor B). Thus, the effect of one independent variable did not depend on the level of the other independent variable and there was no interaction.

Information from tables is often more easily understood by plotting the means of the dependent variable on line graphs. The dependent variable is usually shown along the y-axis in a graph. One of the independent variables will be shown along the x-axis and the other one will be shown as lines on the graph. In Graph 14.1 for our example, mean flavor ratings are shown along the y-axis, the different levels of the spice are shown along the x-axis, and the two different types of vegetables are shown as lines on the graph.

Notice that the lines in the graph are parallel, reflecting the 2-point difference in flavor ratings between the different vegetables across all levels of the amount of spice that was added. Parallel lines where the data points for each line are approximately equidistant apart suggest that there is no interaction between the two independent variables. Lines that are not parallel, or that cross, may be indicative of an interaction between Factors A and B.

**Tip!**

> Lines that are not exactly parallel do not automatically imply an interaction. Their slight non-parallelism could be due to random sampling error.

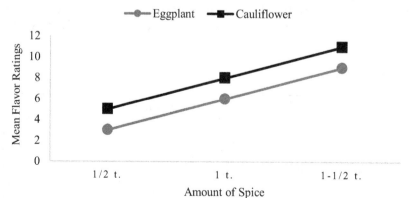

**Graph 14.1** No Interaction

## Table and Graph With an Interaction

Now, let's look at the same example except that we will change the flavor ratings in a way that suggests an interaction. In Table 14.2, notice that cell means for eggplant (Factor $B_1$) *increase* by 3 points as the amount of the spice increases (Factor A). However, cell means for cauliflower ($B_2$) *decrease* by 1 point as the spice increases. This infers an interaction because the effect that one independent variable has on the dependent variable depends on the level of the other independent variable.

The information from the table is illustrated in Graph 14.2. Note that the lines cross and are not parallel. Thus, an interaction is suggested. Graphs can help in conceptualizing whether or not an interaction is present. But, as in the past, determining whether the interaction is significant is something that would have to be determined by means of statistical tests.

## PARTITIONING THE VARIANCE FOR THE *F*-STATISTIC

In the last chapter, you learned that the statistic used for ANOVA is the *F*-statistic, which is a ratio of variances. Recall that total variance was broken down into two different kinds, between-treatments variance which was attributed to treatment (i.e., the effect of the independent variable) and within-treatment variance which was attributed to error. Between-treatments variance examines the differences between the different groups as a result of being treated differently. Within-treatment variance represents the variability among individuals in a particular group who are all treated the same. The same two sources of variance also apply to a two-way ANOVA. However, since we now have more than one independent variable, between-treatments variance is further partitioned into the variance associated with Factor A, the variance associated with Factor B, and the variance associated with the interaction between Factors A and B. Figure 14.1 illustrates this breakdown.

*Table 14.2* Interaction

| | | Amount of Spice (A) | | | |
|---|---|---|---|---|---|
| | | ½ t. ($A_1$) | 1 t. ($A_2$) | 1½ t. ($A_3$) | |
| Vegetable (B) | Eggplant ($B_1$) | 3 | 6 | 9 | $M_{B_1} = 6$ |
| | Cauliflower ($B_2$) | 5 | 4 | 3 | $M_{B_2} = 4$ |
| | | $M_{A_1} = 4$ | $M_{A_2} = 5$ | $M_{A_3} = 6$ | |

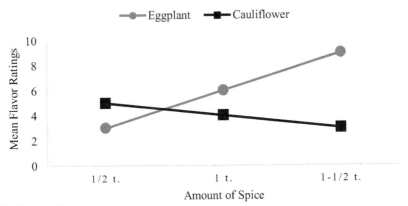

**Graph 14.2** Interaction

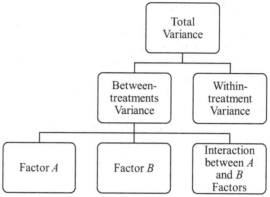

**Figure 14.1** – Partitioning the Variance

As a reminder, the formulations of the $F$-statistic that we used in the last chapter were as follows:

$$F = \frac{\text{Treatment Variance}}{\text{Error Variance}} = \frac{MS_{bet}}{MS_{wi}}$$

Two-way ANOVAs require calculating three different $F$-statistics, one for each component of between-treatments variance. Recall that it takes quite a few steps before we can actually compute the $F$-statistic, first and foremost being the calculations for the different sum of squares values. The good news, however, is that you are already familiar with most of these steps.

## HYPOTHESIS TESTING FOR A FACTORIAL ANOVA

The number of hypotheses to be tested in a factorial ANOVA depends on the number of factors involved. A separate hypothesis test for each factor is needed to determine if any of their main effects are significant. In addition, tests for determining any and all significant interactions between the factors are also necessary. The more factors involved, the more significance tests required. Since we are limiting our application in this chapter to two factors, we will be conducting three significance tests, one for each of the main effects of Factors $A$ and $B$, and one for the interaction between Factors $A$ and $B$. The null and alternative hypotheses for a factorial ANOVA follow the same line of reasoning as other significance tests and will be written as indicated below.

- Main effect for Factor $A$:

  $H_0 : \mu_{A_1} = \mu_{A_2} = \mu_{A_k}$
  $H_1$: Some $\mu_A$s are not equal

- Main effect for Factor $B$:

  $H_0 : \mu_{B_1} = \mu_{B_2} = \mu_{B_k}$
  $H_1$: Some $\mu_B$s are not equal

- Interaction between Factors $A$ and $B$

  $H_0$: Factors $A$ and $B$ do not have a significant interaction.
  $H_1$: Factors $A$ and $B$ have a significant interaction.

## SAMPLE RESEARCH QUESTION WITHOUT AN INTERACTION

A sleep researcher is studying the effects of sleep deprivation on various age groups. For the current study, she uses two groups, teenagers and adults, and measures the number of errors made on a math test after either 3, 6, or 9 hours of sleep. You should recognize this as a $2 \times 3$ ANOVA. One independent variable, age group (Factor $B$), is manipulated at two levels, and the other independent variable, hours of sleep (Factor $A$), is manipulated at three levels. The dependent variable is the number of errors made on the math test. The data for the study are shown in Table 14.3.

*Table 14.3* Sleep Deprivation Study

| | | Hours of Sleep (Factor $A$) | | | | | | |
|---|---|---|---|---|---|---|---|---|
| | | $A_1$ 3 Hours | | $A_2$ 6 Hours | | $A_3$ 9 Hours | | |
| | | $X_1$ | $X_1^2$ | $X_2$ | $X_2^2$ | $X_3$ | $X_3^2$ | |
| | | 8 | 64 | 4 | 16 | 2 | 4 | |
| | | 7 | 49 | 6 | 36 | 1 | 1 | |
| | | 6 | 36 | 5 | 25 | 3 | 9 | |
| | $B_1$ Teenagers | $\Sigma X_{A_1B_1} = 21$ | | $\Sigma X_{A_2B_1} = 15$ | | $\Sigma X_{A_3B_1} = 6$ | | $\Sigma X_{B_1} = 42$ |
| | | $\Sigma X_{A_1B_1}^2 = 149$ | | $\Sigma X_{A_2B_1}^2 = 77$ | | $\Sigma X_{A_3B_1}^2 = 14$ | | $\Sigma X_{B_1}^2 = 240$ |
| | | $n_{A_1B_1} = 3$ | | $n_{A_2B_1} = 3$ | | $n_{A_3B_1} = 3$ | | $N_{B_1} = 9$ |
| | | $M_{A_1B_1} = 7$ | | $M_{A_2B_1} = 5$ | | $M_{A_3B_1} = 2$ | | $M_{B_1} = 4.67$ |
| | | 4 | 16 | 3 | 9 | 2 | 4 | |
| | | 3 | 9 | 2 | 4 | 0 | 0 | |
| | | 2 | 4 | 1 | 1 | 1 | 1 | |
| | $B_2$ Adults | $\Sigma X_{A_1B_2} = 9$ | | $\Sigma X_{A_2B_2} = 6$ | | $\Sigma X_{A_3B_2} = 3$ | | $\Sigma X_{B_2} = 18$ |
| | | $\Sigma X_{A_1B_2}^2 = 29$ | | $\Sigma X_{A_2B_2}^2 = 14$ | | $\Sigma X_{A_3B_2}^2 = 5$ | | $\Sigma X_{B_2}^2 = 48$ |
| | | $n_{A_1B_2} = 3$ | | $n_{A_2B_2} = 3$ | | $n_{A_3B_2} = 3$ | | $N_{B_2} = 9$ |
| | | $M_{A_1B_2} = 3$ | | $M_{A_2B_2} = 2$ | | $M_{A_3B_2} = 1$ | | $M_{B_2} = 2$ |
| | | $\Sigma X_{A_1} = 30$ | | $\Sigma X_{A_2} = 21$ | | $\Sigma X_{A_3} = 9$ | | $\Sigma X_{tot} = 60$ |
| | | $\Sigma X_{A_1}^2 = 178$ | | $\Sigma X_{A_2}^2 = 91$ | | $\Sigma X_{A_3}^2 = 19$ | | $\Sigma X_{tot}^2 = 288$ |
| | | $N_{A_1} = 6$ | | $N_{A_2} = 6$ | | $N_{A_3} = 6$ | | $N_{tot} = 18$ |
| | | $M_{A_1} = 5$ | | $M_{A_2} = 3.5$ | | $M_{A_3} = 1.5$ | | $M_{tot} = 3.33$ |

Age Group (Factor $B$)

All of the notations should look familiar to you from previous procedures. Just be sure that you pay attention to subscripts.

- Each treatment group in factorial ANOVA is referred to as a cell, and each cell is identified by its own subscript. For example, the subscript $A_1B_1$ refers to the treatment group involving teenagers ($B_1$) who received 3 hours of sleep ($A_1$). The subscript $A_3B_2$ refers to the treatment group involving adults ($B_2$) who received 9 hours of sleep ($A_3$). In the calculations for a factorial ANOVA, discussed next, where the subscript "$_{cell}$" is used, the calculations needed for each of the individual cells, or treatment groups, will be performed.
- The values in the row and column margins which are identified by subscripts with a single letter and number represent the values across the various levels of each of the factors. For example, $\Sigma X_{A_1}$ refers to the total of the scores for all of the participants (both teenagers and adults) who received 3 hours of sleep (level one of Factor A). $\Sigma X_{B_2}$ refers to the total of the scores for all of the adults in the study (level two of Factor B). These subscripts will be used when calculating sum of squares values for Factor A ($SS_A$) and Factor B ($SS_B$) below.
- Finally, the subscript "$_{tot}$" represents values across all treatment groups. Adding all of the scores for all levels of A (i.e., $A_1$, $A_2$, and $A_3$) will give you $\Sigma X_{tot}$ (or you could add all of the levels of B and arrive at the same value).

With these understandings, we are now ready to perform the calculations for our sample research question.

## THE CALCULATIONS

The calculations needed for conducting a two-way ANOVA, independent samples design, are the very same calculations as those required for a one-way ANOVA except that there are more of them. In general, we will need to calculate sum of squares values, degrees of freedom, mean square values, and $F$-statistics.

### Sum of Squares (SS)

As with a one-way ANOVA, we will need $SS_{total}$, $SS_{wi}$, and $SS_{bet}$. You are familiar with the formulas for $SS$. We will simply change the notations to reflect the current statistical procedures.

- $SS_{total}$ refers to the total amount of variability from all sources. You may recall that $SS_{total}$ itself is not needed for the $F$-statistic, but it provides a useful check on our calculations because $SS_{wi}$ and $SS_{bet} = SS_{total}$.

$$SS_{total} = \Sigma X_{tot}^2 - \frac{\left(\Sigma X_{tot}\right)^2}{N_{tot}}$$

$$= 288 - \frac{(60)^2}{18}$$

$$= 88$$

- $SS_{wi}$ refers to the variability within each group due to individual differences and experimental error.

$$SS_{wi} = \Sigma \left[ \Sigma X_{cell}^2 - \frac{\left( \Sigma X_{cell} \right)^2}{n_{cell}} \right]$$

$$= \left( 149 - \frac{(21)^2}{3} \right) + \left( 77 - \frac{(15)^2}{3} \right) + \left( 14 - \frac{(6)^2}{3} \right) + \left( 29 - \frac{(9)^2}{3} \right) + \left( 14 - \frac{(6)^2}{3} \right) + \left( 5 - \frac{(3)^2}{3} \right)$$

$$= (149 - 147) + (77 - 75) + (14 - 12) + (29 - 27) + (14 - 12) + (5 - 3)$$

$$= 2 + 2 + 2 + 2 + 2 + 2$$

$$= 12$$

- $SS_{bet}$ refers to the variability between the different groups due, not only to individual differences and experimental error, but also due to Factor $A$, Factor $B$, and the interaction between Factors $A$ and $B$. Thus, in addition to computing $SS_{bet}$, we will break it down into its component parts and calculate $SS_A$, $SS_B$, and $SS_{AB}$.

$$SS_{bet} = \Sigma \left[ \frac{\left( \Sigma X_{cell} \right)^2}{n_{cell}} \right] - \frac{\left( \Sigma X_{tot} \right)^2}{N_{tot}}$$

$$= \frac{(21)^2}{3} + \frac{(15)^2}{3} + \frac{(6)^2}{3} + \frac{(9)^2}{3} + \frac{(6)^2}{3} + \frac{(3)^2}{3} - \frac{(60)^2}{18}$$

$$= 147 + 75 + 12 + 27 + 12 + 3 - 200$$

$$= 76$$

- $SS_A$ measures the amount of variability between Factor $A$ treatment groups while ignoring Factor $B$. In the formula, the column totals are used for each level of Factor $A$ before subtracting the term at the end.

$$SS_A = \frac{\left( \Sigma X_{A_1} \right)^2}{N_{A_1}} + \frac{\left( \Sigma X_{A_2} \right)^2}{N_{A_2}} + \frac{\left( \Sigma X_{A_3} \right)^2}{N_{A_3}} - \frac{\left( \Sigma X_{tot} \right)^2}{N_{tot}}$$

$$= \frac{(30)^2}{6} + \frac{(21)^2}{6} + \frac{(9)^2}{6} - \frac{(60)^2}{18}$$

$$= 150 + 73.5 + 13.5 - 200$$

$$= 37$$

- Similarly, $SS_B$ will ignore Factor $A$, and row totals, rather than column totals, will be used for the different levels of Factor $B$.

$$SS_B = \frac{\left( \Sigma X_{B_1} \right)^2}{N_{B_1}} + \frac{\left( \Sigma X_{B_2} \right)^2}{N_{B_2}} - \frac{\left( \Sigma X_{tot} \right)^2}{N_{tot}}$$

$$= \frac{(42)^2}{9} + \frac{(18)^2}{9} - \frac{(60)^2}{18}$$

$$= 196 + 36 - 200$$

$$= 32$$

- Since between-treatments variability ($SS_{bet}$) is made up of the variability due to Factor $A$ ($SS_A$), Factor $B$ ($SS_B$), and the interaction between Factors $A$ and $B$ ($SS_{AB}$), the easiest way to compute $SS_{AB}$ is by means of subtraction. If we subtract $SS_A$ and $SS_B$ from $SS_{bet}$, what remains will give us $SS_{AB}$. Thus, we will use the following formula:

$$SS_{AB} = SS_{bet} - SS_A - SS_B$$
$$= 76 - 37 - 32$$
$$= 7$$

Let's make sure that we are on the right track by verifying that $SS_{wi} + SS_{bet} = SS_{tot}$. For our calculations: $12 + 76 = 88$. We are now ready to determine the degrees of freedom required for a factorial ANOVA.

## Degrees of Freedom

In addition to a value for total degrees of freedom ($df_{tot}$), we will also need to calculate $df_{wi}$ and three $df_{bet}$ values, one associated with each of the sources of between-treatments variability (i.e., $df_{bet(A)}$, $df_{bet(B)}$, and $df_{bet(AB)}$). The particular computations that we will use for determining the degrees of freedom for a two-way ANOVA are specified below.

$$df_{tot} = N_{tot} - 1$$
$$df_{bet(A)} = A - 1$$
$$df_{bet(B)} = B - 1$$
$$df_{bet(AB)} = (A - 1)(B - 1)$$
$$df_{wi} = N_{tot} - k$$

where $A$ = number of levels of Factor $A$
$B$ = number of levels of Factor $B$
$k$ = number of groups in the study

For our data:

$$df_{tot} = 18 - 1 = 17$$
$$df_{bet(A)} = 3 - 1 = 2$$
$$df_{bet(B)} = 2 - 1 = 1$$
$$df_{bet(AB)} = (3 - 1)(2 - 1) = 2$$
$$df_{wi} = 18 - 6 = 12$$

As with a one-way ANOVA, $df_{tot}$ is not needed but serves as a useful check on our work since $df_{bet(A)} + df_{bet(B)} + df_{bet(AB)} + df_{wi}$ should equal $df_{tot}$. So, let's check our calculations for $df_{tot}$:

$$df_{tot} = df_{bet(A)} + df_{bet(B)} + df_{bet(AB)} + df_{wi}$$
$$= 2 + 1 + 2 + 12$$
$$= 17$$

## Mean Square

Since we will need to calculate an $F$-statistic for each component of the between-treatments variance, we will need three between-treatments mean square values – $MS_A$, $MS_B$, and $MS_{AB}$. In addition, a within-treatments mean square ($MS_{wi}$) will be required for the denominator of the $F$-ratio. These calculations are as follows:

$$MS_A = \frac{SS_A}{df_{bet(A)}} = \frac{37}{2} = 18.5$$

$$MS_B = \frac{SS_B}{df_{bet(B)}} = \frac{32}{1} = 32$$

$$MS_{AB} = \frac{SS_{AB}}{df_{bet(AB)}} = \frac{7}{2} = 3.5$$

$$MS_{wi} = \frac{SS_{wi}}{df_{wi}} = \frac{12}{12} = 1$$

## F-Statistic

Finally, we are in a position to compute the $F$-statistics for this problem:

$$F_A = \frac{MS_A}{MS_{wi}} = \frac{18.5}{1} = 18.5$$

$$F_B = \frac{MS_B}{MS_{wi}} = \frac{32}{1} = 32$$

$$F_{AB} = \frac{MS_{AB}}{MS_{wi}} = \frac{3.5}{1} = 3.5$$

We will need to compare each of our obtained $F$-values with the associated critical values of $F$ in order to determine whether our null hypotheses should be rejected. To do so, we will consult the $F$-distribution table. We are using $\alpha = .05$. $Df_{wi}$ will be the same for all $F$-values but we must use the appropriate $df_{bet}$ value associated with each $F$-statistic.

- For $F_A$, $df_{wi} = 12$, $df_{bet(A)} = 2$. Thus, $F_{crit} = 3.88$.
- For $F_B$, $df_{wi} = 12$, $df_{bet(B)} = 1$. Thus, $F_{crit} = 4.75$.
- For $F_{AB}$, $df_{wi} = 12$, $df_{bet(AB)} = 2$. Thus, $F_{crit} = 3.88$.

## Interpreting Main Effects and Interactions

When interpreting the results of a two-way ANOVA, it is best to first look at the results for any interaction because this result will determine how to proceed with interpreting the main effects. As mentioned earlier, this is facilitated by creating a graph of the cell means. In Graph 14.3, you can see that the lines tend towards being parallel, suggesting no significant interaction.

If your calculations show a non-significant interaction and significant main effects, the main effects can be interpreted in the same way as with a one-way ANOVA. Each factor can be evaluated independently by means of post hoc tests. However, if there is a significant interaction then the main effects cannot be interpreted directly, even if their obtained $F$-value exceeds $F_{crit}$. This is because the interaction makes it necessary to qualify the main effects. Remember that if a significant interaction exists, this means that the effect that one independent variable has on the dependent variable depends on the level of the other independent variable. Thus, the factors cannot be interpreted independently because they are creating a combined effect. This point will come up again with a later example where an interaction is present.

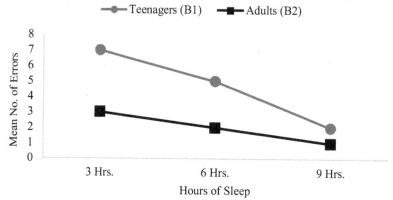

**Graph 14.3** Sleep Deprivation Study

*Table 14.4* Summary Table for Sleep Deprivation Study

| Source | SS | df | MS | F | p |
|--------|-----|-----|------|------|--------|
| Factor A | 37 | 2 | 18.5 | 18.5 | < .05 |
| Factor B | 32 | 1 | 32 | 32 | < .05 |
| Interaction | 7 | 2 | 3.5 | 3.5 | > .05 |
| Within | 12 | 12 | 1 | | |
| Total | 88 | 17 | | | |

As we did before with a one-way ANOVA, we will arrange our obtained values into a summary table as shown in Table 14.4. In this case, the table includes values for SS, df, MS, $F_{obt}$, and p-values for each source of between-treatments variance (i.e., Factors B, A, and the interaction between B and A). The p-values are those associated with our alpha level that will help us to determine whether or not to reject the null hypothesis. Within-treatment variance, which is the variance associated with error, will only include values for SS, df, and MS.

For the current problem, our obtained $F_{AB}$-value was 3.5 and $F_{crit}$ was 3.88. Since $F_{AB}$ does not exceed $F_{crit}$, we can conclude that there was no significant interaction between Factors A and B and we will fail to reject the null hypothesis associated with the interaction. Since that is the case, Factors A and B can each be interpreted separately. For any of the individual factors that have more than two levels and that show significance, researchers will usually follow up with a post hoc test similar to Tukey's HSD that you learned previously. For our purposes here, we will simply note the areas of significance. For Factor A, hours of sleep, our obtained F-value was 18.5 and $F_{crit}$ was 3.88. We can therefore reject the null hypothesis for Factor A and conclude that increasing the number of hours slept resulted in significantly fewer math errors. For Factor B, age group, our obtained F-value was 32 and $F_{crit}$ was 4.75. Thus, the null hypothesis for Factor B can also be rejected and we can conclude that teenagers made significantly more math errors than adults.

## Effect Size

In a factorial ANOVA, an effect size will be calculated for each of the significant results. The same statistic that we used for a one-way ANOVA, eta squared ($\eta^2$), can be used here as well.

In this case, however, three sources of between-treatments variance are possible and so our eta squared formulas will be as follows:

$$\eta_A^2 = \frac{SS_A}{SS_{tot}}$$

$$\eta_B^2 = \frac{SS_B}{SS_{tot}}$$

$$\eta_{AB}^2 = \frac{SS_{AB}}{SS_{tot}}$$

For our problem, since only Factors A and B were significant, only the effect sizes for these variables need to be considered.

For Factor A: $\eta_A^2 = \frac{37}{88} = .42$

For Factor B: $\eta_B^2 = \frac{32}{88} = .36$

The effect size obtained by eta squared for Factor A suggests that 42% of the total variance in the number of errors made can be explained by the number of hours slept. Similarly, 36% of the total variance can be explained by age group (Factor B). In each case, the effect size is substantial.

A drawback to using eta squared in a factorial ANOVA is that, as more variables are added, the proportion of variance accounted for by a single factor automatically decreases. This makes it difficult to interpret the contribution of one factor to the total amount of variability. This problem is sometimes addressed by computing a partial eta squared value which involves subtracting other sources of variability than that being considered from the total variability before calculating $\eta^2$.[1]

However, another effect size value, called omega squared ($\omega^2$), is often recommended as a supplement to $\eta^2$, especially for small samples. The formulas for omega squared are:

$$\omega_A^2 = \frac{SS_A - (df_A)(MS_{wi})}{SS_{tot} + MS_{wi}}$$

$$\omega_B^2 = \frac{SS_B - (df_B)(MS_{wi})}{SS_{tot} + MS_{wi}}$$

$$\omega_{AB}^2 = \frac{SS_{AB} - (df_{AB})(MS_{wi})}{SS_{tot} + MS_{wi}}$$

For our problem, again we need only to consider the omega squared values for Factors A and B separately:

For Factor A: $\omega_A^2 = \frac{37 - (2)(1)}{88 + 1} = .39$

For Factor B: $\omega_B^2 = \frac{32 - (1)(1)}{88 + 1} = .35$

☞ **Your Turn!** 👈

## II. Comprehension Checks for Factorial ANOVA

A. Describe what the following values represent:

$SS_{wi}$:

$SS_{bet}$:

$SS_A$:

$SS_{AB}$:

B. Variance, or mean square, is determined by dividing _____
by _____.

C. In order to reject $H_0$, between-treatments variance must be _____
(larger/smaller) than within-treatment variance.

D. If $df_{bet(A)} = 3$, $df_{bet(B)} = 2$, and $df_{wi} = 36$, how many groups were involved in the study
and how many subjects participated?

E. If results of a factorial ANOVA indicate a significant main effect of Factor $B$ as well
a significant interaction between Factors $A$ and $B$, why should the main effect of
Factor $B$ not be interpreted directly?

---

You can see that the effect sizes obtained by omega squared are somewhat smaller but still sizable. There is a tendency for eta squared to overestimate the size of an effect while omega squared tends to be more conservative.

## SAMPLE RESEARCH QUESTION WITH AN INTERACTION

Now that you have worked through the process of conducting a two-way ANOVA, let's look at an example that involves an interaction using our four-step hypothesis testing procedure.

A political scientist is studying whether interest in politics differs between males and females and if that interest changes as a function of education. She recruits 24 individuals, half male and half female. Four participants from each gender were randomly selected for each group from populations of high school graduates, individuals with some college education (between one and three years), and university graduates with a four-year degree. The Political Interest Survey (PIS) survey was administered to all participants. Higher scores reflect greater political interest. This is a 3 × 2 ANOVA with two independent variables. One independent variable, level of education (Factor $A$), has three levels and the

*Table 14.5* Political Interest Study

| | | Level of Education (Factor $A$) | | | | | | |
|---|---|---|---|---|---|---|---|---|
| | | $A_1$ High School | | $A_2$ Some College | | $A_3$ University | | |
| | | $X_1$ | $X_1^2$ | $X_2$ | $X_2^2$ | $X_3$ | $X_3^2$ | |
| | | 8 | 64 | 18 | 324 | 20 | 400 | |
| | | 9 | 81 | 16 | 256 | 18 | 324 | |
| | | 10 | 100 | 14 | 196 | 16 | 256 | |
| | | 13 | 169 | 8 | 64 | 14 | 196 | |
| | $B_1$ Females | $\Sigma X_{A_1B_1} = 40$ | | $\Sigma X_{A_2B_1} = 56$ | | $\Sigma X_{A_3B_1} = 68$ | | $\Sigma X_{B_1} = 164$ |
| | | $\Sigma X_{A_1B_1}^2 = 414$ | | $\Sigma X_{A_2B_1}^2 = 840$ | | $\Sigma X_{A_3B_1}^2 = 1176$ | | $\Sigma X_{B_1}^2 = 2430$ |
| | | $n_{A_1B_1} = 4$ | | $n_{A_2B_1} = 4$ | | $n_{A_3B_1} = 4$ | | $N_{B_1} = 12$ |
| | | $M_{A_1B_1} = 10$ | | $M_{A_2B_1} = 14$ | | $M_{A_3B_1} = 17$ | | $M_{B_1} = 13.67$ |
| | | 10 | 100 | 13 | 169 | 28 | 784 | |
| | | 8 | 64 | 13 | 169 | 25 | 625 | |
| | | 7 | 49 | 12 | 144 | 23 | 529 | |
| | | 7 | 49 | 10 | 100 | 20 | 400 | |
| | $B_2$ Males | $\Sigma X_{A_1B_2} = 32$ | | $\Sigma X_{A_2B_2} = 48$ | | $\Sigma X_{A_3B_2} = 96$ | | $\Sigma X_{B_2} = 176$ |
| | | $\Sigma X_{A_1B_2}^2 = 262$ | | $\Sigma X_{A_2B_2}^2 = 582$ | | $\Sigma X_{A_3B_2}^2 = 2338$ | | $\Sigma X_{B_2}^2 = 3182$ |
| | | $n_{A_1B_2} = 4$ | | $n_{A_2B_2} = 4$ | | $n_{A_3B_2} = 4$ | | $N_{B_2} = 12$ |
| | | $M_{A_1B_2} = 8$ | | $M_{A_2B_2} = 12$ | | $M_{A_3B_2} = 24$ | | $M_{B_2} = 14.67$ |
| | | $\Sigma X_{A_1} = 72$ | | $\Sigma X_{A_2} = 104$ | | $\Sigma X_{A_3} = 164$ | | $\Sigma X_{tot} = 340$ |
| | | $\Sigma X_{A_1}^2 = 676$ | | $\Sigma X_{A_2}^2 = 1422$ | | $\Sigma X_{A_3}^2 = 3514$ | | $\Sigma X_{tot}^2 = 5612$ |
| | | $N_{A_1} = 8$ | | $N_{A_2} = 8$ | | $N_{A_3} = 8$ | | $N_{tot} = 24$ |
| | | $M_{A_1} = 9$ | | $M_{A_2} = 13$ | | $M_{A_3} = 20.5$ | | $M_{tot} = 14.17$ |

Gender (Factor $B$)

other independent variable, gender (Factor $B$), has two levels. The dependent variable is the degree of interest in politics.

The data for this study are shown in Table 14.5. Analyze the data using a two-factor ANOVA at $\alpha = .05$.

## Step 1: Formulate Hypotheses

- Main effect for Factor $A$:

  $H_0 : \mu_{A_1} = \mu_{A_2} = \mu_{A_3}$
  $H_1$: Some $\mu_A$s are not equal

- Main effect for Factor $B$:

$H_0: \mu_{B_1} = \mu_{B_2} = \mu_{B_3}$
$H_1$: Some $\mu_B$s are not equal
- Interaction between Factors $A$ and $B$

$H_0$: Factors $A$ and $B$ do not have a significant interaction.
$H_1$: Factors $A$ and $B$ have a significant interaction.

## Step 2: Indicate the Alpha Level and Determine Critical Values

$$df_{tot} = N_{tot} - 1 = 24 - 1 = 23$$
$$df_{bet(A)} = A - 1 = 3 - 1 = 2$$
$$df_{bet(B)} = B - 1 = 2 - 1 = 1$$
$$df_{bet(AB)} = (A - 1)(B - 1) = (3 - 1)(2 - 1) = 2$$
$$df_{wi} = N_{tot} - k = 24 - 6 = 18$$

$\alpha = .05$
$F_{crit}$ for Factor $A$ = 3.55
$F_{crit}$ for Factor $B$ = 4.41
$F_{crit}$ for Interaction of $A$ and $B$ = 3.55

## Step 3: Calculate Relevant Statistics

1. Sum of Squares

$$SS_{total} = \Sigma X_{tot}^2 - \frac{\left( \Sigma X_{tot} \right)^2}{N_{tot}}$$

$$= 5612 - \frac{(340)^2}{24}$$

$$= 795.33$$

$$SS_{wi} = \Sigma \left[ \Sigma X_{cell}^2 - \frac{\left( \Sigma X_{cell} \right)^2}{n_{cell}} \right]$$

$$= \left( 414 - \frac{(40)^2}{4} \right) + \left( 840 - \frac{(56)^2}{4} \right) + \left( 1176 - \frac{(68)^2}{4} \right) + \left( 262 - \frac{(32)^2}{4} \right)$$

$$+ \left( 582 - \frac{(48)^2}{4} \right) + \left( 2338 - \frac{(96)^2}{4} \right)$$

$$= (414 - 400) + (840 - 784) + (1176 - 1156) + (262 - 256) + (582 - 576)$$
$$+ (2338 - 2304)$$

$$= 14 + 56 + 20 + 6 + 6 + 34$$

$$= 136$$

$$SS_{bet} = \Sigma \left[ \frac{(\Sigma X_{cell})^2}{n_{cell}} \right] - \frac{(\Sigma X_{tot})^2}{N_{tot}}$$

$$= \frac{(40)^2}{4} + \frac{(56)^2}{4} + \frac{(68)^2}{4} + \frac{(32)^2}{4} + \frac{(48)^2}{4} + \frac{(96)^2}{4} - \frac{(340)^2}{24}$$

$$= 400 + 784 + 1156 + 256 + 576 + 2304 - 4816.67$$

$$= 659.33$$

$$SS_A = \frac{\left(\Sigma X_{A_1}\right)^2}{N_{A_1}} + \frac{\left(\Sigma X_{A_2}\right)^2}{N_{A_2}} + \frac{\left(\Sigma X_{A_3}\right)^2}{N_{A_3}} - \frac{\left(\Sigma X_{tot}\right)^2}{N_{tot}}$$

$$= \frac{(72)^2}{8} + \frac{(104)^2}{8} + \frac{(164)^2}{8} - \frac{(340)^2}{24}$$

$$= 648 + 1352 + 3362 - 4816.67$$

$$= 545.33$$

$$SS_B = \frac{\left(\Sigma X_{B_1}\right)^2}{N_{B_1}} + \frac{\left(\Sigma X_{B_2}\right)^2}{N_{B_2}} - \frac{\left(\Sigma X_{tot}\right)^2}{N_{tot}}$$

$$= \frac{(164)^2}{12} + \frac{(176)^2}{12} - \frac{(340)^2}{24}$$

$$= 2241.33 + 2581.33 - 4816.67$$

$$= 5.99$$

$$SS_{AB} = SS_{bet} - SS_A - SS_B$$

$$= 659.33 - 545.33 - 5.99$$

$$= 108.01$$

2. Mean Square

$$MS_A = \frac{SS_A}{df_{bet(A)}} = \frac{545.33}{2} = 272.67$$

$$MS_B = \frac{SS_B}{df_{bet(B)}} = \frac{5.99}{1} = 5.99$$

$$MS_{AB} = \frac{SS_{AB}}{df_{bet(AB)}} = \frac{108.01}{2} = 54.01$$

$$MS_{wi} = \frac{SS_{wi}}{df_{wi}} = \frac{136}{18} = 7.56$$

3. F-statistics

$$F_A = \frac{MS_A}{MS_{wi}} = \frac{272.67}{7.56} = 36.07$$

$$F_B = \frac{MS_B}{MS_{wi}} = \frac{5.99}{7.56} = .79$$

$$F_{AB} = \frac{MS_{AB}}{MS_{wi}} = \frac{54}{7.56} = 7.14$$

## Step 4: Make a Decision and Report the Results

The results of the study are shown in Table 14.6.

As noted earlier, you should look first to see if there is a significant interaction. If there is, it is the interaction that tells the most complete story and should be the focus of the results. This is because, as you recall, even significant main effects can be misleading if interpreted directly since they do not consider the effect of the other independent variable. This is where a graph of the cell means is helpful. Graph 14.4 illustrates how gender and level of education are related to the mean level of interest in politics. Notice that the lines representing gender intersect dependent on educational attainment, suggesting an interaction.

Even though our obtained results show Factor A (level of education) to be significant, it is not that straightforward because the effect that educational attainment has on political interest depends on gender. It is best to describe interactions by looking at the pattern of cell means. In this case, we can see from the graph that interest in politics for both genders increases slightly along closely parallel lines but then it increases sharply for males with a university education but does not increase at the same rate for females with a university education.[2]

*Table 14.6* Summary Table for Political Interest Study

| Source | SS | df | MS | F | p |
|---|---|---|---|---|---|
| Factor A | 545.33 | 2 | 272.67 | 36.07 | < .05 |
| Factor B | 5.99 | 1 | 5.99 | .79 | > .05 |
| Interaction | 108.01 | 2 | 54 | 7.14 | < .05 |
| Within | 136 | 18 | 7.56 | | |
| Total | 795.33 | 23 | | | |

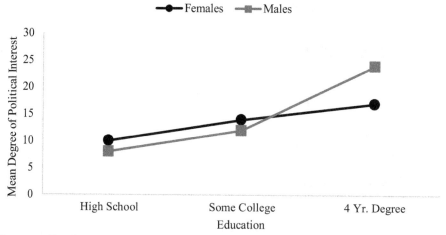

**Graph 14.4** Political Interest Study

In addition to a statement about how the variables interact, effect sizes for each of the main effects and any interactions would also be computed. Since you have learned these techniques previously, they will not be repeated here.

## ASSUMPTIONS AND REQUIREMENTS

The assumptions that should be met for a factorial ANOVA are the same as those for a one-factor ANOVA, independent samples design. These include normal distribution of the dependent variable in the population, independent and random selection of subjects for each group, interval or ratio scores for the dependent variable, and homogeneity of variance of the scores for each treatment group. In addition, the independent samples model that we have examined in this chapter requires that the sample size be the same for each treatment group.

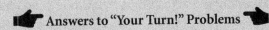 **Answers to "Your Turn!" Problems** 

### I. Factors and Levels

A. Three
B. Study of nootropic drug and memory:

1. Memory
2. One independent variable is the nootropic drug which is being presented at three different levels. The other independent variable is music which is being considered at four different levels.
3. $3 \times 4$

### II. Comprehension Checks for Factorial ANOVA

A. $SS_{wi}$ represents the variability within each group due to individual differences and experimental error.

$SS_{bet}$ represents the variability due to individual differences, experimental error, Factors $A$ and $B$, and the interaction between Factors $A$ and $B$.

$SS_A$ represents the amount of variability between Factor $A$ treatment groups while ignoring Factor $B$.

$SS_{AB}$ represents the variability due to Factors $A$, $B$, and the interaction between Factors $A$ and $B$.

B. Sum of squares; degrees of freedom
C. Larger
D. If $df_{bet(A)} = 3$, then there were 4 groups in condition $A$. If $df_{bet(B)} = 2$, then there were 3 groups in condition $B$. Thus, there were a total of 12 groups in the study. Since $df_{wi} = N_{tot} - k$ and $k = 12$, then $N_{tot}$, the total number of participants, was 48.
E. Caution should be exercised when interpreting main effects if there is a significant interaction because the interaction means that the effect that one independent variable has on the dependent variable depends on the level of the other independent variable. Thus, the factors are creating a combined effect which limits the ability to interpret the factors independently.

## Using Microsoft Excel for Data Analysis

If you are using Excel for the first time for statistical analysis, you may need to load the add-in tool that allows these functions. The information for loading the Data Analysis ToolPak as well as general instructions for using Excel for data analysis are at the beginning of the Excel section in Chapter 4.

### Factorial ANOVA in Excel

To demonstrate how to use Excel for a factorial ANOVA, we will use the sample research study that examines the effect of sleep deprivation on two difference age groups. For this problem, Factor *A* was Hours of Sleep which had three levels (3 hours, 6 hours, and 9 hours). Factor *B* was Age Group which had two levels (teenagers and adults).

- To begin, type the data for this problem into your Excel spreadsheet as follows:

| | A | B | C | D |
|---|---|---|---|---|
| 1 | | 3 Hrs. | 6 Hrs. | 9 Hrs. |
| 2 | Teenagers | 8 | 4 | 2 |
| 3 | | 7 | 6 | 1 |
| 4 | | 6 | 5 | 3 |
| 5 | Adults | 4 | 3 | 2 |
| 6 | | 3 | 2 | 0 |
| 7 | | 2 | 1 | 1 |

- Go to the **Data** tab and click on the **Data Analysis** command.
- From the **Data Analysis** dialog box, highlight **ANOVA: Two Factor with Replication**. Replication simply means that you have more than one score for each combination of the variables.

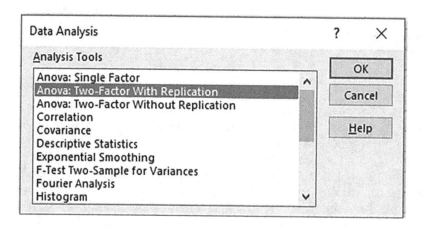

- With your cursor in the window for the **Input Range**, drag your mouse over the cells that contain the data. For this problem, cells A1 through D7 should be highlighted which includes the category labels for both variables. In the **Rows per sample** window, enter 3 (there are 3 scores for teenagers and 3 for adults). We will use the default **Alpha** level of .05. I have selected cell A10 for the **Output Range**. After providing the information, click **OK**.

---

**Anova: Two-Factor With Replication**   ?   ✕

Input
Input Range:   SAS1:SDS7   ⬆

Rows per sample:   3

Alpha:   0.05

Output options
◉ Output Range:   SAS10   ⬆
○ New Worksheet Ply:
○ New Workbook

OK
Cancel
Help

---

- The output will provide summary information for each of the samples (teenagers and adults) as well as summary statistics for the factor combinations (total). What we are interested in, however, is the **ANOVA** table at the bottom which, you will notice, is very much like the summary table in the book for this problem. In Excel's output table, **Sample** refers to Factor $B$ and **Columns** refers to Factor $A$. Actual **P-values** are also included in Excel's ANOVA output as are the $F_{crit}$ values for each Factor and Interaction.

| | ANOVA | | | | | | |
|---|---|---|---|---|---|---|---|
| 32 | *Source of Variation* | *SS* | *df* | *MS* | *F* | *P-value* | *F crit* |
| 34 | Sample | 32 | 1 | 32 | 32 | 0.000106122 | 4.747225347 |
| 35 | Columns | 37 | 2 | 18.5 | 18.5 | 0.00021573 | 3.885293835 |
| 36 | Interaction | 7 | 2 | 3.5 | 3.5 | 0.063469616 | 3.885293835 |
| 37 | Within | 12 | 12 | 1 | | | |
| 38 | | | | | | | |
| 39 | Total | 88 | 17 | | | | |

### Additional Practice Problems

**Answers to odd numbered problems are in Appendix C at the end of the book.**

1. If differences are observed between the means of different treatment groups, can we conclude that these main effects are significant? Why or why not?
2. What is the difference between a main effect and an interaction effect?
3. Explain why within-treatment variance is not influenced by treatment effects but between-treatments variance is.
4. What is the primary benefit of conducting a factorial ANOVA?
5. Using symbolic notation, write the null hypotheses for a study that is examining the effects of four different dosages of medication (Factor A) on three different age groups (Factor B).
6. How do line graphs differ for main effects from line graphs for interaction effects?
7. A $4 \times 3$ ANOVA was conducted with 48 participants distributed equally across all conditions. How many groups were there and what was the sample size of each group?
8. A factorial analysis of variance was conducted with 40 participants distributed equally across the two levels of Factor A and four levels of Factor B. Determine $df_{bet(A)}$, $df_{bet(B)}$, $df_{bet(AB)}$, and $df_{wi}$.
9. In a two-way ANOVA, if $df_{bet(A)} = 2$, $df_{bet(B)} = 4$, and $df_{wi} = 75$, how many treatment groups were involved in the study and how many subjects participated?
10. A group of philanthropists got together and decided to test which of three fund-raising strategies (Factor A) raises the most money for two of their favorite charitable organizations (Factor B). A total of $699 was raised for Charity #1 and $782 was raised for Charity #2. Sum of squares and degrees of freedom values are provided in the table below. Assume an alpha level of $\alpha = .05$.

*Table 14.7* Fundraising Study

| Source | SS | df | MS | F | p |
|---|---|---|---|---|---|
| Factor A | 102 | 2 | _____ | _____ | _____ |
| Factor B | 4600 | 1 | _____ | _____ | _____ |
| Interaction | 620 | 2 | _____ | _____ | _____ |
| Within | 4452 | 18 | _____ | | |
| Total | 9774 | 23 | | | |

a. Complete the table.
b. Determine $F_{crit}$ for each of the main effects and for the interaction effect.
c. Using words, write a statement of conclusion.

11. The managers of a large amusement park studied which rides (Factor A) provided the most enjoyment for various age groups (Factor B). Teenagers gave a mean enjoyment rating of 5 for the Ferris wheel and 20 for the roller coaster. Adults over age 50 gave a mean enjoyment rating of 20 for the Ferris wheel and 5 for the roller coaster. Does there appear to be an interaction effect between Factors A and B? Create a line graph to help make this decision. Put Factor A along the horizontal axis.
12. A television cooking show is testing various methods of cooking different kinds of tofu. For this study, random samples of tasters provided ratings for the flavor profile of either soft or firm tofu that was either oven roasted or pan fried. Factor A was the cooking method and Factor B was the texture of the tofu. Summary values for the study are below. Draw a line graph representing the study with Factor A placed along the horizontal axis and write a statement of conclusion.

Table 14.8 Tofu and Cooking Method

|  | Mean Flavor Ratings | | $F_{obt}$ | $F_{crit}$ |
|---|---|---|---|---|
|  | Oven Roasted | Pan Fried | | |
| | | | Factor $A$ — 6.97 — 4.75 | |
| Firm | 10.5 | 12.50 | Factor $B$ — 55.94 — 4.75 | |
| Soft | 6.5 | 7.75 | Interaction — .19 — 4.75 | |

13. Nutritionists are still trying to determine the best combination of diet and exercise for weight loss. The current study investigates three different types of exercise (brisk walking, swimming, and running) and two different types of diet (low carb and low fat). The amount of weight loss over a three-month period is shown for each of these conditions in the table below. Conduct a two-way ANOVA using $\alpha = .05$. Create a line graph of the cell means with Factor $A$ placed along the vertical axis and write a statement of conclusion.

Table 14.9 Diet and Exercise

| | | Type of Exercise (Factor $A$) | | | |
|---|---|---|---|---|---|
| | | $A_1$ Walking | $A_2$ Swimming | $A_3$ Running | |
| | | $X_1$ $\quad$ $X_1^2$ | $X_2$ $\quad$ $X_2^2$ | $X_3$ $\quad$ $X_3^2$ | |
| | | 5 | 8 | 10 | |
| | | 6 | 6 | 9 | |
| | | 4 | 7 | 12 | |
| | | 5 | 8 | 9 | |
| | $B_1$ Low Carb | $\Sigma X_{A_1B_1} =$ $\Sigma X_{A_1B_1}^2 =$ $n_{A_1B_1} =$ $M_{A_1B_1} =$ | $\Sigma X_{A_2B_1} =$ $\Sigma X_{A_2B_1}^2 =$ $n_{A_2B_1} =$ $M_{A_2B_1} =$ | $\Sigma X_{A_3B_1} =$ $\Sigma X_{A_3B_1}^2 =$ $n_{A_3B_1} =$ $M_{A_3B_1} =$ | $\Sigma X_{B_1} =$ $\Sigma X_{B_1}^2 =$ $N_{B_1} =$ $M_{B_1} =$ |
| | | 7 | 9 | 10 | |
| | | 5 | 7 | 11 | |
| | | 3 | 6 | 12 | |
| | | 4 | 8 | 10 | |
| | $B_2$ Low Fat | $\Sigma X_{A_1B_2} =$ $\Sigma X_{A_1B_2}^2 =$ $n_{A_1B_2} =$ $M_{A_1B_2} =$ | $\Sigma X_{A_2B_2} =$ $\Sigma X_{A_2B_2}^2 =$ $n_{A_2B_2} =$ $M_{A_2B_2} =$ | $\Sigma X_{A_3B_2} =$ $\Sigma X_{A_3B_2}^2 =$ $n_{A_3B_2} =$ $M_{A_3B_2} =$ | $\Sigma X_{B_2} =$ $\Sigma X_{B_2}^2 =$ $N_{B_2} =$ $M_{B_2} =$ |
| | | $\Sigma X_{A_1} =$ $\Sigma X_{A_1}^2 =$ $N_{A_1} =$ $M_{A_1} =$ | $\Sigma X_{A_2} =$ $\Sigma X_{A_2}^2 =$ $N_{A_2} =$ $M_{A_2} =$ | $\Sigma X_{A_3} =$ $\Sigma X_{A_3}^2 =$ $N_{A_3} =$ $M_{A_3} =$ | $\Sigma X_{tot} =$ $\Sigma X_{tot}^2 =$ $N_{tot} =$ $M_{tot} =$ |

Type of Diet (Factor $B$)

## Notes

1  For a discussion of pros and cons of using eta squared or partial eta squared, see Levine, T. R. (2002). Eta squared, partial eta squared, and misreporting of effect size in communication research. *Human Communication Research, 28*(4), 612–625. https://doi.org10.1093/hcr/28.4.612

2  Methods for more thorough interpretations of interactions and main effects in the company of interaction can be found in most intermediate and advanced statistics textbooks. For example, see Kirk, R. E. (2013). *Experimental design: Procedures for the behavioral sciences.* Thousand Oaks, CA: Sage.

# 15

# Correlation and Regression

## INTRODUCTION TO CORRELATION

Is there a relationship between the amount of time you spent studying for the last test you took and the score you earned on that test? Probably so. Thus you have an intuitive understanding of the concept of correlation. Specifically, *correlation research* involves using statistical procedures to analyze the relationship between two variables.

Suppose we wanted to examine the relationship between education level attained and the number of cultural events attended in the last year. We would obtain a representative sample of individuals and collect the data on these two variables, one variable labeled $X$, and the other labeled $Y$. We would then use a statistical formula to determine the direction and strength of the relationship. After doing so, we would end up with a number, called the *correlation coefficient*, that would range from $-1.00$ to $+1.00$.

The *direction* of the relationship, which is indicated by the sign, refers to whether the correlation is positive or negative. **A *positive correlation*** exists when the $X$ and $Y$ scores of each variable proceed in the same direction. In other words, high $X$-scores are associated with high $Y$-scores and low $X$-scores with low $Y$-scores. A positive correlation would be established if we found that individuals with a lot of education (a high score) attended a lot of cultural events (also a high score) and individuals with little education (a low score) attended few cultural events (also a low score). **A *negative correlation***, on the other hand, exists when $X$ and $Y$ scores proceed in opposite directions. Low $X$-scores are associated with high $Y$-scores and high $X$-scores with low $Y$-scores. This is also referred to as an *inverse relationship*. A negative correlation (or inverse relationship) would be established if we found that individuals with a lot of education attended few cultural events, and vice versa.

Tip!

> There is a tendency to think of *positive* as good and *negative* as bad. As applied to correlation, this would be a *mistake*. Think of positive and negative only in terms of the direction of the scores.

☞ **Your Turn!** 🖐

**I. Positive or Negative Correlations?**

For each of the situations below, identify whether the correlations would likely be positive *or* negative.

A Level of happiness and number of kind remarks to others: _____
B. Weight of an automobile and gas mileage: _____
C. Amount of time watching TV and GPA: _____
D. Annual rainfall and number of umbrellas sold: _____
E. Amount of reading and extent of vocabulary: _____
F. A parent's number of children and amount of free time: _____

The *strength* of a relationship is indicated by the absolute numerical value of the correlation coefficient. The stronger the correlation, the closer the numerical value will be to 1.00, regardless of the sign. A correlation of −.90 has the same degree of strength as +.90. A perfect correlation is indicated by a plus or minus 1 (±1.00), which is the strongest relationship possible. Close to a 0 correlation is also possible, meaning that virtually no relationship exists between two variables. There is probably close to a 0 correlation between individuals' intelligence and the length of their arms.

## SCATTERPLOTS

Correlations can also be graphed on a **scatterplot**, which is simply a diagram of the relationship between two variables. *X*-scores are represented along the horizontal axis and *Y*-scores along the vertical axis. Each dot in the diagram corresponds to each person's scores on the two variables.

- The scatterplot below illustrates a *negative correlation*. Less sleep (*X*) is associated with more errors (*Y*), and more sleep is associated with fewer errors.

| X | Y |
|---|---|
| 9 | 0 |
| 8 | 1 |
| 8 | 1 |
| 7 | 0 |
| 7 | 1 |
| 6 | 3 |
| 6 | 2 |
| 6 | 3 |
| 5 | 5 |
| 3 | 6 |
| 3 | 7 |
| 1 | 9 |

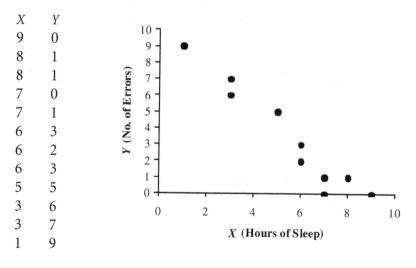

- The following scatterplot illustrates a *positive correlation*. For adult students attending night classes, having fewer children (*X*) is associated with fewer class absences (*Y*), and having more children is associated with more class absences.

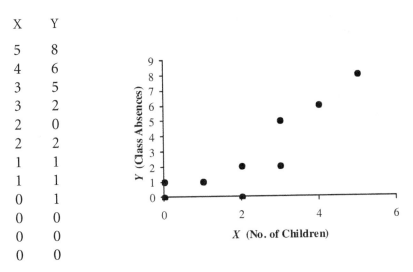

| X | Y |
|---|---|
| 5 | 8 |
| 4 | 6 |
| 3 | 5 |
| 3 | 2 |
| 2 | 0 |
| 2 | 2 |
| 1 | 1 |
| 1 | 1 |
| 0 | 1 |
| 0 | 0 |
| 0 | 0 |
| 0 | 0 |

*Linear* correlations are best described by a straight line in which there is a tendency for the *Y*-scores to move in only one direction in relationship to the *X*-scores. The previous examples represent such correlations. As the number of hours of sleep (*X*) increased, the number of errors (*Y*) tended to decrease (a negative linear correlation). As the number of children (*X*) increased, class absences (*Y*) also tended to increase (a positive linear correlation). The scatterplots below show linear correlations of various strengths and directions:

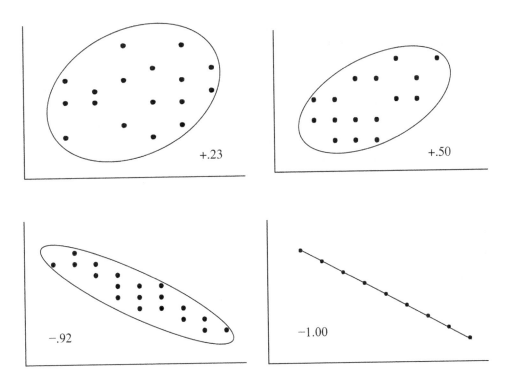

Notice the following:

- When you begin at the left side of the charts, positive correlations ascend to the right. Negative correlations descend to the right.
- The stronger the relationship, the less scatter there is.
- In a perfect correlation, many of the dots will be piled on top of each other and, when connected, will form a straight diagonal line.

Other types of correlations besides linear ones are also possible. For example, *curvilinear* relationships are best described by a curve rather than by a straight line. One example of a curvilinear correlation, known as the Yerkes-Dodson Law,[1] is shown schematically below.

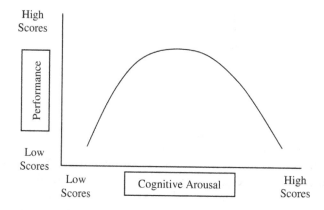

According to the Yerkes-Dodson Law, performance on a task ($Y$) increases with increasing cognitive arousal ($X$) only to a certain point. Thereafter, increases in arousal are associated with decreased performance, hence the curvilinear nature of this relationship.

## PEARSON PRODUCT MOMENT CORRELATION

The method of correlation that we will be learning here is the **Pearson product moment correlation**, which is used for examining linear relationships between variables measured on interval or ratio scales. It is not appropriate to use the Pearson on nonlinear relationships, such as the one represented by the Yerkes-Dodson Law described earlier. Using the Pearson would not capture the true strength of the relationship. Other nonlinear techniques would have to be used. Therefore, our discussion will be limited to linear relationships, which are more common.

The Pearson correlation coefficient is symbolized by $r$. The *definitional formula* is as follows:

$$r = \frac{\Sigma\left(Z_x Z_y\right)}{N}$$

However, this formula requires

- computing means, standard deviations, and z-scores, and
- a lot of number-crunching.

☺ There is a better way!

We are going to use the *computational formula* for calculating Pearson's correlation coefficient:

$$r = \frac{N\Sigma XY - (\Sigma X)(\Sigma Y)}{\sqrt{\left[N\Sigma X^2 - (\Sigma X)^2\right]\left[N\Sigma Y^2 - (\Sigma Y)^2\right]}}$$

The formula looks a bit menacing, but it is really quite friendly. You are familiar with all of the terms in the formula. It is simply a matter of breaking it down into its component parts.

1. Create columns for $X$, $X^2$, $Y$, $Y^2$, and $XY$.
2. Square each $X$ value and place the product in the $X^2$ column. Do the same for the $Y$ values.
3. Multiply each $X$ value by its corresponding $Y$ value to obtain $XY$.
4. Sum the $X$, $Y$, $X^2$, $Y^2$, and $XY$ columns.
5. Plug the values into the formula. $N$ refers to the number of *paired* scores.

## Sample Research Question

A professor collected information from college students on the number of movies they watched per week and the number of hours they spent studying per week. Determine $r$.

| Number of movies | | Hours studying | | |
|---|---|---|---|---|
| X | $X^2$ | Y | $Y^2$ | XY |
| 10 | 100 | 1 | 1 | 10 |
| 7 | 49 | 3 | 9 | 21 |
| 6 | 36 | 9 | 81 | 54 |
| 5 | 25 | 10 | 100 | 50 |
| 3 | 9 | 3 | 9 | 9 |
| 2 | 4 | 22 | 484 | 44 |
| 2 | 4 | 25 | 625 | 50 |
| 1 | 1 | 40 | 1600 | 40 |
| 0 | 0 | 37 | 1369 | 0 |
| $\Sigma X = 36$ | $\Sigma X^2 = 228$ | $\Sigma Y = 150$ | $\Sigma Y^2 = 4278$ | $\Sigma XY = 278$ |

$$r = \frac{N\Sigma XY - (\Sigma X)(\Sigma Y)}{\sqrt{\left[N\Sigma X^2 - (\Sigma X)^2\right]\left[N\Sigma Y^2 - (\Sigma Y)^2\right]}}$$

$$= \frac{(9)(278) - (36)(150)}{\sqrt{\left[(9)(228) - (36)^2\right]\left[(9)(4,278) - (150)^2\right]}}$$

$$= \frac{2,502 - 5,400}{\sqrt{(2,052 - 1,296)(38,502 - 22,500)}}$$

$$= \frac{-2,898}{\sqrt{12,097,512}}$$

$$= -.83$$

**Tip!**

> A correlation will not have a value greater than 1. If the result of your calculation of $r$ is outside the range of $-1.00$ to $+1.00$, a mistake has been made.

## HYPOTHESIS TESTING WITH THE PEARSON CORRELATION

Our familiar four-step hypothesis testing procedure will be used for testing hypotheses about the relationship between two variables in a population. The population correlation is represented by the Greek letter rho and is symbolized by $\rho$.

- The null hypothesis states that no significant relationship exists between the two variables, and that any correlation found is simply due to chance. Thus, the null hypothesis is written as:

$H_0: \rho = 0$ (there is no correlation in the population)

- The alternative hypothesis may be stated as either directional or nondirectional. A nondirectional alternative hypothesis merely asserts a nonzero correlation in the population and calls for a two-tailed test. In this case, either positive or negative obtained $r$-values will reject $H_0$ if they are significant. A nondirectional alternative hypothesis would be written as

$$H_1 : \rho \neq 0 \qquad \left(\text{for } H_0 : \rho = 0\right)$$

A directional alternative hypothesis specifies either a positive or negative correlation and calls for a one-tailed test. In this case, the obtained $r$-value must be significant and in the direction specified before $H_0$ may be rejected. A directional alternative hypothesis for a positive correlation would be written as

$$H_1 : \rho > 0 \qquad \left(\text{for } H_0 : \rho \leq 0\right)$$

A directional alternative hypothesis for a negative correlation would be written as

$$H_1 : \rho < 0 \qquad \left(\text{for } H_0 : \rho \geq 0\right)$$

## THE $r$ DISTRIBUTION TABLE

If the null hypothesis is true, if there is no correlation between $X$ and $Y$ in the population, the value of $r$ will be approximately 0. How much different from 0 the obtained $r$-value must be in order to reject $H_0$ will be determined by comparing it to a theoretical distribution of $r$-values. (Sound familiar?) The table of critical $r$-values for the Pearson correlation is in Table 7 near the end of this book and is similar to the ones we have used for other statistical tests. Guidelines for this table are as follows:

- Along the top, the first row lists various alpha levels for a one-tailed test.
- The second row lists various alpha levels for a two-tailed test.
- In the left column are degrees of freedom (*df*). For the Pearson correlation $df = N - 2$.

- If the degrees of freedom for your particular research problem are not shown, then use the critical values associated with the next-lowest level.
- In order to reject $H_0$, your obtained $r$-value will have to exceed the value listed in the chart.

## SUMMARY OF HYPOTHESIS TESTING PROTOCOL FOR THE PEARSON CORRELATION

A summary of the hypothesis testing procedure for the example given earlier of the relationship between movie watching and studying is as follows:

### Step 1: Formulate Hypotheses

We will use a nondirectional alternative hypothesis. Thus,

$$H_0 : \rho = 0$$
$$H_1 : \rho \neq 0$$

### Step 2: Indicate the Alpha Level and Determine Critical Values

We will test at $\alpha = .05$, two-tailed. Thus,

$$\alpha = .05, \text{two} - \text{ailed}$$
$$df = N - 2$$
$$= 9 - 2$$
$$= 7$$
$$r_{\text{crit}} = \pm .666$$

### Step 3: Calculate Relevant Statistics

$$r = \frac{N\Sigma XY - (\Sigma X)(\Sigma Y)}{\sqrt{\left[ N\Sigma X^2 - (\Sigma X)^2 \right]\left[ N\Sigma Y^2 - (\Sigma Y)^2 \right]}}$$

$$= \frac{(9)(278) - (36)(150)}{\sqrt{\left[ (9)(228) - (36)^2 \right]\left[ (9)(4,278) - (150)^2 \right]}}$$

$$= -.83$$

### Step 4: Make a Decision and Report the Results

There was an inverse relationship between the number of movies watched per week and the amount of time spent studying. Reject $H_0$, $r(7) = -.83, p < .05$.

The format for reporting the results is similar to that of other statistical tests that we have used. The number in parentheses is the degrees of freedom that were used. The negative value of $r$ tells you that the scores on the two variables proceed in opposite directions.

## COEFFICIENTS OF DETERMINATION AND NONDETERMINATION

We have seen in previous chapters that, in addition to determining statistical significance, researchers also like to include a measure of the strength of an obtained statistic. Previously, we looked at effect size for this purpose. The strength of a correlation is often interpreted by calculating the **coefficient of determination,** which is the proportion of variance that two variables have in common. The coefficient of determination is computed by squaring $r$ (i.e., $r^2$).

If there is a correlation between two variables, then the scores tend to change together in predictable ways. As $X$ changes, $Y$ also tends to change in a predictable way. So some of the variability in each set of scores is related. This is the shared common variance between the scores that is assumed to be influenced by the same factors. For example, if there is a correlation of $r = .72$ between students' grades in history and English, the coefficient of determination is $r^2 = .52$. In other words, 52% of the variability between these grades is shared common variance that is assumed to be influenced by the same factors, such as general intelligence, study habits, motivation, and so on. It tells us that 52% of the variance on one variable is explained by the variance in the other. It also means that 52% of this variability can be predicted.

The **coefficient of nondetermination** tells us the proportion of the variability that is not common variance and that is related to factors that do not influence both sets of scores, such as different levels of interest in history and English and different types of assignments for the courses. The coefficient of nondetermination is calculated by subtracting $r^2$ from 1. For the above example, $1 - r^2 = .48$. What this value tells us is that 48% of the variance of one variable is *not* explained by the variance of the other.

Overlapping circles are often used to illustrate this relationship, as follows:

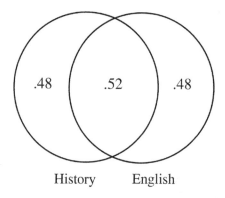

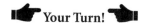

History    English

Each circle represents the total variability (100%) for that variable. Where the circles overlap represents the coefficient of determination, or shared variability (52%), and the areas of nonoverlap (48%) represent the coefficient of nondetermination.

---

☞ **Your Turn!** ☜

### II. Pearson Correlation

*Research Question.* A fifth-grade teacher wanted to determine empirically if there is a link between how much students read and the extent of their vocabulary. He surveyed a random sample of fifth graders in his school, asked them how many books per month they read, and then gave them a vocabulary test. Scores are listed below.

A. Is there a significant relationship between the two variables? Test at $\alpha = .01$, two-tailed.

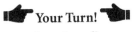

**Your Turn!**

(continued)

| No. of books | Vocabulary score |
|:---:|:---:|
| X | Y |
| 12 | 10 |
| 11 | 9 |
| 11 | 10 |
| 10 | 6 |
| 10 | 8 |
| 8 | 8 |
| 7 | 6 |
| 7 | 9 |
| 6 | 6 |
| 6 | 7 |
| 5 | 8 |
| 5 | 7 |
| 3 | 5 |
| 2 | 6 |
| 1 | 3 |
| 0 | 4 |

Step 1: Formulate Hypotheses

Step 2: Indicate the Alpha Level and Determine Critical Values

Step 3: Calculate Relevant Statistics

Step 4: Make a Decision and Report the Results

B. What proportion of the variance is shared, common variance?

## INTERPRETING THE PEARSON CORRELATION

There are some considerations that should be taken into account when using and interpreting correlations.

1. *Cause and Effect*. That a correlation exists between two variables does not *necessarily* mean that one causes the other. Sometimes relationships exist because of the

effect of other outside influences. For instance, if we found a positive relationship between self-esteem and grades, we could not conclude that high or low self-esteem *causes* students to earn high or low grades. Perhaps low grades cause students to have low self-esteem. Or, perhaps low self-esteem and low grades influence each other in a reciprocal fashion. It is also possible that other outside variables may be influencing the relationship, such as responsive parenting. Perhaps students who have high self-esteem come from nurturing home environments where the parents instill in them a sense of their own value and worth *and* emphasize the importance of education. Although causal relationships cannot be confirmed using the method of correlation, it would also be incorrect to say that the variables involved are definitely *not* causally related. They *may* be, but this cannot be established through correlational procedures. Causal relationships can be demonstrated only through experimentation.

2. *Restricted Range.* Caution should also be exercised when interpreting correlations from a *restricted range* versus a full range of scores. The problem of **restricting the range** occurs when a sample is used that limits the scores on one or both variables more so than would be found in the population. For example, a new car sales manager is interested in knowing if a relationship exists between the personality characteristic of optimism and car sales. She thus administers a standardized optimism assessment scale to all current employees and compares their scores to their car sales quantity. Surprisingly, not much of a correlation was found. This is likely due to the fact that gathering data only for current employees restricted the range of possible scores. More than likely, employees who had low quantities of car sales are no longer employed by the dealership and are likely employees who had a low level of optimism. The scatterplot below illustrates this situation, with the scattered dots to the right of the vertical line representing the restricted range. This correlation appears much weaker than it would be if the entire range of scores had been used.

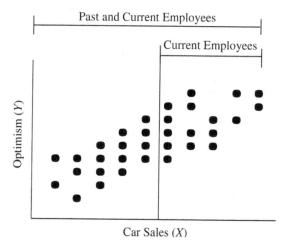

3. *Outliers* are scores on either the $X$ or $Y$ variable that are extreme in comparison to most other scores. **Outliers** are located by visually inspecting the scatterplot. If observed, caution is advised in your interpretation because outliers can have a dramatic effect on the magnitude of the correlation.

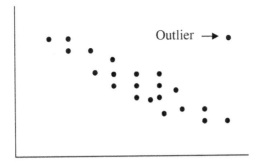

## USES OF THE PEARSON CORRELATION

The Pearson correlation has a number of specific uses, some of which include the following:

1. *Validity*. Correlations are sometimes used to measure the validity of newly developed assessment instruments. By definition, **validity** is the degree to which a test measures what it is supposed to measure. Suppose, for example, a new assessment for depression is being developed. In order to determine if the new assessment instrument in fact measures depression, scores on this test should correlate positively with scores on other standardized measures of depression.
2. *Reliability*. In a similar fashion, correlation is also used to assess the reliability of testing instruments. **Reliability** refers to the consistency or stability of test scores upon repeated administrations of the test (or on alternate forms of the test). For example, suppose you take a test today to measure the personality characteristic of introversion. If it is a reliable instrument, then the scores should be similar if you took the test again two months from now because introversion is a relatively stable personality trait that does not change dramatically in a few weeks' time.
3. *Prediction*. One of the main uses of the Pearson correlation is **prediction.** If there is a strong relationship between two variables, then knowing the score on one variable will enable us to predict the score on the other variable. The stronger the relationship, the more accurate the prediction will be. The weaker the relationship, the less accurate the prediction will be. For instance, we would not be able to predict a person's IQ by knowing the length of his or her arms because there is little, if any, relationship between those two variables. On the other hand, we could probably predict, with some degree of accuracy, students' grades on a test by knowing how many absences they have had. This is because there is a negative correlation between absenteeism and grades on a test.

Remember that the strength of a correlation is often defined by the coefficient of determination ($r^2$) discussed earlier. A correlation coefficient used alone can give a false impression of strength. For instance, a correlation of $r = .50$ seems to be a moderately strong correlation because it falls right in the middle of 0 and 1.00. However, when we compute the coefficient of determination, we find that only 25% of the variability of the scores can be predicted from this relationship. Thus, $r^2$ is a much better measure of the strength and accuracy of our predictions than the correlation coefficient alone.

## REGRESSION ANALYSIS

If a correlation exists between two variables, then we can use the obtained scores on one variable to predict unknown scores on another variable, a procedure called **regression analysis.** Regression analysis can be used to make such predictions as the heights of 21-year-olds based on knowledge of their heights at age 12, or college GPA based on high school GPA.

The variables that are used to estimate values on another variable are called **predictor variables.** The **criterion variable** is the variable that is estimated from predictor variables. In the latter example above, high school GPA would be the predictor variable while college GPA would be the criterion variable. In *multiple regression analysis,* more than one predictor variable is used. For example, in addition to high school GPA, SAT scores could also be used as a predictor variable. Using both variables would result in better estimates of college GPA than either of these variables used alone. Multiple regression analysis is a useful statistical tool, but it is more complex than our discussion permits. We will focus on *simple regression analysis,* which involves only one predictor variable.

We will begin our discussion of simple regression with a visual illustration. Observe the scatterplot below:

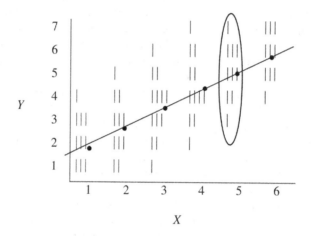

For every score on X, there is a collection of Y-scores. For example, 10 different Y-scores are associated with an X-score of 5. One person who scored 5 on X, scored 3 on Y, two scored 4 on Y, three scored 5 on Y, three scored 6 on Y, and one scored 7 on Y. If we wanted to predict the Y-score for a person who scored 5 on X, we could predict the mean of that collection of Y-scores. In fact, we could calculate the mean Y-value for each value of X and then draw a straight line through, or nearly through, those points. This would give us the **regression line,** or line of best fit, which is used to predict Y-values from given X-values.

*There is a better way!*

We are not going to calculate all those means in order to find the regression line to predict our Y-scores. We are going to use a more sophisticated formula. However, before we use the formula, we need to know two things – the slope of the regression line and the Y-intercept.

- The **slope** (symbolized by the small letter b) tells us how much and in what direction the regression line slants.
- The **Y-intercept** (symbolized by the small letter a) is the point where the regression line cuts across, or intercepts, the Y-axis.

The formulas for obtaining the slope and Y-intercept are below.

<u>Slope (b)</u>

$$b = r\left(\frac{s_y}{s_x}\right)$$

where: $r$ = correlation coefficient
$s_y$ = standard deviation of $Y$
$s_x$ = standard deviation of $X$

<u>Y-intercept (a)</u>

$$a = M_y - b(M_x)$$

where: $M_y$ = mean of $Y$-scores
$b$ = slope
$M_x$ = mean of $X$-scores

Once we have these two pieces of information, we can put them in a formula for the regression equation, as follows:

## Regression Equation

$$Y' = b(X) + a$$

where: $Y'$ = predicted $Y$-value
$b$ = slope
$X$ = $X$-value from which you wish to predict a $Y$-value
$a$ = $Y$-intercept

## For Example

Given: $r$ = .85
$s_x$ = 3
$s_y$ = 24
$M_x$ = 6
$M_y$ = 57

What are the predicted $Y$-scores for the $X$-scores of 4 and 9?

We will first need to find the slope and the $Y$-intercept for our regression equation.

Slope

$$b = r\left(\frac{S_y}{S_x}\right)$$

$$= .85\left(\frac{24}{3}\right)$$

$$= 6.80$$

Y-intercept

$$a = M_y - b(M_x)$$

$$= 57 - 6.80(6)$$

$$= 16.20$$

With this information, we can now determine the regression equation for this problem:

$$Y' = b(X) + a$$
$$= 6.80(X) + 16.20$$

Using this equation, we can now predict the Y-scores for individuals who score 4 and 9 on X.

$$Y' = 6.80(4) + 16.20$$
$$= 43.40$$

$$Y' = 6.80(9) + 16.20$$
$$= 77.40$$

Because we are predicting Y given X, make sure that you assign Y to the variable that you want to predict and X to the variable that is being used to predict it.

**Tip!**

---

**Your Turn!**

### III. Regression Analysis

The correlation between scores on tests of sociability and sense of humor was found to be r = .73. The following summary data were also obtained:

| | Sociability | Humor |
|---|---|---|
| Mean | 47.00 | 36.00 |
| Standard Deviation | 6.81 | 5.22 |

A. What humor score would be predicted for a person with a sociability score of 52?

_____

B. What humor score would be predicted for a person with a sociability score of 25?

_____

Answers to "Your Turn!" Problems

## I. Positive or Negative Correlations?

A. Positive    D. Positive
B. Negative   E. Positive
C. Negative   F. Negative

## II. Pearson Correlation

A. Step 1:           Step 2:
   $H_0: \rho = 0$        $\alpha = .01$
   $H_1: \rho \neq 0$        $df = 14$
                     $r_{crit} = \pm.623$

Step 3:

$$r = \frac{(16)(821)-(104)(112)}{\sqrt{\left[(16)(884)-(104)^2\right]\left[(16)(846)-(112)^2\right]}} = +.82$$

Step 4:

There is a significant positive relationship between reading and vocabulary. Reject $H_0$, $r(14) = +.82$, $p < .01$.

B. $r^2 = .67$

## III. Regression Analysis

A. $Y' = (.56)(52) + 9.68 = 38.80$
B. $Y' = (.56)(25) + 9.68 = 23.68$

---

## Using Microsoft Excel for Data Analysis

If you are using Excel for the first time for statistical analysis, you may need to load the add-in tool that allows these functions. The information for loading the Data Analysis ToolPak as well as general instructions for using Excel for data analysis are at the beginning of the Excel section in Chapter 4.

### Pearson Correlation in Excel

To demonstrate how to use Excel for the Pearson correlation, let's look at the sample research question where you learned this technique about the relationship between the number of movies watched per week and the number of hours spent studying.

- Enter the scores into columns A and B of the spreadsheet, including the labels in row 1.

| | A | B |
|---|---|---|
| 1 | Movies | Studying |
| 2 | 10 | 1 |
| 3 | 7 | 3 |
| 4 | 6 | 9 |
| 5 | 5 | 10 |
| 6 | 3 | 3 |
| 7 | 2 | 22 |
| 8 | 2 | 25 |
| 9 | 1 | 40 |
| 10 | 0 | 37 |
| 11 | | |

- Go to the **Data** tab and click on the **Data Analysis** command.
- From the **Data Analysis** dialog box, scroll down and highlight **Correlation**. Click **OK** and a dialog box for this function will appear.

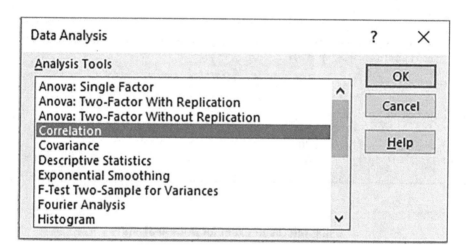

- With your dialog cursor in the window for the **Input Range**, drag your mouse over *all* the scores, including the labels (A1 through B10). The dollar signs that show up in the window between cell locations are references used by Excel and will automatically appear in some types of statistical analyses.
- Check the **Labels** box so that the labels for the variables will appear in the output.
- For **Output options**, the default is to place the output table in a new worksheet. If you prefer, you can include the output table on the same spreadsheet by checking **Output Range** and typing in any empty cell location. Let's enter D1 to keep our output on the same worksheet. Click **OK**.

| Correlation | | ? ✕ |
|---|---|---|

**Input**

Input Range: `$A$1:$B$10` ⬆  OK

Grouped By:  ◉ Columns  Cancel
○ Rows
☑ Labels in first row  Help

**Output options**

◉ Output Range: `D1|` ⬆
○ New Worksheet Ply:
○ New Workbook

You can see that Excel arrived the same correlation coefficient (−.83) that you calculated by hand.

| | A | B | C | D | E | F |
|---|---|---|---|---|---|---|
| 1 | Movies | Studying | | | Movies | Studying |
| 2 | 10 | 1 | | Movies | 1 | |
| 3 | 7 | 3 | | Studying | -0.8332 | 1 |
| 4 | 6 | 9 | | | | |
| 5 | 5 | 10 | | | | |
| 6 | 3 | 3 | | | | |
| 7 | 2 | 22 | | | | |
| 8 | 2 | 25 | | | | |
| 9 | 1 | 40 | | | | |
| 10 | 0 | 37 | | | | |
| 11 | | | | | | |

**Regression in Excel**

Excel can also be used for regression analysis. Let's create the slope and y-intercept for the above problem.

- Enter the scores into columns A and B of the spreadsheet, including the labels in row 1.
- Go to the **Data** tab and click on the **Data Analysis** command.
- From the **Data Analysis** dialog box, scroll down and highlight **Regression**. Click **OK** and a dialog box for this function will appear.

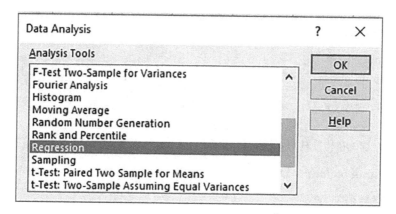

- With your cursor in the window for the **Input Y Range**, drag your mouse over the scores for the Y-variable (studying), including the labels (B1 through B10). With your cursor in the window for the **Input X Range**, drag your mouse over the scores for the X-variable (movies), including the labels (A1 through A10). The dollar signs that show up in the window between cell locations are references used by Excel and will automatically appear in some types of statistical analyses.
- Check the **Labels** box so that the labels for the variables will appear in the output.
- There will be three **Output options.** The default is to place the output table in a new worksheet which is what we will do for this problem. Click **OK** and an output summary will be generated.

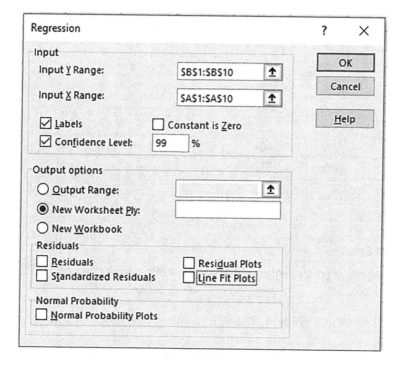

- The output that we are interested in are the Y-intercept (*a*) and the slope (*b*), which is shown at the bottom of the report in rows 17 and 18 under the heading **Coefficients**. The value of the Y-intercept is 32 and the value of the slope is -3.83. If we wanted to predict the amount of time that a student studies who watches *X* number of movies per week, we could now easily do so using the regression equation: $Y' = -3.83(X) + 32$.

| | A | B | C | D | E | F | G | H | I |
|---|---|---|---|---|---|---|---|---|---|
| 1 | SUMMARY OUTPUT | | | | | | | | |
| 2 | | | | | | | | | |
| 3 | *Regression Statistics* | | | | | | | | |
| 4 | Multiple R | 0.83320209 | | | | | | | |
| 5 | R Square | 0.69422572 | | | | | | | |
| 6 | Adjusted R Square | 0.65054368 | | | | | | | |
| 7 | Standard Error | 8.81286938 | | | | | | | |
| 8 | Observations | 9 | | | | | | | |
| 9 | | | | | | | | | |
| 10 | ANOVA | | | | | | | | |
| 11 | | *df* | *SS* | *MS* | *F* | *Significance F* | | | |
| 12 | Regression | 1 | 1234.333333 | 1234.33333 | 15.892704 | 0.005279502 | | | |
| 13 | Residual | 7 | 543.6666667 | 77.6666667 | | | | | |
| 14 | Total | 8 | 1778 | | | | | | |
| 15 | | | | | | | | | |
| 16 | | *Coefficients* | *Standard Error* | *t Stat* | *P-value* | *Lower 95%* | *Upper 95%* | *Lower 99.0%* | *Upper 99.0%* |
| 17 | Intercept | 32 | 4.839760368 | 6.61189761 | 0.000301 | 20.55578526 | 43.4442147 | 15.0633394 | 48.9366606 |
| 18 | Movies | -3.8333333 | 0.961562881 | -3.9865654 | 0.0052795 | -6.10706824 | -1.5595984 | -7.1983066 | -0.4683601 |

*Additional Practice Problems*

**Answers to odd numbered problems are in Appendix C at the end of the book.**

1. Write the null and alternative hypotheses in symbolic form for a two-tailed Pearson correlation.
2. Write the null and alternative hypotheses in symbolic form for a positive Pearson correlation.
3. Calculate a Pearson correlation for the scores below.

| X | Y |
|---|---|
| 7 | 6 |
| 10 | 8 |
| 12 | 10 |
| 17 | 14 |
| 8 | 9 |
| 10 | 7 |

4. Calculate a Pearson correlation for the scores below.

| X | Y |
|---|---|
| 12 | 7 |
| 16 | 8 |
| 22 | 10 |
| 7 | 15 |
| 15 | 6 |
| 18 | 9 |

5. Calculate a Pearson correlation for the scores below.

| X | Y |
|---|---|
| 10 | 6 |
| 9 | 7 |
| 8 | 8 |
| 7 | 9 |
| 6 | 10 |

6. A researcher is studying the relationship between alcohol consumption and cognitive functions. The scores below show the number of alcoholic drinks consumed (X) and number of errors on a math test (Y). Is increased alcohol consumption related to an increased number of errors? Test at $\alpha = .05$, one-tailed.

| X | Y |
|---|---|
| 5 | 4 |
| 1 | 2 |
| 6 | 8 |
| 0 | 1 |
| 2 | 3 |
| 4 | 3 |

7. Is there a relationship between how social a person is and how much anxiety they experience when giving a speech? Below are the scores on assessments for sociability (X) and fear of public speaking (Y). Test at $\alpha = .05$, two-tailed.

| X | Y |
|---|---|
| 15 | 15 |
| 18 | 15 |
| 19 | 16 |
| 23 | 17 |
| 12 | 19 |
| 11 | 22 |
| 20 | 15 |

8. What is meant by the coefficient of determination? How is it calculated?
9. What is meant by the coefficient of nondetermination? How is it calculated?
10. Given $r = .79$, what proportion of the variance on one variable is explained by the variance on the other?
11. There is a negative correlation between alcohol consumption and age at death, thus proving that drinking excessive amounts of alcohol causes people to die at younger ages. Do you agree with this statement? Explain why or why not discussing the third variable problem in your response.
12. What is meant by restricting the range? What effect does it have on the correlation coefficient?
13. What is an outlier? What effect does it have on a correlation coefficient?
14. Based on the summary data below, predict the beginning salary ($Y$) for people whose college GPAs ($X$) were: 1.8, 2.8, and 3.8.

    $r = .78$
    $M_X = 2.8$
    $s_X = .85$
    $M_Y = 64,000$
    $s_Y = 6,976$

15. A regression equation is $Y' = -5X + 92$ with $X$ being the number of class absences during a semester and $Y$ being the scores earned on the final exam. What final exam scores would be predicted for students with 4 and 8 class absences?

## Note

1  Yerkes, R. M., & Dodson, J. D. (1908). The relation of strength of stimulus to rapidity of habit-formation. *Journal of Comparative Neurology and Psychology, 18,* 459–482.

# 16
# Chi-Square

## NONPARAMETRIC TESTS

Remember all those pesky assumptions that were listed for the statistical tests we have performed so far? Those tests, called *parametric tests*, test hypotheses about the parameters of populations and require that certain assumptions be met. Many of those tests, like the *t* test and ANOVA, are robust and can tolerate some violation of the assumptions. However, it is best to avoid such violations if possible in order to avoid increasing the risk of Type I error.

Sometimes, research questions arise but the assumptions required for parametric tests cannot be met. The data may not lend themselves to the mathematical operations permitted with interval- and ratio-level data. The population distribution may be seriously skewed, or some other requirement may not be assumed. Fortunately, there are alternative tests that may be used in such situations, called **nonparametric tests**, which relax many of these assumptions. Nonparametric tests do not require a normal population distribution, homogeneity of variance, or interval- or ratio-level data. Thus, these tests serve a valuable function in answering some types of research questions.

**Tip!**

If parametric assumptions can be met and a choice can be made between parametric and nonparametric tests, it is best to go with a parametric test, such as a *t* test or ANOVA, because these tests are more powerful, meaning that they are more likely to detect statistical significance.

## CHI-SQUARE

The nonparametric test that we will use is called **chi-square**, symbolized by $\chi^2$. Because interval- or ratio-level data are not required, chi-square is often the appropriate test to use for nominal and ordinal data that take the form of frequency counts. With chi- square, we can answer questions such as the following:

- Which of the three leading brands of bottled water do most Americans prefer?
- How does the number of male nurses compare to the number of female nurses in the profession?

- Is there a relationship between gender and the types of movies (e.g., drama, comedy, adventure) watched most?

Notice that each of these questions involves determining the frequencies of observations in various categories.

## THE CHI-SQUARE STATISTIC

The chi-square statistic measures the amount of discrepancy between observed frequencies and the frequencies that would be expected due to chance, or random sampling error. The formula for chi-square is

$$\chi^2 = \Sigma \frac{\left(f_o - f_e\right)^2}{f_e}$$

where: $f_o$ = observed frequencies
$f_e$ = expected frequencies

*Observed frequencies* are the actual frequencies from our sample that fall into each category. *Expected frequencies* are the frequency values that would be expected if the null hypothesis is true. If we find no differences between our observed and expected frequencies, then our obtained $\chi^2$ value will equal 0. But if our observed frequencies differ from those that would be expected, then $\chi^2$ will be greater than 0. How much greater than 0 our chi-square value has to be in order to reject $H_0$ will, of course, be determined by comparing our obtained chi-square value to a theoretical distribution of chi-square values, just as we have done in the past.

Chi-square values will range from 0 to positive infinity. Because $\chi^2$ is calculated from squared deviations (see above formula), there will be no negative values. We will conduct two types of chi-square tests, one called a *goodness of fit test*, and the other called a *test of independence*. Both tests use the same chi-square formula, but they address different types of research questions.

## ASSUMPTIONS

Because chi-square is a nonparametric statistic, the assumptions will be different from those of parametric tests. The assumptions for chi-square include the following:

- *Independent Observations.* Each participant can contribute frequencies to only one category.
- *Minimum Size.* The expected frequency $(f_e)$ for all categories should be a minimum of 5. Using smaller frequencies has a disproportionate effect on the value of $\chi^2$.

## GOODNESS OF FIT

This discussion will focus on the *one-way* goodness of fit test, which examines *one* variable, such as religion, in several categories: Buddhism, Christianity, Hinduism, Islam, Judaism, Taoism, Other. The goodness of fit test is used to determine how well the frequencies observed in our sample match the frequencies that would be expected in the population if the null hypothesis were true.

## Hypothesis Testing for Goodness of Fit

For goodness of fit problems, the null hypothesis will specify that a certain proportion of the population will fall into each category and therefore what frequencies should theoretically be expected in our sample of $n$ subjects if the null hypothesis is true. The alternative hypothesis, as always, will state the opposite.

- *No difference from a known population.* In some cases, a researcher may want to compare the frequencies of a randomly drawn sample to the frequencies of a known population distribution. For instance, a professor collects data to determine if the political affiliations (e.g., Democrat, Republican, Libertarian, Green Party, or Independent) of students who major in political science correspond to the patterns illustrated by voters in the last US presidential election. In this case, the null and alternative hypotheses would be written as:

  $H_0$: The political affiliations of political science students are the same as those of U.S. voters.

  $H_1$: The political affiliations of political science students are different from those of U.S. voters.

If our obtained $\chi^2$ value is greater than would be expected by chance if the null hypothesis is true, then, as always, we reject $H_0$ and assume instead that the political preferences of political science students are different from those of US voters in general.

- *No preference.* At other times, the null hypothesis might predict equal frequencies in each category, or no preference. For example, a candy manufacturer may want to know if there is a preference for one of the five candy bars produced by his company and distributed by a particular store outlet. The null and alternative hypotheses would be written as follows:

  $H_0$: Preferences for candy bars are equally divided.

  $H_1$: Preferences for candy bars are not equally divided.

If our obtained $\chi^2$ value is greater than would be expected by chance if the null hypothesis were true, then, as always, we would reject $H_0$ and assume instead that the preferences for candy bars are not equally divided.

Let us work through some examples to illustrate.

## GOODNESS OF FIT FOR KNOWN PROPORTIONS

### Sample Research Question

A new professor at a midsize college wanted to see if her grade distribution after her first year of teaching was comparable to the overall college grade distribution, which has the following percentages: A – 10%; B – 22%; C – 40%; D – 21%; and F – 7%. The distribution of the new professor's grades for 323 students at the end of her first year was as follows: 38 students received As, 78 received Bs, 139 received Cs, 55 received Ds, and 13 received Fs. Does the new professor's grade distribution fit the overall college's distribution? Test, using $\alpha = .05$.

## Step 1: Formulate Hypotheses

We are using the proportions/percentages from a known population distribution for our comparison. Thus, our hypotheses would be as follows:

$H_0$: The distribution of grades for the new professor fits the overall grade distribution of the college.

$H_1$: The distribution of grades for the new professor does not fit the overall grade distribution of the college.

## Step 2: Indicate the Alpha Level and Determine Critical Values

After we calculate our $\chi^2$ crit value in the next step, we will need to compare it to a critical $\chi^2$ value. The chi-square distribution is in Table 8 near the end of this book. Various alpha levels are listed across the top and $df$ are shown along the left column.

For goodness of fit, $df = \kappa - 1$, where $\kappa$ refers to the number of categories. Our problem has 5 categories (A, B, C, D, and F). Thus,

$\alpha = .05$

$df = k - 1 = 5 - 1 = 4$

$\chi^2_{crit} = 9.488$

## Step 3: Calculate Relevant Statistics

In order to use the chi-square formula presented earlier, observed and expected frequencies are required. Observed frequencies are the actual frequencies obtained from our sample, which are given in the problem. For research questions dealing with a known population distribution, expected frequency is determined by multiplying the known proportion in the population by $n$. In other words,

$$f_e = (\text{known proportion})(n)$$

The null hypothesis specifies that the new professor's grades will not differ significantly from the proportion found in the population. We know that 10% of the college population earned As, 22% earned Bs, and so forth. If we multiply those known proportions by our sample size, then we can determine what frequencies would be expected if $H_0$ were true. Thus,

$A = .10 \times 323 = 32.30$

$B = .22 \times 323 = 71.06$

$C = .40 \times 323 = 129.20$

$D = .21 \times 323 = 67.83$

$F = .07 \times 323 = 22.61$

It is helpful to use a table to keep track of observed and expected frequencies. In the table below, expected frequencies are in parentheses.

| A | B | C | D | F |
|---|---|---|---|---|
| 38 (32.30) | 78 (71.06) | 139 (129.20) | 55 (67.83) | 13 (22.61) |

**Tip!**

Both observed frequency counts and expected frequency values, when added, should equal *n*. If they do not, then you made a mistake in your calculations.

Now we can plug our values into the formula for $\chi^2$. The summation in the formula ($\Sigma$) tells us that the information following that symbol needs to be added for each category.

$$\chi^2_{obt} = \Sigma \frac{(f_o - f_e)^2}{f_e}$$

$$= \frac{(38 - 32.3)^2}{32.3} + \frac{(78 - 71.06)^2}{71.06} + \frac{(139 - 129.2)^2}{129.2} + \frac{(55 - 67.83)^2}{67.83} + \frac{(13 - 22.61)^2}{22.61}$$

$$= 1.01 + .68 + .74 + 2.43 + 4.08$$

$$= 8.94$$

### Step 4: Make a Decision and Report the Results

Our obtained $\chi^2$ value is smaller than $\chi^2$ crit. Consequently, we will not reject $H_0$. We will use the following format for our conclusion. The only new element is the sample size. This is important in chi-square because *df* is based on number of categories rather than sample size. Thus, *n* cannot be determined from *df* and should therefore be reported in the results:

The new professor's grades did not differ significantly from those of the college at large. Fail to reject $H_0$, $\chi^2$ (4 *df*, *n* = 323) = 8.94, *p* > .05.

---

 **Your Turn!**

### I. Goodness of Fit for Known Proportions

*Research Question.* The owner of a large company wants to see if the ethnic diversity of her company reflects the diversity of her state. The breakdown for her state is as follows: White, 63.9%; Black, 14.8%; Hispanic, 13.7%; Asian, 3.7%; Other, 3.9%. The ethnic breakdown of the 1,054 employees of her company is as follows:

| White | Black | Hispanic | Asian | Other |
|-------|-------|----------|-------|-------|
| 607   | 172   | 183      | 52    | 40    |

Does the ethnic diversity of the company reflect that of the state? Test at $\alpha$ = .05. (Hint: Convert the known diversity percentages in the state to proportions in order to determine $f_e$).

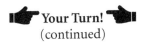

**Your Turn!**
(continued)

Step 1: Formulate Hypotheses

Step 2: Indicate the Alpha Level and Determine Critical Values

Step 3: Calculate Relevant Statistics

Step 4: Make a Decision and Report the Results

## GOODNESS OF FIT FOR NO PREFERENCE

### Sample Research Question

A manufacturer of women's clothing wants to know which of the colors red, blue, green, brown, and black would be preferred for the fall collection. A random sample of 92 women shoppers were asked their preferences. The results were as follows:

| Red | Blue | Green | Brown | Black |
|-----|------|-------|-------|-------|
| 5 | 19 | 19 | 27 | 22 |

Test a no preference null hypothesis using $\alpha = .01$.

### Step 1: Formulate Hypotheses

$H_0$: All colors were equally preferred.
$H_1$: The colors were not equally preferred.

### Step 2: Indicate the Alpha Level and Determine Critical Values

$\alpha = .01$
$df = k - 1 = 5 - 1 = 4$
$\chi^2_{crit} = 13.277$

## Step 3: Calculate Relevant Statistics

For an $H_0$ that specifies no preference, calculate the expected frequency $(f_e)$ by dividing $n$ by the number of categories $(k)$. In other words,

$$f_e = n \div k$$
$$f_e = 92 \div 5 = 18.4 \qquad \text{For our problem, use this value for each category.}$$

| Red | Blue | Green | Brown | Black |
|---|---|---|---|---|
| 5 (18.4) | 19 (18.4) | 19 (18.4) | 27 (18.4) | 22 (18.4) |

$$\chi^2_{obt} = \Sigma \frac{(f_o - f_e)^2}{f_e}$$
$$= \frac{(5-18.4)^2}{18.4} + \frac{(19-18.4)^2}{18.4} + \frac{(19-18.4)^2}{18.4} + \frac{(27-18.4)^2}{18.4} + \frac{(22-18.4)^2}{18.4}$$
$$= 9.76 + .02 + .02 + 4.02 + .70$$
$$= 14.52$$

## Step 4: Make a Decision and Report the Results

Preferences for colors were not equally divided. Reject $H_0$, $\chi^2$ (4 $df$, $n = 92$) = 14.52, $p < .01$.

---

 **Your Turn!**

### II. Goodness of Fit for No Preference

*Research Question.* The owner of a nightclub that specializes in classic modern jazz is going to be buying a series of recordings for the jukebox. Before buying them, he wants to know the customers' preferences for male vocalists, female vocalists, or instrumentals. Seventy-two customers were randomly asked their preferences, with the following results:

| Male | Female | Instrumentals |
|---|---|---|
| 19 | 27 | 26 |

Test for no preferences using $\alpha = .05$.

Step 1: Formulate Hypotheses




Step 2: Indicate the Alpha Level and Determine Critical Values

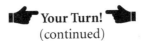 **Your Turn!**
(continued)

Step 3: Calculate Relevant Statistics

Step 4: Make a Decision and Report the Results

## TEST OF INDEPENDENCE

The other type of problem where chi-square has its greatest usefulness is in testing for independence of variables. This test examines the frequencies for *two* variables at different levels in order to determine whether one variable is independent of the other or if the variables are related. In the last chapter, we used the Pearson correlation to test similar hypotheses. However, the Pearson requires interval- or ratio-level data. Now we will test for such relationships using nominal- or ordinal-level data.

### Hypothesis Testing for the Test of Independence

For a test of independence, the null hypothesis states that the two variables are independent and unrelated. Suppose, for example, a researcher wants to know if there is a relationship between gender and introversion. The null hypothesis asserts that the variables are independent and unrelated. The alternative hypothesis asserts the contrary. Thus:

$H_0$: There is no relationship between gender and introversion.
$H_1$: A relationship exists between gender and introversion.

### Contingency Table

The table for the chi-square test of independence is slightly different from the table for one-way goodness of fit because we are now working with *two* variables rather than one. Called a contingency table, it will include rows for the values of one variable and columns that will contain the values of the second variable. Similar to the goodness of fit table, the expected frequencies, after being calculated, will be placed in parentheses in the same cells as the corresponding observed frequencies.

### Sample Research Question

A professor at a veterinary school of medicine is curious about whether or not a relationship exists between gender and type of pets owned in childhood. She randomly asks a sample of $n = 260$ students (132 female and 128 male) about their pet ownership, the frequency of which is recorded in the table below. Is there a relationship between gender and type of pet ownership? Test at $\alpha = .05$.

| Gender | Dogs | Cats | Birds | Reptiles | Rodents | Row total |
|---|---|---|---|---|---|---|
| | | | *Type of pet* | | | |
| Female | 58 | 36 | 22 | 4 | 12 | 132 |
| Male | 62 | 22 | 14 | 10 | 20 | 128 |
| Column total | 120 | 58 | 36 | 14 | 32 | $n = 260$ |

Notice that row totals and column totals have also been computed for the matrix. These are important for determining expected frequencies.

For the test of independence, expected frequency is determined by the following formula.

$$f_e = \frac{(f_c)(f_r)}{n}$$

where $f_c$ = column total
$f_r$ = row total
$n$ = sample size

Using this formula, you can calculate the expected frequencies for each cell. For example, the expected frequency for **females** who owned **dogs** in childhood would be:

$$f_e = \frac{(f_c)(f_r)}{n} = \frac{(120)(132)}{260} = 60.92$$

Using the same procedure, calculate the expected frequencies for all observed frequencies and place them in parentheses in the appropriate cells of the contingency table.

| Gender | Dogs | Cats | Birds | Reptiles | Rodents | Row total |
|---|---|---|---|---|---|---|
| | | | *Type of pet* | | | |
| Female | 58 (60.92) | 36 (29.45) | 22 (18.28) | 4 (7.11) | 12 (16.25) | 132 |
| Male | 62 (59.08) | 22 (28.55) | 14 (17.72) | 10 (6.89) | 20 (15.75) | 128 |
| Column total | 120 | 58 | 36 | 14 | 32 | $n = 260$ |

We can now test our hypotheses in the usual manner.

## Step 1: Formulate Hypotheses

We are using the proportions/percentages from a known population distribution for our comparison. Thus, our hypotheses would be as follows:

$H_0$: Gender and pet ownership are independent and unrelated.
$H_1$: There is a relationship between gender and pet ownership.

## Step 2: Indicate the Alpha Level and Determine Critical Values

For tests of independence, $df = (R - 1)(C - 1)$

where R = number of rows in contingency table
C = number of columns in contingency table

For our example,

$$\alpha = .05$$
$$df = (R-1)(C-1) = (2-1)(5-1) = 4$$
$$\chi^2_{crit} = 9.488$$

Once again, our obtained $\chi^2$ value must exceed $\chi^2$crit in order to reject the null hypothesis.

## Step 3: Calculate Relevant Statistics

$$\chi^2_{obt} = \Sigma \frac{(f_o - f_e)^2}{f_e}$$

$$= \frac{(58 - 60.92)^2}{60.92} + \frac{(36 - 29.45)^2}{29.45} + \frac{(22 - 18.28)^2}{18.28} + \frac{(4 - 7.11)^2}{7.11} + \frac{(12 - 16.25)^2}{16.25}$$

$$+ \frac{(62 - 59.08)^2}{59.08} + \frac{(22 - 28.55)^2}{28.55} + \frac{(14 - 17.72)^2}{17.72} + \frac{(10 - 6.89)^2}{6.89} + \frac{(20 - 15.75)^2}{15.75}$$

$$= .14 + 1.46 + .76 + 1.36 + 1.11 + .14 + 1.50 + .78 + 1.40 + 1.15$$

$$= 9.80$$

## Step 4: Make a Decision and Report the Results

There is a relationship between gender and type of pet owned. Reject $H_0$, $\chi^2$ (4 df, $n = 260) = 9.80, p < .05$.

---

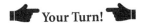 **Your Turn!**

### III. Test of Independence

*Research Question.* A researcher is interested in determining if there is a relationship between handedness and penmanship. To study this question, the researcher submitted writing samples from 100 students to penmanship experts. The samples were rated to be of low, medium, or high penmanship quality. The observed frequencies of these ratings are shown below. Determine if a significant relationship exists between handedness and penmanship quality. Test at $\alpha = .05$.

*(Continued)*

 **Your Turn!**
(continued)

| Handedness | Penmanship quality | | |
|---|---|---|---|
| | Low | Medium | High |
| Left-handed | 8 | 29 | 6 |
| Right-handed | 9 | 37 | 11 |

Step 1: Formulate Hypotheses

Step 2: Indicate the Alpha Level and Determine Critical Values

Step 3: Calculate Relevant Statistics

Step 4: Make a Decision and Report the Results

 **Answers to "Your Turn!" Problems**

### I. Goodness of Fit for Known Proportions

Step 1:

$H_0$: The ethnic diversity of the company is comparable to the ethnic diversity of the state.

$H_1$: The ethnic diversity of the company does not reflect the same diversity of the state.

Step 2:
$\alpha = .05$
$df = 4$
$\chi^2_{crit} = 9.488$

**Answers to "Your Turn!" Problems**
(Continued)

Step 3:

| White | Black | Hispanic | Asian | Other |
|---|---|---|---|---|
| 607 (673.51) | 172 (155.99) | 183 (144.40) | 52 (39) | 40 (41.11) |

$\chi^2_{obt} = 22.89$

Step 4:

The ethnic diversity of the company did not reflect the diversity of the state. The company reflected greater diversity. Reject $H_0$, $\chi^2(4\ df, n = 1054) = 22.89, p < .05$.

## II. Goodness of Fit for No Preference

Step 1:

$H_0$: Preferences for type of jazz are equally divided.
$H_1$: Preferences for type of jazz are not equally divided.

Step 2:

$\alpha = .05$
$df = 2$
$\chi^2_{crit} = 5.991$

Step 3:

| Male | Female | Instrumentals |
|---|---|---|
| 19 (24) | 27 (24) | 26 (24) |

$\chi^2_{obt} = 1.59$

Step 4:

Preferences for types of jazz were equally divided. Fail to reject $H_0$, $\chi^2(2df, n = 72) = 1.59, p > .05$.

## III. Test of Independence

Step 1:

$H_0$: Handedness and penmanship are independent and unrelated.
$H_1$: There is a relationship between handedness and penmanship.

*(Continued)*

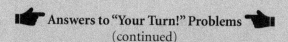

**Answers to "Your Turn!" Problems**
(continued)

Step 2:

$$\alpha = .05$$
$$df = 2$$
$$\chi^2_{crit} = 5.991$$

Step 3:

*Penmanship quality*

| Handedness | Low | Medium | High | Row total |
|---|---|---|---|---|
| Left-handed | 8 (7.31) | 29 (28.38) | 6 (7.31) | 43 |
| Right-handed | 9 (9.69) | 37 (37.62) | 11 (9.69) | 57 |
| Column total | 17 | 66 | 17 | 100 |

$$\chi^2_{obt} = .55$$

Step 4:

There was no evidence of a significant relationship between handedness and quality of penmanship. Fail to reject $H_0$, $\chi^2(2\ df, n = 100) = .55, p > .05$.

---

## Using Microsoft Excel for Data Analysis

If you are using Excel for the first time for statistical analysis, you may need to load the add-in tool that allows these functions. The information for loading the Data Analysis ToolPak as well as general instructions for using Excel for data analysis are at the beginning of the Excel section in Chapter 4.

### Goodness of Fit for Known Proportions

This chapter looked at chi-square for three different kinds of research situations. Here, we will focus on the two types of goodness of fit designs. Excel will calculate chi-square for tests of independence. However, there are numerous steps involved and it is just a easy to do the analysis by hand.

For each of the goodness of fit research problems, we will be providing the formulas and instructing Excel to grab the values needed in the formulas from the cells where they are located in the spreadsheet. We will begin with the chi-square goodness of fit test for known proportions using the sample research question in this chapter about the grade distribution of a new college professor.

First, type in the information shown in the spreadsheet below that will be needed for the calculations. The observed frequencies of the new college professor's grades (column A) were provided in the problem as were the percentages of each letter grade for the college (which we converted into proportions in column C).

| | A | B | C | D | E |
|---|---|---|---|---|---|
| 1 | Grade | Observed | College | Expected | Chi-square |
| 2 | A | 38 | 0.1 | | |
| 3 | B | 78 | 0.22 | | |
| 4 | C | 139 | 0.4 | | |
| 5 | D | 55 | 0.21 | | |
| 6 | F | 13 | 0.07 | | |
| 7 | | | | | |
| 8 | | | | | |
| 9 | Chi-Sq Obs | | | | |
| 10 | Chi-Sq Crit | | | | |

We will now instruct Excel to perform the remaining operations:

1. **Auto Sum.** From the **Formulas** tab, you should see an **Auto Sum** ($\Sigma$) command on the ribbon. With the cursor in cell B7, click on the $\Sigma$ command and press enter. The total for the observed frequencies (323) will appear.
2. **Expected Frequency.** With your cursor in cell D2, type the following exactly as written: =(C2*323) and hit the enter key.

| | A | B | C | D | E |
|---|---|---|---|---|---|
| 1 | Grade | Observed | College | Expected | Chi-square |
| 2 | A | 38 | 0.1 | =(C2*323) | |
| 3 | B | 78 | 0.22 | | |
| 4 | C | 139 | 0.4 | | |
| 5 | D | 55 | 0.21 | | |
| 6 | F | 13 | 0.07 | | |
| 7 | | 323 | | | |
| 8 | | | | | |
| 9 | | | | | |
| 10 | Chi-Sq Obs | | | | |
| 11 | Chi-Sq Crit | | | | |
| 12 | | | | | |

The expected frequency for grades of A (32.3) will appear. Put your cursor in cell D2 so that it is highlighted. Hover your mouse over the lower right corner of the cell box and it will become a crosshair; drag the box down to cell D6. The expected frequencies for all of the grades should now appear. Place your cursor in cell D7, click on the $\Sigma$ command and press enter. The total for the expected frequencies will appear and should be the same as for the observed frequencies.

| | A | B | C | D | E |
|---|---|---|---|---|---|
| 1 | Grade | Observed | College | Expected | Chi-square |
| 2 | A | 38 | 0.1 | 32.3 | |
| 3 | B | 78 | 0.22 | 71.06 | |
| 4 | C | 139 | 0.4 | 129.2 | |
| 5 | D | 55 | 0.21 | 67.83 | |
| 6 | F | 13 | 0.07 | 22.61 | |
| 7 | | 323 | | 323 | |
| 8 | | | | | |
| 9 | | | | | |
| 10 | Chi-Sq Obs | | | | |
| 11 | Chi-Sq Crit | | | | |

3. **Obtained Chi-square Value**. With your cursor in cell E2, type the following exactly as written: =(B2 − D2)^2/D2 and press enter. This is the component of the chi-square formula in which we subtract the expected frequency from the observed frequency (B2–D2), square that value (^2), and divide by the expected frequency (/D2). After you press enter, the contribution of the grades of A to the total chi-square value (1.0058824) will appear. As you did for the expectancy frequency, make sure cell E2 is highlighted, grab the lower right corner of the cell box, drag it down to cell E6 and press enter. The contributions of all of the grades to the chi-square value will now be shown. Place your cursor in cell E9, click on the $\Sigma$ command and press enter. The result will be your obtained chi-square value (8.9383686).

4. **Critical Chi-square Value**. Rather than using the table at the back of your text, Excel will determine your $\chi^2_{crit}$ value. With your cursor in cell E10, go to the **Formulas** tab and click on the **Insert Function (fx)** command from the ribbon. From the **Insert Function** dialog box, click the dropdown box that allows you to select a category; select **Statistical**. From the **Select a function** window, scroll down and highlight **CHISQ.INV.RT**. This is the function that will provide the $\chi^2_{crit}$ value. Click **OK**.

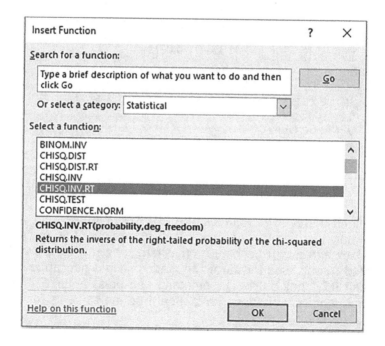

You will need to provide values for probability and degrees of freedom. For this problem, use the alpha level of .05 for probability and $df = 4$. After clicking on **OK**, $\chi^2_{crit}$ will appear in cell E10. You can now compare your own calculations for all elements of the problem with those generated by Excel.

| | A | B | C | D | E |
|---|---|---|---|---|---|
| 1 | Grade | Observed | College | Expected | Chi-square |
| 2 | A | 38 | 0.1 | 32.3 | 1.0058824 |
| 3 | B | 78 | 0.22 | 71.06 | 0.6777878 |
| 4 | C | 139 | 0.4 | 129.2 | 0.7433437 |
| 5 | D | 55 | 0.21 | 67.83 | 2.4267861 |
| 6 | F | 13 | 0.07 | 22.61 | 4.0845688 |
| 7 | | 323 | | 323 | |
| 8 | | | | | |
| 9 | Chi-Sq Obs | | | | 8.9383686 |
| 10 | Chi-Sq Crit | | | | 9.487729 |

## Goodness of Fit for No Preference

To illustrate chi-square goodness of fit for no preference, we will use the sample research question about color preferences for the fall collection of women's clothing. For this problem, we will follow almost all of the same steps as above with the following exceptions:

- You will need to supply the appropriate cell numbers for the calculations rather than those specified for the problem above.
- There will not be a column for known proportions (identified by the "College" label above). This information was needed in order to determine the expected frequency for "known proportions" problems. In "no preference" problems, the expected frequency will be the same for all categories and is determined by simply dividing $n$ by the number of categories.

First, type in the information shown in the spreadsheet below that will be needed for the calculations.

| | A | B | C | D |
|---|---|---|---|---|
| 1 | Colors | Observed | Expected | Chi-Square |
| 2 | Red | 5 | 18.4 | |
| 3 | Blue | 19 | 18.4 | |
| 4 | Green | 19 | 18.4 | |
| 5 | Brown | 27 | 18.4 | |
| 6 | Black | 22 | 18.4 | |
| 7 | | | | |
| 8 | | | | |
| 9 | Chi-Sq Obs | | | |
| 10 | Chi-Sq Crit | | | |

You can use the **Auto Sum ($\Sigma$)** command to get the totals for the observed and expected frequency columns. To get the chi-square contribution for each of the categories, begin with your cursor in cell D2 and type the following exactly as written: =(C2-B2)^2/C2 and hit the enter key. The contribution of the color red to the total chi-square value (9.75869565) will appear. As you did before, grab the lower right corner of the cell box, drag it down to cell D6 and press enter. The contributions of all of the colors to the chi-square value will now be shown. With your cursor in cell D9, use the **Auto Sum ($\Sigma$)** command to obtain your observed chi-square value. Use the same procedure as above to obtain $\chi^2_{crit}$ except be sure to use the alpha level of .01 for this problem as the value for probability instead of .05.

| ◢ | A | B | C | D |
|---|---|---|---|---|
| 1 | Colors | Observed | Expected | Chi-Square |
| 2 | Red | 5 | 18.4 | 9.75869565 |
| 3 | Blue | 19 | 18.4 | 0.01956522 |
| 4 | Green | 19 | 18.4 | 0.01956522 |
| 5 | Brown | 27 | 18.4 | 4.01956522 |
| 6 | Black | 22 | 18.4 | 0.70434783 |
| 7 | | 92 | 92 | |
| 8 | | | | |
| 9 | Chi-Sq Obs | | | 14.5217391 |
| 10 | Chi-Sq Crit | | | 13.2767041 |

---

## Additional Practice Problems

**Answers to odd numbered problems are in Appendix C at the end of the book.**

1. What are the three main parametric assumptions whose violations may lead a researcher to use a nonparametric test such as chi-square?
2. What is the difference between observed and expected frequencies?
3. What formulas determine $df$ and $f_e$ for goodness of fit tests for known population proportions?
4. What formulas determine $df$ and $f_e$ for goodness of fit tests for no preference?
5. What formulas determine $df$ and $f_e$ for chi-square tests of independence?
6. Under what conditions would a researcher use a chi-square goodness of fit test for known proportions, a goodness of fit test for no preference, and a chi-square test of independence?
7. The participants in a national survey were asked to rate the degree of importance that they place on climate change as a priority in the next congressional election. The results were as follows:

   Extremely important – 35%
   Very important – 29%
   Important – 17%
   Somewhat important – 12 %
   Not very important – 4%
   No response – 3%

   A random sample of 245 residents of a particular city was asked about the same issue. What would the expected frequencies be for each category if the null hypothesis is true?

8. A travel agency is putting vacation packages together for the upcoming travel season and asks a sample of 162 potential vacationers which of the following vacation spots would be preferred: Greece, Hawaii, Alaska, the Caribbean, or Australia. If a no preference hypothesis is tested, what is the expected frequency for each category if the null hypothesis is true?

9. A sample of 120 males and 113 females, all between 20 and 35 years of age, were asked which of five activities would be preferred for a Saturday night date. The results are in the table below. If you were to use chi-square to determine if there is a relationship between gender and preferred dating activity, what would the expected frequency be for each category if the null hypothesis is true?

|  | Movie | Concert | Dancing | Sports Event | Play |
|---|---|---|---|---|---|
| Male | 31 | 24 | 18 | 42 | 5 |
| Female | 38 | 15 | 29 | 23 | 8 |

10. A national survey asked if a tax on junk food would be favored with the funds being allocated to educational programs on nutrition. The results were as follows:
    Strongly favor – 26%
    Mildly favor – 27%
    Mildly oppose – 18%
    Strongly oppose – 24%
    No response – 5%
    A city council member administers the same survey to a random sample of 131 residents in her city. The number of responses in each of the categories is shown below:
    Strongly favor – 33
    Mildly favor – 38
    Mildly oppose – 27
    Strongly oppose – 29
    No response – 4
    Do the opinions of the city residents match those of the nation on the issue of a "junk food tax?" Test, using $\alpha = .05$.

11. The athletic director of a university wants to develop an exercise program available to students campus wide. To get a sense of their exercise habits beforehand, he administered a survey that asked, "How much do you exercise?" The results were as follows:

| Frequently | Sometimes | Rarely | Never |
|---|---|---|---|
| 40 | 62 | 68 | 26 |

   Conduct a chi-square goodness of fit test for no preference to determine if the students' current habits have a greater than chance difference from a no preference distribution. Use $\alpha = .01$.

12. A developmental psychologist is interested in studying the pastimes of various age groups. In the current study, she is investigating the relationship between age groups (children and adults) and preferred sports (swimming, baseball, soccer, or basketball). Results are shown in the table below. Conduct a chi-square test of independence to determine if there is a significant relationship between these variables. Use $\alpha = .05$.

|  | Swimming | Baseball | Soccer | Basketball |
|---|---|---|---|---|
| Children | 12 | 25 | 19 | 8 |
| Adults | 22 | 18 | 21 | 14 |

# 17
# Nonparametric Statistics for Ordinal Data

Most of the statistical procedures that have been covered in this text involved parametric tests which required that the dependent variable be measured on an interval or ratio scale. The one exception was in the last chapter where you were introduced to a nonparametric test, chi-square, which used nominal and ordinal level data that was grouped into categories. In this chapter, you will learn additional nonparametric techniques that make use of ordinal data. In this case, the data will maintain its ranked position rather than being treated as categorical data. In addition to ranked data, nonparametric statistics may also be appropriate even if interval or ratio scores are available. One such occasion would be if the assumption of normality cannot be met. It does not matter if the distribution is severely skewed rather than being normal in shape. It is for this reason that nonparametric tests are also called **distribution-free tests**. They do not require that the dependent variable be normally distributed in the population. Another circumstance for which a nonparametric test might be indicated (even with interval or ratio scores) is if the scores come from populations for which the variances are extremely different. Fortunately, homogeneity of variance is also not a requirement for these tests.

To highlight some points from the last chapter, parametric tests are generally considered to be more powerful than nonparametric tests if the assumptions can be met. They are also considered to be fairly robust, meaning that they can withstand *some* infringement of the assumptions. However, if the rules are seriously violated, then the risk of a Type I error becomes too great and a nonparametric test is the better choice. This is especially true if you are working with very small samples.

In sum, if the assumptions can be met, choose a parametric test because they are more likely to reject the null hypothesis (i.e., they are more powerful). On the other hand, if only ordinal level data is available, use a nonparametric test. If interval or ratio level data is available but you are concerned about meeting the assumptions of a parametric test, you can use a nonparametric alternative. In this case, the interval or ratio scores will be ranked and treated as ordinal level data.

There are many nonparametric tests from which to choose. Table 17.1 lists four of the most common that we will examine in this chapter and that are used as alternatives to some of the major parametric tests previously covered.

The same hypothesis testing procedures that apply to parametric statistics apply to these tests as well. As usual, we will assume that the null hypothesis is true unless our analysis

*Table 17.1* Nonparametric Alternatives to Parametric Tests

| Parametric Test | Nonparametric Alternative |
|---|---|
| Independent samples *t* test | Mann-Whitney *U* test |
| Related samples *t* test | Wilcoxon matched-pairs signed-ranks *T* test |
| One-way ANOVA, independent samples design | Kruskal-Wallis *H* test |
| Pearson correlation *r* | Spearman correlation $r_s$ |

demonstrates otherwise. Since you are already well acquainted with the steps involved in hypothesis testing, we will be more general in our approach and not outline the steps individually here. The problems and examples illustrated for each of the tests that follow either make use of data that is measured on an ordinal scale or, if interval or ratio scores are used, we will assume that the researcher is concerned about the shape of the distribution or that homogeneity of variance is questionable. Like parametric tests, nonparametric tests also assume random sampling from the population of interest or random assignment of participants to the different groups involved in the study.

## THE MANN-WHITNEY *U* TEST

The **Mann-Whitney *U* test** is the nonparametric alternative to the independent samples *t* test. The *U* statistic that is generated by this test is appropriate when the size of both samples ($n_1$ and $n_2$) is 20 or less. If the size of either or both samples is greater than 20, the sampling distribution of *U* approximates the normal distribution. In these situations, it is possible to convert your obtained *U* value into a z-value and use the normal distribution curve. We will limit our sample sizes to less than 20.[1]

The Mann-Whitney *U* test will involve comparing two different samples of ranked scores. The null hypothesis for a two-tailed test states that the population distributions from which the samples were drawn are the same. The alternative hypothesis for a two-tailed test states that the population distributions for the two groups are different. A one-tailed alternative hypothesis would specify the ranks from one of the groups to be higher or lower than the ranks from the other group. Notice that it is the difference in the ranks of the two groups that is being compared with this test. With the independent samples *t* test, it was the difference between means that was being examined.

Of course, there will probably always be *some* degree of difference between the ranked scores of the samples due to random sampling error, or chance. The Mann-Whitney *U* test will enable us to determine whether our obtained difference is more likely a chance difference or a real difference in the population.

### Ranking the Scores

In some cases, the scores that you are working with may already be ranked. If they are not, you will need to rank them. The combined scores from both groups will be ranked at the same time. Assign the lowest score a rank of 1. Scores that are tied will all be assigned the average of the tied ranks.

Let's look at the hypothetical scores from two different samples. The scores for Group A are: 25, 33, 21, 13, 31, 17, 21, and 28. The scores for Group B are 24, 24, 15, 18, 12, 24, 36,

*Table 17.2* Ranking Scores for the Mann-Whitney *U* Test

| Group A | Rank | Group B | Rank |
|---------|------|---------|------|
| 13 | 2 | 12 | 1 |
| 17 | 4 | 15 | 3 |
| 21 | 6.5 | 18 | 5 |
| 21 | 6.5 | 22 | 8 |
| 25 | 12 | 24 | 10 |
| 28 | 13 | 24 | 10 |
| 31 | 14 | 24 | 10 |
| 33 | 16 | 32 | 15 |
|  |  | 36 | 17 |
|  | $\Sigma R_1 = 74$ |  | $\Sigma R_2 = 79$ |

22, and 32. To rank the scores, create a table with four columns, one for each set of scores and for their assigned ranks, as in Table 17.2. It will be easier to assign the ranks if you list each set of scores in order from lowest to highest, marking off each score as you list it to keep track.

After you have listed the scores, begin ranking them, assigning the lowest score a rank of 1. Remember, the groups are not ranked separately but together, so be sure to look in both groups for the next score in line.

Notice that in Group A, the score of 21 was achieved by two different participants and so the ranks for both scores will be averaged together and the same rank will be assigned to both. These scores would have been ranked 6 and 7 which, averaged together, is 6.5 $\left(\dfrac{6+7}{2}=6.5\right)$.

We then resume with a rank of 8 for the following score. Next, we encounter a three-way tie with the score of 24 in Group B. Here again, we will average together what the ranks would be for these three scores and each will receive a rank of 10 $\left(\dfrac{9+10+11}{3}=10\right)$. We then move forward with the next rank of 12. Your final rank should be equal to the total number of scores.

## The Calculations

Once we have assigned the ranks, we are ready to perform the calculations for the Mann-Whitney *U* test. First, we will need to sum the ranks for the two groups which we will label $\Sigma R_1$ and $\Sigma R_2$. For our example, $\Sigma R_1 = 74$ for Group A and $\Sigma R_2 = 79$ for group B. We will now calculate two *U*-values, one for each group. The formulas and their application to our problem are as follows:

$$U_1 = (n_1)(n_2) + \frac{n_1(n_1+1)}{2} - \Sigma R_1$$

$$= (8)(9) + \frac{8(8+1)}{2} - 74$$

$$= 72 + 36 - 74$$

$$= 34$$

$$U_2 = (n_1)(n_2) + \frac{n_2(n_2+1)}{2} - \Sigma R_2$$

$$= (8)(9) + \frac{9(9+1)}{2} - 79$$

$$= 72 + 45 - 79$$

$$= 38$$

Tip!

As a check on our calculations, $U_1 + U_2$ should equal $(n_1)(n_2)$. For our problem, $34 + 38 = 72$ and $(8)(9) = 72$.

As with other statistical tests, we will compare our obtained $U$-value with a critical value of $U$ in order to determine if the null hypothesis can be rejected. Although we obtained two values for $U$, it is only the smaller of the two, 34, that will be used for the comparison.

Table 9 toward the end of this book lists the critical values for the Mann-Whitney $U$ test. Alpha levels for a one-tailed test $(\alpha_1)$ are shown in the top row. Alpha levels for a two-tailed test $(\alpha_2)$ are show immediately below that. The left column shows the size of the samples. Once you have located the applicable $U_{crit}$, compare it with your obtained $U$-value. Be careful because, unlike the parametric tests that we have covered in previous chapters where obtained values had to exceed critical values to reach significance, in this case, $U_{obt}$ must be equal to or *smaller* than $U_{crit}$ to reject the null hypothesis. We will use a two-tailed test with an alpha level of .05. The $U_{crit}$-value found in Table 9 at the intersection of $n_1 = 8$ and $n_2 = 9$ and an alpha level of .05 for a two-tailed test is 15. Our obtained $U$-value was 34 which is *larger* than $U_{crit}$. Thus, we will fail to reject the null hypothesis. The distribution of the ranked scores from one group was not significantly different from the ranked scores of the other group.

---

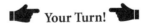 Your Turn!

### I. Parametric versus Nonparametric Tests

Under what circumstances should a nonparametric test be used rather than a parametric test?

### II. Ranking Scores for the Mann-Whitney $U$ Test

Rank the following scores from two different treatment groups. Treatment Group A: 8, 10, 12, 7, 14, 12, and 9. Treatment Group B: 7, 6, 8, 10, 12, and 8.

---

## THE WILCOXON MATCHED-PAIRS SIGNED-RANKS *T* TEST

The *Wilcoxon matched-pairs signed-ranks T test* would be the appropriate test to use in place of the related samples *t* test if only ordinal data is available or if parametric assumptions cannot be met. Recall that there are two types of the related samples $t$ test. The matched pairs design involves a set of scores that have been logically paired together, such as the scores for a set of twins. The repeated measures design involves pre- and post-testing of the same participants. The Wilcoxon matched-pairs signed-ranks $T$ test can be used as a nonparametric choice for either of these designs.

For this test, we will begin with a pair of scores, either from the same subjects or matched for some logical reason. We will then determine the difference between the two sets of scores, rank the difference scores, identify the ranked differences with either a positive or negative sign, and then sum the positive and negative ranks. The null hypothesis for a two-tailed test is that both samples came from populations with the same distribution of scores. If the null hypothesis were true, then the sum of the positive ranks should approximately equal the sum of the negative ranks for our two groups. The alternative hypothesis is, of course, that the population distributions are not equal. A one-tailed alternative hypothesis would specify that the sum of either the positive or negative ranks for one group would be greater than those for the other group.

The Wilcoxon matched-pairs signed-ranks test generates a value for $T_{obt}$ which will be compared to a $T_{crit}$-value.[2] However, the test does not involve the use of a formula. Instead, a series of steps is used to arrive at $T_{obt}$. Let's work through an example as we go through the steps. For this illustration, Table 17.3 shows the hypothetical scores for degree of interest in being in the outdoors for a sample of participants both before and after watching a nature film. Notice that the scores are not listed from lowest to highest because, for this test, it is the difference between the scores and not the scores themselves that are ranked.

The table is completed as follows:

1. Calculate a difference value ($D$) for each pair or scores. For this test, it does not matter which score is subtracted from the other but the order in which the subtraction takes place has to be consistent for all of the pairs.
2. Difference values of 0 are not ranked and are not included in the calculations. Ignoring the signs and any 0 difference values, record the absolute difference values in the $|D|$ column.

*Table 17.3* Interest in the Outdoors Study

| Pair | Before | After | D | $|D|$ | Rank of $|D|$ | Signed Rank |
|------|--------|-------|-----|-----|--------------|-------------|
| 1 | 12 | 17 | −5 | 5 | 6.5 | −6.5 |
| 2 | 8 | 6 | 2 | 2 | 3 | 3 |
| 3 | 5 | 4 | 1 | 1 | 1.5 | 1.5 |
| 4 | 10 | 15 | −5 | 5 | 6.5 | −6.5 |
| 5 | 13 | 19 | −6 | 6 | 8 | −8 |
| 6 | 16 | 16 | 0 | | | |
| 7 | 7 | 10 | −3 | 3 | 4 | −4 |
| 8 | 12 | 16 | −4 | 4 | 5 | −5 |
| 9 | 9 | 16 | −7 | 7 | 9 | −9 |
| 10 | 8 | 9 | −1 | 1 | 1.5 | −1.5 |
| | | | $n = 9$ | | | $\Sigma R_{pos} = 4.5$ |
| | | | | | | $\Sigma R_{neg} = 40.5$ |
| | | | | | | $T_{obt} = 4.5$ |

3. Rank the absolute difference values assigning the lowest score a rank of 1. If there are ties among the $|D|$ values, they will be averaged together in the same way that tied ranks were averaged together for the Mann-Whitney $U$ test.
4. Record the sign of the difference values $(D)$ in the last, *Signed Rank*, column.
5. Add the positive ranks to obtain $\Sigma R_{pos}$ and the negative ranks to obtain $\Sigma R_{neg}$. It is the lowest absolute value of the two sums that will be used as $T_{obt}$ to determine significance.

We will assume a two-tailed test with $\alpha = .05$. Table 10 in the back of the book lists the critical $T$-values for rejecting the null hypothesis. It is similar to the previous table for the Mann-Whitney $U$ test with alpha levels for one- and two-tailed tests across the top rows and sample size along the left column. The number of non-zero difference scores should be used for $n$. For our example, $n = 9$ and $T_{crit} = 5$. Here too, as with the Mann-Whitney $U$ test, $T_{obt}$ has to be equal to or less than $T_{crit}$ in order to reject H$_0$. Since our obtained $T$-value of 4.5 is less than 5, we will reject the null hypothesis that the distributions are the same. The participants rated their degree of interest in the outdoors significantly higher after viewing the nature film.

Remember, both $U_{obt}$ and $T_{obt}$ are significant if they are equal to or *smaller* than the critical values for those tests. Before, our obtained values had to be larger than the critical values in order to reject H$_0$.

Tip!

## THE KRUSKAL-WALLIS *H* TEST

The **Kruskal-Wallis H test** is the nonparametric alternative to a one-way ANOVA, independent samples design. Like the previous nonparametric tests that we have discussed, the Kruskal-Wallis $H$ test can be used for situations in which only ordinal level data is available or if the assumptions of parametric testing cannot be met. In this case, however, we will be working with more than two groups. Technically, the Kruskal-Wallis $H$ test could be used for only two groups but the Mann-Whitney $U$ test is available for those situations. In actuality, the Kruskal-Wallis $H$ test is a further elaboration of the Mann-Whitney $U$ test. Let's again work through an example for which the Kruskal-Wallis $H$ test is appropriate. Keep in mind that a requirement for this test is that a minimum sample size of five is required for each group.

Suppose an investigator is studying the effects of three different types of therapy on depression scores. She is concerned that one or more of the distributions might be skewed and so she decides to use the Kruskal-Wallis $H$ test to analyze the data. The scores for the different types of therapy are as follows: Treatment A: 15, 9, 21, 8, 17; Treatment B: 23, 9, 15, 14, 20; Treatment C: 35, 44, 29, 37, 42. The scores have been placed in Table 17.4. Notice that the scores have been ranked in the same way as for the Mann-Whitney $U$ test with all three groups being ranked at the same time. The sum of the ranks for each group has also been provided.

We will again apply the more commonly used two-tailed test with $\alpha = .05$. Like the Mann-Whitney $U$ test, the null hypothesis is that the samples came from populations with the same distributions of scores (i.e., even after treatment, the distributions of scores for the different treatments groups in the population would be the same). The alternative hypothesis is that the distributions of scores would be different after treatment. And, of course, we hope to be able to reject H$_0$.

*Table 17.4* Depression Study

| Treatment A | Rank | Treatment B | Rank | Treatment C | Rank |
|---|---|---|---|---|---|
| 8 | 1 | 9 | 2.5 | 29 | 11 |
| 9 | 2.5 | 14 | 4 | 35 | 12 |
| 15 | 5.5 | 15 | 5.5 | 37 | 13 |
| 17 | 7 | 20 | 8 | 42 | 14 |
| 21 | 9 | 23 | 10 | 44 | 15 |
| | $\Sigma R_1 = 25$ | | $\Sigma R_2 = 30$ | | $\Sigma R_3 = 65$ |

The formula for the Kruskal-Wallis $H$ test is

$$H = \left[ \frac{12}{N(N+1)} \right]\left[ \Sigma \frac{R_t^2}{n_t} \right] - 3(N+1)$$

where $t$ as a subscript refers to individual sample groups, $n_t$ refers to the number of scores in a sample group, and $N$ refers to the total number of scores in all groups. The term in the middle of the formula instructs you to perform the operations inside the brackets for each group before subtracting the term at the end of the formula. The formula applied to our problem is as follows:

$$H = \left[ \frac{12}{15(15+1)} \right]\left[ \frac{25^2}{5} + \frac{30^2}{5} + \frac{65^2}{5} \right] - 3(15+1)$$

$$= (.0500)(125+180+845) - 48$$

$$= 9.5$$

We now need to compare our obtained $H$-value with a critical value. When the sample size for each group is a minimum of 5, the sampling distribution for $H$ approximates the chi-square distribution. Thus, we can use the critical values for chi-square, found in Table 8, with $df = k - 1$, to determine if $H_{obt}$ is significant. Recall that $k$ refers to the number of groups in the study. If $H_{obt}$ is greater than $\chi^2_{crit}$, then $H_0$ can be rejected. With $\alpha = .05$ and $df = 2$, $\chi^2_{crit} = 5.991$. Since our obtained $H$-value of 9.5 exceeds $\chi^2_{crit}$, we can reject the null hypothesis that the groups represent the same populations. We can conclude instead that at least some of the groups are different. In other words, the three different approaches to treatment for depression did not produce equal results. Here again, post hoc comparisons would be called for in order to determine which groups in particular were different from the others.

As stated earlier, a minimum of five participants in each group is required to use the chi-square distribution. The Kruskal-Wallis $H$ test can, technically, be used for smaller sizes but this is unusual and a table other than the one for the chi-square distribution would be needed. There is no requirement that the samples in each group be the same size in order to use the Kruskal-Wallis $H$ test.

## THE SPEARMAN CORRELATION COEFFICIENT

The last in our exploration of nonparametric statistics is the **Spearman correlation coefficient**, also known as Spearman's rho, symbolized by $r_s$. As you might have guessed, this test is the nonparametric alternative for the Pearson correlation coefficient. Correlation coefficients measure the degree of relationship between two variables. In this case, one or both variables are measured on an ordinal scale. A two-tailed null hypothesis is that the population correlation is 0. The alternative hypothesis for a two-tailed test is that the population correlation is something other than 0. A one-tailed alternative hypothesis will specify the population correlation to be either greater than or less than 0. These were the same hypotheses used for the Pearson correlation. In fact, the Spearman correlation is a simplified version of the Pearson correlation when using rank-order data.

The formula for the Spearman rank-order correlation coefficient is as follows:

$$r_s = 1 - \frac{6\Sigma D^2}{n\left(n^2 - 1\right)}$$

where $D$ = difference between the ranks of the pairs of scores
$\quad n$ = number of pairs of scores

Let's work through an example. Two professors who team taught a humanities course separately ranked their students' capstone projects from 1 to 12. The rankings are shown in Table 17.5. Notice that the variables are ranked separately for this test. Also, be aware that the formula should only be used if there are few or no tied ranks. Some of the accuracy of the formula would be lost if there were several tied ranks.

To use the $r_s$ formula, we first have to determine $\Sigma D^2$. To do so, obtain the difference between the ranked scores, square the difference values and then add them up to obtain $\Sigma D^2$. For the Spearman correlation test, we do not drop the scores that have a 0 difference value from the analysis because they provide important information (i.e., that there was no difference in the ranks of the two scores, thus contributing to a stronger $r_s$ value).

We can now calculate our obtained $r_s$ value:

$$r_s = 1 - \frac{(6)(62)}{12(12^2 - 1)} = 1 - \frac{(372)}{(12)(143)} = 1 - \frac{372}{1716} = 1 - .2168$$

$$= .7832$$

Table 17.5 Spearman Correlation Study

| Student | Rank from Professor X | Rank from Professor Y | D | D² |
|---------|------------------------|------------------------|-----|-----|
| A | 1 | 3 | −2 | 4 |
| B | 3 | 2 | 1 | 1 |
| C | 4 | 1 | 3 | 9 |
| D | 2 | 4 | −2 | 4 |
| E | 6 | 6 | 0 | 0 |
| F | 5 | 5 | 0 | 0 |
| G | 10 | 7 | 3 | 9 |
| H | 7 | 10 | −3 | 9 |
| I | 9 | 9 | 0 | 0 |
| J | 12 | 11 | 1 | 1 |
| K | 11 | 8 | 3 | 9 |
| L | 8 | 12 | −4 | 16 |
| | | | | $\Sigma D^2 = 62$ |

We will use a two-tailed test with $\alpha = .05$. Table 11 at the back of the book lists the critical values of $r_s$ for rejecting $H_0$. Using $n = 12$, we find that $r_{s_{crit}} = .5874$. Significance is indicated if $r_{s_{obt}}$ is equal to or greater than $r_{s_{crit}}$. Since our obtained $r_s$ value meets this standard, we can reject the null hypothesis that there is no relationship between the rankings of the papers by the two professors. Our obtained $r_s$ value of .7832 suggests a strong correlation.

---

 **Your Turn!**

### III. Which Nonparametric Test to Use

For each of the studies that follow, decide whether it would be better to use the (a) Mann-Whitney $U$ test, (b) Wilcoxon $T$ test, (c) Kruskal-Wallis $H$ test, or (d) Spearman $r_s$ test:

A. A random sample of children rates the fonts for four different cereal boxes from most eye-catching to least eye-catching.

B. A new drug is being tested to determine its effectiveness in reducing symptoms of asthma. Twenty participants were randomly assigned to two groups. Half received the new asthma drug and half received a placebo. After two weeks, both groups rated how well their symptoms were controlled on a scale from 1 to 10.

C. A political scientist is studying the relationship between the amount of charitable donations that people make and their attitude toward government sponsored assistance programs.

D. A career researcher is studying various aspects of different occupations. For this study, he randomly selects ten architects and ten engineers and records their annual salary. Since income is known to form a skewed distribution, he converts their annual salaries into ranks in order to determine if the overall ranks of one occupation is significantly higher or lower than the other.

E. A couples counselor is researching the factors that contribute to longevity in relationships. For the current study, a sample of husbands and wives is asked to complete a survey rating their degree of preference for socializing with others as a form of entertainment.

F. Random samples of low-income, moderate-income, and high-income workers complete a survey on the degree of importance that they assign to the candidates' focus on climate change solutions in the upcoming election.

### IV. When to Reject $H_0$

The list below provides information that is needed to use the tables at the back of your text. Locate the critical value from the appropriate table and indicate if $H_0$ should be rejected.

*(Continued)*

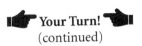
**Your Turn!**
(continued)

*Table 17.6* Using Tables of Critical Values for Nonparametric Tests

| Statistical Test | $\alpha$ Level | One- or Two-Tailed Test | Obtained Value | Critical Value | Reject $H_0$ Yes/No |
|---|---|---|---|---|---|
| Wilcoxon $T$, $n = 12$ | .01 | One-tailed | 10 | | |
| Spearman $r_s$, $n = 10$ | .05 | One-tailed | .78 | | |
| Kruskal-Wallis $H$, $df = 4$ | .05 | N/A | 8.42 | | |
| Mann-Whitney $U$, $n_1 = 9$, $n_2 = 10$ | .01 | Two-tailed | 15 | | |
| Wilcoxon $T$, $n = 13$ | .05 | Two-tailed | 13 | | |
| Spearman $r_s$, $n = 15$ | .05 | Two-tailed | .467 | | |
| Kruskal-Wallis $H$, $df = 3$ | .01 | N/A | 13.56 | | |
| Mann-Whitney $U$, $n_1 = 6$, $n_2 = 8$ | .05 | One-tailed | 8 | | |

## CLOSING REMARKS

This particular leg of your adventure into the world of statistics is over. Some of you will go on to take more advanced courses in statistics or research methods. If you have studied and mastered the concepts in this text, you are well-prepared and can feel confident as you move forward. If you do not continue your studies in other statistics courses, hopefully, you have come to appreciate the value of statistics and the role it plays in science, in understanding the world, and in making informed, educated decisions. Congratulations! You have come a long way.

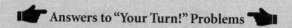 Answers to "Your Turn!" Problems

## I. Factors and Levels

Nonparametric tests should be used if only ordinal level data is available or if there are concerns about meeting the assumptions of normality and homogeneity of variance required for parametric tests.

## II. Ranking Scores

| Group A | Rank | Group B | Rank |
|---|---|---|---|
| 7 | 2.5 | 6 | 1 |
| 8 | 5 | 7 | 2.5 |
| 9 | 7 | 8 | 5 |
| 10 | 8.5 | 8 | 5 |
| 12 | 11 | 10 | 8.5 |
| 12 | 11 | 12 | 11 |
| 14 | 13 | | |

## III. Which Nonparametric Test to Use

A. c
B. a
C. d
D. a
E. b
F. c

## IV. When to Reject $H_0$

| Statistical Test | $\alpha$ Level | One- or Two-Tailed Test | Obtained Value | Critical Value | Reject $H_0$ Yes/No |
|---|---|---|---|---|---|
| Wilcoxon $T$, $n = 12$ | .01 | One-tailed | 10 | 9 | No |
| Spearman $r_s$, $n = 10$ | .05 | One-tailed | .78 | .564 | Yes |
| Kruskal-Wallis $H$, $df = 4$ | .05 | N/A | 8.42 | 9.488 | No |
| Mann-Whitney $U$, $n_1 = 9$, $n_2 = 10$ | .01 | Two-tailed | 15 | 13 | No |
| Wilcoxon $T$, $n = 13$ | .05 | Two-tailed | 13 | 17 | Yes |
| Spearman $r_s$, $n = 15$ | .05 | Two-tailed | .467 | .521 | No |
| Kruskal-Wallis $H$, $df = 3$ | .01 | N/A | 13.56 | 11.345 | Yes |
| Mann-Whitney $U$, $n_1 = 6$, $n_2 = 8$ | .05 | One-tailed | 8 | 10 | Yes |

## Using Online Calculators for Nonparametric Data Analysis

Although it is possible to perform nonparametric statistics tests using Excel, these tests are not built into the program and it is easier to use an online calculator. If you perform an internet search for the nonparametric test you are using (e.g., "Mann-Whitney $U$ test calculator"), several sites with online calculators for that particular test will result. These sites will allow you to type in your data sets, choose between an alpha level of .01 or .05, and choose a one-tailed test or a two-tailed test. The results will include the ranking of the scores, both obtained and critical test values, and p-values. Some will also provide interpretations about whether the obtained test value was significant.

### *Additional Practice Problems*

**Answers to odd numbered problems are in Appendix C at the end of the book.**

1. Why is it better to use a parametric test if the assumptions can be met? Why should one proceed with caution if the assumptions of a parametric test are seriously violated?
2. How is the Mann-Whitney $U$ test different from the Wilcoxon matched-pairs signed-ranks test?
3. How are the Mann-Whitney $U$ test and the Kruskal-Wallis test similar and how are they different?
4. How are the Pearson correlation and the Spearman correlation similar and how are they different?
5. Compare the obtained and critical values for the tests below and determine if the null hypothesis can be rejected.

|     |                         |                          | Y/N |
| --- | ----------------------- | ------------------------ | --- |
| a.  | $r_{s_{obt}} = .6135$   | $r_{s_{crit}} = .5385$   | ___ |
| b.  | $T_{obt} = 18$          | $T_{crit} = 17$          | ___ |
| c.  | $\chi^2_{obt} = 14.36$  | $\chi^2_{crit} = 16.919$ | ___ |
| d.  | $U_{obt} = 3$           | $U_{crit} = 4$           | ___ |

6. What is the $U_{crit}$ for a study that has 12 participants in one group and 14 in another using $\alpha = .01$, two-tailed?
7. What is the $T_{crit}$ for a repeated measures study with a sample size of 18 using $\alpha = .01$, one-tailed?
8. What is the $r_{s_{crit}}$ for a study with a sample size of 9 using $\alpha = .05$, two-tailed?
9. The following interval level scores form skewed distributions. Rank the scores and conduct a Mann-Whitney $U$ test using $\alpha = .05$, two-tailed.
   Treatment A: 13, 38, 10, 16, 12, 10, 42
   Treatment B: 35, 42, 38, 64, 36, 72, 40, 38

10. The following ordinal level scores were obtained before and after a treatment interven-
tion. Conduct a Wilcoxon matched-pairs signed-ranks $T$ test with $\alpha = .05$, one-tailed.
Before: 5, 8, 6, 7, 6, 9, 8, 6
After: 8, 8, 5, 9, 7, 10, 6, 10

11. Rank the following set of ordinal scores from independent samples and conduct a
Kruskal-Wallis $H$ test using $\alpha = .05$.
Group A: 15, 16, 12, 18, 16, 13
Group B: 17, 14, 16, 20, 19, 17
Group C: 23, 20, 25, 22, 23, 24

12. Rank the set of ordinal scores below and calculate the Spearman correlation coefficient. Is
there a significant relationship between the two variables? Test using $\alpha = .05$, two-tailed.
Variable X: 15, 19, 23, 16, 18, 20, 17, 14
Variable Y: 33, 38, 49, 36, 39, 42, 41, 35

13. A podiatrist is testing three different types of foot exercises for people who suffer from
planters fasciitis. Eighteen participants with this condition were randomly assigned to
one of the three exercise groups. They practiced the exercises daily for 3 months and
then rated their level of pain on a scale from 1 to 25, with 25 representing the greatest
amount of pain. Use the appropriate test to determine if there were significant differences among the three different types of exercises. Use $\alpha = .05$, two-tailed.
Exercise A: 18, 12, 16, 14, 20, 15
Exercise B: 5, 9, 15, 12, 8, 6
Exercise C: 16, 14, 11, 15, 19, 18

14. A sleep researcher asks a sample of ten clients to rate their degree of alertness 30 minutes after they wake up in the morning and again at 3:00 p.m. Their scores are listed
below with higher scores indicating a higher level of alertness. Use the appropriate test
to determine if there were significant differences in the morning and afternoon ratings
of alertness. Use $\alpha = .01$, one-tailed.
Morning: 9, 7, 6, 8, 6, 4, 9, 3, 8, 6
Afternoon: 7, 4, 8, 6, 8, 9, 5, 7, 8, 8

15. A new faculty member wanted to see how the grading of student papers aligned with the
grading of established faculty. After grading a sample of her student papers, she ranked
them from 1 to 12. She then removed the students' names and asked a colleague to rank
them. The rankings are listed below. Use the appropriate test to determine if there is
a relationship between the rankings of the new and established faculty members. Use
$\alpha = .01$, two-tailed.

| Student | Ranking by New Faculty | Ranking by Established Faculty |
|---------|------------------------|-------------------------------|
| 1 | 3 | 3 |
| 2 | 5 | 6 |
| 3 | 10 | 10 |
| 4 | 1 | 1 |
| 5 | 7 | 5 |
| 6 | 4 | 2 |
| 7 | 6 | 7 |
| 8 | 9 | 8 |
| 9 | 2 | 4 |
| 10 | 8 | 9 |

16. Two independent samples of grocery shoppers rated two different brands of spaghetti sauce on a scale from 1 to 10 based on how likely it is that they would purchase the product, where 1 = "Would not buy" and 10 = "Would definitely buy." Use the appropriate test to determine if there were significant differences in the ratings. Use $\alpha = .05$, two-tailed.
    Brand X: 6, 4, 7, 5, 4, 3
    Brand Y: 7, 9, 6, 10, 8, 8

## Notes

1 For Mann-Whitney procedures for large samples, see Spatz, C. (2001). *Basic statistics: Tales of distribution* (7th ed.). Belmont, CA: Wadsworth/Thomson.
2 There are other measures besides this test that the letter $T$ is used to symbolize. To avoid confusion, the letter $W$ is sometimes used rather than the letter $T$ to symbolize the Wilcoxon matched-pairs signed-ranks test statistic.

# Glossary of Statistical Terms

**Abscissa**: The horizontal or $x$-axis in a frequency graph, which usually represents the values or categories of the variable being measured.

**Alpha level**: The probability level set by the researcher that defines the point at which the null hypothesis should be rejected.

**Alternative hypothesis**: In hypothesis testing, the hypothesis that attributes differences between observed sample statistics and population parameters to true differences rather than chance differences; the research hypothesis.

**Analysis of variance**: A hypothesis-testing procedure that simultaneously evaluates the means of two or more groups for significance; abbreviated as ANOVA.

**ANOVA**: Acronym for analysis of variance.

**Asymptotic**: A characteristic of the normal distribution curve in which the tails never touch the baseline, illustrating the point that it is based on an infinite number of cases.

**Bar graph**: Graph of a frequency distribution used for qualitative variables that differ in kind, and in which the bars are spatially separated to indicate the discontinuous nature of the measured variable. The heights of the bars reflect the frequencies of each event.

**Between-treatments variance**: In ANOVA, the variability between the treatment groups; made up of individual differences, experimental error, and treatment effects.

**Bimodal distribution**: A distribution that has two scores with high frequencies, and thus two modes.

**Central limit theorem**: Theorem that states that as the size of the sample ($n$) increases, the shape of the sampling distribution of means approximates the shape of a normal distribution with a mean of $\mu$ and a standard deviation of $\sigma/\sqrt{n}$.

**Central tendency**: A single value that describes the most typical or representative score in an entire distribution.

**Chi-square**: Nonparametric procedure that uses nominal and ordinal data and takes the form of frequency counts.

**Class intervals**: Groups of scores of a specified size in a grouped frequency distribution.

**Coefficient of determination**: Proportion of variance that two variables share in common; proportion of the variance on one variable that is explained by the variance of the other.

**Coefficient of nondetermination**: Proportion of variability that is *not* shared, common variance; proportion of the variance on one variable that is *not* explained by the variance of the other.

**Computational formulas**: Formulas that facilitate use with a handheld calculator and that arrive at the same mathematical conclusions as definitional formulas.

**Confidence interval**: Range of values that, with a specified degree of confidence, is expected to include a population parameter.

**Continuous variable**: A variable that can be broken down into fractions or smaller units.

**Control group**: Group in an experiment that is not exposed to experimental treatment; used as a baseline for comparison.

**Correlation coefficient**: A number, ranging from $-1.00$ to $+1.00$, that measures the direction and strength of the relationship between two variables.

**Correlation research**: Method of research in which the values on two variables are analyzed to determine their degree of relationship.

**Counterbalancing**: Procedure used to minimize order effects in a repeated measures design by varying the order in which subjects are exposed to the independent variable.

**Criterion variable**: The variable that is estimated from predictor variables in regression analysis.

**Critical region**: Area of a sampling distribution in which outcomes are unlikely to be due to chance and which therefore lead to rejection of the null hypothesis.

**Critical values**: Values of a sampling distribution that designate the point of rejection of the null hypothesis.

**Cumulative frequency distribution**: A table that lists raw scores in descending order and identifies the frequency of scores that fall at or below a particular score.

**Data**: A set of scores.

**Definitional formulas**: Formulas that are written the way statistics are defined and that facilitate understanding because they guide the learner through the process of what is being measured.

**Degrees of freedom**: An adjustment factor used to estimate population parameters more accurately.

**Dependent variable**: The variable that is measured by the researcher to determine if it has been influenced by the independent variable; the presumed effect in an experiment.

**Descriptive statistics**: Procedures used to condense and summarize a set of scores.

**Deviation score**: A distance score obtained by subtracting the mean from a raw score of a distribution.

**Directional alternative hypothesis**: A hypothesis that specifies the direction of the expected difference between an obtained sample statistic and the value predicted by the null hypothesis.

**Discrete variable**: A variable that cannot be divided or split into intermediate values but can be measured only in whole numbers.

**Distribution-free tests**: Nonparametric tests that make no assumptions about the population distribution.

**Effect size**: A quantitative index of the magnitude of a treatment effect.

**Empirical distribution**: A distribution based on the frequencies of actual scores.

**Expected frequency**: The frequency values that would be expected if the null hypothesis of a chi-square study were true.

**Expected value**: Mean of the sampling distribution of means, which is equal to $\mu$.

**Experimental group**: Group in an experiment that is exposed to some sort of experimental treatment.

**Experimentation**: Research technique that involves manipulating one or more variables to determine if doing so has an effect on another variable; may suggest a cause-and-effect relationship.

**Experiment-wise alpha level**: The accumulated probability of making a Type I error that results from conducting multiple $t$ tests in an experiment.

**Extraneous variable**: A variable that could have an unintended effect on the dependent variable in an experiment, if not controlled.

**Factor**: In research, an independent variable that can be manipulated at several different levels.

**Factorial analysis of variance**: ANOVA performed for a study that involves examining the separate and combined effects of two or more independent variables.

**Frequency distribution**: A table that provides organization to a set of raw scores so that patterns in how the scores are distributed may be detected.

**Frequency polygon**: A graph of a frequency distribution used for quantitative variables that differ in amount. Similar to a histogram except that dots, rather than bars, correspond to the appropriate frequency. The dots are then connected by a straight line.

**Goodness of fit test**: Chi-square test that examines how well the frequencies observed in a sample match the frequencies that would be expected if the null hypothesis were true.

**Grouped frequency distribution**: A table in which raw scores are combined into groups, referred to as class intervals, thus condensing the data and making overall trends more apparent.

**Histogram**: A graph of a frequency distribution used for quantitative variables that differ in amount and in which the bars touch each other to reflect the continuous nature of the measured variable. The heights of the bars reflect the frequencies of each event.

**Homogeneity of variance**: An assumption for some statistical tests that the populations of interest have equal variances.

**Hypothesis testing**: Procedure used in inferential statistics to estimate population parameters based on sample data.

**Independent samples design**: Research design involving separate and unrelated samples for which each subject provides one score; also called between-subjects design.

**Independent variable**: The variable that is manipulated by the researcher to see if it produces a change in the dependent variable; the presumed cause in an experiment.

**Inferential statistics**: Procedures used to estimate and predict the characteristics of a population based on data obtained from a sample.

**Interaction effects**: The case in a factorial ANOVA in which the effect of one independent variable depends on the level of another independent variable.

**Interquartile range**: A measure of variability that describes the range of scores from the middle 50% of a distribution.

**Interval scale**: Measurement scale in which there is equal distance between units but which has an arbitrary zero point.

**Interval size**: The number of scores contained in the class intervals in a grouped frequency distribution.

**Kruskal-Wallis $H$ test**: Nonparametric alternative to a one-way ANOVA, independent samples design; used if only ordinal level data is available or if parametric assumptions cannot be met.

**Main effect**: The effect of a single independent variable in a factorial ANOVA.

**Mann-Whitney $U$ test**: Nonparametric test alternative to the independent samples $t$ test; used for ordinal level data when $n$ is 20 or less.

**Mean**: The sum total of all the scores in a distribution divided by the number of scores. A measure of central tendency.

**Mean square**: A measure of variance in ANOVA obtained by dividing the sum of squares by its corresponding degrees of freedom.

**Median**: The middle point in a distribution such that half the scores will fall above this middle point and half will fall below it. A measure of central tendency.

**Midpoint**: The middle point in a class interval of a grouped frequency distribution.

**Mode**: A measure of central tendency that specifies the most frequently occurring score in a set of scores.

**Negative correlation**: Relationship in which two variables proceed in opposite directions; high $X$-scores are associated with low $Y$-scores, and vice versa.

**Negatively skewed distribution**: An asymmetrical distribution in which most scores are high and there are fewer low scores.

**Nominal scale**: Measurement scale that classifies observations into different categories; has no quantitative value.

**Nondirectional alternative hypothesis**: Hypothesis stating that the population value is other than the one predicted in the null hypothesis; the direction of expected differences is not specified.

**Nonparametric tests**: Statistical procedures that can be used when the assumptions of parametrical procedures cannot be met.

**Normal distribution curve**: A theoretical, symmetrical, bell-shaped curve of probabilities and proportions whose units of measurement are in $z$-scores.

**Null hypothesis**: In hypothesis testing, the hypothesis that attributes differences between observed sample statistics and population parameters to chance, or random sampling error.

**Observed frequency**: The actual frequency count of subjects that fall into each category in a chi-square study.

**One-sample $t$ test**: A test of a hypothesis about a population mean ($\mu$) when the population standard deviation ($\sigma$) is not known.

**One-tailed test**: Statistical test in which sample statistics that fall in only one tail of the critical region of a sampling distribution lead to rejection of the null hypothesis; used when a directional alternative hypothesis is employed.

**One-way analysis of variance**: Analysis of variance performed for studies that involve only one independent variable and two or more groups.

**Order effects**: Effects that take place in a repeated measures design in which the order that the independent variable is presented has an influence on the dependent variable.

**Ordinal scale**: Measurement scale that permits the ordering or ranking of observations; information about more than/less than is provided, but not how much more than/less than.

**Ordinate**: The vertical or $y$-axis in a frequency graph, which usually represents the frequencies of the values or categories being measured.

**Outliers**: Extreme scores in a distribution that are atypical of most of the other scores.

**Parameter**: A numerical value that represents a population and that is usually inferred from a sample.

**Parametric tests**: Statistical procedures that test hypotheses about populations and which require that certain assumptions be met.

**Pearson product moment correlation coefficient**: Method of correlation used for examining linear relationships between variables measured on interval or ratio scales.

**Percentile rank**: The percentage of scores that fall at or below a given score in a distribution.

**Point estimate**: A single value, based on sample data, that is used to estimate the parameter of a population.

**Population**: All members of a group of persons, plants, animals, objects, or events that have something in common.

**Positive correlation**: Relationship in which two variables proceed in the same direction; high $X$-scores are associated with high $Y$-scores, and vice versa.

**Positively skewed distribution**: An asymmetrical distribution in which most scores are low and there are fewer high scores.

**Post hoc tests**: Tests that are conducted after a null hypothesis has been rejected and there are three or more treatment groups; used to pinpoint which means differ significantly.

**Power**: The ability of a statistical test to reject a null hypothesis that is in fact false.

**Predictor variables**: Variables used to estimate values on another variable in regression analysis.

**Probability**: The mathematical likelihood of an event occurring, expressed as a proportion.

**Qualitative variable**: A variable that differs in kind.

**Quantitative variable**: A variable that differs in amount.

**Quartile**: One of the three points that divides a distribution into four equal parts.

**Random assignment**: Method of assigning participants to an experiment in which each participant has an equal chance of being assigned to any one of the groups.

**Random sampling**: Sampling in such a way that all members of a population have the same chance of being selected for inclusion in the sample.

**Range**: A measure of variability that indicates the amount of spread in a distribution of scores as determined by subtracting the lower limit of the lowest score from the upper limit of the highest score.

**Ratio scale**: Measurement scale in which there is an absolute, or true, zero point; permits ratio comparisons such as half as much or four times as many.

**Raw scores**: Scores that have not yet undergone any type of statistical transformation or analysis.

**Real limits**: The upper and lower limits of a reported score's value. These limits extend beyond the reported value by one-half of the unit of measurement in either direction.

**Regression analysis**: Statistical procedure used to predict the value of a score on one variable by knowing the value of the score on another variable.

**Regression line**: The straight line that runs through a scatterplot used for predicting Y-scores from given X-scores; line of best fit.

**Related samples design**: Research design involving scores from the same subjects (repeated measures) or from two samples that are related in some other logical way (matched pairs).

**Relative frequency distribution**: A table that lists raw scores in descending order and identifies the proportion of time that each score occurs.

**Reliability**: The consistency, or stability, of test scores upon repeated administrations of the test (or alternate forms of the test).

**Repeated measures study**: Study in which the same subjects are measured before and after a treatment intervention; also called a within-subjects design.

**Research**: A systematic inquiry in search of knowledge.

**Restricting the range**: Use of a sample that limits the scores on one or both variables more than what would be found in the population.

**Sample**: A subset of a population.

**Sampling distribution**: A theoretical probability distribution that represents a statistic for all possible samples of a given size from a population of interest.

**Sampling distribution of mean differences**: A theoretical probability distribution of all possible mean differences from two related samples of a given size from two related populations of interest.

**Sampling distribution of means**: A theoretical probability distribution of all possible sample means of a given size from a population of interest.

**Sampling distribution of the difference between means**: A theoretical probability distribution of all possible differences between two means from independent samples of a given size from two populations of interest.

**Sampling error:** The amount of error between a sample statistic and a population parameter.

**Sampling frame:** Portion of a population that is accessible and from which samples are drawn.

**Scatterplot:** A diagram of the relationship between two variables.

**Significant:** In statistical testing, refers to a greater-than-chance result, leading to rejection of the null hypothesis.

**Simple frequency distribution:** A table that lists raw scores in descending order and identifies the frequency with which each score occurs.

**Skewed distribution:** An asymmetrical distribution in which scores tend to pile up at either the high or low end of the distribution and trail off at the other end.

**Slope:** Component of the regression equation that tells how much and in what direction the regression line slants.

**Spearman correlation coefficient:** Nonparametric alternative to the Pearson correlation coefficient; used when only rank order data is available.

**Standard deviation:** The square root of the variance. A measure of variability.

**Standard error of difference between means:** The standard deviation of the sampling distribution of the difference between means.

**Standard error of the mean:** The standard deviation of the sampling distribution of means.

**Standard error of the mean difference:** The standard deviation for the sampling distribution of mean differences.

**Standard score:** A score that is expressed relative to a specified mean and standard deviation.

**Statistic:** A numerical value that originates from a sample.

**Statistics:** The procedures used in research for gathering, organizing, and analyzing information.

**Sum of squares:** The sum of the squared deviations of scores from the mean. The numerator in the formula for the standard deviation.

**_t_-distribution:** A theoretical, bell-shaped probability distribution of _t_-values; used when the population standard deviation is not known.

**Test of independence:** Chi-square test that examines the frequencies for two variables to determine if they are independent of each other or if they are related.

**Theoretical distribution:** A distribution based on the mathematical probability of the frequencies of scores in a population.

**Transformed standard score:** A score whose distribution has been altered from the original scale to a new scale with a different mean and standard deviation without altering the relative position of the scores.

**Tukey's Honestly Significant Difference Test:** Post hoc test that makes multiple comparisons between the means in an experiment, two at a time; abbreviated as _HSD_.

**Two-sample _t_ test:** A test of a hypothesis of the difference between two sample means to determine if those means differ significantly.

**Two-tailed test:** Statistical test in which sample statistics that fall in either tail of the critical region of a sampling distribution lead to rejection of the null hypothesis; used when a nondirectional alternative hypothesis is employed.

**Type I error:** Rejecting a null hypothesis that is in reality true; also called an alpha error.

**Type II error:** The failure to reject a null hypothesis that is in reality false.

**Unimodal distribution:** A distribution that has one score with high frequencies, and thus one mode.

**Validity:** The degree to which a test measures what it is supposed to measure.

**Variability:** The amount of spread in a set of scores.

**Variable:** Anything that can be present in more than one form or amount.

**Variance**: The average of the squared deviations of the scores around the mean of a distribution; the standard deviation squared.

**Wilcoxon matched-pairs signed-ranks *T* test**: Nonparametric test alternative to the related samples *t* test; used if only ordinal level data is available or if parametric assumptions cannot be met.

**Within-treatment variance**: In ANOVA, the variability within a particular sample; made up of individual differences and experimental error.

***y*-intercept**: Component of the regression equation that tells the point at which the regression line cuts across the *y*-axis.

***z*-score**: A type of standard score that describes how far a particular raw score deviates from the mean in standard deviation units.

# Appendix B
## Glossary of Statistical Formulas

**ONE-WAY ANALYSIS OF VARIANCE**

$$SS_{total} = \sum X_{tot}^2 - \frac{\left(\sum X_{tot}\right)^2}{N}$$

$$SS_{wi} = \sum \left[ \sum X_t^2 - \frac{\left(\sum X_t\right)^2}{n_t} \right]$$

$$df_{wi} = N - k$$
$$df_{bet} = k - 1$$
$$df_{total} = N - 1$$

$$SS_{bet} = \sum \left[ \frac{\left(\sum X_t\right)^2}{n_t} \right] - \frac{\left(\sum X_{tot}\right)^2}{N}$$

$$MS_{bet} = \frac{SS_{bet}}{df_{bet}} \qquad\qquad MS_{wi} = \frac{SS_{wi}}{df_{wi}}$$

$$F = \frac{MS_{bet}}{MS_{wi}}$$

**FACTORIAL ANALYSIS OF VARIANCE**

$$SS_{total} = \sum X_{tot}^2 - \frac{\left(\sum X_{tot}\right)^2}{N_{tot}}$$

$$df_{tot} = N_{tot} - 1$$
$$df_{bet(A)} = A - 1$$
$$df_{bet(B)} = B - 1$$
$$df_{bet(AB)} = (A - 1)(B - 1)$$
$$df_{wi} = N_{tot} - k$$

$$SS_{wi} = \sum \left[ \sum X_{cell}^2 - \frac{\left(\sum X_{cell}\right)^2}{n_{cell}} \right]$$

$$SS_{bet} = \sum \left[ \frac{\left(\sum X_{cell}\right)^2}{n_{cell}} \right] - \frac{\left(\sum X_{tot}\right)^2}{N_{tot}}$$

$$SS_A = \Sigma \left[ \frac{(\Sigma X_{C\,tot})^2}{N_{C\,tot}} \right] - \frac{(\Sigma X_{tot})^2}{N_{tot}}$$

$$SS_B = \Sigma \left[ \frac{(\Sigma X_{R\,tot})^2}{N_{R\,tot}} \right] - \frac{(\Sigma X_{tot})^2}{N_{tot}}$$

$$SS_{AB} = SS_{bet} - SS_A - SS_B$$

$$MS_A = \frac{SS_A}{df_{bet(A)}}$$

$$MS_B = \frac{SS_B}{df_{bet(B)}}$$

$$MS_{AB} = \frac{SS_{AB}}{df_{bet(AB)}}$$

$$MS_{wi} = \frac{SS_{wi}}{df_{wi}}$$

$$F_A = \frac{MS_A}{MS_{wi}}$$

$$F_B = \frac{MS_B}{MS_{wi}}$$

$$F_{AB} = \frac{MS_{AB}}{MS_{wi}}$$

## CHI-SQUARE

$$\chi^2 = \Sigma \frac{(f_o - f_e)^2}{f_e}$$

## CONFIDENCE INTERVALS

$$\left. \begin{array}{l} LL = M - t(s_M) \\ UL = M + t(s_M) \end{array} \right\} \text{ for one} - \text{sample } t \text{ test}$$

$$\left. \begin{array}{l} LL = (M_1 - M_2) - t(S_{M_1 - M_2}) \\ UL = (M_1 - M_2) + t(S_{M_1 - M_2}) \end{array} \right\} \text{ for independent two} - \text{sample } t \text{ test}$$

$$\left. \begin{array}{l} LL = M_D - t(S_{M_D}) \\ UL = M_D + t(S_{M_D}) \end{array} \right\} \text{ for repeated two} - \text{sample } t \text{ test}$$

## CORRELATION

### Pearson Product Moment Correlation Coefficient

$$r = \frac{N\Sigma XY - (\Sigma X)(\Sigma Y)}{\sqrt{\left[ N\Sigma X^2 - (\Sigma X)^2 \right] \left[ N\Sigma Y^2 - (\Sigma Y)^2 \right]}}$$

**EFFECT SIZE**

$$d = \frac{|M - \mu|}{\sigma} \ (\text{for } z - \text{test}) \qquad\qquad d = \frac{|M - \mu|}{s} \ (\text{for one} - \text{sample } t \text{ test})$$

$$d = \frac{|M_1 - M_2|}{\sqrt{\dfrac{SS_1 + SS_2}{n_1 + n_2 - 2}}} \ (\text{for independent sample } t \text{ test})$$

$$d = \frac{|M_D|}{S_D} \ (\text{for related sample } t \text{ test})$$

$$\eta^2 = \frac{SS_{\text{bet}}}{SS_{\text{total}}} \ (\text{for one} - \text{way ANOVA})$$

(for two-way ANOVA)

$$\eta_A^2 = \frac{SS_A}{SS_{\text{tot}}} \qquad \eta_B^2 = \frac{SS_B}{SS_{\text{tot}}} \qquad \eta_{AB}^2 = \frac{SS_{AB}}{SS_{\text{tot}}}$$

$$\omega_A^2 = \frac{SS_A - (df_A)(MS_{\text{wi}})}{SS_{\text{tot}} + MS_{\text{wi}}} \qquad \omega_B^2 = \frac{SS_B - (df_B)(MS_{\text{wi}})}{SS_{\text{tot}} + MS_{\text{wi}}} \qquad \omega_{AB}^2 = \frac{SS_{AB} - (df_{AB})(MS_{\text{wi}})}{SS_{\text{tot}} + MS_{\text{wi}}}$$

**INTERQUARTILE RANGE**

$$IQR = Q_3 - Q_1$$

**MEAN**

$$\mu = \frac{\Sigma X}{N} \ (\text{population mean}) \qquad M = \frac{\Sigma X}{n} \ (\text{sample mean})$$

$$\mu = \frac{\Sigma fX}{N} \ (\text{for a grouped population frequency distribution})$$

$$M = \frac{\Sigma fX}{n} \ (\text{for a grouped sample frequency distribution})$$

**MEDIAN**

$$Mdn = LL + \left( \frac{50\% \text{ of } N - cf_{\text{below}}}{f_{\text{wi}}} \right) i$$

## NONPARAMETRIC STATISTICS

Mann Whitney $U$

$$U_1 = (n_1)(n_2) + \frac{n_1(n_1+1)}{2} - \Sigma R_1$$

$$U_2 = (n_1)(n_2) + \frac{n_2(n_2+1)}{2} - \Sigma R_2$$

Kruskal-Wallis $H$

$$H = \left[\frac{12}{N(N+1)}\right]\left[\Sigma \frac{R_t^2}{n_t}\right] - 3(N+1)$$

Spearman Correlation

$$r_s = 1 - \frac{6\Sigma D^2}{n(n^2-1)}$$

## RANGE

$$R = X_{UL-High} - X_{LL-Low}$$

## REGRESSION

Slope $(b)$

$$b = r\left(\frac{s_y}{s_x}\right)$$

$Y$ – intercept $(a)$

$$a = M_y - b(M_x)$$

**Regression Equation**

$$Y' = b(X) + a$$

## STANDARD DEVIATION

**Definitional Formulas**

$$\sigma = \sqrt{\frac{\Sigma(X-\mu)^2}{N}} \text{ (for population)}$$

$$s = \sqrt{\frac{\Sigma(X-M)^2}{n-1}} \text{ (for sample)}$$

## COMPUTATIONAL FORMULAS

$$\sigma = \sqrt{\frac{\Sigma X^2 - \frac{(\Sigma X)^2}{N}}{N}} \text{ (for population)}$$

$$s = \sqrt{\frac{\Sigma X^2 - \frac{(\Sigma X)^2}{n}}{n-1}} \text{ (for sample)}$$

## STANDARD ERROR

### Standard Error of the Mean

$$\sigma_M = \frac{\sigma}{\sqrt{n}} \qquad (\text{for } z - \text{test})$$

$$s_M = \frac{s}{\sqrt{n}} \qquad (\text{for one} - \text{sample } t \text{ test})$$

### Standard Error of Difference Between Means

$$S_{M_1 - M_2} = \sqrt{\left(\frac{SS_1 + SS_2}{n_1 + n_2 - 2}\right)\left(\frac{1}{n_1} + \frac{1}{n_2}\right)} \quad (\text{for independent samples } t \text{ test})$$

### Standard Error of Mean Difference

$$s_{M_D} = \frac{s_D}{\sqrt{n}} \qquad (\text{for repeated samples } t \text{ test})$$

## SUM OF SQUARES

### Definitional Formulas

$$SS = \Sigma(X - \mu)^2 \text{ (for population)} \qquad SS = \Sigma(X - M)^2 \text{ (for sample)}$$

### Computational Formula

$$SS = \Sigma X^2 - \frac{(\Sigma X)^2}{N} \text{ (for population)} \qquad SS = \Sigma X^2 - \frac{(\Sigma X)^2}{n} \text{ (for sample)}$$

## t-STATISTIC

$$t = \frac{M - \mu}{s_M} \qquad\qquad (\text{one} - \text{sample } t \text{ test})$$

$$t = \frac{M_1 - M_2}{s_{M_1 - M_2}} \qquad\qquad (\text{independent samples } t \text{ test})$$

$$t = \frac{M_D}{s_{M_D}} \qquad\qquad (\text{repeated samples } t \text{ test})$$

## TUKEY'S POST-HOC TEST FOR EQUAL *ns*

$$HSD = q\left(\sqrt{\frac{MS_{wi}}{n}}\right)$$

## VARIANCE

$$\sigma^2 = \frac{SS}{N}\left(\text{for population}\right)$$

$$s^2 = \frac{SS}{n-1}\left(\text{for sample}\right)$$

## Z-SCORES

$$z = \frac{X - \mu}{\sigma}\left(\text{for raw scores}\right)$$

$$z = \frac{M - \mu}{\sigma_M}\left(\text{for sample means}\right)$$

### Determining Raw Scores From z-Scores

$$X = \mu + z\left(\sigma\right)$$

### Determining Sample Means From Raw Scores

$$M = \mu + \left(z\right)\left(\sigma_M\right)$$

# Appendix C
## Answers to Odd Numbered
## End-of-Chapter Problems

### CHAPTER 1: INTRODUCTION TO STATISTICS

1. Continuous or discrete?

   a. Discrete
   b. Continuous
   c. Continuous
   d. Discrete

3. Scale of measurement?

   a. Nominal
   b. Interval
   c. Ordinal
   d. Ratio

5. Independent variable – Music or silence

   Dependent variable – Exam scores

7. Rounding numbers:

   a. 3.52
   b. 64.59
   c. 19.68
   d. 37.00 (or 37)
   e. 3.86

9. English has the higher percent of females (80% versus 30% in history)
11. Signed numbers:

   a. −4
   b. −1
   c. −12
   d. 20
   e. −4
   f. 4

13. Summation operators:

| X | Y | $X^2$ | $Y^2$ | XY | $(X-1)$ | $(X-1)^2$ |
|---|---|---|---|---|---|---|
| 3 | 2 | 9 | 4 | 6 | 2 | 4 |
| 6 | 4 | 36 | 16 | 24 | 5 | 25 |
| 5 | 4 | 25 | 16 | 20 | 4 | 16 |
| 14 | 10 | 70 | 36 | 50 | 11 | 45 |

a. $\Sigma X = 14$
b. $\Sigma Y = 10$
c. $\Sigma X^2 = 70$
d. $\Sigma Y^2 = 36$
e. $\Sigma XY = 50$
f. $(\Sigma X)(\Sigma Y) = 140$
g. $(\Sigma X)^2 = 196$
h. $\Sigma X^2 + \Sigma Y^2 = 106$
i. $\Sigma X^2 + (\Sigma Y)^2 = 170$
j. $\Sigma(X-1) = 11$
k. $\Sigma(X-1)^2 = 45$

# CHAPTER 2: ORGANIZING DATA USING TABLES AND GRAPHS

1. Type of graph?

   a. bar graph
   b. histogram or frequency polygon
   c. histogram or frequency polygon
   d. bar graph
   e. bar graph
   f. frequency polygon
   g. histogram or frequency polygon

3. Empirical distributions are based on the frequencies of actual scores represented by dots on the graph which are then connected by a straight line. Theoretical distributions are based on the mathematical probability of the frequencies of scores in a population. Since actual scores are not represented, theoretical distributions are drawn with smooth lines without dots.

5. History exam:

   a. $R = 84.5 - 21.5 = 63$
   b. $i = 5$
   c. 20–24

7. Values for cumulative frequency distribution:

   a. $N = 11$
   b. $cf = 4$
   c. P.R. $= 54.55$
   d. Rel $f = .27$

## CHAPTER 3: MEASURES OF CENTRAL TENDENCY

1. The mode specifies the most frequently occurring score in a distribution. It is easy and involves no calculations. However, it is not a very stable measure because a change in one score, if extreme, can have a dramatic effect on the mode. The median is the middle point in a distribution with half of the scores above it and half below it. The median does not have the instability of the mode and it is the most useful measure in a skewed distribution because it is not affected by extreme scores. On the other hand, it does not take all score values into consideration and it is therefore not helpful for further statistical procedures. The mean is the total of all scores in a distribution divided by N. It, therefore, does take all scores into consideration and can be used for further statistical procedures. The sample mean is also an unbiased estimate of the population mean. However, it is affected by extreme scores and therefore should not be used in distributions that are skewed.

3. In a normal distribution, the mode, median, and mean are all in the center of the distribution. In skewed distributions, the mode will be at the peak, the mean will be toward the high end in a positively skewed distribution and toward the low end in a negatively skewed distribution, and the median will be between the mode and the mean.

5. The distribution is negatively skewed.

7. The median should be reported for household incomes in the United States because the mode is not stable and the mean would be influenced by the extremely high incomes of the relatively few multimillionaires and multibillionaires that live in the United States.

9. The mode.

11. The two factors that need to be considered when deciding which measure of central tendency to report are the scale of measurement and shape of the distribution.

13. Values of central tendency measures for given scores:

    a. Mode = 7

    b. Median = 7

    c. Mean = 6

15. Grouped frequency distribution, median, mean, and mode:

$R = 80.5 - 17.5 = 63; i = 5$

| Class Intervals | $f$ | $cf$ | Mid-point | $fX$ |
|---|---|---|---|---|
| 80–84 | 1 | 24 | 82 | 82 |
| 75–79 | 1 | 23 | 77 | 77 |
| 70–74 | 3 | 22 | 72 | 216 |
| 65–69 | 4 | 19 | 67 | 268 |
| 60–64 | 2 | 15 | 62 | 124 |
| 55–59 | 2 | 13 | 57 | 114 |
| 50–54 | 3 | 11 | 52 | 156 |
| 45–49 | 2 | 8 | 47 | 94 |
| 40–44 | 1 | 6 | 42 | 42 |
| 35–39 | 0 | 5 | 37 | 0 |
| 30–34 | 2 | 5 | 32 | 64 |
| 25–29 | 1 | 3 | 27 | 27 |
| 20–24 | 1 | 2 | 22 | 22 |
| 15–19 | 1 | 1 | 17 | 17 |
| | $N = 24$ | | | $\Sigma fX = 1303$ |

$$Mdn = 54.5 + \frac{12-11}{2}(5)$$

$$= 57$$

$$M = 1303 \div 24 = 54.29$$

$$MO = 67$$

## CHAPTER 4: MEASURES OF VARIABILITY

1. The interquartile range is the preferred measure of variability for skewed distributions because, unlike the range and standard deviation, it is not sensitive to extreme scores.

3. Definitional formulas generally require more calculations than computational formulas. However, they are helpful when first learning statistics because they guide the learner through the process of what is measured, thus facilitating understanding of the statistics being calculated.

5. The sample standard deviation is represented by $s$. The population standard deviation is represented by $\sigma$. The formulas for both are the same except that $s$ has $n - 1$ in the denominator because, without this correction, $s$ tends to underestimate $\sigma$.

7. A standard deviation 0 would indicate that there was no variability in the scores. In other words, everyone had the same score.

9. $R = .8150 - .3850 = .43$

11. Standard deviation using definitional formula:

| $X$ | $\mu$ | $X - \mu$ | $(X - \mu)^2$ |
|---|---|---|---|
| 7 | 9 | −2 | 4 |
| 10 | 9 | 1 | 1 |
| 13 | 9 | 4 | 16 |
| 9 | 9 | 0 | 0 |
| 6 | 9 | −3 | 9 |
| $\Sigma X = 45$ | | | $\Sigma(X-\mu)^2 = 30$ |

$$\sigma = \sqrt{\frac{\Sigma(X-\mu)^2}{N}} = \sqrt{\frac{30}{5}} = \sqrt{6} = 2.45$$

$$SS = 30$$

$$\sigma^2 = 6$$

$$\sigma = 2.45$$

13. Population and sample standard deviations:

| $X$ | $X^2$ |
|---|---|
| 6 | 36 |
| 7 | 49 |
| 8 | 64 |
| 9 | 81 |
| 10 | 100 |
| $\Sigma X = 40$ | $\Sigma X^2 = 330$ |

a. $\sigma = \sqrt{\dfrac{\sum X^2 - \dfrac{\sum (X)^2}{N}}{N}} = \sqrt{\dfrac{330 - \dfrac{(40)^2}{5}}{5}} = \sqrt{\dfrac{330 - 320}{5}} = 1.41$

b. $s = \sqrt{\dfrac{330 - 320}{5 - 1}} = 1.58$

c. $s$ is larger. Using $n - 1$ in the formula corrects for the sample's underestimation of the population standard deviation.

## CHAPTER 5: z-SCORES AND OTHER STANDARD SCORES

1. First year: $z = \dfrac{34 - 30}{2} = +2.00$

   Second year: $z = \dfrac{36 - 43}{4} = -1.75$

   Third year: $z = \dfrac{39 - 38}{5} = +.20$

   Fourth year: $z = \dfrac{37 - 42}{3} = -1.67$

   a. Juanita's performance was the best in her second year with a race time of 1.75 standard deviations below the mean for her group.
   b. Juanita's performance was the worst in her first year with a race time of 2 standard deviations above the mean.

3. The mean is 0 and the standard deviation is 1 for a z-distribution.

5. Geology: $z = \dfrac{90 - 87}{6} = +.50$

   Math: $z = \dfrac{90 - 82}{8} = +1.00$

   Brenda scored above the mean of the class on both exams. Her performance was somewhat better on the math exam where she scored one standard deviation above the mean in comparison to her score on the geology exam where she was one half of a standard deviation above the mean.

7. Exam #1: $z = \dfrac{68 - 72}{5} = -.80$

   Exam #2: $z = \dfrac{72 - 66}{4} = +1.50$

   Exam #3: $z = \dfrac{80 - 75}{6} = +.83$

   Exam #4: $z = \dfrac{65 - 68}{3} = -1.00$

   a. Liam's performance was the best on Exam #2 with a z-score of +1.50.
   b. Liam's performance was the worst on Exam #4 with a z-score of −1.00.

9. Equivalent SATs

a. Student A: $z = \dfrac{112 - 108}{11} = +.36$

SAT $= 500 + (.36)(100) = 536$

b. Student B: $z = \dfrac{96 - 108}{11} - 1.09$

SAT $= 500 + (-1.09)(100) = 391$

c. Student C: $z = \dfrac{120 - 108}{11} + 1.09$

SAT $= 500 + (1.09)(100) = 609$

11. Erica's raw score:

a. $X = 65.83 + (-1.12)(5.41) = 59.77$
Gianna's raw score:
b. $X = 65.83 + (1.08)(5.41) = 71.67$

13. $z$-scores for given raw scores:

| $X$ | $X^2$ |
| --- | --- |
| 8 | 64 |
| 7 | 49 |
| 6 | 36 |
| 5 | 25 |
| $\Sigma X = 26$ | $\Sigma X^2 = 174$ |

$\mu = \dfrac{26}{4} = 6.5$

$\sigma = \sqrt{\dfrac{174 - \dfrac{(26)^2}{4}}{4}} = 1.12$

a. $z = \dfrac{5 - 6.5}{1.12} = -1.34$

b. $z = \dfrac{7 - 6.5}{1.12} = +.45$

## CHAPTER 6: PROBABILITY AND THE NORMAL DISTRIBUTION

1. Column A identifies particular $z$-scores.
Column B identifies the proportion in the body of the normal distribution.
Column C identifies the proportion in the tail of the normal distribution.
Column D identifies the proportion between the mean of the distribution and the corresponding $z$-score value shown in Column A.

3. $z$-scores:

a. $-.25$
b. $-.15$
c. $+1.15$

5. $z = -.67$

7. Proportion greater or less than a given score:

a. $z = \dfrac{40-37}{4} = +.75$

$p(X > 40) = .2266$

b. $z = \dfrac{25-37}{4} = -3.00$

$p(X > 25) = .9987$

c. $z = \dfrac{32-37}{4} = -1.25$

$p(X < 32) = .1056$

d. $z = \dfrac{39-37}{4} = +.50$

$p(X < 39) = .6915$

9. Proportion between two scores:

a. $z = \dfrac{42-50}{5} = -1.60$

$z = \dfrac{53-50}{5} = +.60$

Proportion between mean and $-1.60 = .4452$
Proportion between mean and $+.60 = .2257$
$.4452 + .2357 = .6709$

b. $p(42 < X < 53) = .6709$

11. $z = \dfrac{59-57}{8} = +.25$

$z = \dfrac{71-57}{8} = +1.75$

Proportion between mean and $+1.75 = .4599$
Proportion between mean and $+.25 = .0987$
$.4599 - .0987 = .3612$
$p(59 < X < 71) = .3612$

13. $z$-score $= -.47$

$X = 40 + (-.47)(4) = 38.12$

15. 4.5% at each end; $4.5 \div 100 = .0450$

$z$-scores for $.0450 = \pm 1.70$

$X = 71 + (-1.70)(6) = 60.80$
$X = 71 + (+1.70)(6) = 81.20$

# CHAPTER 7: SAMPLING DISTRIBUTION OF MEANS

1. A sampling distribution is a theoretical probability distribution that represents a statistic (such as a mean) for all possible samples of a given size from a population

of interest. It is used to determine the probabilities associated with obtained sample values.

3. It is important to exercise caution when using a sample mean to estimate the population mean because of random sampling error. Sample means will vary somewhat from the population mean just because of the randomness of the sample. The standard error of the mean is used to gauge the amount of error to be expected.

5. The standard error of the mean is the standard deviation of the sampling distribution of means and it represents the average amount that a sample mean is expected to vary from the population mean due to random sampling error. As the size of the sample increases, the size of the estimated standard error decreases. Thus, larger samples generally produce less error and will therefore tend to more accurately predict the population mean.

7. Assertiveness assessment:

a. $\sigma_M = \dfrac{20}{\sqrt{64}} = 2.5$

$z = \dfrac{92 - 90}{2.5} = +.80$

$p(M < 92) = .7881$

b. $z = \dfrac{86 - 90}{2.5} = -1.60$

$p(M > 86) = .9452$

c. $z = \dfrac{96 - 90}{2.5} = +2.4$

$p(M > 96) = .0082$

9. Probability and Proportion:

a. $\sigma_M = \dfrac{14}{\sqrt{44}} = 2.11$

$z = \dfrac{76 - 71}{2.11} = +2.37$

$p(M > 76) = .0089$

b. $\sigma_M = \dfrac{14}{\sqrt{24}} = 2.86$

$z = \dfrac{76 - 71}{2.86} = +1.75$

$p(M < 76) = .9599$

11. Means associated with given probabilities:

a. $\sigma_M = \dfrac{18}{\sqrt{63}} = 2.27$

z-score associated with lower .1000 = $-1.28$

$M = 106 + (-1.28)(2.27) = 103.09$

b. z-score associated with upper .0400 = $+1.75$

$M = 106 + (1.75)(2.27) = 109.97$

13. Range of sample means:

$$\sigma_M = \frac{11}{\sqrt{22}} = 2.35$$

$z$-score associated with upper and lower $.0250 = \pm 1.96$

$$M = 73 + (-1.96)(2.35) = 68.39 \quad \text{and}$$

$$M = 73 + (+1.96)(2.35) = 77.61$$

# CHAPTER 8: HYPOTHESIS TESTING

1. The null hypothesis states that there is no significant difference between the population parameters and our obtained sample statistics, and that any differences found are due to random sampling error. Thus, it claims the independent variable to be ineffective. This is the hypothesis that the researcher usually wants to reject. The alternative hypothesis states that the differences found are true differences due to the effectiveness of the independent variable. The researcher usually wants to obtain support for the alternative hypothesis.

3. The alpha level is a probability level which defines the point at which the null hypothesis can be rejected. This is also the point at which the critical region begins. This is the area of a sampling distribution in which obtained sample means are unlikely to have occurred by chance. They would have a low probability of occurrence if the null hypothesis is true. Thus, when scores are obtained that fall in the critical region, the null hypothesis can be rejected.

5. $H_0$ is more likely to be supported if our obtained sample mean is close in value to the population mean. Our obtained sample mean would not be in the critical region where scores are unlikely if $H_0$ is true. The higher probability associated with the non-critical region makes the null hypothesis more plausible.

7. Step 4 notation:

    a. Fail to reject $H_0$, $p > .01$
    b. Reject $H_0$, $p < .05$
    c. Reject $H_0$, $p < .05$
    d. Fail to reject $H_0$, $p > .01$

9. A Type I error is rejecting a null hypothesis that is actually true. The probability of making a Type I error is the same as the probability set by the alpha level. For example, if alpha is set at .05, the probability of obtaining a sample statistic in the rejection region just by chance alone is .05. Thus, the probability of making a Type I error is .05.

11. Apprehension study:

    a. Step 1:

    $H_0: \mu \geq 80$
    $H_1: \mu < 80$

    Step 2:

    $\alpha = .05$
    $z_{crit} = -1.65$

Step 3:

$$\sigma_M = \frac{12}{\sqrt{44}} = 1.81$$

$$z_{obt} = \frac{76-80}{1.81} = -2.21$$

Step 4:

Attending the workshop significantly reduced apprehension scores. Reject $H_0$, $z = -2.21, p < .05$

b. $d = \dfrac{|76-80|}{12} = .33$, small effect

c. For $\alpha = .01$, $z_{obt}$ would not exceed the $z_{crit}$ value of $-2.33$ and $H_0$ would fail to be rejected.

d. If other factors remain the same, increasing the alpha level increases the power of a statistical test making it more likely that $H_0$ will be rejected. Lower alpha levels set a tougher standard making it more difficult to reject $H_0$.

13. Music and mood study:

a. Step 1:

$H_0: \mu = 65$
$H_1: \mu \neq 65$

Step 2:

$\alpha = .05$
$z_{crit} = \pm 1.96$

Step 3:

$$\sigma_M = \frac{15}{\sqrt{40}} = 2.37 \qquad z_{crit} = \frac{69-65}{2.37} = +1.69$$

Step 4:

Listening to soft piano music did not significantly affect the mood state of the participants. Fail to reject $H_0$, $z_{obt} = 1.69, p > .05$.

b. For a one-tailed test, $z_{crit} = +1.65$. In this case, $p < .05$ so the null hypothesis can be rejected.

c. The power of a statistical test increases by using a one-tailed test because it is easier to reject the null hypothesis. Obtained sample values do not have to be as extreme as those required for a two-tailed test.

## CHAPTER 9: ONE-SAMPLE *t* TEST

1. The normal distribution is based on an infinite number of cases and has a normal bell shape. The *t*-distribution is also bell-shaped but when the sample size is small, the distribution will become flatter and the *t*-values extend further into the tails. This means that more extreme *t*-values will be required in order to reject the null hypothesis.

3. Determine $t_{crit}$ and whether to reject $H_0$:

|  | df | $t_{crit}$ | Reject $H_0$ Y or N |
|---|---|---|---|
| a. | 6 | 3.707 | N |
| b. | 28 | 2.763 | Y |
| c. | 16 | 2.921 | N |
| d. | 40 | 2.704 | Y |

5. Hypotheses for hours of sleep study:

a. The null hypothesis states that college students get equal to or more sleep than the national average of 6.8 hours. The alternative hypothesis states that college students get significantly less sleep than the national average.

b. $H_0: \mu \geq 6.8$
   $H_1: \mu < 6.8$

7. The null hypothesis $(H_0)$ better explains an obtained $t$-value that is not in the critical region. The null hypothesis attributes these values to random sampling error and they have a more frequent probability of occurrence than $t$-values in the critical region.

9. $s_M = \dfrac{12}{\sqrt{100}} = 1.2$

11. $s_M = \dfrac{6}{\sqrt{10}} = 1.9$

$t_{obt} = \dfrac{35 - 40}{1.9} = -2.63$

13. $t_{obt} = \dfrac{48 - 54}{4} = -1.5$

$t_{crit} = -1.753$

$H_0$ would fail to be rejected. Although the sample mean is lower than the population mean, it is not different enough to support the claim that treatment significantly lowered scores.

15. Step 1:

$H_0: \mu \leq 9$
$H_1: \mu > 9$

Step 2:

$\alpha = .05$
$df = 24$
$t_{crit} = +1.711$

Step 3:

$s_M = \dfrac{6}{\sqrt{25}} = 1.2 \qquad t_{obt} = \dfrac{11 - 9}{1.2} = +1.67$

Step 4:

The study did not show that extroverts have significantly more friends than the national average. Fail to reject $H_0$, $t(24) = +1.67$, $p > .05$.

# CHAPTER 10: TWO-SAMPLE $t$ TEST: INDEPENDENT SAMPLES DESIGN

1. Null and alternative hypotheses:

   a. The null hypothesis states that there would be no difference between the means of the population and that any differences found are simply due to chance.
   b. The alternative hypothesis states that there would be differences between the means of the population and that those differences would be due to the groups being treated differently.

3. $s_{M_1-M_2}$ is the standard deviation of the difference between means and it tells us the estimated amount of sampling error that can be expected due to chance alone.

5. $$\frac{SS_1 + SS_2}{n_1 + n_2 - 2} = \frac{163 + 131}{12 + 11 - 2} = 14$$

7. $$s_{M_1-M_2} = \sqrt{\left(\frac{324 + 251}{19 + 16 - 2}\right)\left(\frac{1}{19} + \frac{1}{16}\right)} = 1.39$$

$$t_{obt} = \frac{32 - 28}{1.39} = +2.88$$

9. New medication for memory errors:

   a. $H_0: \mu_1 \geq \mu_2$
      $H_1: \mu_1 < \mu_2$
   b. $df = 14$
      $t_{crit} = -1.761$
   c. $t_{obt} = \dfrac{29 - 25}{2.1} = +1.90$

   No, the memory drug did not result in fewer memory errors. It is important to designate the direction of expected difference in $H_1$ and $t_{crit}$ because if we just looked at the value of $t_{obt}$ without paying attention to the sign, we could mistakenly reject $H_0$ since $t_{obt}$ exceeds $t_{crit}$. However, it is in the wrong direction. The medication actually increased the number of memory errors in group one.

11. Step 1:

   $H_0: \mu_1 = \mu_2$
   $H_1: \mu_1 \neq \mu_2$

   Step 2:

   $\alpha = .05$
   $df = 12$
   $t_{crit} = \pm 2.179$

Step 3:

$$t_{obt} = \frac{63-53}{4.32} + 2.31$$

Step 4:

Yes, there was a significance between the means. Reject $H_0$, $t(12) = +2.31$, $p < .05$.

13. Step 1:

$$H_0: \mu_1 \le \mu_2$$
$$H_1: \mu_1 > \mu_2$$

Step 2:

$$\alpha = .01$$
$$df = 11$$
$$t_{crit} = +2.718$$

Step 3:

| $X_1$ | $X_1^2$ | $X_2$ | $X_2^2$ |
|---|---|---|---|
| 17 | 289 | 18 | 324 |
| 20 | 400 | 12 | 144 |
| 18 | 324 | 16 | 256 |
| 18 | 324 | 13 | 169 |
| 17 | 289 | 15 | 225 |
| 19 | 361 | 17 | 289 |
| 22 | 484 | $\Sigma X_2 = 91$ | $\Sigma X_2^2 = 1407$ |

$$\Sigma X_1 = 131 \qquad \Sigma X_1^2 = 2471$$
$$M_1 = 18.71,$$
$$M_2 = 15.17$$

$$SS_1 = 2471 - \frac{(131)^2}{7} = 19.43$$

$$SS_2 = 1407 - \frac{(91)^2}{6} = 26.83$$

$$SS_{M_1-M_2} = \sqrt{\left(\frac{19.43+26.83}{7+6-2}\right)\left(\frac{1}{7}+\frac{1}{6}\right)} = 1.14$$

$$t = \frac{18.71-15.17}{1.14} = 3.11$$

Step 4:

Participants of the Q&R workshop scored significantly higher on curiosity than the group that did not attend the workshop. Reject $H_0$, $t(11) = +3.11$, $p < .01$.

## CHAPTER 11: TWO-SAMPLE $t$ TEST: RELATED SAMPLES DESIGN

1. The null hypothesis states that pre- and post-testing would show no significant mean difference and that any difference found is simply due to chance. The alternative hypothesis asserts that a mean difference is due to treatment, and not just due to chance.

3. $H_0: \mu_D \geq 0$
   $H_1: \mu_D < 0$

5. A repeated measures design is beneficial because it requires fewer participants since the same subjects are used in more than one treatment condition. Fewer subjects often means less cost and less variability due to individual differences, resulting in less sampling error. Developmental changes can also be tracked using the repeated measures design with the same subjects being tested at different ages.

7. Doreen should have rejected $H_0$. Her $t_{obt}$ exceeded the $t_{crit}$-value of +2.508.

9. A one-sample $t$ test is used to test a hypothesis about a population mean based on the mean of a sample; it is used when the population standard deviation is not known. The independent samples $t$ test is used to compare the means between two separate and unrelated samples to see if they differ significantly. The repeated measures $t$ test uses the same subjects to assess the significance between pre- and post-treatment conditions.

11. Step 1:

$H_0: \mu_D \leq 0$
$H_1: \mu_D > 0$

Step 2:

$\alpha = .01$
$df = 9$
$t_{crit} = +2.821$

Step 3:

| Before Workbook | After Workbook | $D$ | $D^2$ |
|---|---|---|---|
| 40 | 58 | 18 | 324 |
| 45 | 49 | 4 | 16 |
| 58 | 62 | 4 | 16 |
| 32 | 52 | 20 | 400 |
| 48 | 51 | 3 | 9 |
| 47 | 52 | 5 | 25 |
| 50 | 57 | 7 | 49 |
| 52 | 60 | 8 | 64 |
| 46 | 48 | 2 | 4 |
| 49 | 53 | 4 | 16 |
| | | $\Sigma D = 75$ | $\Sigma D^2 = 923$ |

$$s_D = \sqrt{\frac{923 - \frac{(75)^2}{10}}{10-1}} = 6.33$$

$$s_{M_D} = \frac{6.33}{\sqrt{10}} = 2$$

$$M_D = \frac{75}{10} = 7.5$$

$$t_{obt} = \frac{7.5}{2} + 3.75$$

Step 4:

Students scored significantly higher on the practice entrance exam after completing the workbook. Reject $H_0$, $t(9) = +3.75$, $p < .01$.

$$d = \frac{|7.5|}{6.33} = 1.18 \text{, large effect}$$

# CHAPTER 12: CONFIDENCE INTERVAL VERSUS POINT ESTIMATION

1. A point estimate is a single value based on sample data that is used to estimate the parameter of a population. Point estimates don't take sampling error into consideration. Confidence intervals, on the other hand, take sampling error into consideration and establish a range of values within which the population parameter is expected to lie with a specified degree of confidence. Confidence intervals are less specific than point estimates but we can have greater confidence that the true values of the population parameters will be included in the interval.

3. Statistics used for point estimates:

   a. $M$
   b. $M_1 - M_2$
   c. $M_D$

5. $M = \frac{51}{6} = 8.5$

7. Point estimate for $\mu_D$:

| Pre-test | Post-test | D |
|---|---|---|
| 68 | 96 | 28 |
| 75 | 90 | 15 |
| 79 | 89 | 10 |
| 69 | 85 | 16 |
| 80 | 76 | −4 |
| 70 | 87 | 17 |
| | | 82 |

$$M_D = \frac{82}{6} = 13.67$$

9. 95% confidence interval for $\mu_1 - \mu_2$:

   $\alpha = .05$
   $df = 18$
   $t = \pm 2.101$
   $M_1 - M_2 = 8$

$$s_{M_1 - M_2} = \sqrt{\left(\frac{424 + 347}{9 + 11 - 2}\right)\left(\frac{1}{9} + \frac{1}{11}\right)} = 2.93$$

LL = 8 − (2.101)(2.93) = 1.84; UL = 8 + (2.101)(2.93) = 14.16

11. 95% confidence intervals for $\mu$:

LL $= 13.8 - (2.064)(1.11) = 11.51$; UL $= 13.8 + (2.064)(1.11) = 16.09$
We can be 95% confident that the mean age in the population at which the first alcoholic beverage was consumed is between 11.51 and 16.09.

13. 99% confidence interval for $\mu_D$:

LL $= -2.3 - (2.779)(.81) = -4.55$; UL $= -2.3 + (2.779)(.81) = -.05$
We can be 99% confident that the mean decrease in belly fat in the population would be between $-4.55$ and $-.05$.

## CHAPTER 13: ONE-WAY ANALYSIS OF VARIANCE

1. ANOVA should be used for comparing the means for several different groups. It is not appropriate to use repeated $t$ tests for this purpose because doing so would increase the risk of a Type I error.

3. Questions related to results of a one-way ANOVA:

   a. Three groups were involved in the study.
   b. Eighteen subjects participated.
   c. The null hypothesis not rejected, $p > .05$
   d. There is no point in conducting a post hoc test since results of the ANOVA found no significance differences between the group means.

5. If a null hypothesis is rejected, then significant differences exist somewhere among the means. Since ANOVA only detects *if* significance exists and not where, a post hoc test is needed to identify which of the means differ significantly.

7. Complete the ANOVA table and conduct a Tukey's *HSD*.

   a. There were significant differences among the means. Reject $H_0$.

| Source | SS | df | MS | F | p |
|---|---|---|---|---|---|
| Between-treatments | 102.72 | 2 | 51.36 | 7.39 | <.05 |
| Within-treatment | 229.50 | 33 | 6.95 | | |
| Total | 332.22 | 35 | | | |

$$HSD = 3.49\left(\sqrt{\frac{6.95}{12}}\right) = 2.66$$

$$M_2 - M_1 = 13.83 - 10.92 = 2.91\,{}^*$$
$$M_3 - M_1 = 14.92 - 10.92 = 4.00\,{}^*$$
$$M_3 - M_2 = 14.92 - 13.83 = 1.09$$

   Groups 2 and 3 scored significantly higher than Group 1. There was no significant difference between Groups 2 and 3.

9. Completed ANOVA summary table:

| Source | SS | df | MS | F |
|---|---|---|---|---|
| Between-treatments | 129.08 | 2 | 64.54 | 8.13 |
| Within-treatment | 166.75 | 21 | 7.94 | |
| Total | 295.83 | 23 | | |

11. Calculate $SS_{tot}$, $SS_{wi}$, and $SS_{bet}$:

| $X_1$ | $X_1^2$ | $X_2$ | $X_2^2$ | $X_3$ | $X_3^2$ |
|-------|---------|-------|---------|-------|---------|
| 12    | 144     | 8     | 64      | 6     | 36      |
| 14    | 196     | 10    | 100     | 3     | 9       |
| 10    | 100     | 9     | 81      | 7     | 49      |
| 11    | 121     | 8     | 64      | 5     | 25      |

$\Sigma X_1 = 47$

$\Sigma X_1^2 = 561$

$\Sigma X_2 = 35$

$\Sigma X_2^2 = 309$

$\Sigma X_3 = 21$

$\Sigma X_3^2 = 119$

$$\Sigma X_{tot} = 103$$
$$\Sigma X_{tot}^2 = 989$$
$$N = 12$$
$$n_t = 4$$

$$SS_{tot} = 989 - \frac{(103)^2}{12} = 104.92$$

$$SS_{wi} = \left(561 - \frac{(47)^2}{4}\right) + \left(309 - \frac{(35)^2}{4}\right) + \left(119 - \frac{(21)^2}{4}\right) = 20.25$$

$$SS_{bet} = \frac{47^2}{4} + \frac{35^2}{4} + \frac{21^2}{4} - \frac{103^2}{12} = 84.67$$

13. Step 1:

$H_0: \mu_1 = \mu_2 = \mu_3 = \mu_4$
$H_1$: Some $\mu$'s are not equal.

Step 2:

$\alpha = .05$
$df_{wi} = 12$
$df_{bet} = 3$
$F_{crit} = 3.49$

Step 3:

| Quiet | | Low | | Moderate | | Loud | |
|-------|------|-------|------|-------|------|-------|------|
| $X_1$ | $X_1^2$ | $X_2$ | $X_2^2$ | $X_3$ | $X_3^2$ | $X_4$ | $X_4^2$ |
| 2     | 4    | 3     | 9    | 4     | 16   | 6     | 36   |
| 0     | 0    | 1     | 1    | 2     | 4    | 4     | 16   |
| 1     | 1    | 2     | 4    | 2     | 4    | 4     | 16   |
| 1     | 1    | 1     | 1    | 2     | 4    | 3     | 9    |

$$\Sigma X_1 = 4 \qquad \Sigma X_2 = 7 \qquad \Sigma X_3 = 10 \qquad \Sigma X_4 = 17$$

$$\Sigma X_1^2 = 6 \qquad \Sigma X_2^2 = 15 \qquad \Sigma X_3^2 = 28 \qquad \Sigma X_4^2 = 77$$

$$n_1 = 4 \qquad n_2 = 4 \qquad n_3 = 4 \qquad n_4 = 4$$

$$M_1 = 1 \qquad M_2 = 1.75 \qquad M_3 = 2.5 \qquad M_4 = 4.25$$

$$\Sigma X_{tot} = 38$$
$$\Sigma X_{tot}^2 = 126$$
$$N = 16$$
$$k = 4$$

$$SS_{tot} = 126 - \frac{(38)^2}{16} = 35.75$$

$$SS_{wi} = \left( 6 - \frac{(4)^2}{4} \right) + \left( 15 - \frac{(7)^2}{4} \right) + \left( 28 - \frac{(10)^2}{4} \right) + \left( 77 - \frac{(17)^2}{4} \right) = 12.5$$

$$SS_{bet} = \frac{4^2}{4} + \frac{7^2}{4} + \frac{10^2}{4} + \frac{17^2}{4} - \frac{38^2}{16} = 23.25$$

$$MS_{bet} = \frac{23.25}{3} = 7.75$$

$$MS_{wi} = \frac{12.5}{12} = 1.04$$

$$F_{obt} = \frac{7.75}{1.04} = 7.45$$

Step 4:

| Source | SS | df | MS | F | p |
|---|---|---|---|---|---|
| Between-treatments | 23.25 | 3 | 7.75 | 7.45 | <.05 |
| Within-treatment | 12.50 | 12 | 1.04 | | |
| Total | 35.75 | 15 | | | |

Varying levels of noise had a significant influence on concentration. Reject $H_0$.

$$HSD = 4.20 \left( \sqrt{\frac{1.04}{4}} \right) = 2.14$$

$M_2 - M_1 = 1.75 - 1 = .75$    (Low and quiet)
$M_3 - M_1 = 2.5 - 1 = 1.5$    (Moderate and quiet)
$M_4 - M_1 = 4.25 - 1 = 3.25^*$    (Loud and quiet)
$M_3 - M_2 = 2.5 - 1.75 = .75$    (Moderate and low)
$M_4 - M_2 = 4.25 - 1.75 = 2.5^*$    (Loud and low)
$M_4 - M_3 = 4.25 - 2.5 = 1.75$    (Loud and moderate)

The loud noise group made significantly more errors than the quiet and the low noise groups. There were no significant differences between any of the other groups.

# CHAPTER 14: FACTORIAL ANALYSIS OF VARIANCE

1. No, it cannot automatically be assumed that observed differences between means are significant because those differences could have occurred because of random sampling error. Statistical tests are required to determine significance.

3. Within-treatment variance is not influenced by treatment effects because it is only measuring the variability within particular groups, the participants of which have all been treated the same. Treatment effects do influence between-treatments variance because these participants have been treated differently.

$$H_0 : = \mu_{A_1} = \mu_{A_2} = \mu_{A_3} = \mu_{A_4}$$

$$H_0 : = \mu_{B_1} = \mu_{B_2} = \mu_{B_3}$$

$H_0$: Factors $A$ and $B$ do not have a significant interaction.

7. There were 12 groups with 4 participants in each group.

9. If $df_{bet(A)} = 2$, we know that there were 3 groups for Factor $A$ since $df_{bet(A)} = A - 1$. Similarly, we know that there were 5 groups for Factor $B$ ($df_{bet(B)} = B - 1$). Thus, there were a total of 15 groups. Since $df_{wi} = N_{tot} - k$ and $k = 15$, we know that there were 90 participants (75 + 15) with 6 subjects in each group (90 ÷ 15).

11. Amusement park study:

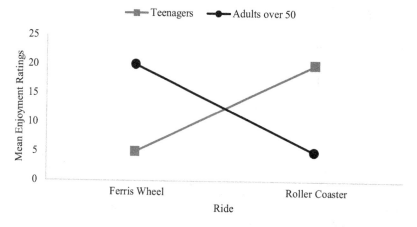

Yes, the graph suggests the presence of an interaction. Whether the Ferris wheel or roller coaster provides the most enjoyment depends upon the age group of the rater.

13. Weight loss study:

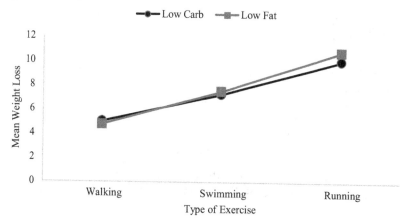

Step 1:

Main effect for Factor $A$:

$H_0: \mu_{A_1} = \mu_{A_2} = \mu_{A_3}$
$H_1$: Some $\mu$'s are not equal.

Main effect for Factor $B$:

$H_0: \mu_{B_1} = \mu_{B_2}$
$H_1$: Some $\mu$'s are not equal.

Interaction between Factors $A$ and $B$:

$H_0$: Factors $A$ and $B$ do not have a significant interaction.
$H_1$: Factors $A$ and $B$ have a significant interaction.

Step 2:

$df_{tot} = 23$
$df_{bet(A)} = 2$
$df_{bet(B)} = 1$
$df_{bet(AB)} = 2$
$df_{wi} = 18$

$\alpha = .05$
$F_{crit}$ for Factor $A = 3.55$
$F_{crit}$ for Factor $B = 4.41$
$F_{crit}$ for Interaction of $A$ and $B = 3.55$

Step 3:
SUM OF SQUARES

$$SS_{total} = \Sigma X_{tot}^2 - \frac{(\Sigma X_{tot})^2}{N_{tot}}$$

$$= 1515 - \frac{(181)^2}{24}$$

$$= 149.96$$

$$SS_{wi} = \left[ X_{cell}^2 - \frac{(X_{cell})^2}{n_{cell}} \right]$$

$$= \left( 102 - \frac{(20)^2}{4} \right) + \left( 213 - \frac{(29)^2}{4} \right) + \left( 406 - \frac{(40)^2}{4} \right) + \left( 99 - \frac{(19)^2}{4} \right) +$$

$$\left( 230 - \frac{(30)^2}{4} \right) + \left( 465 - \frac{(43)^2}{4} \right)$$

$$= (102 - 100) + (213 - 210.25) + (406 - 400) + (99 - 90.25) +$$

$$(230 - 225) + (465 - 462.25)$$

$$= 2 + 2.75 + 6 + 8.75 + 5 + 2.75$$

$$= 27.25$$

$$SS_{bet} = \Sigma \left[ \frac{(\Sigma X_{cell})^2}{n_{cell}} \right] - \frac{(\Sigma X_{tot})^2}{N_{tot}}$$

$$= \frac{(20)^2}{4} + \frac{(29)^2}{4} + \frac{(40)^2}{4} + \frac{(19)^2}{4} + \frac{(30)^2}{4} + \frac{(43)^2}{4} - \frac{(181)^2}{24}$$

$$= 100 + 210.25 + 400 + 90.25 + 225 + 462.25 - 1365.04$$

$$= 122.71$$

$$SS_A = \frac{\left(\Sigma X_{A_1}\right)^2}{N_{A_1}} + \frac{\left(\Sigma X_{A_2}\right)^2}{N_{A_2}} + \frac{\left(\Sigma X_{A_3}\right)^2}{N_{A_3}} - \frac{\left(\Sigma X_{tot}\right)^2}{N_{tot}}$$

$$= \frac{(39)^2}{8} + \frac{(59)^2}{8} + \frac{(83)^2}{8} - \frac{(181)^2}{24}$$

$$= 190.13 + 435.13 + 861.13 - 1365.04$$

$$= 121.35$$

$$SS_B = \frac{\left(\Sigma X_{B_1}\right)^2}{N_{B_1}} + \frac{\left(\Sigma X_{B_2}\right)^2}{N_{B_2}} - \frac{\left(\Sigma X_{tot}\right)^2}{N_{tot}}$$

$$= \frac{(89)^2}{12} + \frac{(92)^2}{12} - \frac{(181)^2}{24}$$

$$= 660.08 + 705.33 - 1365.04$$

$$= .37$$

$$SS_{AB} = SS_{bet} - SS_A - SS_B$$

$$= 221.71 - 121.35 -$$

$$= .99$$

## MEAN SQUARE

$$MS_A = \frac{SS_A}{df_{bet(A)}} = \frac{121.35}{2} = 60.68$$

$$MS_B = \frac{SS_B}{df_{bet(B)}} = \frac{.37}{1} = .37$$

$$MS_{AB} = \frac{SS_{AB}}{df_{bet(AB)}} = \frac{.99}{2} = .50$$

$$MS_{wi} = \frac{SS_{wi}}{df_{wi}} = \frac{27.25}{18} = 1.51$$

## F-STATISTICS

$$F_A = \frac{MS_A}{MS_{wi}} = \frac{60.68}{1.51} = 40.19$$

$$F_B = \frac{MS_B}{MS_{wi}} = \frac{.37}{1.51} = .25$$

$$F_{AB} = \frac{MS_{AB}}{MS_{wi}} = \frac{.50}{1.51} = .33$$

Step 4:

| Source | SS | df | MS | F | p |
|---|---|---|---|---|---|
| Factor A | 121.35 | 2 | 60.68 | 40.19 | <.05 |
| Factor B | .37 | 1 | .37 | .25 | >05 |
| Interaction | .99 | 2 | .50 | .33 | >.05 |
| Within | 27.25 | 18 | 1.51 | | |
| | | | | | |
| Total | 149.96 | 23 | | | |

There was a significant main effect for Factor A. The mean amount of weight loss increased from walking to swimming to running for both the low carb and low fat diets. Post hoc tests should be conducted to determine if all the differences between means for the different exercise groups were significant or only some of them. There was no significant main effect for Factor B, type of diet, and there was no significant interaction between factors A and B.

## CHAPTER 15: CORRELATION AND REGRESSION

1. $H_0: p = 0$
   $H_1: p \neq 0$
3. Pearson correlation:

| X | $X^2$ | Y | $Y^2$ | XY |
|---|---|---|---|---|
| 7 | 49 | 6 | 36 | 42 |
| 10 | 100 | 8 | 64 | 80 |
| 12 | 144 | 10 | 100 | 120 |
| 17 | 289 | 14 | 196 | 238 |
| 8 | 64 | 9 | 81 | 72 |
| 10 | 100 | 7 | 49 | 70 |
| 64 | 746 | 54 | 526 | 622 |

$$r = \frac{(6)(622)-(64)(54)}{\sqrt{\left[(6)(746)-(64)^2\right]\left[(6)(526)-(54)^2\right]}}$$

$$= .9139$$

5. Pearson correlation:

| X | $X^2$ | Y | $Y^2$ | XY |
|---|---|---|---|---|
| 10 | 100 | 6 | 36 | 60 |
| 9 | 81 | 7 | 49 | 63 |
| 8 | 64 | 8 | 64 | 64 |
| 7 | 49 | 9 | 81 | 63 |
| 6 | 36 | 10 | 100 | 60 |
| 40 | 330 | 40 | 330 | 310 |

$$r = \frac{(5)(310)-(40)(40)}{\sqrt{\left[(5)(330)-(40)^2\right]\left[(5)(330)-(40)^2\right]}}$$

$$= -1.00$$

7. Step 1:

$H_0: p = 0$
$H_1: p \neq 0$

Step 2:

$\alpha = .05$
$df = 5$
$r_{crit} = \pm.754$

Step 3:

| X | X² | Y | Y² | XY |
|---|---|---|---|---|
| 15 | 225 | 15 | 225 | 225 |
| 18 | 324 | 15 | 225 | 270 |
| 19 | 361 | 16 | 256 | 304 |
| 23 | 529 | 17 | 289 | 391 |
| 12 | 144 | 19 | 361 | 228 |
| 11 | 121 | 22 | 484 | 242 |
| 20 | 400 | 15 | 225 | 300 |
| 118 | 2104 | 119 | 2065 | 1960 |

$$r = \frac{(7)(1960)-(118)(119)}{\sqrt{\left[(7)(2104)-(118)^2\right]\left[(7)(2065)-(119)^2\right]}}$$

$$= -.6623$$

Step 4:

A significant relationship between sociability and fear of public speaking was not supported. Fail to reject $H_0$, $r(5) = -.6623$, $p > .05$.

9. The coefficient of nondetermination is the proportion of the variability of two variables that is not shared in common and that is assumed to be related to factors that do not influence both sets of scores. It is determined by the formula $1 - r^2$.

11. The statement is incorrect. Just because there is a relationship between two variables doesn't necessarily mean that one causes the other. It may be true that excessive alcohol use causes earlier deaths but this conclusion cannot be verified using the method of correlation. It is possible that some third outside variable may be responsible for the correlation. For example, maybe people who consume high amounts of alcohol also smoke cigarettes and perhaps it is the cigarettes that lead to early death. Only experimental research can demonstrate cause and effect relationships.

13. An outlier is an extreme score that is dissimilar to the majority of the other scores in a distribution or scatterplot. If there are outliers in a distribution of scores, the true strength of the correlation coefficient will not be captured.

15. $Y' = (-5)(4) + 92 = 72$

$Y' = (-5)(8) + 92 = 52$

## CHAPTER 16: CHI-SQUARE

1. The three main assumptions whose violations may lead a researcher to choose a non-parametric test such as chi-square are homogeneity of variance, a normally shaped distribution, and interval or ratio level data.

3. $df = k - 1; f_e = (\text{known proportion})(n)$

5. $df = (R - 1)(C - 1); f_e = \dfrac{(f_c)(f_r)}{n}$

7. Use $f_e = (\text{known proportion})(n)$ for each category:

Extremely important – 85.75
Very important – 71.05
Important – 41.65
Somewhat important – 29.40
Not very important – 9.80
No response – 7.35

9. Expected frequencies: Use $f_e = \dfrac{(f_c)(f_r)}{n}$

|        | Movie       | Concert     | Dancing     | Sports Event | Play       |     |
|--------|-------------|-------------|-------------|--------------|------------|-----|
| Male   | 31 (35.54)  | 24 (20.09)  | 18 (24.21)  | 42 (33.48)   | 5 (6.70)   | 120 |
| Female | 38 (33.46)  | 15 (18.91)  | 29 (22.79)  | 23 (31.52)   | 8 (6.30)   | 113 |
|        | 69          | 39          | 47          | 65           | 13         | 233 |

11. Step 1:

$H_0$: Exercise frequencies are equally distributed across all categories.
$H_1$: Exercise frequencies are not equally distributed.

Step 2:

$\alpha = .01$
$df = 3$
$\chi^2_{\text{crit}} = 11.345$

Step 3:

$f_e = 196 \div 4 = 49$

| Frequency | Sometimes | Rarely   | Never     |
|-----------|-----------|----------|-----------|
| 40 (49)   | 62 (49)   | 68 (49)  | 26 (49)   |

$$\chi^2 = \frac{(40-49)^2}{49} + \frac{(62-49)^2}{49} + \frac{(68-49)^2}{49} + \frac{(26-49)^2}{49}$$

$$= 23.27$$

Step 4:

Exercise frequencies were not equally distributed. Reject $H_0$,
$\chi^2(3df, n = 196) = 23.27$, $p < .01$.

# CHAPTER 17: NONPARAMETRIC STATISTICS FOR ORDINAL DATA

1. It is better to use parametric tests if the assumptions can be met because they are more powerful (i.e., they are more likely to reject $H_0$). Using a parametric test whose assumptions have been violated increases the risk of a Type I error.
3. The Mann-Whitney $U$ test and the Kruskal-Wallis $H$ test are both used for independent samples and for ordinal level data. However, the Mann-Whitney test is appropriate for only two sets of scores while the Kruskal-Wallis test can be used for three or more samples.
5. Reject $H_0$?

   a. Y
   b. N
   c. N
   d. Y

7. $T_{crit} = 32$
9. Mann-Whitney $U$ Test:

| Treatment A | Rank | Treatment B | Rank |
|---|---|---|---|
| 10 | 1.5 | 35 | 6 |
| 10 | 1.5 | 36 | 7 |
| 12 | 3 | 38 | 9 |
| 13 | 4 | 38 | 9 |
| 16 | 5 | 40 | 11 |
| 38 | 9 | 42 | 12.5 |
| 42 | 12.5 | 64 | 14 |
|  |  | 72 | 15 |
|  | $\Sigma R_1 = 36.5$ |  | $\Sigma R_2 = 83.5$ |

$$U_1 = (7)(8) + \frac{7(7+1)}{2} - 36.5 = 47.5$$

$$U_2 = (7)(8) + \frac{8(8+1)}{2} - 83.5 = 8.5$$

For $n_1 = 7$ and $n_2 = 8$, $U_{crit} = 10$. Since $U_{obt}$ of 8.5 is less than $U_{crit}$, we can reject the null hypothesis. The distributions of the ranked scores were significantly different.

11. Kruskal-Wallis $H$ test:

| A | $Rank_1$ | B | $Rank_2$ | C | $Rank_3$ |
|---|---|---|---|---|---|
| 12 | 1 | 14 | 3 | 20 | 12.5 |
| 13 | 2 | 16 | 6 | 22 | 14 |
| 15 | 4 | 17 | 8.5 | 23 | 15.5 |
| 16 | 6 | 17 | 8.5 | 23 | 15.5 |
| 16 | 6 | 19 | 11 | 24 | 17 |
| 18 | 10 | 20 | 12.5 | 25 | 18 |
| | $\Sigma R_1 = 29$ | | $\Sigma R_2 = 49.5$ | | $\Sigma R_3 = 92.5$ |

$$H_{obt} = \left[ \frac{12}{18(18+1)} \right] \left[ \frac{29^2}{6} + \frac{49.5^2}{6} + \frac{92.5^2}{6} \right] - 3(18+1)$$

$$= (.0351)(140.17 + 408.38 + 1426.04) - 57$$

$$= 12.31$$

For $df = 2$, $\chi^2_{crit} = 5.991$. Since $H_{obt}$ exceeds $\chi^2_{crit}$, we can reject $H_0$. There were significant differences among the rankings of the groups.

13. The appropriate test is the Kruskal-Wallis.

| Exercise A | $Rank_1$ | Exercise B | $Rank_2$ | Exercise C | $Rank_3$ |
|---|---|---|---|---|---|
| 12 | 6.5 | 5 | 1 | 11 | 5 |
| 14 | 8.5 | 6 | 2 | 14 | 8.5 |
| 15 | 11 | 8 | 3 | 15 | 11 |
| 16 | 13.5 | 9 | 4 | 16 | 13.5 |
| 18 | 15.5 | 12 | 6.5 | 18 | 15.5 |
| 20 | 18 | 15 | 11 | 19 | 17 |
| | $\Sigma R_1 = 73$ | | $\Sigma R_2 = 27.5$ | | $\Sigma R_3 = 70.5$ |

$$H_{obt} = \left[ \frac{12}{18(18+1)} \right] \left[ \frac{73^2}{6} + \frac{27.5^2}{6} + \frac{70.5^2}{6} \right] - 3(18+1)$$

$$= (.0351)(888.17 + 126.04 + 828.38) - 57$$

$$= 7.67$$

For $df = 2$, $\chi^2_{crit} = 5.991$. Since $H_{obt}$ exceeds $\chi^2_{crit}$, we can reject $H_0$. There were significant differences among the rankings of the exercise groups.

15. The appropriate test is the Spearman correlation.

| Student | Ranking by New Faculty | Ranking by Established Faculty | D | D² |
|---|---|---|---|---|
| 1 | 3 | 3 | 0 | 0 |
| 2 | 5 | 6 | −1 | 1 |
| 3 | 10 | 10 | 0 | 0 |
| 4 | 1 | 1 | 0 | 0 |
| 5 | 7 | 5 | 2 | 4 |
| 6 | 4 | 2 | 2 | 4 |
| 7 | 6 | 7 | −1 | 1 |
| 8 | 9 | 8 | 1 | 1 |
| 9 | 2 | 4 | −2 | 4 |
| 10 | 8 | 9 | −1 | 1 |
| | | | | $\Sigma D^2 = 16$ |

$$r_s = 1 - \frac{6(16)}{10(10^2 - 1)}$$

$$= .903$$

For $n = 10$, $r_{s_{crit}} = .7939$. Since $r_{s_{obt}}$ of .903 is greater than $r_{s_{crit}}$, $H_0$ can be rejected. There is a strong correlation between the rankings of the students papers by both faculty members.

# Tables

Table 1 Table of the Normal Distribution Curve

| Column A z-score | Column B Proportion in body (larger part) | Column C Proportion in tail (smaller part) | Column D Proportion between mean and z | Column A z-score | Column B Proportion in body (larger part) | Column C Proportion in tail (smaller part) | Column D Proportion between mean and z |
|---|---|---|---|---|---|---|---|
| 0.00 | .5000 | .5000 | .0000 | 0.48 | .6844 | .3156 | .1844 |
| 0.01 | .5040 | .4960 | .0040 | 0.49 | .6879 | .3121 | .1879 |
| 0.02 | .5080 | .4920 | .0080 | 0.50 | .6915 | .3085 | .1915 |
| 0.03 | .5120 | .4880 | .0120 | 0.51 | .6950 | .3050 | .1950 |
| 0.04 | .5160 | .4840 | .0160 | 0.52 | .6985 | .3015 | .1985 |
| 0.05 | .5199 | .4801 | .0199 | 0.53 | .7019 | .2981 | .2019 |
| 0.06 | .5239 | .4761 | .0239 | 0.54 | .7054 | .2946 | .2054 |
| 0.07 | .5279 | .4721 | .0279 | 0.55 | .7088 | .2912 | .2088 |
| 0.08 | .5319 | .4681 | .0319 | 0.56 | .7123 | .2877 | .2123 |
| 0.09 | .5359 | .4641 | .0359 | 0.57 | .7157 | .2843 | .2157 |
| 0.10 | .5398 | .4602 | .0398 | 0.58 | .7190 | .2810 | .2190 |
| 0.11 | .5438 | .4562 | .0438 | 0.59 | .7224 | .2776 | .2224 |
| 0.12 | .5478 | .4522 | .0478 | 0.60 | .7257 | .2743 | .2257 |
| 0.13 | .5517 | .4483 | .0517 | 0.61 | .7291 | .2709 | .2291 |
| 0.14 | .5557 | .4443 | .0557 | 0.62 | .7324 | .2676 | .2324 |
| 0.15 | .5596 | .4404 | .0596 | 0.63 | .7357 | .2643 | .2357 |
| 0.16 | .5636 | .4364 | .0636 | 0.64 | .7389 | .2611 | .2389 |
| 0.17 | .5675 | .4325 | .0675 | 0.65 | .7422 | .2578 | .2422 |
| 0.18 | .5714 | .4286 | .0714 | 0.66 | .7454 | .2546 | .2454 |
| 0.19 | .5753 | .4247 | .0753 | 0.67 | .7486 | .2514 | .2486 |
| 0.20 | .5793 | .4207 | .0793 | 0.68 | .7517 | .2483 | .2517 |
| 0.21 | .5832 | .4168 | .0832 | 0.69 | .7549 | .2451 | .2549 |
| 0.22 | .5871 | .4129 | .0871 | 0.70 | .7580 | .2420 | .2580 |
| 0.23 | .5910 | .4090 | .0910 | 0.71 | .7611 | .2389 | .2611 |
| 0.24 | .5948 | .4052 | .0948 | 0.72 | .7642 | .2358 | .2642 |
| 0.25 | .5987 | .4013 | .0987 | 0.73 | .7673 | .2327 | .2673 |
| 0.26 | .6026 | .3974 | .1026 | 0.74 | .7704 | .2296 | .2704 |
| 0.27 | .6064 | .3936 | .1064 | 0.75 | .7734 | .2266 | .2734 |
| 0.28 | .6103 | .3897 | .1103 | 0.76 | .7764 | .2236 | .2764 |
| 0.29 | .6141 | .3859 | .1141 | 0.77 | .7794 | .2206 | .2794 |
| 0.30 | .6179 | .3821 | .1179 | 0.78 | .7823 | .2177 | .2823 |
| 0.31 | .6217 | .3783 | .1217 | 0.79 | .7852 | .2148 | .2852 |
| 0.32 | .6255 | .3745 | .1255 | 0.80 | .7881 | .2119 | .2881 |
| 0.33 | .6293 | .3707 | .1293 | 0.81 | .7910 | .2090 | .2910 |
| 0.34 | .6331 | .3669 | .1331 | 0.82 | .7939 | .2061 | .2939 |
| 0.35 | .6368 | .3632 | .1368 | 0.83 | .7967 | .2033 | .2967 |
| 0.36 | .6406 | .3594 | .1406 | 0.84 | .7995 | .2005 | .2995 |
| 0.37 | .6443 | .3557 | .1443 | 0.85 | .8023 | .1977 | .3023 |
| 0.38 | .6480 | .3520 | .1480 | 0.86 | .8051 | .1949 | .3051 |
| 0.39 | .6517 | .3483 | .1517 | 0.87 | .8078 | .1922 | .3078 |
| 0.40 | .6554 | .3446 | .1554 | 0.88 | .8106 | .1894 | .3106 |
| 0.41 | .6591 | .3409 | .1591 | 0.89 | .8133 | .1867 | .3133 |
| 0.42 | .6628 | .3372 | .1628 | 0.90 | .8159 | .1841 | .3159 |
| 0.43 | .6664 | .3336 | .1664 | 0.91 | .8186 | .1814 | .3186 |
| 0.44 | .6700 | .3300 | .1700 | 0.92 | .8212 | .1788 | .3212 |
| 0.45 | .6736 | .3264 | .1736 | 0.93 | .8238 | .1762 | .3238 |
| 0.46 | .6772 | .3228 | .1772 | 0.94 | .8264 | .1736 | .3264 |
| 0.47 | .6808 | .3192 | .1808 | 0.95 | .8289 | .1711 | .3289 |

(Continued)

*Table 1* Continued

| Column A | Column B | Column C | Column D | Column A | Column B | Column C | Column D |
|---|---|---|---|---|---|---|---|
| z-score | Proportion in body (larger part) | Proportion in tail (smaller part) | Proportion between mean and z | z-score | Proportion in body (larger part) | Proportion in tail (smaller part) | Proportion between mean and z |
| 0.96 | .8315 | .1685 | .3315 | 1.45 | .9265 | .0735 | .4265 |
| 0.97 | .8340 | .1660 | .3340 | 1.46 | .9279 | .0721 | .4279 |
| 0.98 | .8365 | .1635 | .3365 | 1.47 | .9292 | .0708 | .4292 |
| 0.99 | .8389 | .1611 | .3389 | 1.48 | .9306 | .0694 | .4306 |
| 1.00 | .8413 | .1587 | .3413 | 1.49 | .9319 | .0681 | .4319 |
| 1.01 | .8438 | .1562 | .3438 | 1.50 | .9332 | .0668 | .4332 |
| 1.02 | .8461 | .1539 | .3461 | 1.51 | .9345 | .0655 | .4345 |
| 1.03 | .8485 | .1515 | .3485 | 1.52 | .9357 | .0643 | .4357 |
| 1.04 | .8508 | .1492 | .3508 | 1.53 | .9370 | .0630 | .4370 |
| 1.05 | .8531 | .1469 | .3531 | 1.54 | .9382 | .0618 | .4382 |
| 1.06 | .8554 | .1446 | .3554 | 1.55 | .9394 | .0606 | .4394 |
| 1.07 | .8577 | .1423 | .3577 | 1.56 | .9406 | .0594 | .4406 |
| 1.08 | .8599 | .1401 | .3599 | 1.57 | .9418 | .0582 | .4418 |
| 1.09 | .8621 | .1379 | .3621 | 1.58 | .9429 | .0571 | .4429 |
| 1.10 | .8643 | .1357 | .3643 | 1.59 | .9441 | .0559 | .4441 |
| 1.11 | .8665 | .1335 | .3665 | 1.60 | .9452 | .0548 | .4452 |
| 1.12 | .8686 | .1314 | .3686 | 1.61 | .9463 | .0537 | .4463 |
| 1.13 | .8708 | .1292 | .3708 | 1.62 | .9474 | .0526 | .4474 |
| 1.14 | .8729 | .1271 | .3729 | 1.63 | .9484 | .0516 | .4484 |
| 1.15 | .8749 | .1251 | .3749 | 1.64 | .9495 | .0505 | .4495 |
| 1.16 | .8770 | .1230 | .3770 | 1.65 | .9505 | .0495 | .4505 |
| 1.17 | .8790 | .1210 | .3790 | 1.66 | .9515 | .0485 | .4515 |
| 1.18 | .8810 | .1190 | .3810 | 1.67 | .9525 | .0475 | .4525 |
| 1.19 | .8830 | .1170 | .3830 | 1.68 | .9535 | .0465 | .4535 |
| 1.20 | .8849 | .1151 | .3849 | 1.69 | .9545 | .0455 | .4545 |
| 1.21 | .8869 | .1131 | .3869 | 1.70 | .9554 | .0446 | .4554 |
| 1.22 | .8888 | .1112 | .3888 | 1.71 | .9564 | .0436 | .4564 |
| 1.23 | .8907 | .1093 | .3907 | 1.72 | .9573 | .0427 | .4573 |
| 1.24 | .8925 | .1075 | .3925 | 1.73 | .9582 | .0418 | .4582 |
| 1.25 | .8944 | .1056 | .3944 | 1.74 | .9591 | .0409 | .4591 |
| 1.26 | .8962 | .1038 | .3962 | 1.75 | .9599 | .0401 | .4599 |
| 1.27 | .8980 | .1020 | .3980 | 1.76 | .9608 | .0392 | .4608 |
| 1.28 | .8997 | .1003 | .3997 | 1.77 | .9616 | .0384 | .4616 |
| 1.29 | .9015 | .0985 | .4015 | 1.78 | .9625 | .0375 | .4625 |
| 1.30 | .9032 | .0968 | .4032 | 1.79 | .9633 | .0367 | .4633 |
| 1.31 | .9049 | .0951 | .4049 | 1.80 | .9641 | .0359 | .4641 |
| 1.32 | .9066 | .0934 | .4066 | 1.81 | .9649 | .0351 | .4649 |
| 1.33 | .9082 | .0918 | .4082 | 1.82 | .9656 | .0344 | .4656 |
| 1.34 | .9099 | .0901 | .4099 | 1.83 | .9664 | .0336 | .4664 |
| 1.35 | .9115 | .0885 | .4115 | 1.84 | .9671 | .0329 | .4671 |
| 1.36 | .9131 | .0869 | .4131 | 1.85 | .9678 | .0322 | .4678 |
| 1.37 | .9147 | .0853 | .4147 | 1.86 | .9686 | .0314 | .4686 |
| 1.38 | .9162 | .0838 | .4162 | 1.87 | .9693 | .0307 | .4693 |
| 1.39 | .9177 | .0823 | .4177 | 1.88 | .9699 | .0301 | .4699 |
| 1.40 | .9192 | .0808 | .4192 | 1.89 | .9706 | .0294 | .4706 |
| 1.41 | .9207 | .0793 | .4207 | 1.90 | .9713 | .0287 | .4713 |
| 1.42 | .9222 | .0778 | .4222 | 1.91 | .9719 | .0281 | .4719 |
| 1.43 | .9236 | .0764 | .4236 | 1.92 | .9726 | .0274 | .4726 |
| 1.44 | .9251 | .0749 | .4251 | 1.93 | .9732 | .0268 | .4732 |

(*Continued*)

| Column A | Column B | Column C | Column D | Column A | Column B | Column C | Column D |
|---|---|---|---|---|---|---|---|
| | Proportion in body (larger part) | Proportion in tail (smaller part) | Proportion between mean and z | | Proportion in body (larger part) | Proportion in tail (smaller part) | Proportion between mean and z |
| z-score | | | | z-score | | | |
| 1.94 | .9738 | .0262 | .4738 | 2.45 | .9929 | .0071 | .4929 |
| 1.95 | .9744 | .0256 | .4744 | 2.46 | .9931 | .0069 | .4931 |
| 1.96 | .9750 | .0250 | .4750 | 2.47 | .9932 | .0068 | .4932 |
| 1.97 | .9756 | .0244 | .4756 | 2.48 | .9934 | .0066 | .4934 |
| 1.98 | .9761 | .0239 | .4761 | 2.49 | .9936 | .0064 | .4936 |
| 1.99 | .9767 | .0233 | .4767 | 2.50 | .9938 | .0062 | .4938 |
| 2.00 | .9772 | .0228 | .4772 | 2.51 | .9940 | .0060 | .4940 |
| 2.01 | .9778 | .0222 | .4778 | 2.52 | .9941 | .0059 | .4941 |
| 2.02 | .9783 | .0217 | .4783 | 2.53 | .9943 | .0057 | .4943 |
| 2.03 | .9788 | .0212 | .4788 | 2.54 | .9945 | .0055 | .4945 |
| 2.04 | .9793 | .0207 | .4793 | 2.55 | .9946 | .0054 | .4946 |
| 2.05 | .9798 | .0202 | .4798 | 2.56 | .9948 | .0052 | .4948 |
| 2.06 | .9803 | .0197 | .4803 | 2.57 | .9949 | .0051 | .4949 |
| 2.07 | .9808 | .0192 | .4808 | 2.58 | .9951 | .0049 | .4951 |
| 2.08 | .9812 | .0188 | .4812 | 2.59 | .9952 | .0048 | .4952 |
| 2.09 | .9817 | .0183 | .4817 | 2.60 | .9953 | .0047 | .4953 |
| 2.10 | .9821 | .0179 | .4821 | 2.61 | .9955 | .0045 | .4955 |
| 2.11 | .9826 | .0174 | .4826 | 2.62 | .9956 | .0044 | .4956 |
| 2.12 | .9830 | .0170 | .4830 | 2.63 | .9957 | .0043 | .4957 |
| 2.13 | .9834 | .0166 | .4834 | 2.64 | .9959 | .0041 | .4959 |
| 2.14 | .9838 | .0162 | .4838 | 2.65 | .9960 | .0040 | .4960 |
| 2.15 | .9842 | .0158 | .4842 | 2.66 | .9961 | .0039 | .4961 |
| 2.16 | .9846 | .0154 | .4846 | 2.67 | .9962 | .0038 | .4962 |
| 2.17 | .9850 | .0150 | .4850 | 2.68 | .9963 | .0037 | .4963 |
| 2.18 | .9854 | .0146 | .4854 | 2.69 | .9964 | .0036 | .4964 |
| 2.19 | .9857 | .0143 | .4857 | 2.70 | .9965 | .0035 | .4965 |
| 2.20 | .9861 | .0139 | .4861 | 2.71 | .9966 | .0034 | .4966 |
| 2.21 | .9864 | .0136 | .4864 | 2.72 | .9967 | .0033 | .4967 |
| 2.22 | .9868 | .0132 | .4868 | 2.73 | .9968 | .0032 | .4968 |
| 2.23 | .9871 | .0129 | .4871 | 2.74 | .9969 | .0031 | .4969 |
| 2.24 | .9875 | .0125 | .4875 | 2.75 | .9970 | .0030 | .4970 |
| 2.25 | .9878 | .0122 | .4878 | 2.76 | .9971 | .0029 | .4971 |
| 2.26 | .9881 | .0119 | .4881 | 2.77 | .9972 | .0028 | .4972 |
| 2.27 | .9884 | .0116 | .4884 | 2.78 | .9973 | .0027 | .4973 |
| 2.28 | .9887 | .0113 | .4887 | 2.79 | .9974 | .0026 | .4974 |
| 2.29 | .9890 | .0110 | .4890 | 2.80 | .9974 | .0026 | .4974 |
| 2.30 | .9893 | .0107 | .4893 | 2.81 | .9975 | .0025 | .4975 |
| 2.31 | .9896 | .0104 | .4896 | 2.82 | .9976 | .0024 | .4976 |
| 2.32 | .9898 | .0102 | .4898 | 2.83 | .9977 | .0023 | .4977 |
| 2.33 | .9901 | .0099 | .4901 | 2.84 | .9977 | .0023 | .4977 |
| 2.34 | .9904 | .0096 | .4904 | 2.85 | .9978 | .0022 | .4978 |
| 2.35 | .9906 | .0094 | .4906 | 2.86 | .9979 | .0021 | .4979 |
| 2.36 | .9909 | .0091 | .4909 | 2.87 | .9979 | .0021 | .4979 |
| 2.37 | .9911 | .0089 | .4911 | 2.88 | .9980 | .0020 | .4980 |
| 2.38 | .9913 | .0087 | .4913 | 2.89 | .9981 | .0019 | .4981 |
| 2.39 | .9916 | .0084 | .4916 | 2.90 | .9981 | .0019 | .4981 |
| 2.40 | .9918 | .0082 | .4918 | 2.91 | .9982 | .0018 | .4982 |
| 2.41 | .9920 | .0080 | .4920 | 2.92 | .9982 | .0018 | .4982 |
| 2.42 | .9922 | .0078 | .4922 | 2.93 | .9983 | .0017 | .4983 |
| 2.43 | .9925 | .0075 | .4925 | 2.94 | .9984 | .0016 | .4984 |
| 2.44 | .9927 | .0073 | .4927 | 2.95 | .9984 | .0016 | .4984 |

(Continued)

*Table 1* Continued

| Column A | Column B | Column C | Column D | Column A | Column B | Column C | Column D |
|---|---|---|---|---|---|---|---|
| z-score | Proportion in body (larger part) | Proportion in tail (smaller part) | Proportion between mean and z | z-score | Proportion in body (larger part) | Proportion in tail (smaller part) | Proportion between mean and z |
| 2.96 | .9985 | .0015 | .4985 | 3.04 | .9988 | .0012 | .4988 |
| 2.97 | .9985 | .0015 | .4985 | 3.05 | .9989 | .0011 | .4989 |
| 2.98 | .9986 | .0014 | .4986 | 3.06 | .9989 | .0011 | .4989 |
| 2.99 | .9986 | .0014 | .4986 | 3.07 | .9989 | .0011 | .4989 |
| 3.00 | .9987 | .0013 | .4987 | 3.08 | .9990 | .0010 | .4990 |
| 3.01 | .9987 | .0013 | .4987 | 3.09 | .9990 | .0010 | .4990 |
| 3.02 | .9987 | .0013 | .4987 | 3.10 | .9990 | .0010 | .4990 |
| 3.03 | .9988 | .0012 | .4988 | 3.11 | .9991 | .0009 | .4991 |

*Table 2* Critical Values of the *t*-Distribution[1]

| | Level of significance for one-tailed test | | | | | |
|---|---|---|---|---|---|---|
| | .10 | .05 | .025 | .01 | .005 | .0005 |
| | Level of significance for two-tailed test | | | | | |
| df | .20 | .10 | .05 | .02 | .01 | .001 |
| 1 | 3.078 | 6.314 | 12.706 | 31.821 | 63.657 | 636.619 |
| 2 | 1.886 | 2.920 | 4.303 | 6.965 | 9.925 | 31.598 |
| 3 | 1.638 | 2.353 | 3.182 | 4.541 | 5.841 | 12.941 |
| 4 | 1.533 | 2.132 | 2.776 | 3.747 | 4.604 | 8.610 |
| 5 | 1.476 | 2.015 | 2.571 | 3.365 | 4.032 | 6.859 |
| 6 | 1.440 | 1.943 | 2.447 | 3.143 | 3.707 | 5.959 |
| 7 | 1.415 | 1.895 | 2.365 | 2.998 | 3.499 | 5.405 |
| 8 | 1.397 | 1.860 | 2.306 | 2.896 | 3.355 | 5.041 |
| 9 | 1.383 | 1.833 | 2.262 | 2.821 | 3.250 | 4.781 |
| 10 | 1.372 | 1.812 | 2.228 | 2.764 | 3.169 | 4.587 |
| 11 | 1.363 | 1.796 | 2.201 | 2.718 | 3.106 | 4.437 |
| 12 | 1.356 | 1.782 | 2.179 | 2.681 | 3.055 | 4.318 |
| 13 | 1.350 | 1.771 | 2.160 | 2.650 | 3.012 | 4.221 |
| 14 | 1.345 | 1.761 | 2.145 | 2.624 | 2.977 | 4.140 |
| 15 | 1.341 | 1.753 | 2.131 | 2.602 | 2.947 | 4.073 |
| 16 | 1.337 | 1.746 | 2.120 | 2.583 | 2.921 | 4.015 |
| 17 | 1.333 | 1.740 | 2.110 | 2.567 | 2.898 | 3.965 |
| 18 | 1.330 | 1.734 | 2.101 | 2.552 | 2.878 | 3.922 |
| 19 | 1.328 | 1.729 | 2.093 | 2.539 | 2.861 | 3.883 |
| 20 | 1.325 | 1.725 | 2.086 | 2.528 | 2.845 | 3.850 |
| 21 | 1.323 | 1.721 | 2.080 | 2.518 | 2.831 | 3.819 |
| 22 | 1.321 | 1.717 | 2.074 | 2.508 | 2.819 | 3.792 |
| 23 | 1.319 | 1.714 | 2.069 | 2.500 | 2.807 | 3.767 |
| 24 | 1.318 | 1.711 | 2.064 | 2.492 | 2.797 | 3.745 |
| 25 | 1.316 | 1.708 | 2.060 | 2.485 | 2.787 | 3.725 |
| 26 | 1.315 | 1.706 | 2.056 | 2.479 | 2.779 | 3.707 |
| 27 | 1.314 | 1.703 | 2.052 | 2.473 | 2.771 | 3.690 |
| 28 | 1.313 | 1.701 | 2.048 | 2.467 | 2.763 | 3.674 |
| 29 | 1.311 | 1.699 | 2.045 | 2.462 | 2.756 | 3.659 |
| 30 | 1.310 | 1.697 | 2.042 | 2.457 | 2.750 | 3.646 |
| 40 | 1.303 | 1.684 | 2.021 | 2.423 | 2.704 | 3.551 |
| 60 | 1.296 | 1.671 | 2.000 | 2.390 | 2.660 | 3.460 |
| 120 | 1.289 | 1.658 | 1.980 | 2.358 | 2.617 | 3.373 |
| Infinity | 1.282 | 1.645 | 1.960 | 2.326 | 2.576 | 3.291 |

[1] Fisher, R. A., & Yates, F. (1974). *Statistical tables for biological, agricultural, and medical research* (6th ed.). London: Longman Group, Ltd. Reprinted with permission of Addison-Wesley Longman, Ltd.

Table 3 Critical Values of *F* for the .05 Level

| Within groups degrees of freedom ($df_{wi}$) | Between groups degrees of freedom (numerator) ($df_{bet}$) | | | | | | | | | | | | |
|---|---|---|---|---|---|---|---|---|---|---|---|---|---|
| | 1 | 2 | 3 | 4 | 5 | 6 | 7 | 8 | 9 | 10 | 11 | 12 | 14 |
| 1 | 161.00 | 200.00 | 216.00 | 225.00 | 230.00 | 234.00 | 237.00 | 239.00 | 241.00 | 242.00 | 243.00 | 244.00 | 161.00 |
| 2 | 18.51 | 19.00 | 19.16 | 19.25 | 19.30 | 19.33 | 19.36 | 19.37 | 19.38 | 19.39 | 19.40 | 19.41 | 19.42 |
| 3 | 10.13 | 9.55 | 9.28 | 9.12 | 9.01 | 8.94 | 8.88 | 8.84 | 8.81 | 8.78 | 8.76 | 8.74 | 8.71 |
| 4 | 7.71 | 6.94 | 6.59 | 6.39 | 6.26 | 6.16 | 6.09 | 6.04 | 6.00 | 5.96 | 5.93 | 5.91 | 5.87 |
| 5 | 6.61 | 5.79 | 5.41 | 5.19 | 5.05 | 4.95 | 4.88 | 4.82 | 4.78 | 4.74 | 4.70 | 4.68 | 4.64 |
| 6 | 5.99 | 5.14 | 4.76 | 4.53 | 4.39 | 4.28 | 4.21 | 4.15 | 4.10 | 4.06 | 4.03 | 4.00 | 3.96 |
| 7 | 5.59 | 4.74 | 4.35 | 4.12 | 3.97 | 3.87 | 3.79 | 3.73 | 3.68 | 3.63 | 3.60 | 3.57 | 3.52 |
| 8 | 5.32 | 4.46 | 4.07 | 3.84 | 3.69 | 3.58 | 3.50 | 3.44 | 3.39 | 3.34 | 3.31 | 3.28 | 3.23 |
| 9 | 5.12 | 4.26 | 3.86 | 3.63 | 3.48 | 3.37 | 3.29 | 3.23 | 3.18 | 3.13 | 3.10 | 3.07 | 3.02 |
| 10 | 4.96 | 4.10 | 3.71 | 3.48 | 3.33 | 3.22 | 3.14 | 3.07 | 3.02 | 2.97 | 2.94 | 2.91 | 2.86 |
| 11 | 4.84 | 3.98 | 3.59 | 3.36 | 3.20 | 3.09 | 3.01 | 2.95 | 2.90 | 2.86 | 2.82 | 2.79 | 2.74 |
| 12 | 4.75 | 3.88 | 3.49 | 3.26 | 3.11 | 3.00 | 2.92 | 2.85 | 2.80 | 2.76 | 2.72 | 2.69 | 2.64 |
| 13 | 4.67 | 3.80 | 3.41 | 3.18 | 3.02 | 2.92 | 2.84 | 2.72 | 2.77 | 2.63 | 2.63 | 2.60 | 2.55 |
| 14 | 4.60 | 3.74 | 3.34 | 3.11 | 2.96 | 2.85 | 2.77 | 2.70 | 2.65 | 2.60 | 2.56 | 2.53 | 2.48 |
| 15 | 4.54 | 3.68 | 3.29 | 3.06 | 2.90 | 2.79 | 2.70 | 2.64 | 2.59 | 2.55 | 2.51 | 2.48 | 2.43 |
| 16 | 4.49 | 3.63 | 3.24 | 3.01 | 2.85 | 2.74 | 2.66 | 2.59 | 2.54 | 2.49 | 2.45 | 2.42 | 2.37 |
| 17 | 4.45 | 3.59 | 3.20 | 2.96 | 2.81 | 2.70 | 2.62 | 2.55 | 2.50 | 2.45 | 2.41 | 2.38 | 2.33 |
| 18 | 4.41 | 3.55 | 3.16 | 2.93 | 2.77 | 2.66 | 2.58 | 2.51 | 2.46 | 2.41 | 2.37 | 2.34 | 2.29 |
| 19 | 4.38 | 3.52 | 3.13 | 2.90 | 2.74 | 2.63 | 2.55 | 2.48 | 2.43 | 2.38 | 2.34 | 2.31 | 2.26 |
| 20 | 4.35 | 3.49 | 3.10 | 2.87 | 2.71 | 2.60 | 2.52 | 2.45 | 2.40 | 2.35 | 2.31 | 2.28 | 2.23 |
| 21 | 4.32 | 3.47 | 3.07 | 2.84 | 2.68 | 2.57 | 2.49 | 2.42 | 2.37 | 2.32 | 2.28 | 2.25 | 2.20 |
| 22 | 4.30 | 3.44 | 3.05 | 2.82 | 2.66 | 2.55 | 2.47 | 2.40 | 2.35 | 2.30 | 2.26 | 2.23 | 2.18 |
| 23 | 4.28 | 3.42 | 3.03 | 2.80 | 2.64 | 2.53 | 2.45 | 2.38 | 2.32 | 2.28 | 2.24 | 2.20 | 2.14 |
| 24 | 4.26 | 3.40 | 3.01 | 2.78 | 2.62 | 2.51 | 2.43 | 2.36 | 2.30 | 2.26 | 2.22 | 2.18 | 2.13 |
| 25 | 4.24 | 3.38 | 2.99 | 2.76 | 2.60 | 2.49 | 2.41 | 2.34 | 2.28 | 2.24 | 2.20 | 2.16 | 2.11 |
| 26 | 4.22 | 3.37 | 2.98 | 2.74 | 2.59 | 2.47 | 2.39 | 2.32 | 2.27 | 2.22 | 2.18 | 2.15 | 2.10 |
| 27 | 4.21 | 3.35 | 2.96 | 2.73 | 2.57 | 2.46 | 2.37 | 2.30 | 2.25 | 2.20 | 2.16 | 2.13 | 2.08 |
| 28 | 4.20 | 3.34 | 2.95 | 2.71 | 2.56 | 2.44 | 2.36 | 2.29 | 2.24 | 2.19 | 2.15 | 2.12 | 2.06 |
| 29 | 4.18 | 3.33 | 2.93 | 2.70 | 2.54 | 2.43 | 2.35 | 2.28 | 2.22 | 2.18 | 2.14 | 2.10 | 2.05 |

| | | | Between groups degrees of freedom (numerator) $(df_{bet})$ | | | | | | | | | Within groups degrees of freedom |
|---|---|---|---|---|---|---|---|---|---|---|---|---|
| 16 | 20 | 24 | 30 | 40 | 50 | 75 | 100 | 200 | 500 | Infinity | $(df_{wi})$ |
| 246.00 | 248.00 | 249.00 | 250.00 | 251.00 | 252.00 | 253.00 | 253.00 | 254.00 | 254.00 | 254.00 | 1 |
| 19.43 | 19.44 | 19.45 | 19.46 | 19.47 | 19.47 | 19.48 | 19.49 | 19.49 | 19.50 | 19.50 | 2 |
| 8.69 | 8.66 | 8.64 | 8.62 | 8.60 | 8.58 | 8.57 | 8.56 | 8.54 | 8.54 | 8.53 | 3 |
| 5.84 | 5.80 | 5.77 | 5.74 | 5.71 | 5.70 | 5.68 | 5.66 | 5.65 | 5.64 | 5.63 | 4 |
| 4.60 | 4.56 | 4.53 | 4.50 | 4.46 | 4.44 | 4.42 | 4.40 | 4.38 | 4.37 | 4.36 | 5 |
| 3.92 | 3.87 | 3.84 | 3.81 | 3.77 | 3.75 | 3.72 | 3.71 | 3.69 | 3.68 | 3.67 | 6 |
| 3.49 | 3.44 | 3.41 | 3.38 | 3.34 | 3.32 | 3.29 | 3.28 | 3.25 | 3.24 | 3.23 | 7 |
| 3.20 | 3.15 | 3.12 | 3.08 | 3.05 | 3.03 | 3.00 | 2.98 | 2.96 | 2.94 | 2.93 | 8 |
| 2.98 | 2.93 | 2.90 | 2.86 | 2.82 | 2.80 | 2.77 | 2.76 | 2.73 | 2.72 | 2.71 | 9 |
| 2.82 | 2.77 | 2.74 | 2.70 | 2.67 | 2.64 | 2.61 | 2.59 | 2.56 | 2.55 | 2.54 | 10 |
| 2.70 | 2.65 | 2.61 | 2.57 | 2.53 | 2.50 | 2.47 | 2.45 | 2.42 | 2.41 | 2.40 | 11 |
| 2.60 | 2.54 | 2.50 | 2.46 | 2.42 | 2.40 | 2.36 | 2.35 | 2.32 | 2.31 | 2.30 | 12 |
| 2.51 | 2.46 | 2.42 | 2.38 | 2.34 | 2.32 | 2.28 | 2.26 | 2.24 | 2.22 | 2.21 | 13 |
| 2.44 | 2.39 | 2.35 | 2.31 | 2.27 | 2.24 | 2.21 | 2.19 | 2.16 | 2.14 | 2.13 | 14 |
| 2.39 | 2.33 | 2.29 | 2.25 | 2.21 | 2.18 | 2.15 | 2.12 | 2.10 | 2.08 | 2.07 | 15 |
| 2.33 | 2.28 | 2.24 | 2.20 | 2.16 | 2.13 | 2.09 | 2.07 | 2.04 | 2.02 | 2.01 | 16 |
| 2.29 | 2.23 | 2.19 | 2.15 | 2.11 | 2.08 | 2.04 | 2.02 | 1.99 | 1.97 | 1.96 | 17 |
| 2.25 | 2.19 | 2.15 | 2.11 | 2.07 | 2.04 | 2.00 | 1.98 | 1.95 | 1.93 | 1.92 | 18 |
| 2.21 | 2.15 | 2.11 | 2.07 | 2.02 | 2.00 | 1.96 | 1.94 | 1.91 | 1.90 | 1.88 | 19 |
| 2.18 | 2.12 | 2.08 | 2.04 | 1.99 | 1.96 | 1.92 | 1.90 | 1.87 | 1.85 | 1.84 | 20 |
| 2.15 | 2.09 | 2.05 | 2.00 | 1.96 | 1.93 | 1.89 | 1.87 | 1.84 | 1.82 | 1.81 | 21 |
| 2.13 | 2.07 | 2.03 | 1.98 | 1.93 | 1.91 | 1.87 | 1.84 | 1.81 | 1.80 | 1.78 | 22 |
| 2.10 | 2.04 | 2.00 | 1.96 | 1.91 | 1.88 | 1.84 | 1.82 | 1.79 | 1.77 | 1.76 | 23 |
| 2.09 | 2.02 | 1.98 | 1.94 | 1.89 | 1.86 | 1.82 | 1.80 | 1.76 | 1.74 | 1.73 | 24 |
| 2.06 | 2.00 | 1.96 | 1.92 | 1.87 | 1.84 | 1.80 | 1.77 | 1.74 | 1.72 | 1.71 | 25 |
| 2.05 | 1.99 | 1.95 | 1.90 | 1.85 | 1.82 | 1.78 | 1.76 | 1.72 | 1.70 | 1.69 | 26 |
| 2.03 | 1.97 | 1.93 | 1.88 | 1.84 | 1.80 | 1.76 | 1.74 | 1.71 | 1.68 | 1.67 | 27 |
| 2.02 | 1.96 | 1.91 | 1.87 | 1.81 | 1.78 | 1.75 | 1.72 | 1.69 | 1.67 | 1.65 | 28 |
| 2.00 | 1.94 | 1.90 | 1.85 | 1.80 | 1.77 | 1.73 | 1.71 | 1.68 | 1.65 | 1.64 | 29 |

(Continued)

| Within groups degrees of freedom $(df_{wi})$ | Between groups degrees of freedom (numerator) $(df_{bet})$ | | | | | | | | | | | | |
|---|---|---|---|---|---|---|---|---|---|---|---|---|---|
| | 1 | 2 | 3 | 4 | 5 | 6 | 7 | 8 | 9 | 10 | 11 | 12 | 14 |
| 30 | 4.17 | 3.32 | 2.92 | 2.69 | 2.53 | 2.42 | 2.34 | 2.27 | 2.21 | 2.16 | 2.12 | 2.09 | 2.04 |
| 32 | 4.15 | 3.30 | 2.90 | 2.67 | 2.51 | 2.40 | 2.32 | 2.25 | 2.19 | 2.14 | 2.10 | 2.07 | 2.02 |
| 34 | 4.13 | 3.28 | 2.88 | 2.65 | 2.49 | 2.38 | 2.30 | 2.23 | 2.17 | 2.12 | 2.08 | 2.05 | 2.00 |
| 36 | 4.11 | 3.26 | 2.86 | 2.63 | 2.48 | 2.36 | 2.28 | 2.21 | 2.15 | 2.10 | 2.06 | 2.03 | 1.98 |
| 38 | 4.10 | 3.25 | 2.85 | 2.62 | 2.46 | 2.35 | 2.26 | 2.19 | 2.14 | 2.09 | 2.05 | 2.02 | 1.96 |
| 40 | 4.08 | 3.23 | 2.84 | 2.61 | 2.45 | 2.34 | 2.25 | 2.18 | 2.12 | 2.07 | 2.04 | 2.00 | 1.95 |
| 42 | 4.07 | 3.22 | 2.83 | 2.59 | 2.44 | 2.32 | 2.24 | 2.17 | 2.11 | 2.06 | 2.02 | 1.99 | 1.94 |
| 44 | 4.06 | 3.21 | 2.82 | 2.58 | 2.43 | 2.31 | 2.23 | 2.16 | 2.10 | 2.05 | 2.01 | 1.98 | 1.92 |
| 46 | 4.05 | 3.20 | 2.81 | 2.57 | 2.42 | 2.30 | 2.22 | 2.14 | 2.09 | 2.04 | 2.00 | 1.97 | 1.91 |
| 48 | 4.04 | 3.19 | 2.80 | 2.56 | 2.41 | 2.30 | 2.21 | 2.14 | 2.08 | 2.03 | 1.99 | 1.96 | 1.90 |
| 50 | 4.03 | 3.18 | 2.79 | 2.56 | 2.40 | 2.29 | 2.20 | 2.13 | 2.07 | 2.02 | 1.98 | 1.95 | 1.90 |
| 55 | 4.02 | 3.17 | 2.78 | 2.54 | 2.38 | 2.27 | 2.18 | 2.11 | 2.05 | 2.00 | 1.97 | 1.93 | 1.88 |
| 60 | 4.00 | 3.15 | 2.76 | 2.52 | 2.37 | 2.25 | 2.17 | 2.10 | 2.04 | 1.99 | 1.95 | 1.92 | 1.86 |
| 65 | 3.99 | 3.14 | 2.75 | 2.51 | 2.36 | 2.24 | 2.15 | 2.08 | 2.02 | 1.98 | 1.94 | 1.90 | 1.85 |
| 70 | 3.98 | 3.13 | 2.74 | 2.50 | 2.35 | 2.23 | 2.14 | 2.07 | 2.01 | 1.97 | 1.93 | 1.89 | 1.84 |
| 80 | 3.96 | 3.11 | 2.72 | 2.48 | 2.33 | 2.21 | 2.12 | 2.05 | 1.99 | 1.95 | 1.91 | 1.88 | 1.82 |
| 100 | 3.94 | 3.09 | 2.70 | 2.46 | 2.30 | 2.19 | 2.10 | 2.03 | 1.97 | 1.92 | 1.88 | 1.85 | 1.79 |
| 125 | 3.92 | 3.07 | 2.68 | 2.44 | 2.29 | 2.17 | 2.08 | 2.01 | 1.95 | 1.90 | 1.86 | 1.83 | 1.77 |
| 150 | 3.91 | 3.06 | 2.67 | 2.43 | 2.27 | 2.16 | 2.07 | 2.00 | 1.94 | 1.89 | 1.85 | 1.82 | 1.76 |
| 200 | 3.89 | 3.04 | 2.65 | 2.41 | 2.26 | 2.14 | 2.05 | 1.98 | 1.92 | 1.87 | 1.83 | 1.80 | 1.74 |
| 400 | 3.86 | 3.02 | 2.62 | 2.39 | 2.23 | 2.12 | 2.03 | 1.96 | 1.90 | 1.85 | 1.81 | 1.78 | 1.72 |
| 1000 | 3.85 | 3.00 | 2.61 | 2.38 | 2.22 | 2.10 | 2.02 | 1.95 | 1.89 | 1.84 | 1.80 | 1.76 | 1.70 |
| Infinity | 3.84 | 2.99 | 2.60 | 2.37 | 2.21 | 2.09 | 2.01 | 1.94 | 1.88 | 1.83 | 1.79 | 1.75 | 1.69 |

| Between groups degrees of freedom (numerator) ($df_{bet}$) | | | | | | | | | | | Within groups degrees of freedom |
|---|---|---|---|---|---|---|---|---|---|---|---|
| 16 | 20 | 24 | 30 | 40 | 50 | 75 | 100 | 200 | 500 | Infinity | ($df_{wi}$) |
| 1.99 | 1.93 | 1.89 | 1.84 | 1.79 | 1.76 | 1.72 | 1.69 | 1.66 | 1.64 | 1.62 | 30 |
| 1.97 | 1.91 | 1.86 | 1.82 | 1.76 | 1.74 | 1.69 | 1.67 | 1.64 | 1.61 | 1.59 | 32 |
| 1.95 | 1.89 | 1.84 | 1.80 | 1.74 | 1.71 | 1.67 | 1.64 | 1.61 | 1.59 | 1.57 | 34 |
| 1.93 | 1.87 | 1.82 | 1.78 | 1.72 | 1.69 | 1.65 | 1.62 | 1.59 | 1.56 | 1.55 | 36 |
| 1.92 | 1.85 | 1.80 | 1.76 | 1.71 | 1.67 | 1.63 | 1.60 | 1.57 | 1.54 | 1.53 | 38 |
| 1.90 | 1.84 | 1.79 | 1.74 | 1.69 | 1.66 | 1.61 | 1.59 | 1.55 | 1.53 | 1.51 | 40 |
| 1.89 | 1.82 | 1.78 | 1.73 | 1.68 | 1.64 | 1.60 | 1.57 | 1.54 | 1.51 | 1.49 | 42 |
| 1.88 | 1.81 | 1.76 | 1.72 | 1.66 | 1.63 | 1.58 | 1.56 | 1.52 | 1.50 | 1.48 | 44 |
| 1.87 | 1.80 | 1.75 | 1.71 | 1.65 | 1.62 | 1.57 | 1.54 | 1.51 | 1.48 | 1.46 | 46 |
| 1.86 | 1.79 | 1.74 | 1.70 | 1.64 | 1.61 | 1.56 | 1.53 | 1.50 | 1.47 | 1.45 | 48 |
| 1.85 | 1.78 | 1.74 | 1.69 | 1.63 | 1.60 | 1.55 | 1.52 | 1.48 | 1.46 | 1.44 | 50 |
| 1.83 | 1.76 | 1.72 | 1.67 | 1.61 | 1.58 | 1.52 | 1.50 | 1.46 | 1.43 | 1.41 | 55 |
| 1.81 | 1.75 | 1.70 | 1.65 | 1.59 | 1.56 | 1.50 | 1.48 | 1.44 | 1.41 | 1.39 | 60 |
| 1.80 | 1.73 | 1.68 | 1.63 | 1.57 | 1.54 | 1.49 | 1.46 | 1.42 | 1.39 | 1.37 | 65 |
| 1.79 | 1.72 | 1.67 | 1.62 | 1.56 | 1.53 | 1.47 | 1.45 | 1.40 | 1.37 | 1.35 | 70 |
| 1.77 | 1.70 | 1.65 | 1.60 | 1.54 | 1.51 | 1.45 | 1.42 | 1.38 | 1.35 | 1.32 | 80 |
| 1.75 | 1.68 | 1.63 | 1.57 | 1.51 | 1.48 | 1.42 | 1.39 | 1.34 | 1.30 | 1.28 | 100 |
| 1.72 | 1.65 | 1.60 | 1.55 | 1.49 | 1.45 | 1.39 | 1.36 | 1.31 | 1.27 | 1.25 | 125 |
| 1.71 | 1.64 | 1.59 | 1.54 | 1.47 | 1.44 | 1.37 | 1.34 | 1.29 | 1.25 | 1.22 | 150 |
| 1.69 | 1.62 | 1.57 | 1.52 | 1.45 | 1.42 | 1.35 | 1.32 | 1.26 | 1.22 | 1.19 | 200 |
| 1.67 | 1.60 | 1.54 | 1.49 | 1.42 | 1.38 | 1.32 | 1.28 | 1.22 | 1.16 | 1.13 | 400 |
| 1.65 | 1.58 | 1.53 | 1.47 | 1.41 | 1.36 | 1.30 | 1.26 | 1.19 | 1.13 | 1.08 | 1000 |
| 1.64 | 1.57 | 1.52 | 1.46 | 1.40 | 1.35 | 1.28 | 1.24 | 1.17 | 1.11 | 1.00 | Infinity |

Table 4  Critical Values of $F$ for the .01 Level

| Within groups degrees of freedom $(df_{wi})$ | Between groups degrees of freedom (numerator) $(df_{bet})$ | | | | | | | | | | | | |
|---|---|---|---|---|---|---|---|---|---|---|---|---|---|
| | 1 | 2 | 3 | 4 | 5 | 6 | 7 | 8 | 9 | 10 | 11 | 12 | 14 |
| 1 | 4,052 | 4,999 | 5,403 | 5,625 | 5,764 | 5,859 | 5,928 | 5,981 | 6,022 | 6,056 | 6,082 | 6,106 | 6,142 |
| 2 | 98.49 | 99.00 | 99.17 | 99.25 | 99.30 | 99.33 | 99.34 | 99.36 | 99.38 | 99.40 | 99.41 | 99.42 | 99.43 |
| 3 | 34.12 | 30.82 | 29.46 | 28.71 | 28.24 | 27.91 | 29.67 | 27.49 | 27.34 | 27.23 | 27.13 | 27.05 | 26.92 |
| 4 | 21.20 | 18.00 | 16.69 | 15.98 | 15.52 | 15.21 | 14.98 | 14.80 | 14.66 | 14.54 | 14.45 | 14.37 | 14.24 |
| 5 | 16.26 | 13.27 | 12.06 | 11.39 | 10.97 | 10.67 | 10.45 | 10.27 | 10.15 | 10.05 | 9.96 | 9.89 | 9.77 |
| 6 | 13.74 | 10.92 | 9.78 | 9.15 | 8.75 | 8.47 | 8.26 | 8.10 | 7.98 | 7.87 | 7.79 | 7.72 | 7.60 |
| 7 | 12.25 | 9.55 | 8.45 | 7.85 | 7.46 | 7.19 | 7.00 | 6.84 | 6.71 | 6.62 | 6.54 | 6.47 | 6.35 |
| 8 | 11.26 | 8.65 | 7.59 | 7.01 | 6.63 | 6.37 | 6.19 | 6.03 | 5.91 | 5.82 | 5.74 | 5.67 | 5.56 |
| 9 | 10.56 | 8.02 | 6.99 | 6.42 | 6.06 | 5.80 | 5.62 | 5.47 | 5.35 | 5.26 | 5.18 | 5.11 | 5.00 |
| 10 | 10.04 | 7.56 | 6.55 | 5.99 | 5.64 | 5.39 | 5.21 | 5.06 | 4.95 | 4.85 | 4.78 | 4.71 | 4.60 |
| 11 | 9.65 | 7.20 | 6.22 | 5.67 | 5.32 | 5.07 | 4.88 | 4.74 | 4.63 | 4.54 | 4.46 | 4.40 | 4.29 |
| 12 | 9.33 | 6.93 | 5.95 | 5.41 | 5.06 | 4.82 | 4.65 | 4.50 | 4.39 | 4.30 | 4.22 | 4.16 | 4.05 |
| 13 | 9.07 | 6.70 | 5.74 | 5.20 | 4.86 | 4.62 | 4.44 | 4.30 | 4.19 | 4.10 | 4.02 | 3.96 | 3.85 |
| 14 | 8.86 | 6.51 | 5.56 | 5.03 | 4.69 | 4.46 | 4.28 | 4.14 | 4.03 | 3.94 | 3.86 | 3.80 | 3.70 |
| 15 | 8.68 | 6.36 | 5.42 | 4.89 | 4.56 | 4.32 | 4.14 | 4.00 | 3.89 | 3.80 | 3.73 | 3.67 | 3.56 |
| 16 | 8.53 | 6.23 | 5.29 | 4.77 | 4.44 | 4.20 | 4.03 | 3.89 | 3.78 | 3.69 | 3.61 | 3.55 | 3.45 |
| 17 | 8.40 | 6.11 | 5.18 | 4.67 | 4.34 | 4.10 | 3.93 | 3.79 | 3.68 | 3.59 | 3.52 | 3.45 | 3.35 |
| 18 | 8.28 | 6.01 | 5.09 | 4.58 | 4.25 | 4.01 | 3.85 | 3.71 | 3.60 | 3.51 | 3.44 | 3.37 | 3.27 |
| 19 | 8.18 | 5.93 | 5.01 | 4.50 | 4.17 | 3.94 | 3.77 | 3.63 | 3.52 | 3.43 | 3.36 | 3.30 | 3.19 |
| 20 | 8.10 | 5.85 | 4.94 | 4.43 | 4.10 | 3.87 | 3.71 | 3.56 | 3.45 | 3.37 | 3.30 | 3.23 | 3.13 |
| 21 | 8.02 | 5.78 | 4.87 | 4.37 | 4.04 | 3.81 | 3.65 | 3.51 | 3.40 | 3.31 | 3.24 | 3.17 | 3.07 |
| 22 | 7.94 | 5.72 | 4.82 | 4.31 | 3.99 | 3.76 | 3.59 | 3.45 | 3.35 | 3.26 | 3.18 | 3.12 | 3.02 |
| 23 | 7.88 | 5.66 | 4.76 | 4.26 | 3.94 | 3.71 | 3.54 | 3.41 | 3.30 | 3.21 | 3.14 | 3.07 | 2.97 |
| 24 | 7.82 | 5.61 | 4.72 | 4.22 | 3.90 | 3.67 | 3.50 | 3.36 | 3.25 | 3.17 | 3.09 | 3.03 | 2.93 |
| 25 | 7.77 | 5.57 | 4.68 | 4.18 | 3.86 | 3.63 | 3.46 | 3.32 | 3.21 | 3.13 | 3.05 | 2.99 | 2.89 |
| 26 | 7.72 | 5.53 | 4.64 | 4.14 | 3.82 | 3.59 | 3.42 | 3.29 | 3.17 | 3.09 | 3.02 | 2.96 | 2.86 |
| 27 | 7.68 | 5.49 | 4.60 | 4.11 | 3.79 | 3.56 | 3.39 | 3.26 | 3.14 | 3.06 | 2.98 | 2.93 | 2.83 |
| 28 | 7.64 | 5.45 | 4.57 | 4.07 | 3.76 | 3.53 | 3.36 | 3.23 | 3.11 | 3.03 | 2.95 | 2.90 | 2.80 |
| 29 | 7.60 | 5.42 | 4.54 | 4.04 | 3.73 | 3.50 | 3.33 | 3.20 | 3.08 | 3.00 | 2.92 | 2.87 | 2.77 |

| | Between groups degrees of freedom (numerator) ($df_{bet}$) | | | | | | | | | | | Within groups degrees of freedom |
|---|---|---|---|---|---|---|---|---|---|---|---|---|
| *16* | *20* | *24* | *30* | *40* | *50* | *75* | *100* | *200* | *500* | *Infinity* | ($df_{wi}$) |
| 246 | 248 | 249 | 250 | 251 | 252 | 253 | 253 | 254 | 254 | 254 | 1 |
| 19.43 | 19.44 | 19.45 | 19.46 | 19.47 | 19.47 | 19.48 | 19.49 | 19.49 | 19.50 | 19.50 | 2 |
| 8.69 | 8.66 | 8.64 | 8.62 | 8.60 | 8.58 | 8.57 | 8.56 | 8.54 | 8.54 | 8.53 | 3 |
| 5.84 | 5.80 | 5.77 | 5.74 | 5.71 | 5.70 | 5.68 | 5.66 | 5.65 | 5.64 | 5.63 | 4 |
| 4.60 | 4.56 | 4.53 | 4.50 | 4.46 | 4.44 | 4.42 | 4.40 | 4.38 | 4.37 | 4.36 | 5 |
| 3.92 | 3.87 | 3.84 | 3.81 | 3.77 | 3.75 | 3.72 | 3.71 | 3.69 | 3.68 | 3.67 | 6 |
| 3.49 | 3.44 | 3.41 | 3.38 | 3.34 | 3.32 | 3.29 | 3.28 | 3.25 | 3.24 | 3.23 | 7 |
| 3.20 | 3.15 | 3.12 | 3.08 | 3.05 | 3.03 | 3.00 | 2.98 | 2.96 | 2.94 | 2.93 | 8 |
| 2.98 | 2.93 | 2.90 | 2.86 | 2.82 | 2.80 | 2.77 | 2.76 | 2.73 | 2.72 | 2.71 | 9 |
| 2.82 | 2.77 | 2.74 | 2.70 | 2.67 | 2.64 | 2.61 | 2.59 | 2.56 | 2.55 | 2.54 | 10 |
| 2.70 | 2.65 | 2.61 | 2.57 | 2.53 | 2.50 | 2.47 | 2.45 | 2.42 | 2.41 | 2.40 | 11 |
| 2.60 | 2.54 | 2.50 | 2.46 | 2.42 | 2.40 | 2.36 | 2.35 | 2.32 | 2.31 | 2.30 | 12 |
| 2.51 | 2.46 | 2.42 | 2.38 | 2.34 | 2.32 | 2.28 | 2.26 | 2.24 | 2.22 | 2.21 | 13 |
| 2.44 | 2.39 | 2.35 | 2.31 | 2.27 | 2.24 | 2.21 | 2.19 | 2.16 | 2.14 | 2.13 | 14 |
| 2.39 | 2.33 | 2.29 | 2.25 | 2.21 | 2.18 | 2.15 | 2.12 | 2.10 | 2.08 | 2.07 | 15 |
| 2.33 | 2.28 | 2.24 | 2.20 | 2.16 | 2.13 | 2.09 | 2.07 | 2.04 | 2.02 | 2.01 | 16 |
| 2.29 | 2.23 | 2.19 | 2.15 | 2.11 | 2.08 | 2.04 | 2.02 | 1.99 | 1.97 | 1.96 | 17 |
| 2.25 | 2.19 | 2.15 | 2.11 | 2.07 | 2.04 | 2.00 | 1.98 | 1.95 | 1.93 | 1.92 | 18 |
| 2.21 | 2.15 | 2.11 | 2.07 | 2.02 | 2.00 | 1.96 | 1.94 | 1.91 | 1.90 | 1.88 | 19 |
| 2.18 | 2.12 | 2.08 | 2.04 | 1.99 | 1.96 | 1.92 | 1.90 | 1.87 | 1.85 | 1.84 | 20 |
| 2.15 | 2.09 | 2.05 | 2.00 | 1.96 | 1.93 | 1.89 | 1.87 | 1.84 | 1.82 | 1.81 | 21 |
| 2.13 | 2.07 | 2.03 | 1.98 | 1.93 | 1.91 | 1.87 | 1.84 | 1.81 | 1.80 | 1.78 | 22 |
| 2.10 | 2.04 | 2.00 | 1.96 | 1.91 | 1.88 | 1.84 | 1.82 | 1.79 | 1.77 | 1.76 | 23 |
| 2.09 | 2.02 | 1.98 | 1.94 | 1.89 | 1.86 | 1.82 | 1.80 | 1.76 | 1.74 | 1.73 | 24 |
| 2.06 | 2.00 | 1.96 | 1.92 | 1.87 | 1.84 | 1.80 | 1.77 | 1.74 | 1.72 | 1.71 | 25 |
| 2.05 | 1.99 | 1.95 | 1.90 | 1.85 | 1.82 | 1.78 | 1.76 | 1.72 | 1.70 | 1.69 | 26 |
| 2.03 | 1.97 | 1.93 | 1.88 | 1.84 | 1.80 | 1.76 | 1.74 | 1.71 | 1.68 | 1.67 | 27 |
| 2.02 | 1.96 | 1.91 | 1.87 | 1.81 | 1.78 | 1.75 | 1.72 | 1.69 | 1.67 | 1.65 | 28 |
| 2.00 | 1.94 | 1.90 | 1.85 | 1.80 | 1.77 | 1.73 | 1.71 | 1.68 | 1.65 | 1.64 | 29 |

*(Continued)*

| Within groups degrees of freedom $(df_{wi})$ | Between groups degrees of freedom (numerator) $(df_{bet})$ | | | | | | | | | | | | |
|---|---|---|---|---|---|---|---|---|---|---|---|---|---|
| | 1 | 2 | 3 | 4 | 5 | 6 | 7 | 8 | 9 | 10 | 11 | 12 | 14 |
| 30 | 7.56 | 5.39 | 4.51 | 4.02 | 3.70 | 3.47 | 3.30 | 3.17 | 3.06 | 2.98 | 2.90 | 2.84 | 2.74 |
| 32 | 7.50 | 5.34 | 4.46 | 3.97 | 3.66 | 3.42 | 3.25 | 3.12 | 3.01 | 2.94 | 2.86 | 2.80 | 2.70 |
| 34 | 7.44 | 5.29 | 4.42 | 3.93 | 3.61 | 3.38 | 3.21 | 3.08 | 2.97 | 2.89 | 2.82 | 2.76 | 2.66 |
| 36 | 7.39 | 5.25 | 4.38 | 3.89 | 3.58 | 3.35 | 3.18 | 3.04 | 2.94 | 2.86 | 2.78 | 2.72 | 2.62 |
| 38 | 7.35 | 5.21 | 4.34 | 3.86 | 3.54 | 3.32 | 3.15 | 3.02 | 2.91 | 2.82 | 2.75 | 2.69 | 2.59 |
| 40 | 7.31 | 5.18 | 4.31 | 3.83 | 3.51 | 3.29 | 3.12 | 2.99 | 2.88 | 2.80 | 2.73 | 2.66 | 2.56 |
| 42 | 7.27 | 5.15 | 4.29 | 3.80 | 3.49 | 3.26 | 3.10 | 2.96 | 2.86 | 2.77 | 2.70 | 2.64 | 2.54 |
| 44 | 7.24 | 5.12 | 4.26 | 3.78 | 3.46 | 3.24 | 3.07 | 2.94 | 2.84 | 2.75 | 2.68 | 2.62 | 2.52 |
| 46 | 7.21 | 5.10 | 4.24 | 3.76 | 3.44 | 3.22 | 3.05 | 2.92 | 2.82 | 2.73 | 2.66 | 2.60 | 2.50 |
| 48 | 7.19 | 5.08 | 4.22 | 3.74 | 3.42 | 3.20 | 3.04 | 2.90 | 2.80 | 2.71 | 2.64 | 2.58 | 2.48 |
| 50 | 7.17 | 5.06 | 4.20 | 3.72 | 3.41 | 3.18 | 3.02 | 2.88 | 2.78 | 2.70 | 2.62 | 2.56 | 2.46 |
| 55 | 7.12 | 5.01 | 4.16 | 3.68 | 3.37 | 3.15 | 2.98 | 2.85 | 2.75 | 2.66 | 2.59 | 2.53 | 2.43 |
| 60 | 7.08 | 4.98 | 4.13 | 3.65 | 3.34 | 3.12 | 2.95 | 2.82 | 2.72 | 2.63 | 2.56 | 2.50 | 2.40 |
| 65 | 7.04 | 4.95 | 4.10 | 3.62 | 3.31 | 3.09 | 2.93 | 2.79 | 2.70 | 2.61 | 2.54 | 2.47 | 2.37 |
| 70 | 7.01 | 4.92 | 4.08 | 3.60 | 3.29 | 3.07 | 2.91 | 2.77 | 2.67 | 2.59 | 2.51 | 2.45 | 2.35 |
| 80 | 6.96 | 4.88 | 4.04 | 3.56 | 3.25 | 3.04 | 2.87 | 2.74 | 2.64 | 2.55 | 2.48 | 2.41 | 2.32 |
| 100 | 6.90 | 4.82 | 3.98 | 3.51 | 3.20 | 2.99 | 2.82 | 2.69 | 2.59 | 2.51 | 2.43 | 2.36 | 2.26 |
| 125 | 6.84 | 4.78 | 3.94 | 3.47 | 3.17 | 2.95 | 2.79 | 2.65 | 2.56 | 2.47 | 2.40 | 2.33 | 2.23 |
| 150 | 6.81 | 4.75 | 3.91 | 3.44 | 3.14 | 2.92 | 2.76 | 2.62 | 2.53 | 2.44 | 2.37 | 2.30 | 2.20 |
| 200 | 6.76 | 4.71 | 3.88 | 3.41 | 3.11 | 2.90 | 2.73 | 2.60 | 2.50 | 2.41 | 2.34 | 2.28 | 2.17 |
| 400 | 6.70 | 4.66 | 3.83 | 3.36 | 3.06 | 2.85 | 2.69 | 2.55 | 2.46 | 2.37 | 2.29 | 2.23 | 2.12 |
| 1000 | 6.66 | 4.62 | 3.80 | 3.34 | 3.04 | 2.82 | 2.66 | 2.53 | 2.43 | 2.34 | 2.26 | 2.20 | 2.09 |
| Infinity | 6.64 | 4.60 | 3.78 | 3.32 | 3.02 | 2.80 | 2.64 | 2.51 | 2.41 | 2.32 | 2.24 | 2.18 | 2.07 |

| Between groups degrees of freedom (numerator) (df_bet) | | | | | | | | | | | Within groups degrees of freedom |
|---|---|---|---|---|---|---|---|---|---|---|---|
| 16 | 20 | 24 | 30 | 40 | 50 | 75 | 100 | 200 | 500 | Infinity | (df_wi) |
| 2.66 | 2.55 | 2.47 | 2.38 | 2.29 | 2.24 | 2.16 | 2.13 | 2.07 | 2.03 | 2.01 | 30 |
| 2.62 | 2.51 | 2.42 | 2.34 | 2.25 | 2.20 | 2.12 | 2.08 | 2.02 | 1.98 | 1.96 | 32 |
| 2.58 | 2.47 | 2.38 | 2.30 | 2.21 | 2.15 | 2.08 | 2.04 | 1.98 | 1.94 | 1.91 | 34 |
| 2.54 | 2.43 | 2.35 | 2.26 | 2.17 | 2.12 | 2.04 | 2.00 | 1.94 | 1.90 | 1.87 | 36 |
| 2.51 | 2.40 | 2.32 | 2.22 | 2.14 | 2.08 | 2.00 | 1.97 | 1.90 | 1.86 | 1.84 | 38 |
| 2.49 | 2.37 | 2.29 | 2.20 | 2.11 | 2.05 | 1.97 | 1.94 | 1.88 | 1.84 | 1.81 | 40 |
| 2.46 | 2.35 | 2.26 | 2.17 | 2.08 | 2.02 | 1.94 | 1.91 | 1.85 | 1.80 | 1.78 | 42 |
| 2.44 | 2.32 | 2.24 | 2.15 | 2.06 | 2.00 | 1.92 | 1.88 | 1.82 | 1.78 | 1.75 | 44 |
| 2.42 | 2.30 | 2.22 | 2.13 | 2.04 | 1.98 | 1.90 | 1.86 | 1.80 | 1.76 | 1.72 | 46 |
| 2.40 | 2.28 | 2.20 | 2.11 | 2.02 | 1.96 | 1.88 | 1.84 | 1.78 | 1.73 | 1.70 | 48 |
| 2.39 | 2.26 | 2.18 | 2.10 | 2.00 | 1.94 | 1.86 | 1.82 | 1.76 | 1.71 | 1.68 | 50 |
| 2.35 | 2.23 | 2.15 | 2.06 | 1.96 | 1.90 | 1.82 | 1.78 | 1.71 | 1.66 | 1.64 | 55 |
| 2.32 | 2.20 | 2.12 | 2.03 | 1.93 | 1.87 | 1.79 | 1.74 | 1.68 | 1.63 | 1.60 | 60 |
| 2.30 | 2.18 | 2.09 | 2.00 | 1.90 | 1.84 | 1.76 | 1.71 | 1.64 | 1.60 | 1.56 | 65 |
| 2.28 | 2.15 | 2.07 | 1.98 | 1.88 | 1.82 | 1.74 | 1.69 | 1.62 | 1.56 | 1.53 | 70 |
| 2.24 | 2.11 | 2.03 | 1.94 | 1.84 | 1.78 | 1.70 | 1.65 | 1.57 | 1.52 | 1.49 | 80 |
| 2.19 | 2.06 | 1.98 | 1.89 | 1.79 | 1.73 | 1.64 | 1.59 | 1.51 | 1.46 | 1.43 | 100 |
| 2.15 | 2.03 | 1.94 | 1.85 | 1.75 | 1.68 | 1.59 | 1.54 | 1.46 | 1.40 | 1.37 | 125 |
| 2.12 | 2.00 | 1.91 | 1.83 | 1.72 | 1.66 | 1.56 | 1.51 | 1.43 | 1.37 | 1.33 | 150 |
| 2.09 | 1.97 | 1.88 | 1.79 | 1.69 | 1.62 | 1.53 | 1.48 | 1.39 | 1.33 | 1.28 | 200 |
| 2.04 | 1.92 | 1.84 | 1.74 | 1.64 | 1.57 | 1.47 | 1.42 | 1.32 | 1.24 | 1.19 | 400 |
| 2.01 | 1.89 | 1.81 | 1.71 | 1.61 | 1.54 | 1.44 | 1.38 | 1.28 | 1.19 | 1.11 | 1000 |
| 1.99 | 1.87 | 1.79 | 1.69 | 1.59 | 1.52 | 1.41 | 1.36 | 1.25 | 1.15 | 1.00 | Infinity |

*Table 5* Studentized Range Statistic ($q$) for the .05 Level

| Degrees of freedom ($df_{wi}$) | Number of treatments ($k$) | | | | | | | | | | |
|---|---|---|---|---|---|---|---|---|---|---|---|
| | 2 | 3 | 4 | 5 | 6 | 7 | 8 | 9 | 10 | 11 | 12 |
| 5 | 3.64 | 4.60 | 5.22 | 5.67 | 6.03 | 6.33 | 6.58 | 6.80 | 6.99 | 7.17 | 7.32 |
| 6 | 3.46 | 4.34 | 4.90 | 5.30 | 5.63 | 5.90 | 6.12 | 6.32 | 6.49 | 6.65 | 6.79 |
| 7 | 3.34 | 4.16 | 4.68 | 5.06 | 5.36 | 5.61 | 5.82 | 6.00 | 6.16 | 6.30 | 6.43 |
| 8 | 3.26 | 4.04 | 4.53 | 4.89 | 5.17 | 5.40 | 5.60 | 5.77 | 5.92 | 6.05 | 6.18 |
| 9 | 3.20 | 3.95 | 4.41 | 4.76 | 5.02 | 5.24 | 5.43 | 5.59 | 5.74 | 5.87 | 5.98 |
| 10 | 3.15 | 3.88 | 4.33 | 4.65 | 4.91 | 5.12 | 5.30 | 5.46 | 5.60 | 5.72 | 5.83 |
| 11 | 3.11 | 3.82 | 4.26 | 4.57 | 4.82 | 5.03 | 5.20 | 5.35 | 5.49 | 5.61 | 5.71 |
| 12 | 3.08 | 3.77 | 4.20 | 4.51 | 4.75 | 4.95 | 5.12 | 5.27 | 5.39 | 5.51 | 5.61 |
| 13 | 3.06 | 3.73 | 4.15 | 4.45 | 4.69 | 4.88 | 5.05 | 5.19 | 5.32 | 5.43 | 5.53 |
| 14 | 3.03 | 3.70 | 4.11 | 4.41 | 4.64 | 4.83 | 4.99 | 5.13 | 5.25 | 5.36 | 5.46 |
| 15 | 3.01 | 3.67 | 4.08 | 4.37 | 4.59 | 4.78 | 4.94 | 5.08 | 5.20 | 5.31 | 5.40 |
| 16 | 3.00 | 3.65 | 4.05 | 4.33 | 4.56 | 4.74 | 4.90 | 5.03 | 5.15 | 5.26 | 5.35 |
| 17 | 2.98 | 3.63 | 4.02 | 4.30 | 4.52 | 4.70 | 4.86 | 4.99 | 5.11 | 5.21 | 5.31 |
| 18 | 2.97 | 3.61 | 4.00 | 4.28 | 4.49 | 4.67 | 4.82 | 4.96 | 5.07 | 5.17 | 5.27 |
| 19 | 2.96 | 3.59 | 3.98 | 4.25 | 4.47 | 4.65 | 4.79 | 4.92 | 5.04 | 5.14 | 5.23 |
| 20 | 2.95 | 3.58 | 3.96 | 4.23 | 4.45 | 4.62 | 4.77 | 4.90 | 5.01 | 5.11 | 5.20 |
| 24 | 2.92 | 3.53 | 3.90 | 4.17 | 4.37 | 4.54 | 4.68 | 4.81 | 4.92 | 5.01 | 5.10 |
| 30 | 2.89 | 3.49 | 3.85 | 4.10 | 4.30 | 4.46 | 4.60 | 4.72 | 4.82 | 4.92 | 5.00 |
| 40 | 2.86 | 3.44 | 3.79 | 4.04 | 4.23 | 4.39 | 4.52 | 4.63 | 4.73 | 4.82 | 4.90 |
| 60 | 2.83 | 3.40 | 3.74 | 3.98 | 4.16 | 4.31 | 4.44 | 4.55 | 4.65 | 4.73 | 4.81 |
| 120 | 2.80 | 3.36 | 3.68 | 3.92 | 4.10 | 4.24 | 4.36 | 4.47 | 4.56 | 4.64 | 4.71 |
| Infinity | 2.77 | 3.31 | 3.63 | 3.86 | 4.03 | 4.17 | 4.29 | 4.39 | 4.47 | 4.55 | 4.62 |

*Table 6* Studentized Range Statistic ($q$) for the .01 Level

| Degrees of freedom ($df_{wi}$) | Number of treatments ($k$) | | | | | | | | | | |
|---|---|---|---|---|---|---|---|---|---|---|---|
| | 2 | 3 | 4 | 5 | 6 | 7 | 8 | 9 | 10 | 11 | 12 |
| 5 | 5.70 | 6.98 | 7.80 | 8.42 | 8.91 | 9.32 | 9.67 | 9.97 | 10.24 | 10.48 | 10.70 |
| 6 | 5.24 | 6.33 | 7.03 | 7.56 | 7.97 | 8.32 | 8.61 | 8.87 | 9.10 | 9.30 | 9.48 |
| 7 | 4.95 | 5.92 | 6.54 | 7.01 | 7.37 | 7.68 | 7.94 | 8.17 | 8.37 | 8.55 | 8.71 |
| 8 | 4.75 | 5.64 | 6.20 | 6.62 | 6.96 | 7.24 | 7.47 | 7.68 | 7.86 | 8.03 | 8.18 |
| 9 | 4.60 | 5.43 | 5.96 | 6.35 | 6.66 | 6.91 | 7.13 | 7.33 | 7.49 | 7.65 | 7.78 |
| 10 | 4.48 | 5.27 | 5.77 | 6.14 | 6.43 | 6.67 | 6.87 | 7.05 | 7.21 | 7.36 | 7.49 |
| 11 | 4.39 | 5.15 | 5.62 | 5.97 | 6.25 | 6.48 | 6.67 | 6.84 | 6.99 | 7.13 | 7.25 |
| 12 | 4.32 | 5.05 | 5.50 | 5.84 | 6.10 | 6.32 | 6.51 | 6.67 | 6.81 | 6.94 | 7.06 |
| 13 | 4.26 | 4.96 | 5.40 | 5.73 | 5.98 | 6.19 | 6.37 | 6.53 | 6.67 | 6.79 | 6.90 |
| 14 | 4.21 | 4.89 | 5.32 | 5.63 | 5.88 | 6.08 | 6.26 | 6.41 | 6.54 | 6.66 | 6.77 |
| 15 | 4.17 | 4.84 | 5.25 | 5.56 | 5.80 | 5.99 | 6.16 | 6.31 | 6.44 | 6.55 | 6.66 |
| 16 | 4.13 | 4.79 | 5.19 | 5.49 | 5.72 | 5.92 | 6.08 | 6.22 | 6.35 | 6.46 | 6.56 |
| 17 | 4.10 | 4.74 | 5.14 | 5.43 | 5.66 | 5.85 | 6.01 | 6.15 | 6.27 | 6.38 | 6.48 |
| 18 | 4.07 | 4.70 | 5.09 | 5.38 | 5.60 | 5.79 | 5.94 | 6.08 | 6.20 | 6.31 | 6.41 |
| 19 | 4.05 | 4.67 | 5.05 | 5.33 | 5.55 | 5.73 | 5.89 | 6.02 | 6.14 | 6.25 | 6.34 |
| 20 | 4.02 | 4.64 | 5.02 | 5.29 | 5.51 | 5.69 | 5.84 | 5.97 | 6.09 | 6.19 | 6.28 |
| 24 | 3.96 | 4.55 | 4.91 | 5.17 | 5.37 | 5.54 | 5.69 | 5.81 | 5.92 | 6.02 | 6.11 |
| 30 | 3.89 | 4.45 | 4.80 | 5.05 | 5.24 | 5.40 | 5.54 | 5.65 | 5.76 | 5.85 | 5.93 |
| 40 | 3.82 | 4.37 | 4.70 | 4.93 | 5.11 | 5.26 | 5.39 | 5.50 | 5.60 | 5.69 | 5.76 |
| 60 | 3.76 | 4.28 | 4.59 | 4.82 | 4.99 | 5.13 | 5.25 | 5.36 | 5.45 | 5.53 | 5.60 |
| 120 | 3.70 | 4.20 | 4.50 | 4.71 | 4.87 | 5.01 | 5.12 | 5.21 | 5.30 | 5.37 | 5.44 |
| Infinity | 3.64 | 4.12 | 4.40 | 4.60 | 4.76 | 4.88 | 4.99 | 5.08 | 5.16 | 5.23 | 5.29 |

*Table 7* Critical Values for the Pearson Correlation[1]

| df | Level of significance for one-tailed test | | | | df | Level of significance for one-tailed test | | | |
| | .05 | .025 | .01 | .005 | | .05 | .025 | .01 | .005 |
| | Level of significance for two-tailed test | | | | | Level of significance for two-tailed test | | | |
| | .10 | .05 | .02 | .01 | | .10 | .05 | .02 | .01 |
| 1 | .988 | .997 | .9995 | .9999 | 21 | .352 | .413 | .482 | .526 |
| 2 | .900 | .950 | .980 | .990 | 22 | .344 | .404 | .472 | .515 |
| 3 | .805 | .878 | .934 | .959 | 23 | .337 | .396 | .462 | .505 |
| 4 | .729 | .811 | .882 | .917 | 24 | .330 | .388 | .453 | .496 |
| 5 | .669 | .754 | .833 | .874 | 25 | .323 | .381 | .445 | .487 |
| 6 | .622 | .707 | .789 | .834 | 26 | .317 | .374 | .437 | .479 |
| 7 | .582 | .666 | .750 | .798 | 27 | .311 | .367 | .430 | .471 |
| 8 | .549 | .632 | .716 | .765 | 28 | .306 | .361 | .423 | .463 |
| 9 | .521 | .602 | .685 | .735 | 29 | .301 | .355 | .416 | .456 |
| 10 | .497 | .576 | .658 | .708 | 30 | .296 | .349 | .409 | .449 |
| 11 | .476 | .553 | .634 | .684 | 35 | .275 | .325 | .381 | .418 |
| 12 | .458 | .532 | .612 | .661 | 40 | .257 | .304 | .358 | .393 |
| 13 | .441 | .514 | .592 | .641 | 45 | .243 | .288 | .338 | .372 |
| 14 | .426 | .497 | .574 | .623 | 50 | .231 | .273 | .322 | .354 |
| 15 | .412 | .482 | .558 | .606 | 60 | .211 | .250 | .295 | .325 |
| 16 | .400 | .468 | .542 | .590 | 70 | .195 | .232 | .274 | .302 |
| 17 | .389 | .456 | .528 | .575 | 80 | .183 | .217 | .256 | .283 |
| 18 | .378 | .444 | .516 | .561 | 90 | .173 | .205 | .242 | .267 |
| 19 | .369 | .433 | .503 | .549 | 100 | .164 | .195 | .230 | .254 |
| 20 | .360 | .423 | .492 | .537 | | | | | |

Note: To be significant, the sample correlation, r, must be greater than or equal to the critical value in the table.

[1] Fisher, R. A., & Yates, F. (1974). *Statistical tables for biological, agricultural, and medical research* (6th ed.). London: Longman Group Ltd. Adapted and reprinted with permission of Addison-Wesley Longman, Ltd.

*Table 8* Critical Values for Chi-Square[1] and Kruskal-Wallis

| df | .05 level | .01 level | .001 level |
|----|-----------|-----------|------------|
| 1 | 3.841 | 6.635 | 10.827 |
| 2 | 5.991 | 9.210 | 13.815 |
| 3 | 7.815 | 11.345 | 16.268 |
| 4 | 9.488 | 13.277 | 18.465 |
| 5 | 11.070 | 15.086 | 20.517 |
| 6 | 12.592 | 16.812 | 22.457 |
| 7 | 14.067 | 18.475 | 24.322 |
| 8 | 15.507 | 20.090 | 26.125 |
| 9 | 16.919 | 21.666 | 27.877 |
| 10 | 18.307 | 23.209 | 29.588 |
| 11 | 19.675 | 24.725 | 31.264 |
| 12 | 21.026 | 26.217 | 32.909 |
| 13 | 22.362 | 27.688 | 34.528 |
| 14 | 23.685 | 29.141 | 36.123 |
| 15 | 24.996 | 30.578 | 37.697 |
| 16 | 26.296 | 32.000 | 39.252 |
| 17 | 27.587 | 33.409 | 40.790 |
| 18 | 28.869 | 34.805 | 42.312 |
| 19 | 30.144 | 36.191 | 43.820 |
| 20 | 31.410 | 37.566 | 45.315 |
| 21 | 32.671 | 38.932 | 46.797 |
| 22 | 33.924 | 40.289 | 48.268 |
| 23 | 35.172 | 41.638 | 49.728 |
| 24 | 36.415 | 42.980 | 51.179 |
| 25 | 37.652 | 44.314 | 52.620 |
| 26 | 38.885 | 45.642 | 54.052 |
| 27 | 40.113 | 46.963 | 55.476 |
| 28 | 41.337 | 48.278 | 56.893 |
| 29 | 42.557 | 49.588 | 58.302 |
| 30 | 43.773 | 50.892 | 59.703 |

[1] Fisher, R. A., & Yates, F. (1974). *Statistical tables for biological, agricultural, and medical research* (6th ed.). London: Longman Group Ltd.

*Table 9* Critical Values for the Mann-Whitney *U* Test[1]

**Block 1**

| $\alpha_1$ | .05 | .025 | .01 | .005 |
|---|---|---|---|---|
| $\alpha_2$ | .10 | .05 | .02 | .01 |
| $n_1$ $n_2$ | | | | |
| 2 2 | – | – | – | – |
| 2 3 | – | – | – | – |
| 2 4 | – | – | – | – |
| 2 5 | 0 | – | – | – |
| 2 6 | 0 | – | – | – |
| 2 7 | 0 | – | – | – |
| 2 8 | 1 | 0 | – | – |
| 2 9 | 1 | 0 | – | – |
| 2 10 | 1 | 0 | – | – |
| 2 11 | 1 | 0 | – | – |
| 2 12 | 2 | 1 | – | – |
| 2 13 | 2 | 1 | 0 | – |
| 2 14 | 3 | 1 | 0 | – |
| 2 15 | 3 | 1 | 0 | – |
| 2 16 | 3 | 1 | 0 | – |
| 2 17 | 3 | 2 | 0 | – |
| 2 18 | 4 | 2 | 0 | – |
| 2 19 | 4 | 2 | 1 | 0 |
| 2 20 | 4 | 2 | 1 | 0 |
| 2 21 | 5 | 3 | 1 | 0 |
| 2 22 | 5 | 3 | 1 | 0 |
| 2 23 | 5 | 3 | 1 | 0 |
| 2 24 | 6 | 3 | 1 | 0 |
| 2 25 | 6 | 3 | 1 | 0 |
| 3 3 | 0 | – | – | – |
| 3 4 | 0 | – | – | – |
| 3 5 | 1 | 0 | – | – |
| 3 6 | 2 | 1 | – | – |
| 3 7 | 2 | 1 | 0 | – |
| 3 8 | 3 | 2 | 0 | – |
| 3 9 | 4 | 2 | 1 | 0 |
| 3 10 | 4 | 3 | 1 | 0 |
| 3 11 | 5 | 3 | 1 | 0 |
| 3 12 | 5 | 4 | 2 | 1 |
| 3 13 | 6 | 4 | 2 | 1 |
| 3 14 | 7 | 5 | 2 | 1 |
| 3 15 | 7 | 5 | 3 | 2 |
| 3 16 | 8 | 6 | 3 | 2 |
| 3 17 | 9 | 6 | 4 | 2 |
| 3 18 | 9 | 7 | 4 | 2 |
| 3 19 | 10 | 7 | 4 | 3 |
| 3 20 | 11 | 8 | 5 | 3 |
| 3 21 | 11 | 8 | 5 | 3 |
| 3 22 | 12 | 9 | 6 | 4 |
| 3 23 | 13 | 9 | 6 | 4 |
| 3 24 | 13 | 10 | 6 | 4 |
| 3 25 | 14 | 10 | 7 | 5 |
| 4 4 | 1 | 0 | – | – |
| 4 5 | 2 | 1 | 0 | – |
| 4 6 | 3 | 2 | 1 | 0 |
| 4 7 | 4 | 3 | 1 | 0 |
| 4 8 | 5 | 4 | 2 | 1 |
| 4 9 | 6 | 4 | 3 | 1 |
| 4 10 | 7 | 5 | 3 | 2 |
| 4 11 | 8 | 6 | 4 | 2 |
| 4 12 | 9 | 7 | 5 | 3 |
| 4 13 | 10 | 8 | 5 | 3 |
| 4 14 | 11 | 9 | 6 | 4 |
| 4 15 | 12 | 10 | 7 | 5 |
| 4 16 | 14 | 11 | 7 | 5 |
| 4 17 | 15 | 11 | 8 | 6 |
| 4 18 | 16 | 12 | 9 | 6 |
| 4 19 | 17 | 13 | 9 | 7 |
| 4 20 | 18 | 14 | 10 | 8 |
| 4 21 | 19 | 15 | 11 | 8 |
| 4 22 | 20 | 16 | 11 | 9 |
| 4 23 | 21 | 17 | 12 | 9 |
| 4 24 | 22 | 17 | 13 | 10 |
| 4 25 | 23 | 18 | 13 | 10 |

**Block 2**

| $\alpha_1$ | .05 | .025 | .01 | .005 |
|---|---|---|---|---|
| $\alpha_2$ | .10 | .05 | .02 | .01 |
| $n_1$ $n_2$ | | | | |
| 5 5 | 4 | 2 | 1 | 0 |
| 5 6 | 5 | 3 | 2 | 1 |
| 5 7 | 6 | 5 | 3 | 1 |
| 5 8 | 8 | 6 | 4 | 2 |
| 5 9 | 9 | 7 | 5 | 3 |
| 5 10 | 11 | 8 | 6 | 4 |
| 5 11 | 12 | 9 | 7 | 5 |
| 5 12 | 13 | 11 | 8 | 6 |
| 5 13 | 15 | 12 | 9 | 7 |
| 5 14 | 16 | 13 | 10 | 7 |
| 5 15 | 18 | 14 | 11 | 8 |
| 5 16 | 19 | 15 | 12 | 9 |
| 5 17 | 20 | 17 | 13 | 10 |
| 5 18 | 22 | 18 | 14 | 11 |
| 5 19 | 23 | 19 | 15 | 12 |
| 5 20 | 25 | 20 | 16 | 13 |
| 5 21 | 26 | 22 | 17 | 14 |
| 5 22 | 28 | 23 | 18 | 14 |
| 5 23 | 29 | 24 | 19 | 15 |
| 5 24 | 30 | 25 | 20 | 16 |
| 5 25 | 32 | 27 | 21 | 17 |
| 6 6 | 7 | 5 | 3 | 2 |
| 6 7 | 8 | 6 | 4 | 3 |
| 6 8 | 10 | 8 | 6 | 4 |
| 6 9 | 12 | 10 | 7 | 5 |
| 6 10 | 14 | 11 | 8 | 6 |
| 6 11 | 16 | 13 | 9 | 7 |
| 6 12 | 17 | 14 | 11 | 9 |
| 6 13 | 19 | 16 | 12 | 10 |
| 6 14 | 21 | 17 | 13 | 11 |
| 6 15 | 23 | 19 | 15 | 12 |
| 6 16 | 25 | 21 | 16 | 13 |
| 6 17 | 26 | 22 | 18 | 15 |
| 6 18 | 28 | 24 | 19 | 16 |
| 6 19 | 30 | 25 | 20 | 17 |
| 6 20 | 32 | 27 | 22 | 18 |
| 6 21 | 34 | 29 | 23 | 19 |
| 6 22 | 36 | 30 | 24 | 21 |
| 6 23 | 37 | 32 | 26 | 22 |
| 6 24 | 39 | 33 | 27 | 23 |
| 6 25 | 41 | 35 | 29 | 24 |
| 7 7 | 11 | 8 | 6 | 4 |
| 7 8 | 13 | 10 | 7 | 6 |
| 7 9 | 15 | 12 | 9 | 7 |
| 7 10 | 17 | 14 | 11 | 9 |
| 7 11 | 19 | 16 | 12 | 10 |
| 7 12 | 21 | 18 | 14 | 12 |
| 7 13 | 24 | 20 | 16 | 13 |
| 7 14 | 26 | 22 | 17 | 15 |
| 7 15 | 28 | 24 | 19 | 16 |
| 7 16 | 30 | 26 | 21 | 18 |
| 7 17 | 33 | 28 | 23 | 19 |
| 7 18 | 35 | 30 | 24 | 21 |
| 7 19 | 37 | 32 | 26 | 22 |
| 7 20 | 39 | 34 | 28 | 24 |
| 7 21 | 41 | 36 | 30 | 25 |
| 7 22 | 44 | 38 | 31 | 27 |
| 7 23 | 46 | 40 | 33 | 29 |
| 7 24 | 48 | 42 | 35 | 30 |
| 7 25 | 50 | 44 | 36 | 32 |
| 8 8 | 15 | 13 | 9 | 7 |
| 8 9 | 18 | 15 | 11 | 9 |
| 8 10 | 20 | 17 | 13 | 11 |
| 8 11 | 23 | 19 | 15 | 13 |
| 8 12 | 26 | 22 | 17 | 15 |
| 8 13 | 28 | 24 | 20 | 17 |
| 8 14 | 31 | 26 | 22 | 18 |
| 8 15 | 33 | 29 | 24 | 20 |

**Block 3**

| $\alpha_1$ | .05 | .025 | .01 | .005 |
|---|---|---|---|---|
| $\alpha_2$ | .10 | .05 | .02 | .01 |
| $n_1$ $n_2$ | | | | |
| 8 16 | 36 | 31 | 26 | 22 |
| 8 17 | 39 | 34 | 28 | 24 |
| 8 18 | 41 | 36 | 30 | 26 |
| 8 19 | 44 | 38 | 32 | 28 |
| 8 20 | 47 | 41 | 34 | 30 |
| 8 21 | 49 | 43 | 36 | 32 |
| 8 22 | 52 | 45 | 38 | 34 |
| 8 23 | 54 | 48 | 40 | 35 |
| 8 24 | 57 | 50 | 42 | 37 |
| 8 25 | 60 | 53 | 45 | 39 |
| 9 9 | 21 | 17 | 14 | 11 |
| 9 10 | 24 | 20 | 16 | 13 |
| 9 11 | 27 | 23 | 18 | 16 |
| 9 12 | 30 | 26 | 21 | 18 |
| 9 13 | 33 | 28 | 23 | 20 |
| 9 14 | 36 | 31 | 26 | 22 |
| 9 15 | 39 | 34 | 28 | 24 |
| 9 16 | 42 | 37 | 31 | 27 |
| 9 17 | 45 | 39 | 33 | 29 |
| 9 18 | 48 | 42 | 36 | 31 |
| 9 19 | 51 | 45 | 38 | 33 |
| 9 20 | 54 | 48 | 40 | 36 |
| 9 21 | 57 | 50 | 43 | 38 |
| 9 22 | 60 | 53 | 45 | 40 |
| 9 23 | 63 | 56 | 48 | 43 |
| 9 24 | 66 | 59 | 50 | 45 |
| 9 25 | 69 | 62 | 53 | 47 |
| 10 10 | 27 | 23 | 19 | 16 |
| 10 11 | 31 | 26 | 22 | 18 |
| 10 12 | 34 | 29 | 24 | 21 |
| 10 13 | 37 | 33 | 27 | 24 |
| 10 14 | 41 | 36 | 30 | 26 |
| 10 15 | 44 | 39 | 33 | 29 |
| 10 16 | 48 | 42 | 36 | 31 |
| 10 17 | 51 | 45 | 38 | 34 |
| 10 18 | 55 | 48 | 41 | 37 |
| 10 19 | 58 | 52 | 44 | 39 |
| 10 20 | 62 | 55 | 47 | 42 |
| 10 21 | 65 | 58 | 50 | 44 |
| 10 22 | 68 | 61 | 53 | 47 |
| 10 23 | 72 | 64 | 55 | 50 |
| 10 24 | 75 | 67 | 58 | 52 |
| 10 25 | 79 | 71 | 61 | 55 |
| 11 11 | 34 | 30 | 25 | 21 |
| 11 12 | 38 | 33 | 28 | 24 |
| 11 13 | 42 | 37 | 31 | 27 |
| 11 14 | 46 | 40 | 34 | 30 |
| 11 15 | 50 | 44 | 37 | 33 |
| 11 16 | 54 | 47 | 41 | 36 |
| 11 17 | 57 | 51 | 44 | 39 |
| 11 18 | 61 | 55 | 47 | 42 |
| 11 19 | 65 | 58 | 50 | 45 |
| 11 20 | 69 | 62 | 53 | 48 |
| 11 21 | 73 | 65 | 57 | 51 |
| 11 22 | 77 | 69 | 60 | 54 |
| 11 23 | 81 | 73 | 63 | 57 |
| 11 24 | 85 | 76 | 66 | 60 |
| 11 25 | 89 | 80 | 70 | 63 |
| 12 12 | 42 | 37 | 31 | 27 |
| 12 13 | 47 | 41 | 35 | 31 |
| 12 14 | 51 | 45 | 38 | 34 |
| 12 15 | 55 | 49 | 42 | 37 |
| 12 16 | 60 | 53 | 46 | 41 |
| 12 17 | 64 | 57 | 49 | 44 |
| 12 18 | 68 | 61 | 53 | 47 |
| 12 19 | 72 | 65 | 56 | 51 |
| 12 20 | 77 | 69 | 60 | 54 |

**Block 4**

| $\alpha_1$ | .05 | .025 | .01 | .005 |
|---|---|---|---|---|
| $\alpha_2$ | .10 | .05 | .02 | .01 |
| $n_1$ $n_2$ | | | | |
| 12 21 | 81 | 73 | 64 | 58 |
| 12 22 | 85 | 77 | 67 | 61 |
| 12 23 | 90 | 81 | 71 | 64 |
| 12 24 | 94 | 85 | 75 | 68 |
| 12 25 | 98 | 89 | 78 | 71 |
| 13 13 | 51 | 45 | 39 | 34 |
| 13 14 | 56 | 50 | 43 | 38 |
| 13 15 | 61 | 54 | 47 | 42 |
| 13 16 | 65 | 59 | 51 | 45 |
| 13 17 | 70 | 63 | 55 | 49 |
| 13 18 | 75 | 67 | 59 | 53 |
| 13 19 | 80 | 72 | 63 | 57 |
| 13 20 | 84 | 76 | 67 | 60 |
| 13 21 | 89 | 80 | 71 | 64 |
| 13 22 | 94 | 85 | 75 | 68 |
| 13 23 | 98 | 89 | 79 | 72 |
| 13 24 | 103 | 94 | 83 | 75 |
| 13 25 | 108 | 98 | 87 | 79 |
| 14 14 | 61 | 55 | 47 | 42 |
| 14 15 | 66 | 59 | 51 | 46 |
| 14 16 | 71 | 64 | 56 | 50 |
| 14 17 | 77 | 69 | 60 | 54 |
| 14 18 | 82 | 74 | 65 | 58 |
| 14 19 | 87 | 78 | 69 | 63 |
| 14 20 | 92 | 83 | 73 | 67 |
| 14 21 | 97 | 88 | 78 | 71 |
| 14 22 | 102 | 93 | 82 | 75 |
| 14 23 | 107 | 98 | 87 | 79 |
| 14 24 | 113 | 102 | 91 | 83 |
| 14 25 | 118 | 107 | 95 | 87 |
| 15 15 | 72 | 64 | 56 | 51 |
| 15 16 | 77 | 70 | 61 | 55 |
| 15 17 | 83 | 75 | 66 | 60 |
| 15 18 | 88 | 80 | 70 | 64 |
| 15 19 | 94 | 85 | 75 | 69 |
| 15 20 | 100 | 90 | 80 | 73 |
| 15 21 | 105 | 96 | 85 | 78 |
| 15 22 | 111 | 101 | 90 | 82 |
| 15 23 | 116 | 106 | 94 | 87 |
| 15 24 | 122 | 111 | 99 | 91 |
| 15 25 | 128 | 117 | 104 | 96 |
| 16 16 | 83 | 75 | 66 | 60 |
| 16 17 | 89 | 81 | 71 | 65 |
| 16 18 | 95 | 86 | 76 | 70 |
| 16 19 | 101 | 92 | 82 | 74 |
| 16 20 | 107 | 98 | 87 | 79 |
| 16 21 | 113 | 103 | 92 | 84 |
| 16 22 | 119 | 109 | 97 | 89 |
| 16 23 | 125 | 115 | 102 | 94 |
| 16 24 | 131 | 120 | 108 | 99 |
| 16 25 | 137 | 126 | 113 | 104 |
| 17 17 | 96 | 87 | 77 | 70 |
| 17 18 | 102 | 93 | 82 | 75 |
| 17 19 | 109 | 99 | 88 | 81 |
| 17 20 | 115 | 105 | 93 | 86 |
| 17 21 | 121 | 111 | 99 | 91 |
| 17 22 | 128 | 117 | 105 | 96 |
| 17 23 | 134 | 123 | 110 | 102 |
| 17 24 | 141 | 129 | 116 | 107 |
| 17 25 | 147 | 135 | 122 | 112 |
| 18 18 | 109 | 99 | 88 | 81 |
| 18 19 | 116 | 106 | 94 | 87 |
| 18 20 | 123 | 112 | 100 | 92 |
| 18 21 | 130 | 119 | 106 | 98 |
| 18 22 | 136 | 125 | 112 | 104 |

**Block 5**

| $\alpha_1$ | .05 | .025 | .01 | .005 |
|---|---|---|---|---|
| $\alpha_2$ | .10 | .05 | .02 | .01 |
| $n_1$ $n_2$ | | | | |
| 18 23 | 143 | 132 | 118 | 109 |
| 18 24 | 150 | 138 | 124 | 115 |
| 18 25 | 157 | 145 | 130 | 121 |
| 19 19 | 123 | 113 | 101 | 93 |
| 19 20 | 130 | 119 | 107 | 99 |
| 19 21 | 138 | 126 | 113 | 105 |
| 19 22 | 145 | 133 | 120 | 111 |
| 19 23 | 152 | 140 | 126 | 117 |
| 19 24 | 160 | 147 | 133 | 123 |
| 19 25 | 167 | 154 | 139 | 129 |
| 20 20 | 138 | 127 | 114 | 105 |
| 20 21 | 146 | 134 | 121 | 112 |
| 20 22 | 154 | 141 | 127 | 118 |
| 20 23 | 161 | 149 | 134 | 125 |
| 20 24 | 169 | 156 | 141 | 131 |
| 20 25 | 177 | 163 | 148 | 138 |
| 21 21 | 154 | 142 | 128 | 118 |
| 21 22 | 162 | 150 | 135 | 125 |
| 21 23 | 170 | 157 | 142 | 132 |
| 21 24 | 179 | 165 | 150 | 139 |
| 21 25 | 187 | 173 | 157 | 146 |
| 22 22 | 171 | 158 | 143 | 133 |
| 22 23 | 179 | 166 | 150 | 140 |
| 22 24 | 188 | 174 | 158 | 147 |
| 22 25 | 197 | 182 | 166 | 155 |
| 23 23 | 189 | 175 | 159 | 148 |
| 23 24 | 198 | 183 | 167 | 155 |
| 23 25 | 207 | 192 | 175 | 163 |
| 24 24 | 207 | 192 | 175 | 164 |
| 24 25 | 217 | 201 | 184 | 172 |
| 25 25 | 227 | 211 | 192 | 180 |
| 26 26 | 247 | 230 | 211 | 198 |
| 27 27 | 268 | 250 | 230 | 216 |
| 28 28 | 291 | 272 | 250 | 235 |
| 29 29 | 314 | 294 | 271 | 255 |
| 30 30 | 338 | 317 | 293 | 276 |
| 31 31 | 363 | 341 | 315 | 298 |
| 32 32 | 388 | 365 | 339 | 321 |
| 33 33 | 415 | 391 | 363 | 344 |
| 34 34 | 443 | 418 | 388 | 369 |
| 35 35 | 471 | 445 | 414 | 394 |
| 36 36 | 501 | 473 | 441 | 420 |
| 37 37 | 531 | 503 | 469 | 447 |
| 38 38 | 563 | 533 | 498 | 475 |
| 39 39 | 595 | 564 | 528 | 504 |
| 40 40 | 628 | 596 | 558 | 533 |
| 41 41 | 662 | 628 | 590 | 564 |
| 42 42 | 697 | 662 | 622 | 595 |
| 43 43 | 733 | 697 | 655 | 627 |
| 44 44 | 770 | 732 | 689 | 660 |
| 45 45 | 808 | 769 | 724 | 694 |
| 46 46 | 846 | 806 | 760 | 729 |
| 47 47 | 886 | 845 | 797 | 765 |
| 48 48 | 926 | 884 | 835 | 802 |
| 49 49 | 968 | 924 | 873 | 839 |
| 50 50 | 1010 | 965 | 913 | 877 |

*Table 10* Critical Values for Wilcoxon's Signed-Ranks $T$ Test[2]

| $\alpha_1$ | .05 | .025 | .01 | .005 |
|---|---|---|---|---|
| $\alpha_2$ | .10 | .05 | .02 | .01 |
| $n$ | | | | |
| 1 | – | – | – | – |
| 2 | – | – | – | – |
| 3 | – | – | – | – |
| 4 | – | – | – | – |
| 5 | 0 | – | – | – |
| 6 | 2 | 0 | – | – |
| 7 | 3 | 2 | 0 | – |
| 8 | 5 | 3 | 1 | 0 |
| 9 | 8 | 5 | 3 | 1 |
| 10 | 10 | 8 | 5 | 3 |
| 11 | 13 | 10 | 7 | 5 |
| 12 | 17 | 13 | 9 | 7 |
| 13 | 21 | 17 | 12 | 9 |
| 14 | 25 | 21 | 15 | 12 |
| 15 | 30 | 25 | 19 | 15 |
| 16 | 35 | 29 | 23 | 19 |
| 17 | 41 | 34 | 27 | 23 |
| 18 | 47 | 40 | 32 | 27 |
| 19 | 53 | 46 | 37 | 32 |
| 20 | 60 | 52 | 43 | 37 |
| 21 | 67 | 58 | 49 | 42 |
| 22 | 75 | 65 | 55 | 48 |
| 23 | 83 | 73 | 62 | 54 |
| 24 | 91 | 81 | 69 | 61 |
| 25 | 100 | 89 | 76 | 68 |

| $\alpha_1$ | .05 | .025 | .01 | .005 |
|---|---|---|---|---|
| $\alpha_2$ | .10 | .05 | .02 | .01 |
| $n$ | | | | |
| 26 | 110 | 98 | 84 | 75 |
| 27 | 119 | 107 | 92 | 83 |
| 28 | 130 | 116 | 101 | 91 |
| 29 | 140 | 126 | 110 | 100 |
| 30 | 151 | 137 | 120 | 109 |
| 31 | 163 | 147 | 130 | 118 |
| 32 | 175 | 159 | 140 | 128 |
| 33 | 187 | 170 | 151 | 138 |
| 34 | 200 | 182 | 162 | 148 |
| 35 | 213 | 195 | 173 | 159 |
| 36 | 227 | 208 | 185 | 171 |
| 37 | 241 | 221 | 198 | 182 |
| 38 | 256 | 235 | 211 | 194 |
| 39 | 271 | 249 | 224 | 207 |
| 40 | 286 | 264 | 238 | 220 |
| 41 | 302 | 279 | 252 | 233 |
| 42 | 319 | 294 | 266 | 247 |
| 43 | 336 | 310 | 281 | 261 |
| 44 | 353 | 327 | 296 | 276 |
| 45 | 371 | 343 | 312 | 291 |
| 46 | 389 | 361 | 328 | 307 |
| 47 | 407 | 378 | 345 | 322 |
| 48 | 426 | 396 | 362 | 339 |
| 49 | 446 | 415 | 379 | 355 |
| 50 | 466 | 434 | 397 | 373 |

| $\alpha_1$ | .05 | .025 | .01 | .005 |
|---|---|---|---|---|
| $\alpha_2$ | .10 | .05 | .02 | .01 |
| $n$ | | | | |
| 51 | 486 | 453 | 416 | 390 |
| 52 | 507 | 473 | 434 | 408 |
| 53 | 529 | 494 | 454 | 427 |
| 54 | 550 | 514 | 473 | 445 |
| 55 | 573 | 536 | 493 | 465 |
| 56 | 595 | 557 | 514 | 484 |
| 57 | 618 | 579 | 535 | 504 |
| 58 | 642 | 602 | 556 | 525 |
| 59 | 666 | 625 | 578 | 546 |
| 60 | 690 | 648 | 600 | 567 |
| 61 | 715 | 672 | 623 | 589 |
| 62 | 741 | 697 | 646 | 611 |
| 63 | 767 | 721 | 669 | 634 |
| 64 | 793 | 747 | 693 | 657 |
| 65 | 820 | 772 | 718 | 681 |
| 66 | 847 | 798 | 742 | 705 |
| 67 | 875 | 825 | 768 | 729 |
| 68 | 903 | 852 | 793 | 754 |
| 69 | 931 | 879 | 819 | 779 |
| 70 | 960 | 907 | 846 | 805 |
| 71 | 990 | 936 | 873 | 831 |
| 72 | 1020 | 964 | 901 | 858 |
| 73 | 1050 | 994 | 928 | 884 |
| 74 | 1081 | 1023 | 957 | 912 |
| 75 | 1112 | 1053 | 986 | 940 |

| $\alpha_1$ | .05 | .025 | .01 | .005 |
|---|---|---|---|---|
| $\alpha_2$ | .10 | .05 | .02 | .01 |
| $n$ | | | | |
| 76 | 1144 | 1084 | 1015 | 968 |
| 77 | 1176 | 1115 | 1044 | 997 |
| 78 | 1209 | 1147 | 1075 | 1026 |
| 79 | 1242 | 1179 | 1105 | 1056 |
| 80 | 1276 | 1211 | 1136 | 1086 |
| 81 | 1310 | 1244 | 1168 | 1116 |
| 82 | 1345 | 1277 | 1200 | 1147 |
| 83 | 1380 | 1311 | 1232 | 1178 |
| 84 | 1415 | 1345 | 1265 | 1210 |
| 85 | 1451 | 1380 | 1298 | 1242 |
| 86 | 1487 | 1415 | 1332 | 1275 |
| 87 | 1524 | 1451 | 1366 | 1308 |
| 88 | 1561 | 1487 | 1400 | 1342 |
| 89 | 1599 | 1523 | 1435 | 1376 |
| 90 | 1638 | 1560 | 1471 | 1410 |
| 91 | 1676 | 1597 | 1507 | 1445 |
| 92 | 1715 | 1635 | 1543 | 1480 |
| 93 | 1755 | 1674 | 1580 | 1516 |
| 94 | 1795 | 1712 | 1617 | 1552 |
| 95 | 1836 | 1752 | 1655 | 1589 |
| 96 | 1877 | 1791 | 1693 | 1626 |
| 97 | 1918 | 1832 | 1731 | 1664 |
| 98 | 1960 | 1872 | 1770 | 1702 |
| 99 | 2003 | 1913 | 1810 | 1740 |
| 100 | 2045 | 1955 | 1850 | 1779 |

*Table 11* Critical Values for Spearman's Rank Correlation Coefficient[3]

| $\alpha_1^R$ | .05 | .025 | .01 | .005 |
|---|---|---|---|---|
| $\alpha_2$ | .10 | .05 | .02 | .01 |
| $n$ | | | | |
| 1 | – | – | – | – |
| 2 | – | – | – | – |
| 3 | – | – | – | – |
| 4 | 1.0000 | – | – | – |
| 5 | 0.9000 | 1.0000 | 1.0000 | – |
| 6 | 0.8286 | 0.8857 | 0.9429 | 1.0000 |
| 7 | 0.7143 | 0.7857 | 0.8929 | 0.9286 |
| 8 | 0.6429 | 0.7381 | 0.8333 | 0.8810 |
| 9 | 0.6000 | 0.7000 | 0.7833 | 0.8333 |
| 10 | 0.5636 | 0.6485 | 0.7455 | 0.7939 |
| 11 | 0.5364 | 0.6182 | 0.7091 | 0.7545 |
| 12 | 0.5035 | 0.5874 | 0.6783 | 0.7273 |
| 13 | 0.4835 | 0.5604 | 0.6484 | 0.7033 |
| 14 | 0.4637 | 0.5385 | 0.6264 | 0.6791 |
| 15 | 0.4464 | 0.5214 | 0.6036 | 0.6536 |
| 16 | 0.4294 | 0.5029 | 0.5824 | 0.6353 |
| 17 | 0.4142 | 0.4877 | 0.5662 | 0.6176 |
| 18 | 0.4014 | 0.4716 | 0.5501 | 0.5996 |
| 19 | 0.3912 | 0.4596 | 0.5351 | 0.5842 |
| 20 | 0.3805 | 0.4466 | 0.5218 | 0.5699 |
| 21 | 0.3701 | 0.4364 | 0.5091 | 0.5558 |
| 22 | 0.3608 | 0.4252 | 0.4975 | 0.5438 |
| 23 | 0.3528 | 0.4160 | 0.4862 | 0.5316 |
| 24 | 0.3443 | 0.4070 | 0.4757 | 0.5209 |
| 25 | 0.3369 | 0.3977 | 0.4662 | 0.5108 |
| 26 | 0.3306 | 0.3901 | 0.4571 | 0.5009 |
| 27 | 0.3242 | 0.3828 | 0.4487 | 0.4915 |
| 28 | 0.3180 | 0.3755 | 0.4401 | 0.4828 |
| 29 | 0.3118 | 0.3685 | 0.4325 | 0.4749 |
| 30 | 0.3063 | 0.3624 | 0.4251 | 0.4670 |

| $\alpha_1^R$ | .05 | .025 | .01 | .005 |
|---|---|---|---|---|
| $\alpha_2$ | .10 | .05 | .02 | .01 |
| $n$ | | | | |
| 31 | 0.3012 | 0.3560 | 0.4185 | 0.4593 |
| 32 | 0.2962 | 0.3504 | 0.4117 | 0.4523 |
| 33 | 0.2914 | 0.3449 | 0.4054 | 0.4455 |
| 34 | 0.2871 | 0.3396 | 0.3995 | 0.4390 |
| 35 | 0.2829 | 0.3347 | 0.3936 | 0.4328 |
| 36 | 0.2788 | 0.3300 | 0.3882 | 0.4268 |
| 37 | 0.2748 | 0.3253 | 0.3829 | 0.4211 |
| 38 | 0.2710 | 0.3209 | 0.3778 | 0.4155 |
| 39 | 0.2674 | 0.3168 | 0.3729 | 0.4103 |
| 40 | 0.2640 | 0.3128 | 0.3681 | 0.4051 |
| 41 | 0.2606 | 0.3087 | 0.3636 | 0.4002 |
| 42 | 0.2574 | 0.3051 | 0.3594 | 0.3955 |
| 43 | 0.2543 | 0.3014 | 0.3550 | 0.3908 |
| 44 | 0.2513 | 0.2978 | 0.3511 | 0.3865 |
| 45 | 0.2484 | 0.2945 | 0.3470 | 0.3822 |
| 46 | 0.2456 | 0.2913 | 0.3433 | 0.3781 |
| 47 | 0.2429 | 0.2880 | 0.3396 | 0.3741 |
| 48 | 0.2403 | 0.2850 | 0.3361 | 0.3702 |
| 49 | 0.2378 | 0.2820 | 0.3326 | 0.3664 |
| 50 | 0.2353 | 0.2791 | 0.3293 | 0.3628 |
| 51 | 0.2329 | 0.2764 | 0.3260 | 0.3592 |
| 52 | 0.2307 | 0.2736 | 0.3228 | 0.3558 |
| 53 | 0.2284 | 0.2710 | 0.3198 | 0.3524 |
| 54 | 0.2262 | 0.2685 | 0.3168 | 0.3492 |
| 55 | 0.2242 | 0.2659 | 0.3139 | 0.3460 |
| 56 | 0.2221 | 0.2636 | 0.3111 | 0.3429 |
| 57 | 0.2201 | 0.2612 | 0.3083 | 0.3400 |
| 58 | 0.2181 | 0.2589 | 0.3057 | 0.3370 |
| 59 | 0.2162 | 0.2567 | 0.3030 | 0.3342 |
| 60 | 0.2144 | 0.2545 | 0.3005 | 0.3314 |

| $\alpha_1^R$ | .05 | .025 | .01 | .005 |
|---|---|---|---|---|
| $\alpha_2$ | .10 | .05 | .02 | .01 |
| $n$ | | | | |
| 61 | 0.2126 | 0.2524 | 0.2980 | 0.3287 |
| 62 | 0.2108 | 0.2503 | 0.2956 | 0.3260 |
| 63 | 0.2091 | 0.2483 | 0.2933 | 0.3234 |
| 64 | 0.2075 | 0.2463 | 0.2910 | 0.3209 |
| 65 | 0.2058 | 0.2444 | 0.2887 | 0.3185 |
| 66 | 0.2042 | 0.2425 | 0.2865 | 0.3161 |
| 67 | 0.2027 | 0.2407 | 0.2844 | 0.3137 |
| 68 | 0.2012 | 0.2389 | 0.2823 | 0.3114 |
| 69 | 0.1997 | 0.2372 | 0.2802 | 0.3092 |
| 70 | 0.1982 | 0.2354 | 0.2782 | 0.3070 |
| 71 | 0.1968 | 0.2337 | 0.2762 | 0.3048 |
| 72 | 0.1954 | 0.2321 | 0.2743 | 0.3027 |
| 73 | 0.1940 | 0.2305 | 0.2724 | 0.3006 |
| 74 | 0.1927 | 0.2289 | 0.2706 | 0.2986 |
| 75 | 0.1914 | 0.2274 | 0.2688 | 0.2966 |
| 76 | 0.1901 | 0.2259 | 0.2670 | 0.2947 |
| 77 | 0.1888 | 0.2244 | 0.2652 | 0.2928 |
| 78 | 0.1876 | 0.2229 | 0.2635 | 0.2909 |
| 79 | 0.1864 | 0.2215 | 0.2619 | 0.2891 |
| 80 | 0.1852 | 0.2201 | 0.2602 | 0.2872 |
| 82 | 0.1829 | 0.2174 | 0.2570 | 0.2837 |
| 84 | 0.1807 | 0.2147 | 0.2539 | 0.2804 |
| 86 | 0.1785 | 0.2122 | 0.2510 | 0.2771 |
| 88 | 0.1765 | 0.2097 | 0.2481 | 0.2740 |
| 90 | 0.1745 | 0.2074 | 0.2453 | 0.2709 |
| 92 | 0.1725 | 0.2051 | 0.2426 | 0.2680 |
| 94 | 0.1707 | 0.2029 | 0.2400 | 0.2651 |
| 96 | 0.1689 | 0.2008 | 0.2375 | 0.2623 |
| 98 | 0.1671 | 0.1987 | 0.2351 | 0.2597 |
| 100 | 0.1654 | 0.1967 | 0.2327 | 0.2571 |

## Notes

1  Neave, H. R. (2012). *Elementary statistical tables* (2nd ed.). London: Routledge. Adapted and reprinted with permission of Routledge/Taylor & Francis Group.
2  Neave, H. R. (2012). *Elementary statistical tables* (2nd ed.). London: Routledge. Adapted and reprinted with permission of Routledge/Taylor & Francis Group.
3  Neave, H. R. (2012). *Elementary statistical tables* (2nd ed.). London: Routledge. Adapted and reprinted with permission of Routledge/Taylor & Francis Group.

# Index

Note: Page numbers in **bold** indicate a table.